Role of AI in Producing, Evaluating, and Interpreting Literary Materials

Andi Asrifan
Universitas Negeri Makassar, Indonesia

IGI Global
Scientific Publishing
Publishing Tomorrow's Research Today

Vice President of Editorial	Melissa Wagner
Director of Acquisitions	Mikaela Felty
Director of Book Development	Jocelynn Hessler
Production Manager	Mike Brehm
Cover Design	Jose Rosado

Published in the United States of America by
IGI Global Scientific Publishing
701 East Chocolate Avenue
Hershey, PA, 17033, USA
Tel: 717-533-8845
Fax: 717-533-7115
Website: https://www.igi-global.com E-mail: cust@igi-global.com

Library of Congress Cataloging-in-Publication Data
Names: Asrifan, Andi, 1985- editor http://id.loc.gov/rwo/agents/n2025006247

Title: Role of AI in producing, evaluating, and interpreting literary materials / edited by Andi Asrifan.
Description: Hershey, PA : IGI Global Scientific Publishing, 2026. | Includes bibliographical references and index. | Summary: "AI tools are helping writers write stories and generate poetry in the digital age, enabling new creativity. AI-powered apps are also changing literary evaluations by providing data-driven insights into themes, styles, and emotional resonance. AI is helping readers and scholars understand subtle meanings through enhanced text analysis and natural language processing. This book examines these intersections and the pros and cons of AI in literature"-- Provided by publisher.
Identifiers: LCCN 2025000753 (print) | LCCN 2025000754 (ebook) | ISBN 9798337310572 hardcover | ISBN 9798337310589 paperback | ISBN 9798337310596 ebook
Subjects: LCSH: Literature and technology http://id.loc.gov/authorities/subjects/sh85077575 | Authorship--Technological innovations | Criticism--Data processing | Creation (Literary, artistic, etc.) http://id.loc.gov/authorities/subjects/sh85033827 | Artificial intelligence http://id.loc.gov/authorities/subjects/sh85008180 | Artificial intelligence--Educational applications http://id.loc.gov/authorities/subjects/sh87006783 | LCGFT: Essays http://id.loc.gov/authorities/genreForms/gf2014026094
Classification: LCC PN56.T37 R75 2025 (print) | LCC PN56.T37 (ebook) | DDC 802.85/63--dc23/eng/20250225
LC record available at https://lccn.loc.gov/2025000753
LC ebook record available at https://lccn.loc.gov/2025000754

British Cataloguing in Publication Data
A Cataloguing in Publication record for this book is available from the British Library.

Table of Contents

Detailed Table of Contents

This chapter analyzes the changing role of artificial intelligence (AI) in literature, emphasizing the intricate dynamics of originality and authenticity in AI-generated creations. As AI systems progressively engage with human authors or generate independent literature, inquiries emerge regarding authorship, emotional profundity, and creative authenticity. The research examines the philosophical underpinnings of originality, the functional role of algorithms, and the difficulties in evaluating the literary merit of machine-generated texts. It also examines audience perceptions of AI-generated literature and its cultural implications. Ethical aspects, such as copyright, representation, and creative purpose, are emphasized to promote appropriate utilization of AI in literary creation. This interdisciplinary investigation advocates for a balanced methodology that recognizes the advantages and constraints of AI, promoting collaborative creation while safeguarding human expression in the digital literary domain.

Artificial Intelligence (AI) has transformed literary criticism by introducing advanced tools to analyze complex literary elements such as themes, symbolism, and emotional depth. This chapter explores AI's impact on both contemporary and classic literature, demonstrating how Natural Language Processing (NLP) and machine learning algorithms uncover recurring motifs, narrative structures, and cultural variations beyond human perception. AI's role in interpreting symbolism and identifying thematic connections across genres is examined, alongside its limitations in capturing abstract meanings compared to human intuition. The chapter also investigates AI's effectiveness in assessing emotional resonance using sentiment analysis and tonal evaluation to measure audience engagement. Ultimately, this chapter presents AI as both an innovative tool and a disruptive force, reshaping literary analysis in the digital age.

Artificial Intelligence (AI) is transforming historical studies by introducing innovative methodologies enriched with philosophical insights. Historical narratives, inherently interpretative, are shaped by concepts of causality, morality, and volition. This chapter explores how AI acts as a conceptual tool, blending moral philosophy, existentialism, and socio-political theory into narrative creation. By augmenting historical facts with philosophical frameworks, AI enables speculative reconstructions that address ethical dilemmas, existential questions, and socio-political issues. These AI-driven narratives challenge traditional historiographical boundaries while raising concerns about the distortion of facts and the distinction between history and philosophical invention. Using global examples, the chapter demonstrates how AI broadens access to history while addressing methodological intersectionality. It advocates for the responsible application of AI in history and philosophy to extend historical knowledge and tackle modern challenges, redefining how we engage with the past.

The intersection of artificial intelligence and literary creation presents both exhilarating possibilities and profound philosophical questions. This chapter explores how AI is transforming the ways we produce, understand, and value fiction, poetry, and drama. Far from simply automating the writing process, AI reshapes the creative landscape—serving as collaborator, tool, and sometimes even provocateur. By analyzing contemporary examples of AI-assisted literature and examining how machine learning models engage with narrative structures, poetic forms, and dramatic dialogue, this chapter seeks to uncover what is gained—and potentially lost—when creativity becomes entangled with code. It reflects on the evolving identity of the writer, the shifting boundaries of originality and authorship, and the broader cultural implications of letting machines into the sacred space of storytelling. Rather than offering definitive answers, this inquiry invites readers to wrestle with the complexities of a literary future that is not just human but also hybrid.

creativity, authorship, and emotional expression in literature. The evolution of AI poetry generators, particularly through models like GPT-2, GPT-3, and GPT-4, highlights the increasing sophistication of natural language processing (NLP) technologies that enable machines to analyze and replicate human poetic styles. This chapter also explores the features and functionalities of five prominent AI poem generators: ToolBaz, EditPad, BoredHumans, Vondy.com, and CapitalizeMyTitle.com. AI-generated poetry utilizes advanced algorithms and extensive datasets to produce text that adheres to established poetic conventions, offering a novel perspective on creativity that is both innovative and sometimes unpredictable. It further explores the implications of AI's role in artistic expression, raising critical questions about authorship, creativity, and the definition of poetry itself.

Chapter 8
Transformation of Literary Culture in the Digital Era Through the Use of Artificial Intelligence as a Form of Copyright Protection 177
Junaidi Junaidi, Sjakhyakirti University, Indonesia

Artificial Intelligence (AI) is one of the many innovations that have emerged in the digital era. Most people believe that artificial intelligence (AI) can do many things, such as creating stories or literary works. As artificial intelligence (AI) becomes more popular in society, cases of plagiarism have increased. In the Industrial Revolution 5.0, artificial intelligence (AI) is an important part of the revolution. This advancement has benefited many industries, such as literary development. Input data is essential to the development of artificial intelligence (AI) for various purposes. This is because the way artificial intelligence (AI) systems are built and the methods that will be used to solve problems depend largely on the availability of data. The use of input data for the development of artificial intelligence (AI) derived from copyrighted works may raise legal issues if done without observing the provisions of the Agreement on Trade-Related Aspects of Intellectual Property Rights (TRIPs) and Berne Convention for the Protection of Literary and Artistic Works

Chapter 9
Artificial Intelligence (AI) in Cultural and Historical Literary Analysis 205
Ipseeta Satpathy, KSOM, KIIT University, Bhubaneswar, India
Arpita Nayak, KIIT School of Liberal Studies, KIIT University, Bhubaneswar, India
Vishal Jain, Sharda University, India

The employment of AI in cultural and historical literary processing has become a new way of reading texts and studying literature evolution. The current chapter aims at a discussion of possibilities of utilizing the AI for discovering the culture in the historical documents and identifying trends in the literature throughout the centuries. Only using algorithms such as NLP or using sentiment analysis and

Preface

INTRODUCTION

In an era marked by the seamless integration of technology into nearly every facet of our lives, the realm of literature is no exception. The growing presence of Artificial Intelligence in the literary domain is not just a technological trend; it is a transformative force redefining how we create, critique, and comprehend literary works. As editor of this volume, *Role of AI in Producing, Evaluating, and Interpreting Literary Materials*, I am pleased to introduce a timely and forward-looking exploration of the shifting boundaries between human imagination and machine intelligence.

This book was conceived out of a recognition that literature, long held as a deeply human, intuitive art form, is now intersecting with advanced algorithms and machine learning systems. These technologies, once tools of science and computation, have become capable of composing poetry, developing narrative arcs, analyzing stylistic choices, and even interpreting symbolic themes with remarkable sophistication. The implications of such developments are both exhilarating and complex.

Role of AI in Producing, Evaluating, and Interpreting Literary Materials brings together an array of scholars, practitioners, and technologists to engage with these complexities. The chapters offer a rich tapestry of insights, theoretical frameworks, and case studies that illuminate the evolving relationship between AI and literature. Topics range from AI-assisted storytelling and genre prediction to the use of Natural Language Processing in textual interpretation to ethical debates around originality, authorship, and authenticity.

CHAPTER OVERVIEWS

The opening chapter, *Navigating the Fine Line: Originality and Authenticity in AI-Generated Literature*, introduces a central tension at the heart of this volume: the contested space between machine-generated creativity and human literary tradition. This chapter delves into the philosophical and practical complexities of defining originality and authenticity when AI becomes a co-author or even sole creator of literary works. It raises critical questions around authorship, emotional depth, audience reception, and ethical boundaries, setting the tone for an ongoing dialogue on human-AI collaboration in the arts.

The second chapter, *AI-Powered Literary Analysis: Redefining Themes, Symbolism, and Emotional Resonance in Contemporary Literature*, highlights how AI is revolutionizing literary criticism. By leveraging NLP and machine learning, scholars can now identify hidden themes, analyze sentiment, and track symbolism across vast corpora. While offering powerful insights, the chapter also acknowledges the boundaries of algorithmic interpretation and the continued necessity of human intuition in discerning abstract literary meaning.

AI and Historical Narratives: Reconstructing the Past Through Philosophy presents a compelling interdisciplinary approach, merging AI tools with philosophical inquiry to revisit and reinterpret historical narratives. The chapter underscores how AI can enrich historiography by embedding moral, existential, and socio-political dimensions into digital reconstructions of the past, while cautioning against the risks of factual distortion and narrative manipulation.

In *AI and the Future of Literary Creation: Transforming Fiction, Poetry, and Drama*, we explore the transformative impact of AI on literary genres and creative identity. The chapter examines how machines are engaging with plot structures, poetic meters, and dramatic dialogue, while reflecting on the evolving role of the author in a world where creativity is increasingly shared with intelligent systems. It invites readers to consider what it means to tell stories in an age of hybrid authorship.

Chapter five, *Interpreting Literature Through an AI Lens: Cross-Cultural Dynamics and Insights*, investigates how AI facilitates deeper cross-cultural literary understanding. With examples from global literature and translation studies, the chapter illustrates AI's potential to reveal universal motifs and cultural nuances, while also examining critical issues around bias, inclusivity, and responsible data use in literary scholarship.

In *Scripts and Stories: AI's Role in Modern Creative Writing*, the seventh chapter offers practical insights into how AI is transforming narrative construction, especially in screenwriting and fiction. The chapter presents real-world applications where AI tools assist with character arcs and dialogue generation, while also engaging with ethical concerns surrounding intellectual property, creativity, and the preservation of human narrative agency.

Chapter seven, *Verse by Algorithm: AI's Impact on Poetry Writing and Literary Insight*, brings a focused discussion on AI-generated poetry. By analyzing various AI tools and poetic models, the chapter explores how machines replicate poetic structures and styles, raising questions about what constitutes creativity and authorship in lyrical expression. The chapter also highlights the unpredictability and innovation that AI introduces to poetic experimentation.

Transformation of Literary Culture in the Digital Era Through the Use of Artificial Intelligence as a Form of Copyright Protection, the ninth chapter, shifts the lens toward legal frameworks and the role of AI in literary copyright enforcement. In a world of increased digital content generation, the chapter addresses the legal ramifications of using copyrighted material to train AI and the implications of TRIPs and Berne Convention compliance. It emphasizes the need for ethical AI development aligned with global intellectual property standards.

In *Artificial Intelligence in Cultural and Historical Literary Analysis*, chapter ten, the reader is introduced to the application of AI in tracing cultural patterns and historical evolution in literary texts. This chapter underscores how AI tools like NLP and pattern recognition reveal hidden connections and social themes across time, offering fresh perspectives on literary history and its societal impact.

Chapter ten, *Integration of Multiculturalism in AI-Based Literature: A Social Perspective*, explores the opportunities and tensions in using AI to generate and analyze multicultural content. While AI offers a promising path toward global literary inclusion, the chapter confronts challenges such as cultural erasure, homogenization, and algorithmic bias. It advocates for ethical, inclusive frameworks that promote cultural diversity and protect marginalized literary traditions.

The final chapter, *Perceptions, Roles, Considerations, and Practices in Literary Criticism in the Age of AI*, brings the conversation full circle by examining how AI is reshaping literary criticism itself. Drawing on the views of literature educators and graduate students, the chapter presents a grounded, human-centered framework for integrating AI responsibly in literary evaluation. It underscores the enduring role of human judgment and ethical reflection, even as AI tools become more capable in offering textual analysis.

CONCLUSION

At the heart of this volume lies an effort to balance optimism and critique. While AI presents exciting possibilities for enhancing creativity and accessibility, it also challenges long-held notions of literary value, human expression, and the role of authors and critics. Can a machine understand the emotional depth of a human experience? Should AI-generated narratives be considered art? How do we protect cultural nuance and authenticity in algorithmically constructed texts? These are not merely academic questions. They are fundamental concerns for educators, writers, publishers, and readers navigating the rapidly shifting literary landscape.

This book seeks to spark a dialogue between the worlds of technology and the humanities, encouraging multidisciplinary collaboration and a shared understanding of how artificial intelligence might coexist with, complement, or even redefine literary practices. Whether you are a literature scholar intrigued by AI, a technologist delving into the humanities, an educator integrating digital tools into teaching, or a reader curious about the future of storytelling, this book offers valuable perspectives and provocations.

I would like to express my gratitude to the contributors, whose diverse voices and thoughtful analyses give this volume its depth and vibrancy. Together, they help chart a course for understanding and shaping the future of literature in the age of artificial intelligence. It is my hope that this work serves not only as a resource, but also as an invitation to critically engage with the possibilities AI offers and the responsibilities it demands in the creative and intellectual work of literature.

Andi Asrifan
Universitas Negeri Makassar, Indonesia

Chapter 1
Navigating the Fine Line: Originality and Authenticity in AI-Generated Literature

Supriadi Supriadi
https://orcid.org/0009-0002-0285-2920
Universitas Islam Makassar, Indonesia

Andi Asrifan
https://orcid.org/0000-0002-9934-6129
Universitas Negeri Makassar, Indonesia

ABSTRACT

This chapter analyzes the changing role of artificial intelligence (AI) in literature, emphasizing the intricate dynamics of originality and authenticity in AI-generated creations. As AI systems progressively engage with human authors or generate independent literature, inquiries emerge regarding authorship, emotional profundity, and creative authenticity. The research examines the philosophical underpinnings of originality, the functional role of algorithms, and the difficulties in evaluating the literary merit of machine-generated texts. It also examines audience perceptions of AI-generated literature and its cultural implications. Ethical aspects, such as copyright, representation, and creative purpose, are emphasized to promote appropriate utilization of AI in literary creation. This interdisciplinary investigation advocates for a balanced methodology that recognizes the advantages and constraints of AI, promoting collaborative creation while safeguarding human expression in the digital literary domain.

DOI: 10.4018/979-8-3373-1057-2.ch001

1. UNDERSTANDING AI AND LITERATURE

1.1 The Evolution of AI in Creative Writing

The convergence of artificial intelligence (AI) and literature has markedly progressed over recent decades, mirroring broader technological breakthroughs and changes in cultural perceptions of creativity (Campedelli, 2021). The historical setting of AI in literature originates from the nascent period of computing, when academics first investigating the capacity of machines to produce human-like prose. During the 1960s, programs such as ELIZA, created by Joseph Weizenbaum, demonstrated computers' capacity to emulate conversation, establishing a foundation for further inquiries into AI's involvement in creative writing.

During the 1980s and 1990s, artificial intelligence research increasingly concentrated on natural language processing (NLP), enhancing robots' capabilities to comprehend and produce text more proficiently. These advancements facilitated the establishment of primitive text-generation systems capable of producing basic narratives or poems according to predetermined guidelines (Odden et al., 2021). Nevertheless, the outputs frequently exhibited a formulaic nature and were devoid of the depth and complexity typical of human writing.

The turn of the millennium signified a substantial transformation in AI's creative writing abilities, primarily attributable to progress in machine learning and the accessibility of extensive textual material (Radanliev 2024). In 2014, the introduction of the neural network model termed Long Short-Term Memory (LSTM) significantly enhanced the quality of text production. LSTMs can assimilate context and generate more coherent and contextually pertinent tales, facilitating the development of more advanced AI writing instruments.

In 2018, a significant milestone was achieved with the launch of OpenAI's GPT-2, a language model proficient in producing human-like writing in several genres and styles. The capacity to generate coherent and contextually nuanced passages has prompted inquiries regarding originality and authorship, as the differentiation between human and machine-generated content increasingly becomes indistinct (Huang et al., 2025). The subsequent launch of GPT-3 in 2020, including enhanced capabilities, greatly increased the discourse about AI's role in literature.

As AI technologies advance, they are progressively incorporated into creative writing processes, enabling authors to work with machines in innovative manners. The advent of AI-assisted writing tools has ignited discussions over the essence of creativity and the ramifications for originality and authenticity in literature (Zhao, 2024). Writers currently confront the difficulty of balancing the utilization of AI's capabilities with the preservation of human expression. The progression of AI in creative writing underscores technical developments and raises significant inquiries regarding the future of literature.

1.2 Defining AI-Generated Literature

AI-generated literature denotes any text that is created, either whole or partially, by artificial intelligence systems. These systems employ algorithms and machine learning methodologies to scrutinize extensive datasets of current literature, allowing them to produce new content that emulates human writing styles, structures, and themes (Danesi, 2024). AI-generated literature can include several literary forms, such as poetry, short stories, essays, and novels, contingent upon the sophistication of the underlying technology.

The definition of AI-generated text is chiefly influenced by the extent of human involvement and the methodologies utilized by the AI. In certain instances, AI can autonomously construct text based on user-provided cues, resulting in content that is wholly machine-produced (Ranade et al., 2025). In alternative situations, human authors may partner with AI technologies to augment their writing or produce concepts, culminating in a hybrid literary style that integrates both human and machine contributions. This collaborative method prompts significant inquiries regarding authorship and the creative process, obscuring the distinctions between conventional literary composition and machine-generated content.

The distinctions between AI-generated and human-generated literature are complex. A notable difference resides in the creative process. Human authors leverage personal experiences, emotions, and cultural contexts, imbuing their work with authenticity and depth derived from their own viewpoints (Younas et al. 2023). Conversely, AI systems are devoid of awareness and personal experience; they produce text by recognizing patterns in existing data without comprehending the underlying meanings or feelings. Although AI may generate logical and contextually appropriate language, it may lack the subtle emotional depth that defines most of human literature.

A significant distinction is the aspect of intention. Human authors compose with distinct objectives, whether to communicate a message, elicit emotions, or stimulate contemplation. Their decisions are frequently shaped by personal convictions and experiences. AI functions without purpose or emotional comprehension, producing language only based on mathematical probabilities resulting from its training data (Zhao et al. 2023). The lack of intent may yield outputs that, although technically adept, can appear sterile or devoid of authentic emotional connection.

In summary, delineating AI-generated literature necessitates comprehending the processes of its creation and acknowledging the intrinsic distinctions between machine-generated and human-generated works. As AI advances, the literary landscape will progressively embody these distinctions, inciting continuous discourse over originality, authenticity, and the future of creative expression.

1.3 The Role of Algorithms in Creativity

Algorithms are fundamental in AI-generated writing, constituting the foundation of systems that replicate human creativity. Fundamentally, algorithms are collections of rules or directives that direct data processing. In creative writing, these algorithms examine extensive textual data to discern patterns, structures, and stylistic features characteristic of human-authored literature (Sarker, 2021). Through the analysis of this data, AI systems can produce language that mirrors the intricacy and depth of human creativity, but via a fundamentally distinct methodology.

Algorithms emulate human creativity by employing deep learning methodologies, especially neural networks. These networks are engineered to identify patterns within data, enabling the AI to produce coherent and contextually relevant text. For instance, when assigned to compose a poem, an AI may scrutinize thousands of existing poems to comprehend meter, rhyme schemes, and thematic components (Anantrasirichai & Bull, 2022). This allows the AI to generate new poems that conform to analogous norms, yielding outcomes that can be unexpectedly artistic. It is crucial to recognize that although the output may seem inventive, it is fundamentally a result of statistical correlations rather than authentic inspiration or emotional profundity.

The influence of training data on AI output is a crucial element of the creative process. The caliber and variety of data employed to train AI models profoundly affect the characteristics of the produced text. If an AI is predominantly trained on a limited range of genres or styles, its output will likely exhibit such constraints, potentially leading to repetitious or derivative creations (Hashemi et al. 2024). In contrast, a model trained on a large range of texts can provide more diversified and original outputs, as it utilizes a wider diversity of literary influences.

Furthermore, the biases inherent in the training data can influence the AI's creative outputs. If the training data lacks representation of specific voices or viewpoints, the produced literature may unintentionally reinforce stereotypes or omit minority narratives (Chiarella et al. 2022). This prompts significant ethical questions regarding the obligation of developers to curate training datasets that foster tolerance and diversity.

In conclusion, algorithms function as a potent instrument for emulating human creativity in AI-generated literature, utilizing deep learning and vast training data to generate prose that can resemble human writing. The limits and biases inherent in these algorithms underscore the persistent difficulty in balancing originality and authenticity in AI-generated creations. As technology progresses, comprehending the function of algorithms in creativity will be essential for both producers and consumers within the literary domain.

2. THE CONCEPT OF ORIGINALITY

2.1 The Philosophy of Originality in Literature

The notion of originality has historically been fundamental to literary theory, influencing our comprehension of creativity and artistic expression. Traditionally, originality has been seen as the defining characteristic of exceptional literature, frequently linked to an author's own voice and perspective. This viewpoint gained prominence during the Romantic era of the late 18th and early 19th centuries, when authors like William Wordsworth and Samuel Taylor Coleridge highlighted the significance of personal expression and emotional veracity (McArthur, 2023). The Romantic ideal asserted that authentic work emerges from the creator's inner experiences, fostering the notion that uniqueness is inherently connected to the author's own journey and discoveries.

Nevertheless, the concept of originality is fraught with complications. The conflict between originality and imitation has been a persistent issue throughout literary history. Numerous esteemed literary works have derived inspiration from prior texts, exemplifying a legacy of intertextuality in which authors interact with and respond to the creations of their ancestors (Pack & Maloney, 2023). Classic Greek tragedies usually appropriated concepts and structures from prior mythology, but Shakespeare's plays generally reinterpreted established narratives and historical occurrences. In this context, imitation is not inherently regarded as a negative attribute; instead, it is perceived as an essential component of the creative process that facilitates the development of ideas and styles.

The differentiation between originality and imitation prompts significant inquiries regarding the essence of creativity. If originality is defined exclusively by the lack of influence, then a significant portion of literature may be considered derivative. Conversely, if we acknowledge that all writers are inspired by their predecessors, we must reevaluate our criteria for assessing originality (Haase & Hanel, 2023). This philosophical question is more relevant in the era of AI-generated writing, where algorithms can replicate established styles and topics.

In modern discourse, originality is frequently perceived as a manifestation of creativity and distinctiveness. Critics contend that genuine originality encompasses not only the generation of novel concepts but also the capacity to recontextualize preexisting ideas in manners that appeal with modern audiences (Verhaal & Dobrev, 2022). This viewpoint underscores the significance of cultural and chronological settings in influencing literary originality, indicating that perceptions of originality may change throughout various epochs and societies.

In exploring the delicate balance between originality and authenticity in AI-generated fiction, these philosophical reflections underscore the intrinsic complexity of the creative process. The relationship among inspiration, imitation, and invention persistently complicates our comprehension of originality in authorship within a technology-driven landscape.

2.2 Measuring Originality in AI Texts

Assessing originality in AI-generated works has distinct issues, as conventional literary evaluation techniques may not be applicable in the same manner as they are for human authors. As AI generates ever advanced writing, the necessity for effective tools and measures to evaluate originality becomes essential (Mazzi, 2024). Various methodologies have arisen to assess the originality of AI-generated content, each possessing distinct advantages and drawbacks.

A prevalent technique for evaluating originality involves the use of plagiarism detection software, which juxtaposes AI-generated texts with extensive databases of existing material. Instruments such as Turnitin and Copyscape can proficiently discern similarities between AI-generated content and existing publications, facilitating the identification of probable plagiarism (Amirzhanov et al. 2025). Nevertheless, these technologies frequently emphasize exact text matches and may insufficiently consider the subtle methods via which AI can produce original content by recontextualizing concepts or utilizing innovative phrase combinations.

An alternative method employs stylistic analysis and linguistic metrics to assess the distinctiveness of AI-generated writings. Researchers may examine the frequency of particular syntactic structures, lexical diversity, and thematic components to ascertain if a written work has traits indicative of originality (Yang et al., 2024). Advanced algorithms can be utilized to assess aspects such as lexical richness and grammatical complexity, offering insights into the comparison between AI-generated texts and human-authored literature. Nonetheless, these criteria may be subjective and might fail to encapsulate the core of genuine innovation.

Case studies of AI-generated creations further exemplify the intricacies of assessing originality. A prominent instance is the poetry "Sunspring," generated by an AI called Benjamin, which was developed using a recurrent neural network trained on a corpus of science fiction scripts. The poem attracted notice because to its atypical structure and bizarre images, inciting discussions over its originality (Sönmez, 2025). Critics observed that although the poem was distinctive in its structure, it relied significantly on established tropes and themes common in science fiction literature, prompting inquiries over the limits of originality in AI-generated works.

Another instance is the short novel "The Day a Computer Writes a Novel," authored by an AI system named Hitoshi Matsubara (Subagiyo & Wibisono, 2024). This narrative was entered into a literary contest in Japan and successfully navigated the preliminary evaluation, demonstrating the capability of AI to generate content that may be indistinguishable from human authorship. The reception of the narrative underscored the persistent discourse on originality, as it contested conventional concepts of creativity and the standards used to assess literary value.

In summary, assessing originality in AI-generated texts necessitates a comprehensive strategy that incorporates both quantitative and qualitative measurements. As AI advances, our approaches to evaluating originality must also adapt, sparking continuous discourse over the ramifications for literature and creativity in the digital era.

2.3 Ethical Implications of Originality

The emergence of AI-generated literature has raised substantial ethical concerns, especially with copyright matters and the discourse surrounding authorship and attribution (Watiktinnakorn et al. 2023). As AI systems progressively generate coherent and stylistically advanced texts, the issue of ownership rights for these creations has become a sensitive subject within literary and legal circles.

Copyright law conventionally safeguards original works of writing, conferring exclusive rights to creators over their creations. The applicability of these regulations to AI-generated content is complicated. Due to the absence of mind and intent, AI cannot be regarded as an author in the conventional sense (Cañas, 2022). This prompts the inquiry: who possesses the copyright to a literary work generated by an AI? Is the responsibility attributed to the AI developers, the people who led the AI to produce the text, or maybe the AI itself? Existing legal systems fail to deliver definitive solutions, resulting in ambiguity and possible conflicts about ownership rights.

In numerous nations, copyright law mandates that a work must be produced by a human to be eligible for protection. This constraint presents difficulties for AI-generated literature, as it may exist in a legal ambiguity where it is neither completely safeguarded nor wholly unprotected (Chesterman, 2025). Consequently, creators of AI-generated content may encounter a perilous situation, uncertain about their rights and responsibilities concerning the utilization and dissemination of such works.

The discourse surrounding authorship and attribution further confuses the ethical framework. The emergence of AI-generated text prompts the inquiry of whether human users engaging with these systems merit acknowledgment for their contribution to the creative process (Černe et al. 2022). For example, if a writer employs an AI tool to produce ideas or complete passages, should they be acknowledged as co-authors, or does the AI's involvement undermine their assertion of originality? This predicament interrogates conventional concepts of authorship and prompts significant inquiries regarding the essence of creativity.

Moreover, the capacity of AI to emulate established styles and subjects prompts apprehensions over the safeguarding of varied voices in writing. If AI-generated content mostly mirrors the biases and constraints of its training data, there exists a danger that minority viewpoints may be neglected or inaccurately portrayed (Nguyen et al. 2024). This underscores the ethical need of both developers and users to guarantee that AI systems are trained on varied and representative datasets.

In summary, the ethical ramifications of originality in AI-generated writing involve various concerns, such as copyright, authorship, and representation. As technology progresses, it is imperative for legal frameworks and literary communities to maintain continuous discourse to address these difficulties, ensuring the rights of all creators—both human and machine—are honored and preserved. The problem is to achieve a balance that respects the innovative capabilities of AI while preserving the integrity of human creativity.

3. AUTHENTICITY IN LITERARY EXPRESSION

3.1 Defining Authenticity in Literature

Authenticity in literature is a complex notion that includes the author's voice, aim, and the emotional impact of a work. Authenticity fundamentally denotes the extent to which a written work embodies sincere expression, personal experience, and a cohesive worldview (Negus & Astor, 2022). It is sometimes linked to the notion that a literary piece has to express the distinct viewpoints and sentiments of its author, thereby forging a relationship with readers that appears authentic and approachable.

The author's voice is a fundamental aspect in a work's authenticity. This unique style includes the selection of vocabulary and syntax, as well as the fundamental ideas and emotional nuances that pervade the work. A genuine voice resonates with readers, imparting a sense of personality and personal veracity (Luo, 2024). The candid, confessional style of authors such as Sylvia Plath and the evocative narrative of Gabriel García Márquez illustrate how a distinctive voice may establish a profound connection with an audience, drawing them into the author's inner realm.

Intent is also essential in determining genuineness. The author's intentions—be it to stimulate contemplation, elicit emotion, or narrate a story—mold the narrative and affect readers' perceptions of the work. Authenticity is frequently associated with the sincerity of intentions; when an author composes from a position of genuine emotion or conviction, the resultant work typically resonates more profoundly with its audience (Roos & Reccius, 2024). Conversely, writing that seems formulaic or lacking explicit purpose may be regarded as inauthentic, irrespective of the text's technical proficiency.

In the realm of AI-generated writing, the issue of authenticity grows increasingly intricate. AI systems, lacking consciousness and human experience, produce language based on patterns derived from existing works. Consequently, the "voice" of AI-generated writing is a synthesis of diverse influences rather than a solitary, genuine statement (Mindner et al. 2023). Although AI may generate cohesive and artistically remarkable prose, it lacks the emotional profundity and purpose inherent in human-created masterpieces.

The lack of personal experience prompts significant inquiries on the essence of authenticity in literature. Can a work produced by an algorithm be deemed authentic if it lacks true human feeling or intent? Bishop and Kant, 2023 The difficulty is to reconcile AI's capabilities with our conventional notions of authenticity, leading to continuous discourse on the future of literary expression in a progressively mechanized society.

In conclusion, determining authenticity in writing necessitates an analysis of the relationship among the author's voice, intent, and emotional impact. As we traverse the intricacies of AI-generated writings, comprehending these components will be crucial for assessing the legitimacy of literary works in the digital era. The discourse on authenticity will persist in its evolution, mirroring wider cultural transformations and the dynamic realm of innovation.

3.2 Authenticity Challenges with AI

The emergence of AI-generated literature prompts critical inquiries on the legitimacy of the texts created by these systems. A primary challenge is whether AI can truly create authentic literature—works that connect with readers on a human level (Amirjalili et al., 2024). Authenticity is frequently linked to the emotional profundity, personal experiences, and deliberate intent underlying a written work. Given that AI is devoid of consciousness, emotions, and experiential knowledge, its outputs are inherently distinct from those produced by human authors. AI generates writing based on patterns and information derived from extensive datasets, rather than personal ideas or emotions. This mechanical approach casts skepticism on AI's capacity to produce writing that can be considered genuinely authentic.

The readers' perception of authenticity significantly influences the reception of AI-generated writing. Readers frequently pursue connections with authors, seeking a sense of shared experience or emotional authenticity in the words they encounter. When a reader confronts a literary work perceived as devoid of authentic human feeling or intention, they may scrutinize its authenticity (Lee et al. 2025). This skepticism may create a disconnection between the text and its audience, as readers may perceive AI-generated works as simple imitations or simulations of human creativity rather than genuine representations of thinking and emotion.

Some readers may engage with AI-generated fiction out of curiosity, valuing the innovation and experimentation inherent in its production. For example, "Sunspring," a short film authored by an AI, has attracted interest due to its unorthodox plots and distinctive stylistic elements. Some viewers acknowledge the constraints of AI in expressing genuine human experience, while others appreciate the novel methods by which AI may reinterpret language and narrative (Świerczyńska-Kaczor, 2024). This dichotomy in perception mirrors wider cultural attitudes towards technology and creativity, with some individuals embracing the potential of AI, while others express reservations regarding its impact on artistic integrity.

The context in which AI-generated texts are displayed can affect perceptions of authenticity. When presented as experimental or collaborative endeavors, readers may exhibit greater receptivity to engaging with AI-generated writing on its own merits (Lee et al. 2025). Nonetheless, when offered as substitutes for human authorship, the legitimacy of these texts frequently encounters suspicion.

In conclusion, the issues of authenticity in AI-generated literature arise from the fundamental distinctions between human and machine-generated works. Although AI may generate cohesive and stylistically remarkable texts, the absence of emotional profundity and human experience prompts inquiries over their validity. Reader perceptions are crucial in this discussion, as individuals contend with the intricacies of interacting with literature in an era where technology increasingly influences creative expression. As discussions on AI and authenticity progress, it is crucial to examine how these factors may shape the future of literary expression.

3.3 The Human Element in AI-Generated Works

The advancement of AI technology underscores the significance of the human element in AI-generated writing. Although AI systems may generate cohesive and stylistically diverse material, the incorporation of human oversight and feedback is crucial for guaranteeing that the resultant works authentically resonate with readers (Ramesh et al. 2023). Human authors infuse their writing with extensive experience, emotion, and intentionality—attributes that AI inherently cannot emulate. This partnership between human authors and AI technologies can provide unique literary works that capitalize on the strengths of both parties while mitigating the limits of AI.

Human supervision is essential in the AI writing process, as it directs the trajectory and tone of the produced text. Writers can furnish context, delineate topics, and establish parameters that influence the AI's production (Holzinger et al., 2024). A writer may utilize an AI tool to brainstorm concepts or produce preliminary drafts, subsequently improving the writing to reflect their distinctive voice and purpose. This collaborative method fosters a symbiotic relationship in which the AI serves as an assistant, augmenting the creative process instead of supplanting the human author. Integrating human judgment and emotional depth enables the final product to attain a level of authenticity that just AI-generated texts may lack.

Collaborations between artificial intelligence and human authors are currently being investigated in diverse literary contexts. Contemporary authors are utilizing AI as a collaborative partner, employing machine-generated text as a foundation for further investigation (Ramesh et al. 2023). Authors may enter particular prompts or topics into an AI system, which subsequently creates a variety of responses. The author can choose, modify, and elaborate on these responses, crafting a more nuanced narrative that embodies their personal insights and emotional veracity. This technique improves creativity and fosters a conversation between human intuition and algorithmic production.

Furthermore, incorporating human viewpoints can assist in mitigating the ethical issues associated with AI-generated writing. By incorporating various perspectives and experiences in the training data and creative process, human writers can reduce the risks of prejudice and exclusion that AI systems may unintentionally propagate (Varsha2023). This collaboration promotes diversity and authenticity, enhancing the literary environment with a broader range of narratives.

In conclusion, the human component is essential in the domain of AI-generated literature. By means of supervision and cooperation, human authors can direct AI systems to generate content that genuinely connects with readers. By integrating human creativity with AI skills, authors can investigate novel creative avenues while maintaining the emotional depth and intentionality characteristic of genuine literature. The collaboration between humans and machines will be pivotal in determining the future of literary expression as we traverse this changing world.

4. READER RECEPTION AND CULTURAL IMPACT

4.1 Audience Perception of AI Literature

As AI-generated literature gains prominence, comprehending audience perception is essential for assessing its influence on the literary environment. Research has examined reader responses to AI-generated writings, uncovering a nuanced relationship between enjoyment and appreciation (Lee et al. 2025). Some readers may like the novelty of AI-generated works, while others question their legitimacy and literary value.

Recent polls reveal an increasing interest among readers in AI-generated fiction. A significant number of respondents indicate a readiness to engage with works produced by AI, captivated by the possibilities for novel storytelling and distinctive narrative frameworks (Gibson and Green 2025). This fascination frequently arises from the acknowledgment that AI might generate literature that contradicts conventional literary norms, providing novel insights and unforeseen developments. Nonetheless, the pleasure obtained from interacting with AI fiction does not invariably convert into authentic appreciation for its artistic merit.

The differentiation between enjoyment and appreciation is crucial for comprehending reader attitudes. Enjoyment may stem from the novelty of AI-generated content, since readers are frequently attracted to the concept of robots engaging in creative endeavors. The enjoyment derived from encountering unexpected phrases or unorthodox storylines might enhance the reading experience (Lin and Ng 2024). Appreciation entails a profound engagement with the text, wherein readers evaluate the work's emotional depth, thematic intricacy, and overall literary merit. Numerous readers may like AI-generated writing for its entertainment value while also questioning its authenticity and artistic integrity.

Research indicates that the impression of AI literature differs markedly among various demographics. Younger readers, typically better acquainted with technology and its applications, sometimes display a more favorable disposition towards AI-generated works (Alghamdi et al. 2025). They frequently perceive these texts as components of a dynamic literary environment, welcoming the possibility of collaboration between human creativity and machine learning. Conversely, elder readers can engage with AI fiction with skepticism, favoring conventional authorship and voicing apprehensions regarding the effects of AI on creativity and originality.

Moreover, the setting in which AI-generated literature is introduced significantly influences audience perception. When presented as experimental or new, readers may exhibit greater willingness to engage with AI-generated writings (De et al. 2025). Conversely, if regarded as alternatives to human authorship, doubt may emerge, prompting apprehensions on the future of creative expression.

In conclusion, audience reception of AI-generated literature is complex, encompassing a variety of attitudes from curiosity and delight to skepticism and critique. As readers confront the intricacies of interacting with AI-generated texts, the differentiation between enjoyment and appreciation becomes increasingly significant. Comprehending these relationships will be crucial for authors, publishers, and scholars as they investigate the cultural influence of AI in literature and its ramifications for the future of storytelling.

4.2 The Role of AI Literature in Contemporary Culture

The prevalence of AI-generated writing is rendering its place in current culture and the literary canon increasingly significant. This nascent genre contests conventional concepts of authorship, originality, and the fundamental definition of literature (Amirjalili et al., 2024). Examining the role of AI literature within the literary canon enhances our comprehension of its impact on nascent literary trends and the wider cultural milieu.

AI literature is establishing a distinct position within the literary canon, inciting debates on the criteria for a respectable literary work. Although traditional literature is frequently lauded for its emotional profundity and exploration of the human condition, AI-generated works present a novel paradigm that prioritizes innovation and experimentation (Stelmach, 2025). The emergence of AI-generated works that challenge traditional storytelling methods prompts inquiries regarding the standards used to assess literary value. This changing environment prompts literary scholars and critics to reevaluate the limits of the canon, potentially resulting in a more broad comprehension of literature's possibilities.

The impact of AI literature on nascent literary trends is already apparent in multiple aspects. A notable trend is the fusion of genres and styles, as AI systems can effortlessly integrate components from several literary traditions. This genre-defying method inspires writers to explore hybrid formats, yielding inventive narratives that contest traditional norms (Ramesh et al. 2023). AI-generated poetry may amalgamate aspects of science fiction, surrealism, and classical lyricism, resulting in a distinctive reading experience that encapsulates the intricacies of modern existence.

Moreover, AI literature is cultivating an increasing fascination with collaborative writing processes, wherein human authors collaborate with AI systems to produce new works. This collaboration enhances creative opportunities for writers and fosters a conversation between technology and human expression (Nguyen et al. 2024). As more authors adopt AI technologies, we may observe a transformation in the production and consumption of literature, with readers increasingly interacting with texts that embody the synergy between human creativity and machine intelligence.

The cultural influence of AI literature transcends conventional publishing. As AI-generated material increasingly permeates digital platforms, social media, and online communities, it affects the manner in which narratives are exchanged and transmitted (Feher & Katona, 2021). Readers now encounter a broader spectrum of narratives, frequently produced in real-time, which can democratize the literary domain and facilitate the emergence of multiple voices.

In conclusion, AI fiction is securing its position in modern culture and the literary canon, necessitating a reassessment of conventional concepts of authorship and creativity. Its impact on nascent literary trends fosters experimentation and collaboration, simultaneously transforming the methods of story creation and dissemination. As we traverse this novel landscape, the function of AI writing will persist in its evolution, mirroring the intricacies of a progressively digitized and networked society. The current discourse on AI-generated writings is crucial for comprehending their cultural importance and the future of literary expression.

4.3 Case Studies of Notable AI-Generated Works

With the rise of AI-generated literature, several significant works have surfaced that illustrate the potential and obstacles of this emerging genre. Examining these pieces offers insight into their reception and the critiques they encounter within literary circles, emphasizing the continuous discourse on originality and authenticity in AI-generated literature.

A notable instance is “Sunspring,” a short film entirely scripted by an AI called Benjamin. “Sunspring,” developed with a recurrent neural network with a dataset of science fiction screenplays, debuted at the 2016 Sci-Fi-London Film Festival. The film's atypical narrative and strange dialogues generated much curiosity and discussion (Danesi, 2024). Some viewers applauded the originality of an AI-generated narrative, while others condemned its coherence and emotional profundity, contending that it lacked the deep comprehension of human experience essential for effective storytelling. The film's reception highlights the conflict between innovation and quality in AI-generated creations, as viewers contend with the ramifications of machine-generated artistry.

A notable example is the short narrative “The Day a Computer Writes a Novel,” authored by the AI system Hitoshi Matsubara. This narrative was entered into a literary contest in Japan and successfully navigated the preliminary evaluation, illustrating the capability of AI to generate content that may be indistinguishable from human authorship (Fusillo & Lino, 2024). The story's inclusion in a literary competition sparked debates regarding authorship and the standards for literary excellence. Critics lauded the story's innovative idea but expressed apprehensions regarding the ramifications of AI involvement in literary competitions, questioning its potential to devalue human innovation.

The collaboration between AI and human poets in poetry has yielded fascinating outcomes. The poetry book “1 the Road,” produced by the AI model GPT-2 in conjunction with human poet Ross Goodwin, exemplifies the possibilities of hybrid literary forms (Hussain and Qazi 2023). The collection, influenced by diverse styles, garnered mixed reviews. Some critics praised its experimental character and unique approach, while others voiced doubt, contending that it lacked the emotional depth of conventional poetry.

The reception of AI-generated works underscores the intricacies of assessing writing created by robots. Literary communities are frequently polarized, with some advocating for the innovation and experimentation of AI-generated work, while others critique its authenticity and emotional profundity (Amirjalili et al., 2024). This ongoing discussion illustrates wider cultural perspectives on technology and creativity, raising inquiries about the future of literary expression.

In conclusion, case studies of significant AI-generated works illustrate the complex nature of public reception and critique. As AI fiction progresses, comprehending the reactions of literary communities will be crucial for addressing the difficulties and opportunities posed by this novel genre. The discourse around these pieces will influence the future of AI-generated literature and its position within the wider cultural context.

5. THE FUTURE OF AI IN LITERATURE

5.1 Trends in AI and Creative Writing

The future of AI in literature is poised to be dynamic and transformational, as continuous technological developments redefine the realm of creative writing (Amankwah-Amoah et al. 2024). As AI-generated literature becomes increasingly accepted, some significant tendencies are emerging that will likely shape its future course.

A notable development is the growing incorporation of AI tools into the writing process. As more authors engage in AI-assisted writing, an increase in hybrid works that amalgamate human creativity with machine-generated content is anticipated. These collaborations will enable writers to investigate novel narrative possibilities, augmenting their creative repertoire while preserving their own voice (Marzuki et al. 2023). This movement may result in the birth of novel literary forms that contest existing genres and conventions, prompting authors to expand the limits of storytelling.

A further forecast for the future of AI-generated literature is the advancement of more intricate algorithms capable of creating progressively complicated and nuanced texts. Progress in natural language processing (NLP) and machine learning will enhance AI systems' comprehension of context, tone, and emotional nuances (Khan et al., 2023). As these technologies advance, AI-generated literature may demonstrate increased depth and complexity, potentially diminishing the disparity between human and machine-generated writing. This advancement may result in more acceptance of AI-generated work within literary communities, as the quality of the production rises.

The democratization of literature via AI presents an intriguing opportunity. As AI tools become increasingly available, aspiring authors from varied backgrounds will have the ability to utilize these technologies to articulate their thoughts and narratives. This openness may yield a more diverse literary landscape, showcasing a broader spectrum of voices and opinions that embody the intricacies of modern life (Cupać et al., 2024). The capacity of AI to enhance marginalized tales could promote a more egalitarian literary culture, contesting the conventional gatekeeping practices of publication.

Nonetheless, the future of AI in literature presents certain obstacles. Ethical issues about authorship, originality, and representation will persist in generating discourse as AI-generated content becomes increasingly common (Mazzi, 2024). Resolving these issues necessitates continuous discourse among authors, engineers, and literary critics to create frameworks that respect both human creativity and the inventive capabilities of AI.

In conclusion, the future of AI in literature is set for substantial expansion and evolution. As trends in artificial intelligence and creative writing progress, the incorporation of sophisticated technologies will facilitate novel avenues for collaboration and expression. Although the prospects are exhilarating, it is crucial to address the ethical ramifications and obstacles that emerge in this swiftly evolving environment. By cultivating a deliberate discourse regarding the function of AI in literature, we can guarantee that the future of storytelling remains vibrant, varied, and genuine.

5.2 Balancing Originality and Authenticity

As AI assumes a more significant role in literature, achieving a balance between originality and authenticity is essential. Writers, educators, and literary communities must design solutions to incorporate AI into literary processes while preserving the integrity of human creation (Anantrasirichai & Bull, 2022). This equilibrium is crucial for maintaining the worth of literature and enhancing comprehension of the interaction between human and machine-generated content.

An effective technique for incorporating AI into literary practices is to encourage collaborative writing processes. Authors can utilize AI tools as collaborative collaborators to produce ideas, investigate novel story structures, or draft segments of text. By perceiving AI as an adjunct rather than a substitute, writers can preserve their distinctive voice and purpose while leveraging the inventive potential of AI (Nguyen et al. 2024). Workshops and writing programs that promote experimenting with AI technologies can enhance collaboration, enabling writers to investigate the limits of creativity while maintaining authenticity.

A crucial strategy is to formulate explicit standards and ethical frameworks for the application of AI in literature. These recommendations assist authors in navigating the intricacies of originality and authorship, ensuring responsible and transparent usage of AI-generated work (Sadek et al. 2024). By cultivating an atmosphere of ethical consciousness, literary communities can motivate authors to reveal their utilization of AI tools, enabling readers to interact with the work knowledgeably. This transparency can elevate the idea of authenticity, as readers value the collaborative aspect of the creative process.

Education is crucial in cultivating comprehension of AI's influence on literature. Integrating talks on AI and its ramifications into literary courses can equip future writers and readers to adeptly traverse this emerging world (Walter2024). By examining the ethical, philosophical, and practical dimensions of AI-generated literature, students can cultivate critical thinking abilities that will allow them to engage critically with both human and machine-produced writings. Educators can underscore the significance of many voices and viewpoints in AI training datasets, emphasizing the necessity for inclusion in the literary domain.

Moreover, public dialog regarding AI-generated literature should be promoted, engaging authors, critics, and technologists in discussions about the future of storytelling (Danesi, 2024). Conferences, seminars, and online forums serve as venues for disseminating insights and experiences with AI in literature, cultivating a collaborative community that prioritizes both originality and authenticity.

In conclusion, reconciling originality and authenticity in the era of AI necessitates deliberate ways for incorporating technology into literary activities. Through the promotion of collaboration, the establishment of ethical rules, and the encouragement of education and public discourse, we can effectively address the complexity of AI-generated literature while safeguarding the integrity of human creativity. As we harness the promise of AI in narrative, it is crucial to maintain a literary environment that is rich, diverse, and real, accurately representing the nuances of the human experience.

5.3 Navigating the Fine Line

In concluding our examination of AI-generated literature, it is imperative to encapsulate the principal insights that have arisen during this discourse. The incorporation of artificial intelligence into the literary domain offers both prospects and obstacles, significantly transforming our comprehension of originality and authenticity in artistic expression (Mazzi, 2024). The interaction between human creativity and machine-generated content requires a thorough analysis of its implications for authors, consumers, and the wider cultural landscape.

A key finding is the acknowledgment that AI can function as a potent instrument for augmenting the creative process. Through collaboration with AI systems, authors can broaden their creative boundaries, producing innovative ideas and investigating unusual narrative frameworks (Finn & Wylie, 2021). This collaboration promotes innovation while enabling writers to preserve their distinct voice and purpose. It is essential to engage in this partnership with a comprehensive awareness of the ethical implications related to authorship and originality, guaranteeing that AI-generated work is utilized ethically and transparently.

The continuous interaction between technology and creativity is essential for influencing the future of literature. As artificial intelligence advances, literary societies must deliberate on AI's role in storytelling, examining its capacity to democratize writing and enhance various voices (Law, 2024). By promoting inclusion in AI training datasets and advocating for ethical methods, we can guarantee that the literary environment encompasses a diverse range of perspectives and experiences.

Education is essential in this discourse, providing future generations of writers and readers with the critical thinking abilities required to comprehend the intricacies of AI-generated literature (Gibson and Green 2025). Integrating considerations of AI into literary curricula enables educators to equip students to engage critically with both human and machine-generated literature, so enhancing their comprehension of the creative process.

The primary difficulty is reconciling the inventive capabilities of AI with the necessity for authenticity in literature. While we explore the potential of AI-generated material, we must remain attentive to maintaining the emotional depth and intentionality that define genuine literary expression (Werdiningsih et al., 2024). The discourse on AI and creativity will persist in evolving, mirroring wider societal transformations and the dynamic essence of storytelling.

In conclusion, traversing the delicate boundary between originality and authenticity in AI-generated fiction necessitates a cooperative strategy that appreciates both human ingenuity and technical advancement. Through continuous dialogue, the establishment of ethical frameworks, and the promotion of education, we may cultivate a literary future that is rich, diverse, and authentic. The evolving interplay between technology and creativity will persist in shaping the literary environment, prompting exploration of new narratives and a redefinition of storytelling in the digital era.

6. CONCLUSION

The advent of AI-generated writing offers a revolutionary possibility and poses a philosophical problem for modern literary practice. This research has examined how the distinction between originality and authenticity becomes increasingly ambiguous when machines engage in the creative process. Although AI may replicate styles, produce content, and interact with human writers, it essentially lacks emotional experience and intentionality—two essential components typically linked to genuine literary expression.

AI-generated works typically exhibit originality that is algorithmically built, relying on extensive datasets and probabilistic models rather than introspective insight. However, when adeptly directed by human authors, AI can function as a significant creative collaborator, providing structural innovation and stylistic variety. Authenticity is inherently challenging to recreate, as it is fundamentally anchored in voice, purpose, and emotional resonance—attributes that AI cannot independently provide.

This changing dynamic compels literary societies to reevaluate traditional concepts of authorship, innovation, and worth. The incorporation of AI into literary culture is further complicated by legal and ethical issues related to authorship, copyright, and bias. Nonetheless, with collaboration, openness, and critical engagement, AI might enhance human creativity instead of diminishing it.

In conclusion, traversing the convergence of AI and literature necessitates a judicious, morally grounded methodology. By maintaining the human aspect in storytelling and integrating technical advancements, we may cultivate a literary future that is diverse, inclusive, and representative of both human creativity and machine proficiency. The future of writing may be shaped not solely by humans or machines, but by the developing collaboration between the two.

REFERENCES

Alghamdi, S. A., Alashban, Y., Alhailiy, A. B., Alharbi, F. F., & Al-Nahrawi, A. E. (2025). Perceptions of artificial intelligence among computed tomography technologists in Saudi Arabia: Influence of demographics and training on AI adoption. *Journal of Radiation Research and Applied Sciences, 18*(2), 101355. DOI: 10.1016/j.jrras.2025.101355

Amankwah-Amoah, J., Abdalla, S., Mogaji, E., Elbanna, A., & Dwivedi, Y. K. (2024). The impending disruption of creative industries by generative AI: Opportunities, challenges, and research agenda. *International Journal of Information Management, 79*, 102759. DOI: 10.1016/j.ijinfomgt.2024.102759

Amirjalili, F., Neysani, M., & Nikbakht, A. (2024). Exploring the boundaries of authorship: A comparative analysis of AI-generated text and human academic writing in English literature. *Frontiers in Education, 9*, 1347421. Advance online publication. DOI: 10.3389/feduc.2024.1347421

Amirzhanov, A., Turan, C., & Makhmutova, A. (2025). Plagiarism types and detection methods: A systematic survey of algorithms in text analysis. *Frontiers of Computer Science, 7*, 1504725. Advance online publication. DOI: 10.3389/fcomp.2025.1504725

Anantrasirichai, N., & Bull, D. (2022). Artificial intelligence in the creative industries: A review. *Artificial Intelligence Review, 55*(1), [page range]. https://doi.org/ DOI: 10.1007/s10462-021-10039-7

Bishop, S., & Kant, T. (2023). Algorithmic autobiographies and fictions: A digital method. *The Sociological Review, 71*(5), 1012–1036. DOI: 10.1177/00380261221146403

Campedelli, G. M. (2021). Where are we? Using Scopus to map the literature at the intersection between artificial intelligence and research on crime. *Journal of Computational Social Science, 4*(2), 503–530. DOI: 10.1007/s42001-020-00082-9

Cañas, J. J. (2022). AI and ethics when human beings collaborate with AI agents. *Frontiers in Psychology, 13*, 836650. Advance online publication. DOI: 10.3389/fpsyg.2022.836650 PMID: 35310226

Černe, M., Bunjak, A., Wong, S. I., & Moh'd, S. S. (2022). I'm creative and deserving! From self-rated creativity to creative recognition. *Creativity and Innovation Management, 31*(4), 664–679. DOI: 10.1111/caim.12518

Chesterman, S. (2024). Good models borrow, great models steal: Intellectual property rights and generative AI. *Policy and Society, 44*(1), 23–45. DOI: 10.1093/polsoc/puae006

Chiarella, S. G., Torromino, G., Gagliardi, D. M., Rossi, D., Babiloni, F., & Cartocci, G. (2022). Investigating the negative bias towards artificial intelligence: Effects of prior assignment of AI-authorship on the aesthetic appreciation of abstract paintings. *Computers in Human Behavior*, *137*, 107406. Advance online publication. DOI: 10.1016/j.chb.2022.107406

Cupać, J., Schopmans, H., & Tuncer-Ebetürk, İ. (2024). Democratization in the age of artificial intelligence: Introduction to the special issue. *Democratization*, *31*(5), 899–921. DOI: 10.1080/13510347.2024.2338852

Danesi, M. (2024). *AI-Generated Cinema*. In *AI-Generated Popular Culture: A Semiotic Perspective* (pp. 37–60). Springer. DOI: 10.1007/978-3-031-54752-2_3

Danesi, M. (2024). *AI-Generated Literature*. In *AI-Generated Popular Culture: A Semiotic Perspective* (pp. 61–85). Springer. https://doi.org/DOI: 10.1007/978-3-031-54752-2_2

De Cicco, R., Francioni, B., Curina, I., & Cioppi, M. (2025). AI, human or a blend? How the educational content creator influences consumer engagement and brand-related outcomes. *Journal of Services Marketing*, *39*(10), 52–70. DOI: 10.1108/JSM-10-2024-0539

Fehér, K., & Katona, A. I. (2021). Fifteen shadows of socio-cultural AI: A systematic review and future perspectives. *Futures*, *132*, 102817. Advance online publication. DOI: 10.1016/j.futures.2021.102817

Finn, E., & Wylie, R. (2021). Collaborative imagination: A methodological approach. *Futures*, *132*, 102788. Advance online publication. DOI: 10.1016/j.futures.2021.102788

Fusillo, M., & Lino, M. (2024). Inter-mediality in digital media environment. *New Techno-Humanities*, *4*(1), 58–64. DOI: 10.1016/j.techum.2024.11.002

Gibson, B., & Green, C. N. (2025). Teaching literature in the age of AI: A collaborative approach to engaged learning. In *Navigating AI in Academic Libraries: Implications for Academic Research* (pp. 179–210). IGI Global.

Haase, J., & Hanel, P. H. P. (2023). Artificial muses: Generative artificial intelligence chatbots have risen to human-level creativity. *Journal of Creativity*, *33*(3), 100066. Advance online publication. DOI: 10.1016/j.yjoc.2023.100066

Hashemi, A., Shi, W., & Corriveau, J. P. (2024). AI-generated or AI touch-up? Identifying AI contribution in text data. *International Journal of Data Science and Analytics*, *8*(4), 1–12. DOI: 10.1007/s41060-024-00693-9

Holzinger, A., Zatloukal, K., & Müller, H. (2025). Is human oversight to AI systems still possible? *New Biotechnology*, *85*, 59–62. DOI: 10.1016/j.nbt.2024.12.003 PMID: 39675423

Huang, B., Chen, C., & Shu, K. (2025). Authorship attribution in the era of LLMs: Problems, methodologies, and challenges. *SIGKDD Explorations*, *27*(1), 45–63. DOI: 10.1145/3715073.3715076 PMID: 40276161

Hussain, A., & Qazi, K. A. (2023). Textual alchemy: AI, authorship and the shifting paradigms of interpretation. *Rupkatha Journal on Interdisciplinary Studies in Humanities*, *15*(4), 1–12. DOI: 10.21659/rupkatha.v15n4.08

Khan, W., Daud, A., Khan, K., & Muhammad, S. (2023). Exploring the frontiers of deep learning and natural language processing: A comprehensive overview of key challenges and emerging trends. *Journal of Natural Language Processing*.

Law, L. (2024). Application of generative artificial intelligence (GenAI) in language teaching and learning: A scoping literature review. *Computers and Education Open*, *6*, 100174. Advance online publication. DOI: 10.1016/j.caeo.2024.100174

Lee, D. C., Jhang, J., & Baek, T. H. (2025). AI-generated news content: The impact of AI writer identity and perceived AI human-likeness. *International Journal of Human-Computer Interaction*, •••, 1–13. Advance online publication. DOI: 10.1080/10447318.2025.2477739

Lin, Z., & Ng, Y. L. (2024). Unraveling gratifications, concerns, and acceptance of generative artificial intelligence. *International Journal of Human-Computer Interaction*, •••, 1–18. Advance online publication. DOI: 10.1080/10447318.2024.2436749

Luo, J. (2024). A critical review of GenAI policies in higher education assessment: A call to reconsider the "originality" of students' work. *Assessment & Evaluation in Higher Education*. Advance online publication. DOI: 10.1080/02602938.2024.2436748

Marzuki, W., Widiati, U., Rusdin, D., Darwin, , & Indrawati, I. (2023). The impact of AI writing tools on the content and organization of students' writing: EFL teachers' perspective. *Cogent Education*, *10*(2), 2236469. DOI: 10.1080/2331186X.2023.2236469

Mazzi, F. (2024). Authorship in artificial intelligence-generated works: Exploring originality in text prompts and AI outputs through philosophical foundations of copyright and collage protection. *The Journal of World Intellectual Property*, *27*(3), 410–427. DOI: 10.1111/jwip.12310

McArthur, J. (2023). Rethinking authentic assessment: Work, well-being, and society. *Higher Education*, *85*(1), 85–101. DOI: 10.1007/s10734-022-00822-y PMID: 35194229

Mindner, L., Schlippe, T., & Schaaff, K. (2023, December). Classification of human- and AI-generated texts: Investigating features for ChatGPT. In Abbas, M., & Freihat, A. A. (Eds.), *Proceedings of the 6th International Conference on Natural Language and Speech Processing (ICNLSP 2023)* (pp. 1–10). Association for Computational Linguistics. https://doi.org/DOI: 10.1007/978-981-99-7947-9_12

Negus, K., & Astor, P. (2022). Authenticity, empathy, and the creative imagination. *Rock Music Studies*, *9*(2), 157–175. DOI: 10.1080/19401159.2021.1989272

Nguyen, A., Hong, Y., Dang, B., & Huang, X. (2024). Human–AI collaboration patterns in AI-assisted academic writing. *Studies in Higher Education*, *49*(5), 847–864. DOI: 10.1080/03075079.2024.2323593

Nguyen, H., Nguyen, V., Ludovise, S., & Santagata, R. (2024). Misrepresentation or inclusion: Promises of generative artificial intelligence in climate change education. *Learning, Media and Technology*, *49*(1), 1–17. DOI: 10.1080/17439884.2024.2435834

Odden, T. O. B., Marin, A., & Rudolph, J. L. (2021). How has Science Education changed over the last 100 years? An analysis using natural language processing. *Science Education, 105*(4), 653–680. DOI: 10.1002/sce.21623

Pack, A., & Maloney, J. (2023). Using generative artificial intelligence for language education research: Insights from using OpenAI's ChatGPT. *TESOL Quarterly*, *57*(4), 1571–1582. DOI: 10.1002/tesq.3253

Radanliev, P. (2024). Artificial intelligence: Reflecting on the past and looking towards the next paradigm shift. *Journal of Experimental & Theoretical Artificial Intelligence*, *36*(2), 1–18. DOI: 10.1080/0952813X.2024.2323042

Ramesh, R., Venkatesh, M., & Girish, G. P. (2023, October). The symbiosis of AI and human agency in digital authorship: Redefining the landscape of contemporary literature. In *International Conference on Intelligent Computing & Optimization* (pp. 255–262). Springer Nature Switzerland. https://doi.org/DOI: 10.1007/978-3-031-50887-5_12

Ranade, N., Saravia, M., & Johri, A. (2025). Using rhetorical strategies to design prompts: A human-in-the-loop approach to make AI useful. *AI & Society*, *40*(2), 711–732. DOI: 10.1007/s00146-024-01905-3

Roos, M., & Reccius, M. (2024). Narratives in economics. *Journal of Economic Surveys*, *38*(2), 303–341. DOI: 10.1111/joes.12576

Sadek, M., Kallina, E., Bohné, T., Mougenot, C., Calvo, R. A., & Cave, S. (2024). Challenges of responsible AI in practice: Scoping review and recommended actions. *AI & Society*, *40*(1), 199–215. DOI: 10.1007/s00146-024-01880-9

Sarker, I. H. (2021). Machine learning: Algorithms, real-world applications and research directions. *SN Computer Science*, *2*(3), 160. Advance online publication. DOI: 10.1007/s42979-021-00592-x PMID: 33778771

Sönmez, S. (2025). Artificial Intelligence in screenplay: ChatGPT application. In *Transforming Cinema with Artificial Intelligence* (pp. 37–52). IGI Global Scientific Publishing., DOI: 10.4018/979-8-3693-3916-9.ch003

Stelmach, M. (2025). Canonization/quantification: Film canon as an empirical matter. *Studies in Eastern European Cinema*, *16*(1), 136–148. DOI: 10.1080/2040350X.2024.2430798

Subagiyo, D. T., & Wibisono, H. (2025). The urgency of artificial intelligence regulation from a joint authorship perspective on copyright infringement. *Indonesia Private Law Review*, *5*(2), 135–156. DOI: 10.25041/iplr.v5i2.3962

Świerczyńska-Kaczor, U. (2024). Empirical insights into traditional and AI-enhanced interactive narratives based on children's fables. *Journal of Economics and Management*, *46*(1), 25–54. DOI: 10.22367/jem.2024.46.02

Varsha, P. S. (2023). How can we manage biases in artificial intelligence systems–A systematic literature review. *International Journal of Information Management Data Insights*, *3*(1), 100165. Advance online publication. DOI: 10.1016/j.jjimei.2023.100165

Verhaal, J. C., & Dobrev, S. D. (2022). The authenticity paradox: Why the returns to authenticity on audience appeal decrease in popularity and iconicity. *Journal of Management*, *48*(4), 873–899. DOI: 10.1177/0149206320950414

Walter, Y. (2024). Embracing the future of Artificial Intelligence in the classroom: The relevance of AI literacy, prompt engineering, and critical thinking in modern education. *International Journal of Educational Technology in Higher Education*, *21*(1), 15. Advance online publication. DOI: 10.1186/s41239-024-00448-3

Watiktinnakorn, C., Seesai, J., & Kerdvibulvech, C. (2023). Blurring the lines: How AI is redefining artistic ownership and copyright. *Discover Artificial Intelligence*, *3*(1), 37. Advance online publication. DOI: 10.1007/s44163-023-00088-y

Werdiningsih, I., Wibisono, H., & Rusdin, D. (2024). Balancing AI and authenticity: EFL students' experiences with ChatGPT in academic writing. *Cogent Arts & Humanities*, *11*(1), 2392388. Advance online publication. DOI: 10.1080/23311983.2024.2392388

Yang, S., Chen, S., Zhu, H., Lin, J., & Wang, X. (2024). A comparative study of thematic choices and thematic progression patterns in human-written and AI-generated texts. *System, 126*, 103494. Advance online publication. DOI: 10.1016/j.system.2024.103494

Younas, A., Fàbregues, S., Durante, A., Escalante, E. L., Inayat, S., & Ali, P. (2023). Proposing the "MIRACLE" Narrative Framework for Providing Thick Description in Qualitative Research. *International Journal of Qualitative Methods*, *22*, 16094069221147162. Advance online publication. DOI: 10.1177/16094069221147162

Zhao, D. (2024). The impact of AI-enhanced natural language processing tools on writing proficiency: An analysis of language precision, content summarization, and creative writing facilitation. *Education and Information Technologies*, *30*(6), 8055–8086. DOI: 10.1007/s10639-024-13145-5

Zhao, Y., Cheng, B., Huang, Y., & Wan, Z. (2023). Beyond Words: An intelligent human-machine dialogue system with multimodal generation and emotional comprehension. *International Journal of Intelligent Systems*, *38*(1), 1–15. DOI: 10.1002/int.20386

Chapter 2
AI-Powered Literary Analysis:
Redefining Themes, Symbolism, and Emotional Resonance in Contemporary Literature

Vishal Jain
https://orcid.org/0000-0003-1126-7424
Sharda University, Greater Noida, India

Archan Mitra
https://orcid.org/0000-0002-1419-3558
NITTE Institute of Communication, India

Sanchita Paul
https://orcid.org/0009-0006-6437-3991
Neil Patel Digital India, India

ABSTRACT

Artificial Intelligence (AI) has transformed literary criticism by introducing advanced tools to analyze complex literary elements such as themes, symbolism, and emotional depth. This chapter explores AI's impact on both contemporary and classic literature, demonstrating how Natural Language Processing (NLP) and machine learning algorithms uncover recurring motifs, narrative structures, and cultural variations beyond human perception. AI's role in interpreting symbolism and identifying thematic connections across genres is examined, alongside its limitations in capturing abstract meanings compared to human intuition. The chapter also investigates AI's effectiveness in assessing emotional resonance using sentiment analysis and tonal evaluation to measure audience engagement. Ultimately, this

DOI: 10.4018/979-8-3373-1057-2.ch002

chapter presents AI as both an innovative tool and a disruptive force, reshaping literary analysis in the digital age.

1. INTRODUCTION

1.1 Background & Significance

The integration of Artificial Intelligence (AI) in literary analysis represents a transformative shift in the way scholars, critics, and educators engage with literary texts. Traditionally, literary interpretation has relied on human intuition, close reading, and cultural contextualization. However, with advancements in Natural Language Processing (NLP) and Machine Learning (ML), AI has introduced new methodologies that offer objective, data-driven insights into themes, symbolism, and emotional resonance in literature (Khurana et al., 2023). This intersection of AI and literary studies is not merely an academic curiosity but a significant evolution that influences both research and pedagogy.

One of the most profound contributions of AI to literary analysis is its ability to process vast amounts of text efficiently. Through NLP, AI can detect recurring themes and patterns that may go unnoticed by human readers. For instance, AI models trained on extensive corpora can identify intertextual references, analyze linguistic styles, and map out historical shifts in literary trends (Dabhade & Narula, 2023). This capability has led to the emergence of computational literary studies, which use machine learning techniques to classify texts based on stylistic elements and thematic content (Hatzel et al., 2023). By automating certain aspects of literary interpretation, AI allows scholars to engage with literature in ways that were previously impractical due to time and resource constraints.

Sentiment analysis, another key AI-driven technique, enables researchers to quantify the emotional tone of literary works. This approach has been particularly useful in studying historical literature, where AI can track shifts in sentiment over time, providing valuable insights into cultural and social evolution (Gandhi et al., 2023). AI's ability to evaluate tonal nuances in texts also extends to contemporary literature, where it aids in understanding audience engagement and reception. Such applications underscore AI's growing role in bridging the gap between qualitative literary critique and quantitative computational analysis.

Academia has shown an increasing interest in AI-driven literary studies. Universities are incorporating AI tools into humanities research, fostering interdisciplinary collaborations between computer scientists and literary scholars (Hutson et al., 2022). AI is also being integrated into digital humanities courses, enabling students to use computational methods for textual analysis. This shift indicates a broader acceptance of AI's role in reshaping literary scholarship, despite ongoing debates about its interpretive limitations.

While AI offers numerous advantages, it also presents challenges. One major concern is whether AI-driven interpretations can fully capture the depth and complexity of literary texts. Symbolism and thematic nuances often require cultural and historical contextualization, which AI, despite its advanced algorithms, may struggle to comprehend accurately (Yadav, 2024). Additionally, issues such as algorithmic bias and the ethical implications of machine-generated critiques raise important questions about the reliability and authenticity of AI-assisted literary analysis. These concerns highlight the need for a balanced approach where AI complements, rather than replaces, human literary interpretation.

The growing integration of AI into literary analysis represents a significant evolution in humanities research. By leveraging computational techniques, scholars can uncover patterns and insights that were previously inaccessible. However, the limitations of AI necessitate continued human engagement to ensure that literary criticism remains nuanced and contextually informed. This study seeks to explore the capabilities and challenges of AI in literary analysis, addressing its implications for contemporary scholarship.

1.2 Research Problem

Despite AI's advancements in textual analysis, its role in literary criticism remains a subject of debate. AI-driven methodologies provide new insights into themes and symbolism, but their accuracy and interpretative depth are frequently questioned. One of the primary concerns is AI's ability to capture subjective elements, such as metaphorical language and emotional depth, which are often central to literary meaning. While AI excels in pattern recognition, it struggles with abstract literary concepts that require human intuition and contextual awareness.

Additionally, there is a need for comparative analysis to determine whether AI can serve as a complementary tool or a potential replacement for traditional literary interpretation. Many scholars argue that AI should enhance human critique rather than substitute it, ensuring that literary studies retain their depth and interpretive richness. However, the increasing reliance on AI raises ethical concerns, particularly regarding algorithmic biases and the potential for misrepresentation of complex literary structures. This research aims to critically examine these issues and assess AI's evolving role in literary analysis.

1.3 Research Objectives

- To explore AI's role in literary interpretation, particularly in analyzing themes, symbolism, and emotional resonance.
- To assess the strengths and weaknesses of AI-driven literary analysis compared to traditional human approaches.
- To evaluate the effectiveness of AI models in sentiment analysis and tonal assessment in literature.
- To investigate AI's integration in academic research and pedagogy and its implications for literary education.
- To examine ethical concerns such as algorithmic biases and their impact on literary authenticity.

1.4 Significance of the Study

The significance of this study lies in its contribution to the growing discourse on AI's role in literary analysis. As computational methods become more prevalent in the humanities, understanding their implications is crucial for both scholars and educators. This research provides a comprehensive examination of AI's capabilities and limitations, offering valuable insights into how machine learning and NLP can enhance literary studies.

Furthermore, this study addresses the ethical dimensions of AI-driven literary analysis. With AI models increasingly influencing academic research, concerns about algorithmic biases and interpretive reliability must be critically evaluated. By exploring these issues, the research highlights the need for a balanced approach where AI serves as a tool to augment, rather than replace, human literary interpretation.

The findings of this study will also have pedagogical implications. As AI tools become integrated into literary education, understanding their potential benefits and drawbacks is essential for educators. This research will provide recommendations for best practices in utilizing AI for textual analysis while ensuring that literary criticism retains its depth and contextual relevance. By bridging technological advancements with traditional humanities scholarship, this study contributes to an evolving field that is reshaping the future of literary analysis.

2. AI IN LITERARY ANALYSIS: A CONCEPTUAL OVERVIEW

2.1 Evolution of AI in Humanities Research

The integration of Artificial Intelligence (AI) into literary studies marks a significant shift in humanities research, merging computational methods with traditional literary criticism. Over the decades, AI has evolved from simple word frequency analysis to sophisticated models capable of thematic interpretation, sentiment analysis, and stylistic evaluation. This transformation has allowed scholars to explore literature at an unprecedented scale, uncovering patterns and intertextual relationships that might otherwise remain unnoticed (Hutson et al., 2022). Despite its potential, AI's application in literary criticism raises fundamental questions about interpretation, objectivity, and the role of human intuition in understanding complex texts.

The roots of AI in literary studies can be traced back to the mid-20th century when early computational linguistics experiments sought to automate language processing. One of the earliest endeavors was machine translation in the 1950s, where researchers attempted to develop systems capable of converting text between languages using rule-based approaches (Ahdritz, 2022). As computational power increased, scholars began employing quantitative techniques to analyze literary texts, focusing on aspects such as word frequency, syntax, and stylistic markers. A key development in AI-driven literary analysis was the emergence of corpus linguistics in the 1980s. By compiling vast digital collections of texts, researchers gained the ability to analyze language patterns across different genres and historical periods (Ye et al., 2025). The rise of Natural Language Processing (NLP) in the 1990s and early 2000s further expanded the capabilities of computational literary analysis, enabling machines to extract meaning from text, recognize entities, and generate summaries (Yadav, 2024). These early applications laid the foundation for modern AI-driven literary criticism, which now leverages deep learning and machine learning models to conduct more nuanced and large-scale analyses.

Traditional literary criticism has long relied on human intuition, close reading, and historical contextualization. Scholars have sought to interpret texts by considering factors such as authorial intent, cultural influences, and reader reception. However, AI has introduced new analytical possibilities by offering a data-driven approach to literary interpretation (Zong & Guan, 2024). AI-assisted methods, such as topic modeling and thematic clustering, allow researchers to detect latent structures within texts that may not be immediately apparent through conventional reading. One of the major advantages of AI in literary analysis is its ability to process massive corpora quickly and efficiently. Large-scale comparative studies, once impractical due to time constraints, are now feasible using AI-powered tools (Biagini, 2025). For instance, sentiment analysis can be applied to thousands of novels to track shifts in emotional tone over centuries, revealing historical changes in literary expression (Bizzoni et al., 2023). Similarly, AI models can detect stylistic trends across different authors and periods, offering insights into the evolution of literary techniques.

Despite these benefits, AI's role in literary interpretation is not without challenges. Unlike human critics, AI lacks the ability to engage with literature on a deeply subjective and philosophical level. The nuances of symbolism, irony, and metaphor often require cultural and historical awareness, which AI struggles to replicate (Arcilla, 2024). Moreover, AI-generated analyses are inherently shaped by the data on which models are trained, raising concerns about algorithmic biases and their impact on interpretive accuracy (Yadav, 2024). As a result, while AI serves as a powerful tool for augmenting literary research, it is unlikely to replace human criticism entirely. Instead, AI should be viewed as a complementary asset that enhances traditional methods by providing new perspectives and expanding the scope of literary inquiry.

2.2 Core AI Technologies Used in Literary Analysis

The effectiveness of AI in literary analysis is largely attributed to three primary technologies: Natural Language Processing (NLP), Machine Learning Algorithms, and Large Language Models (LLMs). These technologies enable AI to analyze texts at multiple levels, from surface-level sentiment analysis to deeper thematic and symbolic interpretation.

Natural Language Processing (NLP) is a branch of AI that focuses on enabling machines to understand, interpret, and generate human language (Bonnel, 2023). In literary analysis, NLP is used to perform semantic analysis, which involves identifying meaning in texts, and sentiment analysis, which gauges the emotional tone of literary works. AI-driven semantic analysis helps in mapping relationships between words, phrases, and concepts within a text. This technique allows researchers to detect implicit themes and associations that might not be evident in a straightforward textual reading (Yadav, 2024). Additionally, by analyzing the emotional tone of a text, AI can classify passages as positive, negative, or neutral, providing insights into character emotions, narrative mood shifts, and thematic evolution (Troiano, 2023).

Machine learning (ML) algorithms are instrumental in recognizing complex literary patterns and clustering texts based on thematic similarities. These models are trained on extensive literary datasets and can classify texts according to genre, authorial style, and period-specific linguistic trends (Li et al., 2024). ML models can detect recurring motifs, syntactic structures, and word usage patterns, helping scholars trace stylistic evolution across different authors and literary movements (Allam et al., 2025). Additionally, AI can group texts based on shared themes, even when the themes are expressed through different linguistic and narrative structures.

This clustering helps in understanding cross-cultural literary influences and intertextual relationships (Yang et al., 2022).

Large Language Models (LLMs), such as OpenAI's GPT series and Google's BERT, have revolutionized AI-driven textual analysis by enabling models to generate human-like interpretations of literary works (Slocombe & Liveley, 2024). These models use deep learning to process large amounts of text, allowing them to produce coherent and contextually relevant literary critiques. LLMs can generate summaries, thematic analyses, and stylistic evaluations of literary texts, mimicking the analytical depth of human critics (Zhang et al., 2024). Despite their capabilities, LLMs lack true comprehension of literature. Their interpretations are based on statistical correlations rather than genuine understanding, making them prone to misinterpretation and bias (Yadav, 2024).

2.3 AI vs. Traditional Literary Criticism

The debate over AI's role in literary criticism centers on the strengths and weaknesses of machine-driven interpretation compared to human analysis. AI can analyze thousands of texts within minutes, making it a valuable tool for large-scale literary research. Its data-driven approach reduces subjective bias, enabling more consistent thematic classification (Wagner et al., 2022). AI can also compare texts across languages and literary traditions, uncovering global literary patterns that might escape human critics. However, AI struggles with the deep cultural, philosophical, and emotional nuances that human critics naturally grasp (Dobson, 2020). Furthermore, AI models are trained on existing datasets, which may reflect cultural biases, leading to skewed literary interpretations (Yadav, 2024). Literature often involves an element of aesthetic and philosophical reflection that AI cannot fully comprehend. Thus, while AI provides valuable insights and enhances traditional literary criticism, human interpretation remains essential for capturing the full depth of literary meaning.

3. AI IN IDENTIFYING AND ANALYZING THEMES & SYMBOLISM

3.1 Automated Detection of Themes

Artificial Intelligence (AI) has emerged as a transformative tool in literary analysis, particularly in the detection of recurring themes across diverse texts. Unlike traditional methods that rely on human interpretation and close reading, AI leverages Natural Language Processing (NLP) and Machine Learning (ML) to systematically identify thematic structures. These AI models analyze vast corpora, recognize patterns, and extract key concepts that contribute to overarching themes in literature (Khurana et al., 2023). AI-based thematic analysis enables researchers to uncover subtle narrative structures and cross-cultural motifs that might otherwise go unnoticed due to human subjectivity and cognitive limitations (Régis et al., 2024).

AI models use topic modeling techniques such as Latent Dirichlet Allocation (LDA) and Non-negative Matrix Factorization (NMF) to analyze the probability distribution of words and phrases across texts. These probabilistic methods categorize literature into clusters based on linguistic features, providing an empirical foundation for identifying dominant and latent themes (Yadav, 2024). Additionally, word embedding techniques, including Word2Vec and GloVe, map relationships between words, enabling AI to detect nuanced thematic elements that evolve across different literary periods and genres.

One significant advantage of AI-driven thematic detection is its ability to perform cross-text analysis, comparing multiple works across different historical and cultural contexts. For instance, AI can analyze the presence of themes such as social justice, gender dynamics, and existentialism in 19th-century European literature and compare them with contemporary global narratives. By doing so, AI provides a macroscopic view of literary evolution, shedding light on how themes persist, adapt, or fade over time (Christou, 2024)

A study applied AI to analyze over 1000 19th-century British and American novels, aiming to detect dominant themes in Victorian literature. The NLP-driven analysis revealed recurring themes such as social class struggle, industrialization, and gender roles, which were prevalent in novels by Charles Dickens, Elizabeth Gaskell, and Henry James. Interestingly, AI identified a previously under-explored thematic shift: an increasing focus on individual psychological struggles in late Victorian literature, suggesting a transition from collective social concerns to personal introspection (Kim, 2022). This AI-driven discovery has influenced literary scholars to reconsider how the Victorian novel gradually evolved toward modernist self-exploration.

3.2 AI in Symbolism Interpretation

Interpreting symbolism has long been one of the most complex tasks in literary studies, given that symbolic meanings often rely on historical, cultural, and philosophical contexts. AI models, particularly those trained on deep learning algorithms, are now capable of detecting and classifying symbolic references by analyzing co-occurrence patterns, metaphor usage, and figurative language structures. AI's ability to recognize symbolic associations through deep neural networks allows for a systematic approach to metaphor and allegory interpretation (Skrynnikova, 2024)

One of the key techniques employed in AI-driven symbolism analysis is vector space modeling, where words and phrases are mapped into multidimensional spaces. This approach enables AI to recognize associative meanings, such as how the word 'light' is frequently linked to knowledge or enlightenment, while 'darkness' is associated with mystery or fear Luger, 2021). AI also employs sentiment analysis to measure the emotional weight of symbolic references, distinguishing between positive and negative connotations in metaphorical expressions.

However, one of the major challenges in AI-based symbolism detection is its difficulty in contextual interpretation. Unlike human critics, AI lacks the ability to fully grasp the historical and philosophical significance of symbols beyond their linguistic patterns. This limitation suggests that AI should serve as an assistive tool rather than an independent literary critic, working alongside human scholars to validate symbolic interpretations and provide additional layers of analysis (Sarker, 2022).

During his final year at Princeton, Fernando Avilés-García, a researcher at Princeton, took on the challenge of analyzing 700-year-old literature with a groundbreaking approach—developing an AI-powered tool to examine the language of Dante Alighieri's *Divine Comedy*. Using word embeddings and NLP-driven sentiment analysis, AI successfully mapped recurring symbols such as fire, darkness, and ascent/descent metaphors throughout the text. AI recognized 'fire' as a dual symbol, representing both punishment and divine purification, while 'darkness' consistently appeared in negative emotional contexts, reinforcing themes of despair and ignorance. However, while AI accurately categorized these symbols, it struggled with more nuanced theological allegories, such as the hierarchical structuring of hell as a representation of divine justice. The study concluded that AI could efficiently assist in quantifying symbolic recurrence and thematic associations, but deeper interpretative insight still required human expertise (Senior Thesis Spotlight: AI and Italian, 2024).

3.3 Comparison of AI-Generated Interpretations with Human Literary Criticism

While AI excels in identifying patterns, recurrences, and linguistic associations, its interpretations often lack the depth and subjectivity that human literary critics bring to analysis. AI can effectively quantify symbol frequency and thematic clusters, but it cannot fully understand philosophical intentions, cultural allegories, or authorial purpose (Dobson, 2020). For instance, in analyzing Shakespeare's *Hamlet*, AI models successfully identified dominant themes such as revenge, madness, and existentialism, but struggled to interpret metaphysical dilemmas such as Hamlet's famous soliloquy *"To be or not to be"*. Unlike AI, human critics contextualize this passage within Renaissance humanism, theological anxiety, and existential philosophy, which AI cannot inherently grasp (Ehrett et al., 2024).

Another key difference is AI's inability to account for intertextual relationships beyond direct textual evidence. Human critics draw upon historical, philosophical, and artistic influences, whereas AI primarily relies on textual data (Umphrey, et al., 2024). This limitation suggests that AI is best used as a quantitative supplement rather than a qualitative replacement for human literary scholarship.

4. AI IN EVALUATING EMOTIONAL RESONANCE IN LITERATURE

4.1 Sentiment Analysis in Literary Texts

Sentiment analysis, a subset of Natural Language Processing (NLP), has been increasingly used in literary studies to assess emotional resonance in texts. AI employs computational tools to quantify the affective and tonal elements within literature, enabling researchers to map out emotional trajectories across narratives (Mao et al., 2024). These techniques analyze linguistic cues, sentiment polarity, and affective markers to determine the emotional intensity and progression within a text.

Computational approaches such as lexicon-based sentiment analysis, machine learning classifiers, and deep learning models facilitate the measurement of emotional depth in literature (Gandhi et al., 2023). Lexicon-based methods rely on predefined sentiment dictionaries, like VADER (Valence Aware Dictionary and sEntiment Reasoner) and AFINN, which score words based on their emotional valence. However, these models often struggle with contextual sentiment shifts and complex literary devices such as irony and sarcasm. Machine learning-based sentiment analysis, particularly models trained on large corpora, like Support Vector Machines (SVM) and Random Forest classifiers, improves the precision of sentiment scoring by recognizing contextual variations (Yadav, 2024). More recently, deep learning models such as Long Short-Term Memory (LSTM) networks and Bidirectional Encoder Representations from Transformers (BERT) have enhanced sentiment analysis by capturing nuanced emotional expressions and complex syntactic structures (Bizzoni et al., 2023).

One of the key applications of AI-driven sentiment analysis is in tracking tonal shifts within narratives. By segmenting texts into passages and analyzing sentiment scores, AI models generate sentiment arcs that reveal emotional progressions across a novel or poem (Nasser El Erafy, 2023). This methodology has been particularly useful in studying modern and classic literature, allowing scholars to quantify shifts from despair to hope, conflict to resolution, or love to loss.

In a study, AI-based sentiment analysis was applied to Shakespeare's *Othello* to track the play's emotional trajectory. Using NLP sentiment scoring techniques, researchers found that the play's tonal progression closely aligned with narrative turning points, particularly Othello's descent into jealousy and paranoia. The sentiment arc highlighted significant emotional downturns in moments of deception, especially in scenes involving Iago's manipulation. While AI successfully mapped emotional patterns, it struggled with interpreting the layered irony and dramatic subtext, reinforcing the need for human critical oversight in AI-driven literary analysis (Mao et al., 2024).

4.2 AI vs. Human Interpretation of Emotional Resonance

AI's ability to quantify emotional tones in literature provides an objective framework for understanding narrative affect. However, compared to human interpretation, AI struggles with capturing subtle emotional undertones, irony, and cultural context (Huffaker, 2023)). While sentiment analysis assigns numeric scores to words and phrases, human literary critics draw upon historical, psychological, and cultural factors to interpret emotional depth beyond mere word polarity.

AI's role in predicting audience engagement has been tested in several large-scale studies where sentiment analysis has been used to compare reader reactions with AI-generated emotional arcs. Studies suggest that emotionally volatile texts—those with pronounced tonal shifts—tend to evoke stronger reader engagement and literary impact (Davis & Grierson, 2022). This aligns with traditional literary theories that emphasize conflict and catharsis as central components of compelling narratives.

5. AI INTEGRATION IN ACADEMIC RESEARCH AND PEDAGOGY

5.1 Enhancing Literary Studies with AI

Artificial Intelligence (AI) has begun reshaping academic research and pedagogy in literary studies, offering innovative tools that enhance both textual analysis and interpretive methodologies. Universities are integrating AI into humanities curricula, where it serves as an assistive tool for linguistic analysis, thematic detection, and literary pattern recognition (V. S and A, 2024). AI's ability to analyze vast textual corpora enables students and researchers to identify recurring motifs, stylistic features, and narrative structures, providing deeper insights into literary works.

AI-powered tools such as Voyant Tools, Google's BERT, and OpenAI's GPT models assist students in conducting sentiment analysis, topic modeling, and lexical frequency analysis, allowing for a computational approach to literature (Tu et al., 2024). These technologies enable researchers to assess emotional resonance, rhetorical structures, and intertextual connections, fostering interdisciplinary collaboration between literary studies and computational linguistics. The accessibility of AI-driven text analysis platforms has democratized literary research, empowering scholars to conduct large-scale comparative studies that were once time-consuming and resource-intensive (Yadav, 2024).

One of the most promising applications of AI in literary pedagogy is the development of adaptive learning systems. AI-driven platforms customize literary learning experiences based on students' reading proficiency, comprehension levels, and analytical skills. For example, NLP-based educational tools provide real-time feedback on students' textual interpretations, guiding them towards deeper analytical reasoning (Mandour, 2025). Such advancements have the potential to bridge gaps in literary education, particularly in non-native English-speaking contexts, where AI can aid in linguistic and thematic comprehension. Students who utilized AI-based literary analysis tools demonstrated enhanced critical engagement, as they could compare their interpretations with AI-generated insights. Furthermore, AI helped identify linguistic nuances and stylistic consistencies across different authors, allowing students to explore intertextual relationships beyond their immediate reading scope (Zheng, 2024). However, researchers also noted that while AI improved efficiency and pattern recognition, students still relied on human interpretative skills to analyze symbolism, historical context, and philosophical depth. The study concluded that AI serves as a powerful complementary tool in literary pedagogy but cannot replace traditional humanistic inquiry.

5.2 Challenges in Academic Adoption

Despite the advantages of AI in literary studies, its integration into academic research and pedagogy has met with resistance. Many scholars argue that AI lacks the critical reasoning, cultural awareness, and interpretive depth required for literary analysis. AI's reliance on data-driven analysis often fails to account for the subjective and philosophical dimensions of literature, leading to concerns about algorithmic oversimplification (Kingbeil et al., 2024).

Another significant challenge is the potential biases in AI models. Since AI learns from existing literary corpora, it inherits linguistic and cultural biases embedded in training datasets. Studies have shown that Western literary traditions dominate many AI training datasets, leading to an underrepresentation of non-Western literary perspectives (Vinodini & Adithya Pothan, 2024)). Such biases can skew AI-driven interpretations, reinforcing dominant narratives while marginalizing diverse literary traditions.

Furthermore, ethical concerns arise when AI-generated literary critiques are misattributed or over-relied upon. Some fear that automated interpretations may devalue traditional literary scholarship, reducing critical inquiry to algorithmic pattern recognition rather than human-led discourse. The overuse of AI in literary studies might lead to a dependency where students prioritize machine-generated insights over their analytical abilities, diminishing the depth and originality of literary interpretation (Yadav, 2024).

6. ETHICAL AND THEORETICAL CHALLENGES IN AI-DRIVEN LITERARY ANALYSIS

6.1 Bias in AI Interpretations

Artificial Intelligence (AI) has revolutionized literary analysis by enabling large-scale textual studies, but it also introduces ethical challenges, particularly in terms of bias and interpretive limitations. AI models are trained on existing textual corpora, which often reflect historical, cultural, and linguistic biases. These biases can manifest in AI-generated literary interpretations, potentially reinforcing dominant narratives while overlooking marginalized voices (Abdelgadir Mohamed et al., 2024)

One of the primary concerns in AI-driven literary analysis is linguistic bias. AI models, particularly those trained on Western-centric datasets, tend to prioritize English-language literature and canonical Western authors, often neglecting non-Western literary traditions. As a result, AI may fail to accurately interpret themes, symbolism, and stylistic nuances in texts from underrepresented cultures (Yadav, 2024). Furthermore, gender and racial biases embedded in training data can influence sentiment analysis and thematic clustering, leading to skewed representations of characters and narratives (Elkins, 2022).

AI's algorithmic constraints further exacerbate its limitations. Machine learning models rely on statistical patterns rather than human intuition, which means they struggle with metaphors, intertextuality, and allegory—critical components of literary meaning. While AI can efficiently detect word patterns, it often misinterprets complex narrative structures and fails to grasp the historical and ideological contexts of literary works (Nishant et al., 2024)).

Additionally, AI models trained primarily on Western literary corpora exhibited difficulty in recognizing oral traditions and indigenous storytelling structures, which are essential components of African literature (Yadav, 2024). Several studies have highlighted AI's Eurocentric biases, demonstrating the need for diverse and inclusive training datasets to ensure a more equitable approach to literary analysis. Researchers concluded that while AI can assist in analyzing African literature, human scholarly intervention remains crucial in contextualizing and correcting AI's interpretative errors.

6.2 Implications for Literary Authenticity

Another major concern in AI-driven literary analysis is whether machine-generated interpretations distort an author's original intent. AI models analyze texts based on linguistic structures and statistical probabilities, often producing decontextualized readings that differ from traditional human interpretations (Barbierato & Gatti, 2024). This raises questions about literary authenticity, particularly in cases where AI-generated insights conflict with established scholarly interpretations.

A key issue is the reduction of literary meaning to quantifiable metrics. AI systems often classify texts based on sentiment scores, word frequencies, and thematic clusters, yet literature is inherently subjective, requiring human intuition and interpretive depth (Karjus, 2025). The reliance on computational analysis risks oversimplifying complex narratives, leading to misinterpretations that overlook philosophical, historical, and ideological subtexts.

Moreover, authorial intent plays a crucial role in literary studies, yet AI cannot discern an author's personal motivations or sociopolitical influences with certainty. Literary authenticity depends on cultural context, philosophical discourse, and historical positioning, aspects that AI models struggle to incorporate meaningfully (Bearman et al., 2023). While AI excels at identifying patterns and linguistic trends, it remains an assistive tool rather than a definitive analytical authority.

7. CONCLUSION

The integration of Artificial Intelligence in literary analysis has significantly expanded the scope of textual interpretation, enabling scholars to identify themes, symbolism, and emotional resonance with computational precision. AI-driven models have demonstrated remarkable efficiency in detecting recurring motifs, categorizing sentiment shifts, and performing large-scale text comparisons that would be impractical through traditional literary criticism. Despite these advancements, AI remains an assistive tool rather than a replacement for human interpretation. While it excels at pattern recognition and thematic clustering, its limitations in contextual understanding, cultural awareness, and emotional depth highlight the continued need for human literary scholars to provide nuanced analysis and philosophical insights.

As AI continues to evolve, its role in literary studies is likely to shift towards a more collaborative framework where computational analysis complements human critique. Hybrid approaches, where AI assists in processing vast literary corpora while scholars provide interpretative depth, could lead to more comprehensive and multidimensional readings of literature. Future developments in AI should focus on refining its ability to understand metaphor, irony, and intertextuality, areas where machine learning models currently struggle. Expanding training datasets to include diverse literary traditions will also help mitigate biases and improve AI's capacity to analyze non-Western literary works with greater accuracy.

Further research should explore the integration of AI's emotional interpretation capabilities through models that combine sentiment analysis with human intuition. Developing AI tools that incorporate historical, philosophical, and cultural contexts will enhance its interpretative accuracy. By fostering interdisciplinary collaboration between AI developers and literary scholars, the field can ensure that technological advancements enrich rather than diminish the depth of literary criticism.

REFERENCES

Abdelgadir Mohamed, Y., Mohamed, A. H. H. M., Khanan, A., Bashir, M., Adiel, M. A. E., & Elsadig, M. A. (2024). Navigating the ethical terrain of AI-generated text tools: A review. *IEEE Access : Practical Innovations, Open Solutions, 12*, 197061–197120. DOI: 10.1109/ACCESS.2024.3521945

Ahdritz, A. (2022). Language in the Age of Artificial Intelligence.

Allam, H., Makubvure, L., Gyamfi, B., Graham, K. N., & Akinwolere, K. (2025). Text classification: How machine learning is revolutionizing text categorization. *Information (Basel), 16*(2), 130. DOI: 10.3390/info16020130

Arcilla, F. E.Jr. (2024). Poetic devices, thematic significance, and social realities in poetry: A critical literature review. *Randwick International of Education and Linguistics Science Journal*, *5*(1), 70–85. DOI: 10.47175/rielsj.v5i1.935

Barbierato, E., & Gatti, A. (2024). The challenges of machine learning: A critical review. *Electronics (Basel), 13*(2), 416. DOI: 10.3390/electronics13020416

Bearman, M., Ryan, J., & Ajjawi, R. (2023). Discourses of artificial intelligence in higher education: A critical literature review. *Higher Education*, *86*(2), 369–385. DOI: 10.1007/s10734-022-00937-2

Biagini, G. (2025). Towards an AI-Literate Future: A Systematic Literature Review Exploring Education, Ethics, and Applications. *International Journal of Artificial Intelligence in Education*. Advance online publication. DOI: 10.1007/s40593-025-00466-w

Bizzoni, Y., Moreira, P., Thomsen, M. R., & Nielbo, K. (2023, July). Sentimental matters: Predicting literary quality by sentiment analysis and stylometric features. In Proceedings of the 13th Workshop on Computational Approaches to Subjectivity, Sentiment, & Social Media Analysis (pp. 11–18). Association for Computational Linguistics. DOI: 10.18653/v1/2023.wassa-1.2

Bonnell, J. R. (2023). Natural language processing in cultural heritage domains: Integrating pretrained language models with rule-based systems for historical Japanese corpora (Doctoral dissertation, University of Miami).

Christou, P. (2024). Thematic analysis through artificial intelligence (AI). *The Qualitative Report*, *29*(2), 21603715. DOI: 10.46743/2160-3715/2024.7046

Dabhade, A., & Narula, S. (2023). Artificial Intelligence in English Literature: Revolutionizing Research Methodologies, unveiling insights, and catalyzing Social Transformation. *Journal of Thematic Analysis*, *4*(1), 88–100.

Davis, G., & Grierson, M. (2022). Investigating attitudes of professional writers to GPT text generation AI based creative support tools.

Ehrett, C., Ghita, L., Ranwala, D., & Menezes, A. (2024). Shakespeare machine: New AI-based technologies for textual analysis. *Digital Scholarship in the Humanities*, *39*(2), 522–531. DOI: 10.1093/llc/fqae021

Elkins, K. (2022). *The shapes of stories: Sentiment analysis for narrative*. Cambridge University Press. DOI: 10.1017/9781009270403

Gandhi, A., Adhvaryu, K., Poria, S., Cambria, E., & Hussain, A. (2023). Multimodal sentiment analysis: A systematic review of history, datasets, multimodal fusion methods, applications, challenges and future directions. *Information Fusion*, *91*, 424–444. DOI: 10.1016/j.inffus.2022.09.025

Glass, G. (n.d.). Fidelity, remix, and the adaptive potential: Leveraging AI and ML techniques in literary adaptation theory. Source Name. Retrieved from https://www.proquest.com/openview/b157b50eb80b8a8d41cb21c37c443001/1?pq-origsite=gscholar&cbl=18750&diss=y

Hatzel, H. O., Stiemer, H., Biemann, C., & Gius, E. (2023). Machine learning in computational literary studies. *IT-Information Technology*, *65*(4–5), 200–217. DOI: 10.1515/itit-2023-0041

Huffaker, J. (2023). Social Reference Processing with Collaborative Human-AI Systems (Doctoral dissertation, University of Michigan). DOI: 10.7302/8321

Hutson, J., Jeevanjee, T., Vander Graaf, V., Lively, J., Weber, J., Weir, G., & Edele, S. (2022). Artificial intelligence and the disruption of higher education: Strategies for integrations across disciplines. *Creative Education*, *13*(12), 3953–3980. Advance online publication. DOI: 10.4236/ce.2022.1312253

Karjus, A. (2025). Machine-assisted quantitizing designs: Augmenting humanities and social sciences with artificial intelligence. *Humanities & Social Sciences Communications*, *12*(1), 1–18. DOI: 10.1057/s41599-025-04503-w

Khurana, D., Koli, A., Khatter, K., & Singh, S. (2023). Natural language processing: State of the art, current trends and challenges. *Multimedia Tools and Applications*, *82*(3), 3713–3744. DOI: 10.1007/s11042-022-13428-4 PMID: 35855771

Kim, H. (2022). Computational approaches in the humanities: From sentiment analysis to deep learning colorization (Doctoral dissertation, Texas A&M).

Klingbeil, A., Grützner, C., & Schreck, P. (2024). Trust and reliance on AI: An experimental study on the extent and costs of overreliance on AI. *Computers in Human Behavior*, *160*, 108352. DOI: 10.1016/j.chb.2024.108352

Li, D., Wu, K., & Lei, V. L. (2024). Applying topic modeling to literary analysis: A review. *Digital Studies in Language and Literature*, *1*(1–2), 113–141. DOI: 10.1515/dsll-2024-0010

Luger, G. F. (2021). Association and connectionist approaches to AI. In *Book Title* (pp. 105–141). Springer., DOI: 10.1007/978-3-030-71873-2_5

Mandour, W. S. (2025). AI-powered tools for linguistic and sentiment analysis in language learning: Applications using Google Sheets and large language models. In *Using AI tools in text analysis, simplification, classification, and synthesis* (pp. 67–112). IGI Global Scientific Publishing. DOI: 10.4018/979-8-3693-9511-0.ch003

Mao, Y., Liu, Q., & Zhang, Y. (2024). Sentiment analysis methods, applications, and challenges: A systematic literature review. *Journal of King Saud University. Computer and Information Sciences*, *36*(4), 102048. DOI: 10.1016/j.jksuci.2024.102048

Nasser El Erafy, A. (2023). Applications of artificial intelligence in the field of media. *International Journal of Artificial Intelligence and Emerging Technology*, *6*(2), 19–41. DOI: 10.21608/ijaiet.2024.275179.1006

Nishant, R., Schneckenberg, D., & Ravishankar, M. N. (2024). The formal rationality of artificial intelligence-based algorithms and the problem of bias. *Journal of Information Technology*, *39*(1), 19–40. DOI: 10.1177/02683962231176842

Régis, C., Denis, J. L., Axente, M. L., & Kishimoto, A. (Eds.). (2024). *Human-centered AI: A multidisciplinary perspective for policy-makers, auditors, and users*. CRC Press. DOI: 10.1201/9781003320791

Sarker, I. H. (2022). AI-based modeling: Techniques, applications and research issues towards automation, intelligent and smart systems. *SN Computer Science*, *3*(2), 158. DOI: 10.1007/s42979-022-01043-x PMID: 35194580

Senior thesis spotlight: AI and Italian. (2024, June 17). Princeton University. https://www.princeton.edu/news/2024/06/17/senior-thesis-spotlight-perfect-marriage-science-and-humanities

Skrynnikova, I. V. (2024). Interpreting metaphorical language: A challenge to artificial intelligence. Vestnik Volgogradskogo Gosudarstvennogo Universiteta, Seriya 2. *Yazykoznanie*, *23*(5), 99–107. DOI: 10.15688/jvolsu2.2024.5.8

Slocombe, W., & Liveley, G. (2024). Introduction: Why AI and literature? In The Routledge handbook of AI and literature (pp. 3–16). Routledge.

Troiano, E. (2023). Where are emotions in text? A human-based and computational investigation of emotion recognition and generation. Source Name. https://doi.org/ DOI: 10.21248/jlcl.37.2024.253

Tu, X., He, Z., Huang, Y., Zhang, Z., Yang, M., & Zhao, J. (2024). An overview of large AI models and their applications. *Visual Intelligence*, *2*(1), 34. Advance online publication. DOI: 10.1007/s44267-024-00065-8

Umphrey, R., Roberts, J., & Roberts, L. (2024). *Investigating Expert-in-the-Loop LLM Discourse Patterns for Ancient Intertextual Analysis*. ArXiv.org. https://arxiv .org/abs/2409.01882 DOI: 10.18653/v1/2024.nlp4dh-1.4

Vinodini, S., & Adithya Pothan Raj, V. (2024). Enhancing literary analysis through artificial intelligence and machine learning: Insights from The Alchemist. In 2024 2nd International Conference on Recent Advances in Information Technology for Sustainable Development (ICRAIS) (pp. 136–141). Publisher Name. DOI: 10.1109/ ICRAIS62903.2024.10811737

Wagner, G., Lukyanenko, R., & Paré, G. (2022). Artificial intelligence and the conduct of literature reviews. *Journal of Information Technology*, *37*(2), 209–226. DOI: 10.1177/02683962211048201

Yadav, D. (2024). The role of artificial intelligence in literary analysis: A computational approach to understand literary styles. Source Name. https://doi.org/xxxxx

Yang, D., Zhou, Y., Zhang, Z., Li, T. J. J., & Lc, R. (2022, March). AI as an Active Writer: Interaction strategies with generated text in human-AI collaborative fiction writing. In *Joint proceedings of the ACM IUI workshops* (Vol. 10, pp. 1–11). CEUR-WS Team.

Ye, X., Huang, L., & Wang, Z. (2025). Exploration of the human-computer synergy paradigm for literary creation via the lens of digital humanities. *Humanities and Social Science Research*, *8*(2), 1–1. DOI: 10.30560/hssr.v8n2p1

Zhang, R., Zhao, W., & Eger, S. (2024). How good are LLMs for literary translation, really? Literary translation evaluation with humans and LLMs. arXiv. https://doi .org//arXiv.2410.18697DOI: 10.48550

Zheng, W. (2024). AI vs. Human: A Comparative Study of Cohesion and Coherence in Academic Texts between Human-Written and ChatGPT-Generated Texts.

Zong, Z., & Guan, Y. (2024). AI-driven intelligent data analytics and predictive analysis in Industry 4.0: Transforming knowledge, innovation, and efficiency. *Journal of the Knowledge Economy*, *16*(1), 864–903. DOI: 10.1007/s13132-024-02001-z

Chapter 3
AI and Historical Narratives:
Reconstructing the Past Through Philosophy

Sooraj Kumar Maurya
https://orcid.org/0000-0002-6974-5508
Zakir Husain Delhi College (Evening), University of Delhi, India

Vikash Ranjan Singh
https://orcid.org/0009-0006-9130-6997
Zakir Husain Delhi College (Evening), University of Delhi, India

ABSTRACT

Artificial Intelligence (AI) is transforming historical studies by introducing innovative methodologies enriched with philosophical insights. Historical narratives, inherently interpretative, are shaped by concepts of causality, morality, and volition. This chapter explores how AI acts as a conceptual tool, blending moral philosophy, existentialism, and socio-political theory into narrative creation. By augmenting historical facts with philosophical frameworks, AI enables speculative reconstructions that address ethical dilemmas, existential questions, and socio-political issues. These AI-driven narratives challenge traditional historiographical boundaries while raising concerns about the distortion of facts and the distinction between history and philosophical invention. Using global examples, the chapter demonstrates how AI broadens access to history while addressing methodological intersectionality. It advocates for the responsible application of AI in history and philosophy to extend historical knowledge and tackle modern challenges, redefining how we engage with the past.

DOI: 10.4018/979-8-3373-1057-2.ch003

INTRODUCTION

The emergence of AI has created a new wave in many fields such as history, philosophy to rewrite history in a number of ways through new methodologies. AI's capacity for assimilating massive data sets, for identifying features or themes, and for creating novel materials has broadened its scope from computational problems and made it a tool that can address fundamental humanistic concerns — concerns arguably best expressed as questions. When applied to the field of history, AI offers a possibility of redefining history both in the philosophical and empirical sense by questioning traditional historical writing and thereby offering new ways of exploring the ethical, existential, and socio-political aspects of history. History is a set of narratives that are not just reports of what happened but constructs based on presence of philosophical investigations and reflections on concepts of cause, justice, and actors. Historians such as Leopold von Ranke stressed on narration of facts where they really were "writing history as it is" (Ranke, 1981). However, more contemporary voices, for instance, Hayden White has maintained that historical writing is inherently relativistic in that it is always and already situated with in the frameworks of meaning, language, and culture (White, 1973). Other schools of thought such as Hegelian and Marxian historicism also support the assessments indicating that the histories propagated are in adherence to the subjective and moral outlooks of the cultures they stem from (Hegel, 2017).

AI's ability to process large amounts of data and generate speculative stories offers new options for incorporating philosophical paradigms into historical writing. The use of ethical dilemmas, existential queries, and socio-political concepts within AI-generated histories allows one to present histories that open up the spectator to critical reflection on aspects of the human' Lebenswelt. For instance, AI written narratives could retell significant events in human history such as the end of slavery in every country, the French Revolution or even modern events like Brexit or Trump's presidency in the frameworks of utilitarianism, existentialism, post-colonialism, patriarchal oppression or any other school of thought and present new opportunities for philosophical reflections on human history.

Philosophical Foundations of Historical Narratives

Historical discourses that are actually presented as the plots in Historical novels are not linear chronicles at all: they are philosophical schools of thoughts superimposed on historical plots. They do thus demonstrate the manner in which the human mind finds pattern, cause, blame and purpose where there is, in fact, none, thus fitting neatly into the tradition characteristic of many earlier disciplines. Obviously the historian and the philosophers who tried to make sense out of history over the times questioned several issues that include what is history?; how can we compare the relative significance of process and persons in history?; and what can be learned from it? The importance of critical philosophical thinking in relation to history refers to the awareness of the philosophical assumptions of historical representations as it enables dealing with the interpretive nature and effects of ideologies and power and the ethical issues involved.

Historical Narratives as Interpretive Constructs

It is crucial to understand that the narrative of history is not purely fact-oriented, but interpretive in nature, which has been known before. Whereas Leopold von Ranke insisted that history must depict events in "how they really were" (Ranke, 1981), the annalistic narrative approach emphasizes positivist empiricism, other neorealist thinkers such as Hayden White have claimed that historical writing is a form of storytelling heavily influenced by narrative structures and ethical worldviews (White 1973). In the same vein, the choice of emplotment – whether the historical account is offered up as a tragedy, a comedy or a romance – is seen as the interpretative stance of the historian. It implies that history writing is not simply a reporting of facts about the past but is strongly influenced by philosophical beliefs of determinism, rationalism, positivism, and enlightenment. The idea of agency and structure has also been discussed in regard to philosophical conceptions of history. Does history progress due to individual effort, which became a notion in historical works through Thomas Carlyle 'Great Man Theory (Carlyle, 1841), or is it an effect of huge structures that has been highlighted in the works of Marx and Foucault? These questions pose the philosophical problems that exist precisely in historical narratives, which is why these themes are so promising.

Hegel: Historical Progress as a Dialectical Process

The German philosopher who developed one of the most popular and appealing historical visions was Georg Wilhelm Friedrich Hegel. Like all great idealists, Hegel also has some concrete explanation to offer about the world and that is his dialectical history which is divided into the thesis, the antithesis and the synthesis. This dialectical movement leads to the advancement of the World Spirit (Weltgeist), as Hegel defined as the process of reason and freedom's development in history. For Hegel, history is not random or purposeless; it has a goal: the attainment of liberty and the pursuit of happiness. As he sees it, each epoch is the next stage in this narrative that is defined by the wars and their resolution. In Hegel's dialectical approach history is made part of the philosophical category, with key themes being freedom, morality, humanity. For instance, he saw the French Revolution not just in terms of a political revolution but a revolution of spirit seeking freedom. According to Hegel, the revolution represents a logical stage of history and encompasses both liberty and its contradictions that were later to be worked out in other historical processes (Hegel, 2017). This of course, aligns with his view that anything historical is not isolated but exists in a grand scheme of things, which is reasonably rational.

However, one of the valuable Hegel's insights is the recognition of the philosophical perspective in historical accounts. He disagreed with the postmodern view that history is just a reconstruction of events that have occurred but a process that has been predetermined by principles that Strozier termed the Great Story. This narrative is an intentionalist, posing history a coherent, progressive movement towards the final goal of free will. The ideas espoused by Hegel refer to the advancement of historical interpretation where one is forced to probe in search of other meanings of historical occurrences and their positive impact on the advancement of humankind. This vision counters simplistic explanations of historical progress and calls for history to be viewed as a complex intercommunication of ideas, struggle, and solutions that define the Human experience and its pursuit of liberty.

Marx: Material Conditions and Class Struggles Shaping History

The strongest influence of Hegelianism with regard to historical narrating can best be demonstrated in the work of Karl Marx, who did not accept the concept of the "World Spirit" as has been postulated by the idealist Hegelicians. According to Marx, history is not a continuous development of ideas but a process that is characterized by conflict that results from the economic structure of human society (Marx, 1859). His famous interpretation of history, historical materialism, contends that the relations of production – the manner in which a society deals with work and resources determines its other relations, political, social, and cultural.

The dialectic approach shifts historical events into a war of material forces where one force represents the opposite of the other force, be it the bourgeoisie and the proletariat. For instance, when speaking about the Industrial Revolution, it is possible to examine the views of Marx and open that it is the process of the working class' exploitation and alienation that may lead to revolutionary action (Marx & Engels, 1848). By reiterating the importance of material circumstances, Marx throws light on the performative decisions historians have to make when drawing a narrative, where they have to define what kind of forces – economic, cultural or political – played the greatest roles in determining the course of history.

Foucault: Power Dynamics and Discursive Formations in Historiography

Foucault's approach to the history overturns the insights of the conventional historical narrative and a cause-and-effect scheme. Unlike Althusser, for whom history is a series of processes culminating in a terminal stage, Foucault stresses the places of power and discourse in the construction of history (Foucault, 1988). According to Foucault, history was not just the chronicle of events but an analysis of how forms of knowledge and power shaped history and specific genres of history writing. Another one of Foucault's discoveries is the idea of "discursive formations" which focuses on how exactly some kinds of knowledge, some norms, some practices come to dominate the field and other kinds remain on the outskirts. For example, in his work Madness and Civilization, he considers the historical representation of madness in order to discover that the concepts of sanity and insanity are actually based on the dynamics of power rather than the specific realities of the existing world (Foucault, 1988). According to Foucault historical narratives are not innocent and straightforward but inscribed with power relations that condition memory and its meaning.

Philosophical Questions Underlying Historical Narratives

The works of Hegel, Marx, and Foucault illustrate that historical narratives are shaped by enduring philosophical questions:

1. **Causality**: What drives historical change? Is it the actions of individuals, structural forces, or a combination of both? Hegel's dialectical process, Marx's class struggles, and Foucault's power dynamics offer competing answers to this question.
2. **Morality**: How should we interpret the ethical and moral dimensions of history? Philosophers like Hegel viewed history as a moral progression toward freedom, while Marx emphasized the exploitation inherent in economic systems. Foucault, in contrast, questioned whether historical narratives can ever escape the power dynamics that shape them.
3. **Human Agency**: What role do individuals play in shaping history? While Hegel emphasized the "great men" who embody the spirit of their times, Marx viewed individuals as shaped by material conditions, and Foucault focused on the broader discourses that constrain and enable human action.

Shaping the Way History is Written and Understood

Fundamentally, the subject of philosophy has transformed how history has been written and the understanding that is given to such work. For instance, the French historical school known as the Annales School in the twentieth century borrowed from Marxist social theory that considered the social and economic processes going on in the society rather than focusing on facts and events in the society. Like Foucault, postmodern historians have also cast doubts on the idea of an objective history and the role of narration and interpretation to history (White, 1988). Therefore, these philosophical influences indicate that historical accounts are not frozen because new philosophy questions and techniques continued to arise. Old as they are, these debates assume new meanings in the age of AI. The capability of creating stories from data highlight the philosophical assumptions that underly AI. For example, can an interpretation created by an AI be deterministic or contain contingencies and moral ambiguity? Thus, it is important to understand how exactly AI can challenge traditional philosophical assumptions about agency and causality in history.

Thus, by posing such questions to consideration, historians and philosophers can systematically clarify the inherently hermeneutical nature of historical representational and writing, as well as the brilliantly moral and epistemological questions prompted by the increasingly ubiquitous technologies.

AI as a Tool for Philosophical and Historical Inquiry

Artificial Intelligence (AI) has emerged as an intesive and revolutionary tool for synthesizing complex datasets, enabling new possibilities for philosophical and historical discussions. Beyond its coventional applications in data analysis and automation, AI holds the potential to reinterpret history through a philosophical lens. By incorporating ethical, existential, and socio-political perspectives into historical narratives, AI enables us to reimagine the past in ways that provoke critical reflection on timeless questions of human agency, morality, and societal structures.

The Role of AI in Synthesizing Historical Data and Philosophical Perspectives

Historical investigation has conventionally been an interpretative exercise that was performed by human beings who are inherently weak cognitive processors and who may not necessarily have been privy to all the source material available to them. AI, however, allows to process large amounts of historical data and find those patterns and relationships that would hardly be seen by a human. Even more significantly,

AI is able to generate the historical scenarios which would include the philosophical issues and discussions and thereby, give a broader perspective of history.

For instance, AI algorithms, when powered with historical texts, can evaluate the phenomenon of competing narratives of history and synthesize critical viewpoints and epistemologies like Marxist historiography, postcolonial theory, or even the feminism method of criticism as conceived by Hayden White (1973). Further, these narratives have potential to be developed with philosophical concepts, including determinism/indeterminism, ethical foundations of violent action, or the Dialektik des Politischen (Hegel, 2017). This synthesis not only expands out knowledge of historical occurrences but also closes the gap between empirical historical studies and strictly philosophical musings.

At the same time it is able to bring change to historiographical writing by including more voices of marginalised groups. By incorporating overlooked files, probe stories, and documentation that remained unnoticed, AI enables a better understanding of history from a more diverse perspective. In an ethical perspective this falls under justice and equity since it breaks away from mainstream thinking that reflects the sociopolitical biases of given time (Fanon, 1963).

Applications of AI in Reimagining Historical Narratives

AI's generative capabilities make it an ideal tool for creating historical narratives that integrate moral, existential, and socio-political philosophy. Below, we explore its applications in these domains.

1. Moral Philosophy: Revisiting Ethical Dilemmas in History

Many historical books raise the issue: Was a particular war morally justified? Did revolutionary leaders act ethically?

One can understand the ethical arguments behind the American Civil War or World War II, for example. Working with methods like utilitarianism, deontology and virtue ethics, AI is capable of creating stories to explain the thought process behind making important choices. A speculative narrative might reimagine Abraham Lincoln's decision to issue the Emancipation Proclamation, examining it through Kantian ethics, which emphasizes duty and universal moral laws, versus utilitarianism, which focuses on the greatest good for the greatest number (Kant, 1785).

2. Existential Philosophy: Freedom, Choice, and Agency in Historical Contexts

In existential philosophy, freedom, choice and agency are key and these subjects are crucial for understanding historical narratives. In many cases, what happens in history relies on big decisions by people or groups, making us wonder if human choices have a strong impact on history. By rethinking crucial events involving freedom, AI-designed narratives can look at these important existential questions. An AI-created story could look at the French Revolution using existentialism as a lens, showing the clash between personal liberty and being part of a community. Taking Sartre's and Camus's ideas in mind, this narrative might look at how revolutionary leaders chose between their moral beliefs and what needed to be done for political progress (Sartre, 2018). AI stories often emphasize how history depends on chance and individual choices instead of being simply predictable. This is related to philosophical inquiries on causality & contingency.

3. Socio-Political Philosophy: Reinterpreting Revolutions, Governance, and Power Dynamics

Socio-political philosophy helps explain revolutions, the way countries are governed and how power is distributed. According to Marx, Foucault and Gramsci, in the manner common men understand history is affected by the structures society, the economy and power ties. AI's capacity to ponder over the ideas and synthesize socio-political theories enables it to originate narratives that interrogate these dynamics. For example, an AI-driven reinterpretation of the Russian Revolution could incorporate Marx's inquiry of class struggle alongside Foucault's thoughts into the relationship between power & discourse. The narrative could focus on how speeches from revolutionaries changed opinions, how financial hardship influenced outcomes in politics and how power transitioned as the revolution was carried out and continued (as explained by Marx in his 1859 work). By integrating socio-political philosophy, AI-generated narratives not only reinterpret the past but also offer insights into the power dynamics of the present.

Case Studies: Speculative AI-Generated Narratives on Key Historical Events

The change AI brings to history can be seen most clearly in its use for speculative restorations of important events. With the help of such narratives, people might explore ideas from the philosophies, understand them in the context of history and reflect on their ethics. There are many interesting cases that reveal how watching moving films can help us grasp the moral, existential and political meanings of the past. The end of slavery shows why we need to look at history from multiple perspectives. An AI-based text might consider slavery from a utilitarian viewpoint, pointing out that it was inefficient economically and caused social problems, as well as according to Kantian ideas which contend that it violated the moral and human dignity of all people. The narrative could integrate postcolonial understanding to outline how abolishing slavery did not always address the greater structures of racial and economic injustice (Fanon, 1963). The story can highlight the decisions history took such as continuing with slavery, to make readers reflect on how things might have developed differently and why inequality still persists.

The French Revolution can also inspire new thinking about philosophy. According to Hegelian dialectics, the Revolution could be understood as a combination of liberty and authority, of equality and hierarchy which led to new ideas in the political world (Hegel, 2017). Through existential perspectives, we can see that during the Reign of Terror, people facing both important moral questions and tough challenges, as revolutionary concepts struggled with the difficulties of meeting survival needs and governing the country (Sartre, 2018). With both a structural and an existential perspective, we are able to understand better both the ambitions and contradictions found in revolutionary movements. India's independence struggle and other decolonization movements from the twentieth century can be restyled using stories generated by AI. For some, these ideas fit together Gandhi's ideas about non-violence and following your moral duty, along with Fanon's strong denunciation of colonialism and cultural domination (Gandhi, 1938; Fanon, 1963). This type of story could focus on leaders' challenges, the choices facing resisters and the joys and disappointments of establishing independence for a country. Blending both philosophies can help AI-generated accounts portray the challenges involved in gaining political freedom. All of these show that speculative AI storytelling goes beyond writing purely about the past and can be a way to discuss important questions about it. Using AI, we can rethink important events from history, challenge accepted stories and consider new thoughts on how we carry on history.

Ethical and Epistemological Implications

While AI's potential for generating philosophical and historical narratives is immense, it also raises ethical and epistemological questions. Considerations about how reliable these accounts are, whether they introduce bias and what blurring fact and fiction means. By dealing with these problems, we make sure AI narratives are a valuable resource for historical and philosophical exploration.

The Philosophy of Interpretation in AI Narratives

Understanding philosophy and history involves interpreting sources. It's important to share the history, but it's even more important to understand the reasons for these events and their meaning. It further examines how to interpret events, by revealing the real meaning and situations occurring in people's lives and within societies. By merging, Artificial Intelligence (AI) makes it possible to seamlessly mix philosophical symbolism, allegory and debate in the creation of narratives. According to Hans-Georg Gadamer, interpretation means discovering the truth but, more importantly, interacting with the historical and cultural contexts in which knowledge is created (Gadamer, 2013). When building a picture of the past, researchers must interpret evidence that is often incomplete, relate this to larger stories and give it its own significance. White (1973) claimed that people tell their history by shaping it with narrative forms such as tragedy or comedy. Basically, these acts are philosophical, since they rely on certain assumptions about how actions result, what is moral and how human beings function. AI makes it possible to study many types of information at once and creates new narratives, thus adding value to interpretation. When philosophical symbolism and allegory are combined with AI-generated narratives, users can better understand the past and think about it more deeply. For instance, an AI narrative might reinterpret the Industrial Revolution as an allegory for humanity's struggle between progress and alienation, echoing Marx's critique of capitalism (Marx, 1859).

AI's ability to incorporate philosophical symbolism into historical storytelling lies in its capacity to synthesize diverse intellectual traditions. For a long time, philosophers and historians have used symbolism to explain abstract ideas clearly. AI is able to recognize and use symbols in stories which helps the writings become richer in meaning. In the context of a speculative novel, chains might symbolize the oppression faced by slaves and also represent a wider meaning for others oppressed by a system. By involving allegory, AI can use historical events to probe the ethical and existential issues they bring up for the audience. (Stanford HAI, 2022) Additionally, AI's capacity for multidimensional analysis enables it to juxtapose competing philosophical perspectives within a single narrative.

Philosophical Debates in AI-Generated Narratives

AI-generated narratives open new possibilities for engaging with perennial philosophical debates, particularly those surrounding causality, determinism, contingency, and agency. These debates shape not only how history is written but also how it is understood and interpreted.

Causality and Determinism in History

It is important to consider whether history is shaped mostly by big forces or by individual actions. According to Hegel, there is a definite system to the events of history (Hegel, 2017). Consequently, existentialists argued that people have the ultimate choice of made their own decisions and aren't limited by pre-set systems (Sartre, 2018).

AI can approach these debates by producing stories exploring different reasons behind similarities and differences. An example would be an AI narrative about World War I which might cover both the main reasons behind the war (alliances, militarism and imperialism) and the role of a single individual's decision (the killing of Archduke Franz Ferdinand). Bringing these perspectives together may lead readers to think about the connection between main forces and single actions in the past.

Contingency and Chance in Shaping Events

The question of contingency in history, events determined by chance or beyond predetermination, is another philosophical debate. For instance, indeed the lead thinker in modernity, Jacques Derrida, postmodern theorists proposed that history was, rather, not a linear progression, but rather, as a series of contingent events which disrupt the line and, indeed, the dominant narrative (Derrida, 1997). AI's ability to simulate counterfactual scenarios makes it uniquely suited to explore the role of contingency. So, what is one speculative narrative doing? It's speculating an alternative outcome to historic events. The task of such narratives is to challenge deterministic accounts and incorporate philosophical reflections on chance and necessity, to show what is unknowable in history.

Free Will vs. Structural Constraints

The tension between free will and structural constraints is another enduring philosophical question. While existentialists champion human freedom, structuralist and poststructuralist thinkers, like Marx and Foucault, emphasize the constraints imposed by economic, social, and discursive systems (Marx, 1859). AI narratives address these questions by using several ways to analyze the issue. In the same way, a tale about the Civil Rights Movement could show how Martin Luther King Jr. was able to guide the movement despite facing challenges like racism and income inequality everywhere. By bringing these views next to each other, the narrative might explain how social change is pushed by more than just individual acts.

Examples of AI-Generated Speculative Narratives Enriched by Philosophical Frameworks

1. **Reimagining the Abolition of Slavery** An AI-generated narrative could reinterpret the abolition of slavery through diverse philosophical lenses. Drawing on utilitarian ethics, it might explore the economic inefficiencies of slavery and their role in abolitionist arguments. Simultaneously, Kantian ethics could be invoked to emphasize the moral imperative of human dignity and universal rights (Kant, 1785). The narrative might also incorporate postcolonial critiques, examining how abolition failed to dismantle broader structures of racial inequality (Fanon, 1963).
2. **The spread of digital surveillance** could be depicted in a speculative narrative as one aspect of continuing arguments about authority and control. Using Foucault's concept of the panopticon, the narrative might analyze how surveillance technologies replicate historical systems of discipline and punishment. If the story includes deep ideas about privacy and autonomy, it might challenge us to rethink the ethics underlying technological governance.
3. **The French Revolution** A reimagined narrative of the French Revolution could juxtapose Hegelian dialectics with Sartrean existentialism to explore the contradictions and choices faced by revolutionary leaders. For instance, the narrative might examine the moral dilemmas of using violence to achieve liberty, reflecting on the tension between collective goals and individual ethics (Hegel, 2017; Sartre, 2018).
4. **Decolonization Movements** Narratives about decolonization could draw on postcolonial theory to examine the psychological and cultural dimensions of liberation struggles. For example, an AI narrative about India's independence might integrate Gandhian non-violence with Fanon's critique of colonial violence, exploring how these philosophies shaped the movement's strategies and outcomes (Gandhi, 1938; Fanon, 1963).

Interpretation philosophy in AI-generated narratives provides a useful way to revise history. Through the use of symbolic concepts, discussing major topics and coming up with thought experiments, AI goes past basic history writing and creates narratives that are both categorical and appealing. At the same time, these stories encourage us to ask about the honesty, objectivity and the place of lies or fantasies when examining history.

Ethical and Epistemological Implications of AI-Generated Historical Narratives

The integration of Artificial Intelligence (AI) into historical storytelling is transformative but fraught with ethical and epistemological challenges. The reasons for these challenges lie in how accurate or true stories are, the difficult choices often present in future stories and the issues about what makes historical knowledge real. It is important to handle these issues to maintain that AI-generated narratives are smart, fair and well-grounded.

Philosophical Authenticity: Challenges in Maintaining Intellectual Rigor

Maintaining philosophical authenticity in AI-generated historical narratives requires adherence to established intellectual traditions and frameworks. Philosophy, as a discipline, emphasizes precision, consistency, and the careful articulation of ideas. When AI engages with philosophical themes, there is a risk of diluting or misinterpreting complex concepts due to the limitations of algorithmic design and training data. For instance, when generating narratives about historical revolutions, an AI system trained on superficial summaries of Marx's materialist philosophy might oversimplify the nuanced relationship between economic conditions and class struggle (Marx, 1859).Similarly, attempting to incorporate Foucault's theories of power and discourse into speculative narratives might result in reductive interpretations that fail to capture the complexity of his ideas. For example, AI produced content is backed by the knowledgeable experts that made sure that it follows the main ideas of the philosophy behind it. AI-based approaches to history also face difficulties related to working across different academic fields. Even though historiography and philosophy use different methods, their fusion through artificial intelligence means they must delicately balance using evidence and imagination. It refers to being faithful to historical information and making a real effort to think analytically and ask questions like philosophers.

Ethical Dilemmas in AI-Generated Historical Narratives

1. Risks of Misrepresenting Historical Truths

It is an urgent concern that AI may present distorted versions of history. All types of historical accounts are involve interpretation, however the introduction of possible or imagined facts by AI increases the problems involved. As an example, if an AI narrative debates whether colonialism was ethical, it might actually strengthen stereotypes or support unjust systems, even when its goal is to argue against them (Fanon, 1963). It is more possible for misrepresentation to happen because many AI algorithms are not completely transparent. It is common for machine learning systems to use methods that are difficult to examine. Certainly, when AI-generated stories depart from the facts or misunderstand important philosophies, it becomes an issue of accountability. It is necessary to make algorithm design transparent and show output results to expert reviewers to reduce these risks (Binns, 2018).

2. Responsibilities in Creating Speculative or Counterfactual Narratives

These types of narratives are helpful for studying how things might have been and can reflect on important debates, but they must still be ethically responsible. It is important to clearly label these narratives as fiction to maintain confidence in history. If someone made a narrative imagining World War II had turned out differently, it could bring up philosophical issues, even though it would likely ignore the true losses and pain experienced. We should always respect the expected rules and not hide the truth or distort our ideas when speculating. It is necessary that fictional narratives admit their arguments are possible and that their philosophical grounding is notable. The goal of AI-generated speculative fictions should be to inspire questioning and second thoughts, rather than simply support and spread ideological views (White, 1973).

Epistemological Boundaries in AI-Generated Historical Narratives

1. Distinction Between Historical Fact and Philosophical Fiction

Oftentimes, the lines between true history and imagined philosophy are hazy in AI-written stories of the past. By blending philosophical ideas, this approach helps storytelling but also brings up questions about what history is and how we learn it. Traditionally, historians try to depict the past using evidence, while philosophers handle abstract ideas and discuss them. When these areas come together under AI, the age-old difference between fact and fiction becomes unclear. If we use existential philosophy to look at the Industrial Revolution again, it may draw attention to issues like loneliness and independence, yet it might also skew the truth if it lacks historical evidence from primary sources (Marx, 1859; Sartre, 2018). It is important to define what epistemological goal AI-generated narratives have: Are these stories meant to copy historical events, probe philosophical ideas or mix both aspects? The separation between historical fact and philosophical fiction impacts how reliable historiography is. If AI stories seem to mix history and fiction too much, they might weaken people's faith in historians. It is necessary for scholars and practitioners to create ways to assess if these narratives carry valid knowledge, so they can be useful in historical and philosophical conversations (Gadamer, 2013).

2. How AI-Generated Narratives Blur Traditional Historiographical Boundaries

The ability of AI to connect different viewpoints and imagine multiple outcomes questions the established rules of writing history. The blending of categories does not have to be an issue; it can, in fact, add new ways for us to understand history. That means we must reconsider what historians consider to be proper study of the past.

By including various types of stories, AI technologies can become more just and inclusive. Yet, this expansion of historiography must be accompanied by rigorous evaluation to ensure that these narratives are not merely tokenistic but contribute to a deeper understanding of history's complexity (Spivak, 1988). Some AI-generated stories might get criticism from historians, as certain traditional ones thrive on using facts and evidence instead of new ideas in their written accounts.

Ethical Frameworks to Guide the Responsible Use of AI in Historical Storytelling

Now that AI is involved in the way we tell history, it is necessary to create rules that help ensure its proper use. It's essential for these frameworks to tie together timeless philosophies and current AI ethics. If AI is not carefully supervised, its narratives about history could lead to incorrect facts, bias or alterations in people's perceptions of history. This means that the ethical use of AI in this field should be guided by transparency, inclusivity, clear philosophy and the cooperation of different fields.

1. Transparency and Accountability

Algorithms and narratives must be made transparent for them to serve their purpose. It is important for developers and scholars to reveal where the data for training was gathered which models they employed and the concepts guiding the story outline. This way, everyone can reflect on their own work and help each other improve. Transparency also aligns with the philosophical value of intellectual honesty, which emphasizes open dialogue, rational critique, and the democratic sharing of knowledge (Habermas, 1984). Having transparent AI in this way enables users to check its results and avoid blindly believing what the model produces.

2. Inclusivity and Equity

An ethical historiography of artificial intelligence should include numerous voices and perspectives. Because standard historical stories have overlooked many groups, it is necessary for AI-written histories to specifically include narratives from women, Indigenous peoples and communities from the Global South. But including all voices should mean more than just showing a diversity of characters. It demands that you study the historical and philosophical basis of exclusion and examine the hidden ways power works. Following Fanon's call for decolonizing history and consciousness, AI narratives should aim to unsettle dominant paradigms and contribute to a more equitable and pluralistic historical discourse (Fanon, 1963).

3. Ethical Use of Speculation

Though speculative AI-generated histories can be fascinating and philosophical, they should be clearly declared as creative stories rather than as factual events. The texts should include warnings and notes explaining that these pieces are meant for examining ethics and topics in philosophy. For example, a speculative retelling of the French Revolution might use philosophical allegory to examine tensions between liberty, equality, and fraternity, but must make clear that it is a theoretical exercise and not an empirical chronicle (Hegel, 2017). This way, we preserve the history, letting people ask deeper questions about it.

4. Interdisciplinary Collaboration

Creating and applying narratives made with AI ought to be done by collaborating with many individuals. For these accounts to be correct, progressive and ethical, experts from different fields have to collaborate. This helps create a knowledge system that works from data through to philosophical perspectives. Drawing from Hayden White's understanding of history as both narrative and interpretation, such collaboration ensures a balance between factual historiography and speculative thought (White, 1973). All in all, using AI in stories should include a framework that is open, open to every background, informed by philosophy and developed together by everyone. Only with this approach can AI serve as a useful tool for looking at history, instead of simply giving distorted or repeated images.

Applications in Philosophy and History

The combination of AI and philosophy or history can enable new forms of storytelling that prompt ethical thoughts, update traditional perspectives and unite different fields of education. By joining philosophical ideas with historical knowledge, AI-based writing can both increase our understanding of history and address important issues happening in the world today.

One important field for its use is philosophical storytelling which involves creating stories that prompt questions about ethics, morality and existence. Major historical events often lead to significant moral questions, including debates about war, colonization and social justice. AI can be applied to analyze these narratives from a moral philosophy viewpoint to encourage different ethical actions. AI could, for example, explore different historical ways in which the abolition of slavery was decided, looking at issues using both utilitarian and deontological reasoning. According to a utilitarian standpoint such stories highlight the happiness of all achieved following the end of slavery, whereas from a Kantian viewpoint, slavery is wrong simply because it harms people morally, without taking outcomes into account (Kant, 1785). Doing history like this, students and researchers may look at old events from a new perspective which encourages them to reflect on their values and develop critical thinking. AI-created stories can also make effective use of existential philosophy. Freedom, choice and human action can be seen as aspects of revolutions and wars. A retelling of the French Revolution, for instance, might highlight themes from Sartre's existentialism—freedom in action, collective responsibility, and the formation of identity through struggle (Sartre, 2018). With these narratives, we can revisit important events in history and ponder today's issues connected to liberty, responsibility and resistance.

AI also plays a role in changing how traditional histories are understood, specifically by incorporating new scholars' ideas. A lot of historical writing focuses on stories centered in the West and ignores views from non-Western and Indigenous cultures. Using AI, it is possible to bring in other ways of understanding and experiencing the world. For example, an AI-generated narrative could integrate Indigenous conceptions of cyclical time and intergenerational memory, in contrast to the linear, progress-oriented logic of Western historiography (Battiste, 2000). AI assists in shifting the focus away from European history and opening up opportunities for fairer and diverse portrayals of earlier times. AI makes it possible to examine colonial times with critical postcolonial theory as well. Narratives shaped by Frantz Fanon's perspective on decolonization and cultural resistance (Fanon, 1963) can offer deeper insights into the legacies of empire, displacement, and identity. These interpretations help change the way history is viewed in each nation and are also part of larger talks about history and justice.

AI narratives can also bring in philosophies that are rarely discussed, helping to make historical accounts more interesting. Many traditional histories tend to overlook the interesting ethical and community lessons found in Confucianism, Ubuntu and Dharmic philosophy. For example, a narrative about Mughal governance could be interpreted through Dharmic ethics—emphasizing dharma (duty), ahimsa (non-violence), and the balance between ruler and subject. Similarly, an AI-generated account of precolonial African societies could draw on Ubuntu philosophy, emphasizing interconnectedness and collective well-being (Mbiti, 1990). They promote discussions between cultures and question the cultural homogeneity found in ordinary history lessons. All things considered, using AI in philosophy and history provides more than just a technical benefit; it also opens ethical and knowledge-based opportunities. It helps rewrite histories from different ethical viewpoints, gives voice to those who were once overlooked and promotes a better understanding of philosophical thoughts worldwide. If used responsibly, AI can improve how we think about and share our historical knowledge with others.

Using Generated Narratives in Philosophy and History Education

The use of AI-written narratives in education is very effective, as they can help students learn from both philosophy and history. Bringing historical data and philosophical foundations together, AI allows students to better engage with difficult concepts. These accounts relate important philosophical ideas to actual historical happenings, helping students observe how both are connected over time. An example is an AI-made story discussing the Enlightenment, pointing out the conflict between rationalism and empiricism by looking at what occurred in the French Revolution or American Declaration of Independence. As a result, it presents the events of history and ties them to current dialogues in philosophy (Habermas, 1984). Using this approach, students are led to consider how history and philosophy influence each other. These narratives often inspire students to think about morality and analyze situations critically in class. It could be interesting to consider a possible situation where new types of inventions helped the Industrial Revolution. It might cause students to reflect on labor, the environment and growth and consider ways to use philosophy to resolve ongoing problems. Encouraging students to talk about and reconsider topics, AI-produced material helps them think about ethics more deeply. AI plays a major role in helping students become more engaged in their learning. The use of such accounts allows students to see different views, reflect on what they believe, compare different explanations and notice how history is complex. For example, an AI-created account of the Holocaust could focus on ethical and existential questions about surviving and resisting, taking inspiration from Hannah Arendt's insights on totalitarianism (Arendt, 1951). It promotes students to go beyond the basic details and think about the moral significance of various events in history.

AI helps students take the lead in their learning. Students can use innovative AI narratives to understand historical subjects and different philosophies in a more creative way. By engaging in learning activities, students become responsible for their learning and develop critical thinking abilities that are important in modern life. AI helps bring philosophy and history together which can improve our teaching styles and insights into the past. The use of various philosophies, highlighting the stories of marginalized groups and prompting reflection on global issues widens the range of traditional history. By this account, this approach helps academics, but more importantly, it lets us grasp our past, handle today and imagine a fairer future (Özmutlu, 2025). So, bringing AI into philosophical and historical education is not just a tech feature but also involves ideas about morality and teaching. It leads to a different style of writing history—one that reflects, is open to all and is meaningful for today's problems and dreams.

Future Directions for AI in Philosophical and Historical Storytelling

As Artificial Intelligence (AI) continues to evolve, so does its capacity to transform philosophical and historical storytelling. The progress of AI-driven stories is connected to technological advances as well as by involving various experts, making historical knowledge available and stimulating creative visions of history. These new approaches show that AI can help make historiography more original, fair and ethical. AI can help historians, philosophers and technologists join forces and work together. By bringing together experts from different areas, it is possible to produce philosophical and historically accurate narratives. Technological developments are helped by the knowledge of historians, philosophers and scientists on interpretation, ethics and forming narratives. As an example, a project could have historians organize historical materials, philosophers add their ethical perspectives and AI developers create tools to combine the results. This cooperation ensures that AI-generated narratives avoid reductive interpretations and instead reflect nuanced, multi-layered perspectives (Binns, 2018).

In addition, AI may help unite experts from different fields. AI now makes it possible to examine topics such as causality, morality and human influence, by studying history and philosophy together. A narrative of the Industrial Revolution, for example, could merge philosophical debates about progress and labor with historical insights into socio-economic change (Marx, 1859). It not only helps us understand more but also creates the chance for scholars to work together more. AI is also playing a major part in giving everyone access to historical knowledge. Historical study has frequently given preference to the stories of those with power, leaving out the voices of women, Indigenous peoples and groups living outside their homeland. By using AI, we can ensure that stories represent a wider variety of people. A feminist-informed AI narrative, for example, could explore the role of women in anti-colonial resistance (Fraser, 2014), while Indigenous histories could be told through frameworks of interconnectedness and cyclical time (Battiste, 2000). By amplifying marginalized voices, AI-driven storytelling aligns with broader efforts to address historical injustice and promote equity in historical discourse (Fanon, 1963).

Furthermore, AI's skills in dealing with big data and communicating in different languages make it possible for overlooked stories to be told by more people. It is possible to digitize and make sense of archival documents from non-Western regions, allowing everyone around the world to use them. This democratization of history has particular value in education, where AI-generated tools can offer students diverse perspectives and foster critical thinking and cross-cultural understanding (Spivak, 1988). AI is also exploring and developing imaginative new approaches in historical storytelling. AI enables the generation of new historical narratives that challenge old interpretations and present new perspectives. They are used not just to interpret events but also to examine philosophical concepts. Reimagining the American Civil War through theories of justice or forgiveness (Derrida, 2001), or framing the French Revolution through allegories of liberty and fraternity (Hegel, 2017), enriches historical understanding while making philosophical ideas accessible and engaging. Still, artificial intelligence in speculative histories creates important ethical issues. These kinds of stories should identify themselves as interpretive or speculative, not based on actual facts. Being open about information sources, pointing out potential guesswork and accepting many scholarly opinions play a key role in sticking to ethical standards (Binns, 2018). When used correctly, these studies can contribute something new to our understanding of the past without changing the facts. To sum up, there are many promising aspects and complexities when it comes to AI in philosophical and historical storytelling. Being an interdisciplinary technology, AI can improve knowledge sharing, promote equitable and ethical stories and help us explore and see the past in different ways. We should not only build stronger AI systems but also tell stories that reflect historical facts, philosophical concepts and social realities. Through working together, AI can assist us in learning about the past, observing and considering the present and imagining a better and fairer future.

CONCLUSION

AI technology added to history gives a better view of how it is studied now. This chapter reveals that history also includes understanding what it all means with the guidance of philosophy. Philosophy is important throughout human history and can be understood by considering Hegel's ideas of dialectic or Foucault's concepts of history and power. AI is able to handle and link many variables and ideas and it brings creative ways to explore such philosophies and restate their histories. There is potential for AI and philosophy to change how moral philosophy, existentialism and socio-political stories are understood. For instance, narrative creation from AI can bring different perspectives to already settled and debated issues like colonialism, wars or migration, which are historical events (Sartre, 2018). All these methods challenge the typical storyline and push viewers to think more thoroughly. For this reason, we will need to handle the new ethical and knowledge problems from AI by telling real information from fake. History's credibility has led us to doubt the processes used by historians and the difference between history and art. In addition to reshaping history writing, AI brings new questions about historical ethics. It exposes the prejudice underlying how history is built and it thereby questions the official accounts of past happenings. It can also bring out the silenced voices that could enrich a fairer representation of history while incorporating Graphics Processing Units.(Zimeta, 2023) The accented focus on both philosophical foundation and ethical standpoint best captures the innovation that AI introduces to the task of historiography (Binns, 2018). AI helps people connect better with old documents and also offers new techniques for both studying and interpreting history, leading to a more thoughtful and helpful way of understanding historical events.

In the modern world, Artificial Intelligence influences how history is written by making historiographic writings more open to questioning and expansion. Bias, exclusion, and systematic marginalization of any histories has been an issue throughout historical scholarship.(Kammerath, 2025) However, AI does not have such limitations, as it creates multiple and inclusive as well as speculative narratives regarding history. The roots of the sociology of knowledge can be seen in the way Weber separated historical development into a progression of stages taking place in European civilization. The ability of AI to introduce non-Western epistemologies, for instance Indigenous cyclical temporality or Ubuntu, challenges such paradigms and enhances the interpretation of past events thus revealing their exclusion (Battiste, 2000; Mbiti, 1990). Similarly, AI can rewrite the conventional histories based on feminist or postcolonial approach, which shifts the paradigms and brings out voices that are often silenced (Fraser, 2014). AI also views it as a unique possibility to explore ideas that would not appear in reality. Because of this, the realm of historical and philosophical questions is more open to ideas. Thus, analysing the Industrial Revolution through the Marxist and existentialist approaches could open up the aspects of ethical intention and socialization of technologies (Sartre, 2018). These narratives both question the accepted version of history and also help expand and modify history, going outside conventional systems.

It is evident from all this that using AI to create historical stories needs close cooperation. This situation arises as AI narratives introduce historical, philosophical, technological and ethical difficulties for which input from historians, philosophers, technologists and ethicists are crucial. Historians assure independence in finding facts and bring experience to make the narratives given by machines more reliable.

Philosophers investigate these stories by suggesting how to analyze them, raising questions on causes and outcomes, morality and the role of personal decisions. This way, technologists develop the algorithms that would write the stories from the data, while ethicists make sure that those algorithms should be developed with respect to the principles of inclusion, openness, and accountability (Binns, 2018; Derrida, 2001). These fields can reach new heights with joint, interdisciplinary projects that encourage discussion and knowledge sharing. For example, imaginative socio-historical projects involve historians, technology engineers, who build intricate and effective AI reconstructions of stories by marginalized peoples; and philosophers and ethicists responsible for reviewing and perfecting their terms. It makes AI-driven storytelling better and it paves the way for artists to mix their creative skills with those of AI experts.

Since AI, philosophy and history are so closely related, these fields have created a new way of understanding the past today and in the future. While AI allows for accurate reconstructions of the past, it is also a platform that motivates people to reflect on eternal problems in philosophy. In addition to history, using philosophy in stories about the past deepens the application of AI by adding understanding and answers to crucial questions related to freedom, justice and agency. Speculative narratives produced by AI involve us in ethical and existential questions which render such history not simply documentation of the past but a means of practising critical thinking about the present and the future (Arendt, 1958). Moreover, the ability of AI to make more historical resources available and emphasize underrepresented experiences fits well with ethical and social goals. AI is valuable for history because, through creating various and inclusive history, AI promotes justice in historiography and understanding of human history's richness and diversity (Fanon, 1963; Battiste, 2000). All things considered, there are many possibilities and reasons to be hopeful about using AI in historical and philosophical narratives. The use of interdisciplinary methods with AI could bring about a rewriting of history that is accurate and important to society. With this possibility, we could address real aspects of life, suggest something different about thinking and invite people to act in favor of justice and new ideas.

REFERENCES

Arendt, H. (1958). *The human condition*. University of Chicago Press.

Battiste, M. (2000). *Reclaiming Indigenous voice and vision*. UBC Press.

Binns, R. (2018). Fairness in machine learning: Lessons from political philosophy. *Proceedings of the 2018 Conference on Fairness, Accountability, and Transparency*, 149–159. DOI: 10.1145/3287560.3287592

Camus, A. (1947). *The plague*. Random House.

Carlyle, T. (1841). *On heroes, hero-worship, and the heroic in history*. Chapman and Hall.

Derrida, J. (1997). *Of grammatology*. Johns Hopkins University Press.

Derrida, J. (2001). *On cosmopolitanism and forgiveness*. Routledge.

Fanon, F. (1963). *The wretched of the earth* (Vol. 36). Grove Press.

Foucault, M. (1961). *Madness and civilization: A history of insanity in the age of reason*. Pantheon Books. DOI: 10.4324/9780203278796

Fraser, N. (2014). *Justice interruptus: Critical reflections on the "postsocialist" condition*. Routledge. DOI: 10.4324/9781315822174

Gadamer, H.-G. (2013). *Truth and method*. Bloomsbury Academic.

Gandhi, M. (1938). *Hind Swaraj*. Navajivan Publishing.

Habermas, J. (1984). *The theory of communicative action*. Beacon Press.

Hegel, G. W. F. (2017). *Elements of the philosophy of right*. Cambridge University Press.

Kammerath, J. (2025). Decolonizing AI: Countermeasures against model biases. *Medium*. https://medium.com/@jankammerath/decolonizing-ai-countermeasures-against-model-biases-e25d95b826ea

Kant, I. (1785). *Groundwork of the metaphysics of morals*. Harper & Row.

Marx, K. (1859). *A contribution to the critique of political economy*. Progress Publishers.

Marx, K., & Engels, F. (1848). *The communist manifesto*. Progress Publishers.

Mbiti, J. S. (1990). *African religions and philosophy*. Heinemann.

Mundre, A. (2025). Epistemic injustice in AI-generated histories. *eScholarship*. https://escholarship.org/content/qt92z102k6/qt92z102k6.pdf

Özmutlu, M. (2025). Uncovering historical silences with AI. *Historica*. https://www.historica.org/blog/ai-unexpected-role-in-uncovering-historical-silences

Ranke, L. (1981). *The secret of world history: Selected writings on the art and science of history*. Harvard University Press.

Sartre, J.-P. (2018). *Being and nothingness: An Essay in phenomenological ontology*. Routledge.

Spivak, G. C. (1988). Can the subaltern speak? In C. Nelson & L. Grossberg (Eds.), *Marxism and the interpretation of culture* (pp. 271–313). University of Illinois Press.

Stanford, H. A. I. (2022). The movement to decolonize AI: Centering dignity over dependency. *Stanford HAI*. https://hai.stanford.edu/news/movement-decolonize-ai-centering-dignity-over-dependency

White, H. (1973). *Metahistory: The historical imagination in nineteenth-century Europe*. Johns Hopkins University Press.

White, H. (1988). *The content of the form: Narrative discourse and historical representation*. Johns Hopkins University Press.

Zimeta, M. (2023). Why AI must be decolonized to fulfill its true potential. *Chatham House*. https://www.chathamhouse.org/publications/the-world-today/2023-10/why-ai-must-be-decolonized-fulfill-its-true-potential

Chapter 4
AI and the Future of Literary Creation:
Transforming Fiction, Poetry, and Drama

Mustafa Kayyali
https://orcid.org/0000-0003-3300-262X
Maaref University of Applied Sciences, Syria

ABSTRACT

The intersection of artificial intelligence and literary creation presents both exhilarating possibilities and profound philosophical questions. This chapter explores how AI is transforming the ways we produce, understand, and value fiction, poetry, and drama. Far from simply automating the writing process, AI reshapes the creative landscape—serving as collaborator, tool, and sometimes even provocateur. By analyzing contemporary examples of AI-assisted literature and examining how machine learning models engage with narrative structures, poetic forms, and dramatic dialogue, this chapter seeks to uncover what is gained—and potentially lost—when creativity becomes entangled with code. It reflects on the evolving identity of the writer, the shifting boundaries of originality and authorship, and the broader cultural implications of letting machines into the sacred space of storytelling. Rather than offering definitive answers, this inquiry invites readers to wrestle with the complexities of a literary future that is not just human but also hybrid.

DOI: 10.4018/979-8-3373-1057-2.ch004

INTRODUCTION

Literature has always been shaped by the tools of its time. From the oral traditions of ancient storytellers to the invention of the printing press, from the typewriter to the digital word processor, each innovation has left its imprint on the way stories are told and shared (JOURNEY, 2024). Today, we stand at the edge of another monumental shift—not merely in medium, but in agency. The arrival of artificial intelligence (AI) as a creative collaborator, and in some cases as a semi-autonomous literary "author," signals a profound change in the very nature of literary creation. What was once the exclusive domain of human imagination is now being co-inhabited by machines capable of generating poetry, crafting narratives, and even improvising dialogue. This chapter begins with a recognition that the growing presence of AI in literary spaces is not a passing trend or a technological gimmick, but rather a development with deep implications for how we understand authorship, originality, and creativity itself. As large language models become more advanced, the line between human and machine-generated text becomes increasingly difficult to draw. This blurring challenges our long-held assumptions about what it means to write—and to be a writer. Can a machine possess a literary voice? What role does intention play in meaning-making? And how do we evaluate literary merit when the creator may not be sentient? These questions are not merely philosophical (Edmond, 2019). They strike at the heart of literary practice and pedagogy, editorial judgment, and even the marketplace for books and ideas.

Writers today are already using AI to brainstorm plots, rephrase prose, generate poetic stanzas, and simulate character dialogue (Gero, 2023). Some authors are transparent about their use of AI; others integrate it quietly into their workflows. In either case, the relationship between human and machine is complex and evolving. Rather than viewing AI as a replacement for the human writer, many artists are beginning to see it as a new kind of creative partner—one that can provoke, challenge, and amplify their work in unexpected ways. But the enthusiasm surrounding AI's potential must be tempered by a sober analysis of its limitations and risks. The models that generate language do not "understand" the world as humans do. They predict text based on patterns in data, not lived experience or emotional insight.

Figure 1. Human vs AI literary capabilities

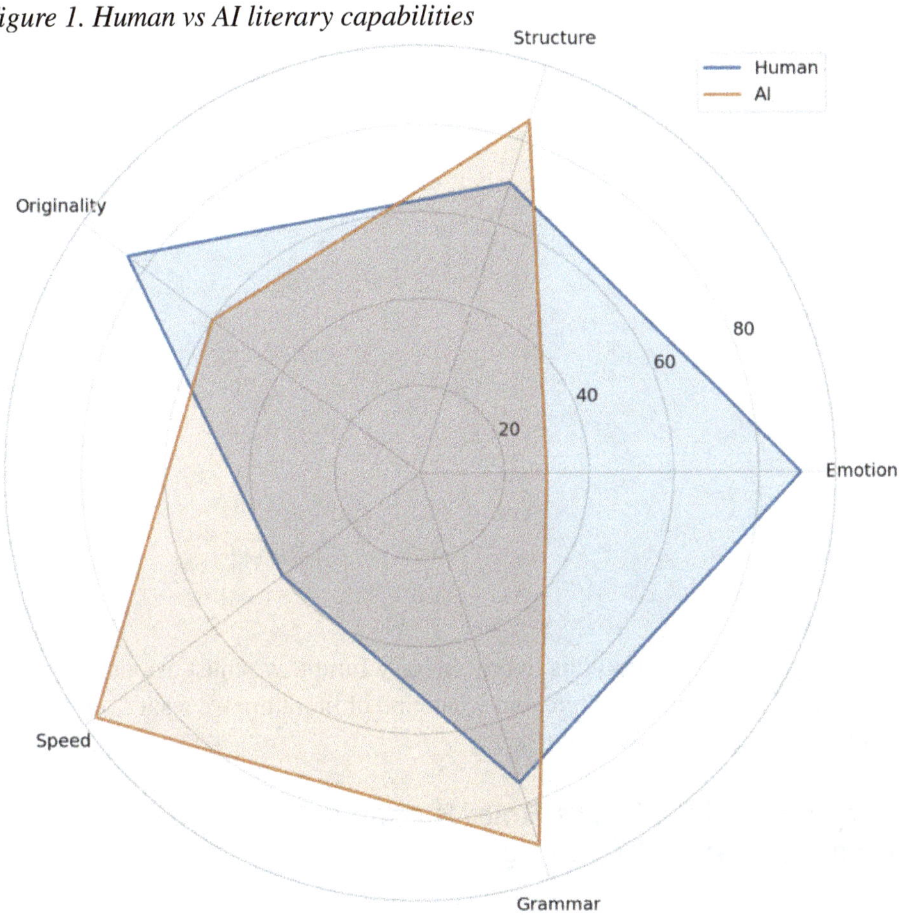

This has implications not only for the quality and depth of AI-generated literature but also for the values it reproduces—often unconsciously—through biased training data or culturally homogenized outputs. As such, the integration of AI into literary creation demands not only technical skill but also critical literacy and ethical reflection. This chapter explores the transformation of literary creation through the lens of fiction, poetry, and drama—three genres that each present unique challenges and opportunities for AI integration. It traces the trajectory of AI's involvement in the creative process, from simple tools for word suggestion to complex systems capable of co-authoring entire works. It also considers the aesthetic, cultural, and moral questions that arise from this transformation.

Figure 2. Growth of AI integration across literary genres

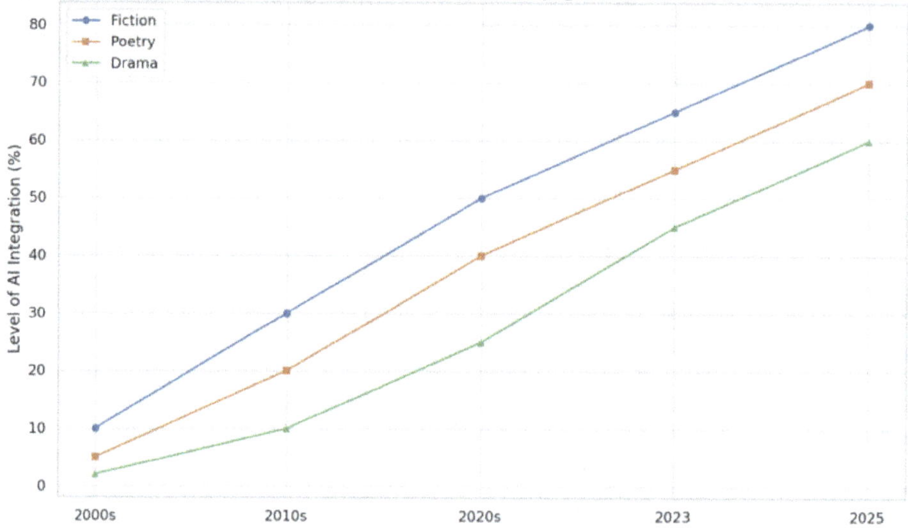

As we move deeper into this hybrid literary future, we must ask ourselves not only what AI can do for literature, but what kind of literature we want to create, and what kind of society we want it to serve.

Reimagining the Writer's Role: Human Creativity in an AI-Driven Age

There is a quiet, almost imperceptible revolution unfolding in the world of literary creation—a shift not announced with fanfare or manifestos, but whispered through subtle changes in how stories are conceived, how words are assembled, and how ideas come into being. At the heart of this transformation lies a fundamental question: what does it mean to be a writer in an era where machines can write? For centuries, the image of the writer has been steeped in romanticism—solitary, imaginative, wrestling with language to give voice to thoughts too elusive for everyday speech (Sharples & y Pérez, 2022). The writer was seen as a kind of cultural alchemist, turning lived experience, memory, and emotion into something enduring: a story, a poem, a play. But now, with the advent of artificial intelligence, that image is beginning to blur. The once-sacrosanct creative process—so long considered uniquely human—is being reconfigured, augmented, and, in some cases, imitated by algorithms.

And yet, perhaps surprisingly, this is not a lament. It is not the death of writing, nor the disappearance of the writer. Rather, it is an invitation—a chance to rethink the role of the human creator, to explore creativity not as a static identity but as an evolving relationship between mind, machine, and meaning. To understand this shift, it helps to consider what AI is and what it is not. These systems—however sophisticated—do not possess consciousness, intention, or desire. They are not creative in the sense that they feel compelled to express themselves. What they do is process: they sort through massive amounts of language data, identify patterns, and generate output based on probabilities. That output can be dazzling. It can mimic style, structure, rhythm. It can sound "like" something a human would write. But it does not come from experience. It does not emerge from the messy, intuitive, often painful terrain of being alive. And yet, for the human writer, AI can be a mirror, a muse, a collaborator (Jung, 2023). Not because it replicates human creativity, but because it challenges the writer to see the creative process differently. When a machine offers ten variations of a phrase you've been struggling with, it might not give you the perfect sentence—but it opens a door. It helps you think laterally, pushing you past the limits of your own linguistic habits. In this way, AI becomes less a rival and more a provocation—asking not "What can I write for you?" but "What have you not yet considered?"

Writers today are navigating this terrain with a mix of curiosity, caution, and courage. Some embrace AI as a tool to break through writer's block, to play with structure, to experiment with genre. Others worry—rightfully—about originality, about voice, about the dilution of artistic integrity. But perhaps the most meaningful way forward is not to retreat from these technologies, nor to romanticize them, but to engage them critically and creatively. In this new landscape, the writer's role becomes less about guarding the borders of authorship and more about guiding the interplay between human intuition and machine-generated possibility. The writer is no longer just the originator of content, but the curator, the interpreter, the ethical center. It is the writer who chooses what to keep, what to discard, what to rework. It is the writer who infuses the text with meaning, context, and resonance. In short, the human remains the heartbeat of the literary endeavor. This shift echoes other moments in literary history when new tools or technologies disrupted traditional modes of creation. The typewriter was once considered a threat to the sanctity of handwriting. The computer, too, was met with suspicion. But over time, each of these innovations became extensions of the writer's hand and mind. What distinguishes AI is not just its capacity to assist, but its capacity to imitate—to produce prose that can feel eerily lifelike. And that, precisely, is what makes the writer's discernment more essential than ever.

Figure 3. Contemporary writer attitudes toward AI

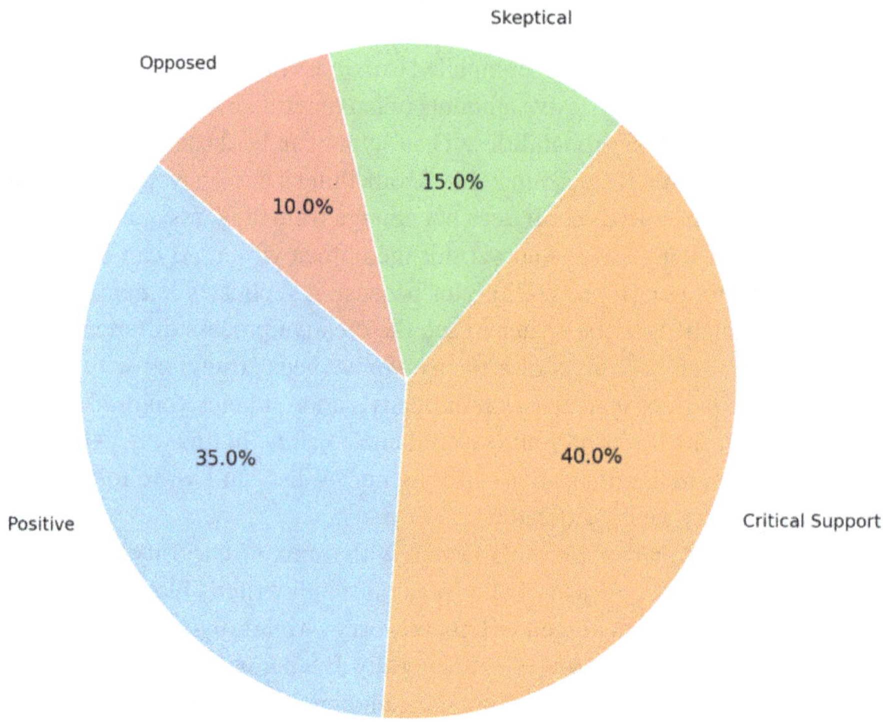

The challenge, then, is not to compete with the machine but to deepen the humanity in our writing (Vallor, 2024). To write not faster, not more efficiently, but more vulnerably, more precisely, more honestly. AI can help us generate a metaphor, but only we can know which metaphor wounds us, which one redeems us (Gero & Chilton, 2019). It can draft dialogue, but only we can understand the silence between the lines. That is where the writer lives—in the subtext, in the contradiction, in the emotional residue that no algorithm can replicate. In this sense, the presence of AI might actually push literature toward greater authenticity. When readers know that a machine can produce technically competent prose, they will crave more than competence. They will seek out the strange, the raw, the unmistakably human. They will value not just polished syntax but idiosyncratic voice, emotional depth, and moral complexity. In a world where machines can write, the writer's task is to make sure we still have something to say. There is also a certain humility that comes with this shift. When we see machines generate language that resembles our own, we are reminded that much of what we do—especially at the surface level—is formulaic. We lean on clichés, on genre conventions, on linguistic shortcuts. AI, in all its mimicry, exposes this. And in doing so, it invites us to go deeper. To break patterns. To unlearn. To return to the blank page not with fear, but with renewed purpose.

But there is more at stake here than individual practice. The role of the writer has always extended beyond the personal. Writers bear witness. They record, question, imagine. They shape the cultural narratives that influence how we see ourselves and each other. In an age of AI-generated content, the writer's social and ethical responsibilities grow even more significant (Lehtimäki, 2024). Who decides what stories are told? Who ensures that the voices of the marginalized are not drowned out by the dominant data sets that feed machine learning? Who holds space for ambiguity, for dissent, for nuance?

These are not questions a machine can answer. They require human judgment, empathy, and accountability. And so the writer, far from being rendered obsolete, is being called upon more urgently than ever—not only to write, but to reflect, to interrogate, to lead. Of course, this reimagined role is not without tension. Writers may feel pressure to adapt, to keep pace with technologies they don't fully understand. They may worry about the erosion of labor, about the commodification of creativity. These are valid concerns. And they point to the need for broader conversations—not just about what is possible, but about what is desirable. About the kind of literary culture we want to build and sustain. Ultimately, the future of writing will not be determined by AI alone, but by the choices writers make in relation to it (Amirjalili et al, 2024). It will be shaped by how we define creativity, how we value originality, and how we protect the soul of storytelling in a world increasingly tempted by speed, convenience, and automation. To reimagine the writer's role in an AI-driven age is not to surrender authorship, but to reclaim it in a more expansive and conscious way. It is to see writing not as a fixed identity, but as a dynamic practice—one that evolves, adapts, and resists. It is to honor both the tools we use and the truths we seek. And most of all, it is to remember that while machines can write, only we can mean.

From Inspiration to Execution: How AI Tools Shape the Creative Process

There is something inherently mysterious about the creative process. At its core, creativity resists being pinned down, defined, or replicated. It emerges unpredictably, often from strange collisions—an overheard conversation, a half-forgotten dream, the shape of shadows on a wall. Writers have long revered this unpredictability, treating inspiration as something sacred, ephemeral, almost divine. But now, in the age of intelligent tools and automated assistance, inspiration has a new companion: the machine. The introduction of AI into the creative process doesn't erase mystery, but it changes its texture (Miller, 2019). What used to be a solitary endeavor, where writers waited patiently (or impatiently) for a flash of insight, is increasingly becoming an interactive exchange—between human instinct and algorithmic suggestion, between the raw emotion of an idea and the statistical patterns that AI can surface. It's not that the muse has disappeared. She's still there. But now she speaks in part through prompts and pattern recognition, through probabilistic phrasing and semantic predictions. The challenge for the writer is to learn how to listen—to both.

What surprises many writers is not that machines can produce coherent language, but that they can spark genuine creative movement (Sharples & y Pérez, 2022). AI tools, when used thoughtfully, don't replace inspiration. They provoke it. They stir the still water. A writer might begin with nothing more than a vague sense—a feeling, a mood, a sentence fragment—and feed that into a text generator. What comes back may not be profound or even usable, but it might trigger a new direction, a line of thought the writer hadn't considered. It's in this moment of dialogue—this back-and-forth—that something genuinely new can emerge. Of course, it would be naive to romanticize this entirely. AI can also mislead, distract, flatten. It can suggest phrases that are technically correct but emotionally empty. It can steer a story toward cliché or generic structure. Writers quickly learn that machine-generated content, for all its fluency, lacks intuition. It has no inner voice. No yearning. No awareness of silence or rhythm. What it offers, then, is not completion but invitation. It gives the writer something to respond to, to push against, to reshape with intention and care.

This is perhaps the most profound way in which AI tools shape the creative process: they reposition the writer as editor, conductor, interpreter. No longer is writing solely about pouring forth original content from some deep interior well. It becomes, increasingly, an act of selection—of recognizing which parts of the machine's output resonate, and why. This demands a different kind of sensitivity. It asks the writer to be attuned not just to what is written, but to what is missing. To what needs to be undone, reimagined, humanized. There's a strange paradox here. In using a machine to help generate text, the writer may actually become more human. More deliberate. More self-aware. Faced with the uncanny mimicry of language that sounds real but feels hollow, the writer is called to dig deeper, to make meaning that the machine cannot access. In this sense, AI is not a threat to creativity but a kind of provocation—a tool that, in exposing the limits of mechanical writing, reveals the essence of authentic voice (Tsao & Nogues, 2024). This interplay is particularly visible in the early stages of writing. In the past, the blank page was both a space of possibility and a source of fear. Now, writers can begin with a nudge—a prompt, a suggested phrase, a quick brainstorm with a digital partner. This lowers the barrier to entry. It demystifies the start. But it also raises new questions: where is the origin of the idea? Who holds the spark? These are not simple questions, and they won't have simple answers. But they force us to think more critically about authorship, intention, and collaboration.

As the writing process moves from inspiration toward execution, the influence of AI becomes more technical—but no less complex. Writers now use tools that assist with grammar, tone, pacing, even stylistic imitation (Dehghanian et al, 2023). Some use these tools to tighten their prose. Others to mimic the voice of another writer, or to match a particular genre. In doing so, they walk a fine line between adaptation and imitation. The tools are powerful, yes. But they require restraint, judgment, and an underlying vision. Without that, the work risks becoming mechanical—not because a machine helped write it, but because the writer relinquished too much control. Execution, in this context, is not just about finishing a text. It's about refining intention. It's about making choices—what to keep, what to discard, what to revise with greater care. AI tools can assist with all of this, but they do not guide the heart of the work. They do not know what the writer is trying to say, or why it matters. That remains a profoundly human concern. Perhaps the most interesting tension in this process is not between man and machine, but between ease and depth. AI tools can make writing faster (Abinaya & Vadivu, 2024). More fluid. But speed is not always a friend to insight. The risk is that writers begin to favor convenience over exploration. That they settle too soon. That they confuse fluency with meaning. The challenge, then, is to use AI not as a shortcut, but as a tool for discovery—to slow down, even as the technology speeds things up. Writers who do this well approach AI not as a magic solution, but as a sparring partner. They test its outputs. They ask questions of the suggestions it makes. They use it to push their own boundaries—not to define them. In this way, the creative process becomes more dialogic, more layered. There is still solitude, yes. But it is punctuated by interaction, by experimentation, by the friction of divergent logics—human and computational—meeting on the page.

There's also a communal dimension to this new process. Writers are beginning to share not just their finished work, but their methods—their experiments with tools, their prompts, their surprises and missteps (Smith, 2020). This openness invites new conversations about craft. It demystifies writing in a way that is oddly generous. It reminds us that inspiration does not have to be solitary, or even secretive. It can be shared, co-created, tangled in the feedback loop of collective creativity. What this all points to is a redefinition of authorship—not in terms of ownership, but in terms of agency. The writer, in this AI-assisted process, is not less important. In fact, they may be more central than ever. Because now, their role is not just to write, but to decide. To shape. To care. To ensure that what emerges is not merely coherent, but alive. And maybe this is the most human part of it all—that despite all the tools, all the shortcuts, all the computational elegance, writing still comes down to something ineffable. A moment of clarity. A sentence that feels exactly right. A rhythm that breaks the surface of the ordinary and becomes something you can feel in your chest. AI can help us get closer to that moment. But it cannot give it to us. That still belongs to the writer, and perhaps always will.

Narrative Mechanics and Machine Learning: Fiction in the Age of Algorithms

There's something sacred about storytelling—something elemental, almost primal. Long before the written word, long before printing presses and publishing contracts, we sat around fires and made sense of the world through narrative. Fiction was never just about entertainment; it was how we taught, how we remembered, how we imagined lives beyond our own (Currie, 2020). It is a practice as old as language itself, shaped by intuition, emotion, and the ineffable rhythms of human experience. So, what happens when that age-old practice meets something as calculated and mathematical as machine learning? What happens when the delicate act of weaving a story—a novel, a fable, a confession disguised as fiction—is no longer the sole province of the human imagination? We live in a time where algorithms can write stories. Not just summaries or reports, but narratives—complete with characters, settings, conflict, and resolution. These machines don't "feel" or "understand" in any traditional sense, but they can mimic the structure of storytelling remarkably well. They can generate dialogue, evoke setting, even play with style. And while the results are uneven, sometimes uncanny, there's no denying that something is shifting—something profound.

At the heart of fiction is structure. Writers, even if they claim to reject rules, are almost always working within invisible scaffolds. Rising action, climax, denouement. Character arcs. Point of view. Narrative tension. These elements give stories their shape, their emotional pull. And it turns out that machines, trained on vast archives of literature, are very good at identifying these patterns. They can learn what a love story "sounds like," how horror builds suspense, what beats appear in a hero's journey. They don't invent these mechanics, but they recognize them and replicate them with a kind of eerie precision. This has complicated consequences. On one hand, it democratizes fiction. Someone who struggles with plotting might use an AI tool to sketch out a basic narrative arc (Chen et al, 2023). A writer unsure of dialogue might lean on the algorithm for rhythm or tone. In this way, machine learning becomes a kind of tutor—a silent, tireless collaborator who offers structure where there was once uncertainty. And for many, this is empowering. It reduces the paralysis of the blank page. It opens doors. But fiction is not just mechanics. It's not just the scaffolding. It's the pause in a sentence that reveals a character's hesitation. It's the awkward, messy, too-honest line of dialogue that doesn't quite fit, but feels heartbreakingly true. It's the unresolved ending, the moral ambiguity, the contradiction that lingers. These are things that resist pattern. They are gestures, instincts, ruptures. They are what make fiction not just readable, but human.

Figure 4. AI use cases across literary genres

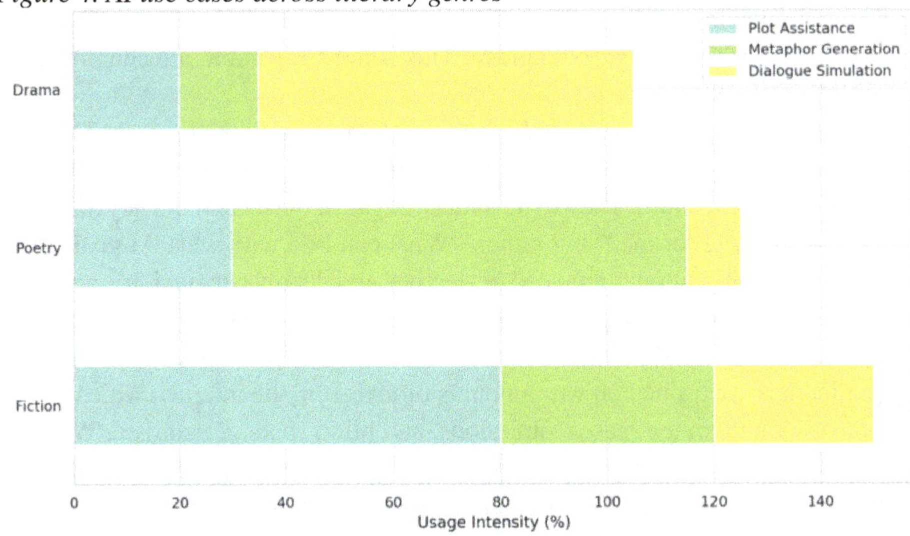

And this is where the machine falls short—not because it fails to emulate, but because it lacks what cannot be emulated. It lacks memory. Not data memory, but the kind that lives in a scar or a secret. It lacks yearning. It lacks the irrational leaps we make when we write from pain or joy or love. A character, to a machine, is a cluster of traits and actions. To a human, a character is a mirror, a ghost, a dare. That difference is everything. Still, the presence of machine learning in fiction is not something to fear blindly. It is something to reckon with, to interrogate. For some, it may become part of the process—a brainstorming partner, a generative springboard. For others, it may serve as a foil, a reminder of what fiction is and must remain. Either way, it forces a confrontation with our assumptions: What makes a story "good"? What makes it authentic? Is it the originality of its form? The honesty of its voice? The emotional resonance it leaves behind?

There's also the question of saturation. As machine-generated fiction becomes more common, we may find ourselves surrounded by texts that are perfectly structured, linguistically smooth, but strangely hollow (Danesi, 2024). The risk is not that readers won't know the difference—it's that we'll stop expecting more. That we'll grow used to fiction that satisfies but doesn't surprise, that entertains but doesn't challenge. This is where the role of the human writer becomes not less important, but more urgent. In a world flooded with artificial narrative, the raw, imperfect, vulnerable voice will stand out like never before. Some writers already see this coming and are pushing back—not with hostility, but with intention. They are leaning into the messiness of storytelling. They are writing stories that resist easy summary, that break rules, that speak in voices that algorithms can't quite imitate. They are embracing silence, contradiction, discontinuity—those very elements that machine learning struggles to grasp. This is not a rejection of technology, but a reassertion of art.

Others are experimenting, blending the mechanical with the organic. They use AI to generate fragments, and then respond to those fragments like a jazz musician riffing off a familiar chord. They write with and against the machine. They don't ask, "What can AI write for me?" but rather, "What can I do with what AI gives me?" This kind of collaboration is nuanced, reflective, and deeply personal. It's not about replacing creativity. It's about expanding its boundaries—cautiously, critically, and with care. We also need to consider the cultural and ethical implications. Most AI writing models are trained on vast amounts of text from the internet, which means they carry with them the biases, omissions, and blind spots of that data. When an algorithm writes fiction, it writes from a place of statistical majority. This can reinforce stereotypes, erase nuance, and marginalize already underrepresented voices. Writers have a responsibility to be aware of this, to question not just the outputs, but the inputs. To ask: Whose stories are we training machines to tell? Whose voices are being echoed, and whose are being silenced?

In fiction, as in life, voice matters. Perspective matters. And while machines can generate language, they do not have perspective. They do not grow up in a particular family, walk through a particular city, feel the sting of a particular loss. They do not live in bodies marked by race, gender, disability, or desire. They do not carry generational memory. And so, they cannot tell certain stories—not truthfully, not meaningfully. That responsibility remains with us. Still, there is room for experimentation. There is room to explore what fiction becomes when it's born from hybrid authorship. We might one day read novels co-written by humans and machines that offer something genuinely new—not because the machine is "creative," but because it disrupts our habits, challenges our assumptions, makes us see the page differently (Yang et al, 2022). The key is not to pretend that machines are storytellers, but to acknowledge that they are tools—and like all tools, they reflect the hand that wields them. Narrative, at its best, is not just about plot. It's about consciousness. It's about how we experience time, how we interpret change, how we make meaning from chaos. Machine learning can simulate aspects of this, but only we can feel it. Only we can recognize when a story touches something that hasn't been touched before. That remains the great miracle of fiction: its ability to take the singular, the deeply personal, and render it universal. So perhaps the question is not whether fiction will survive the age of algorithms. Of course it will. The question is: What kind of fiction do we want to write? What kind of stories will we insist on telling, even when a machine can imitate the telling?

The answer, I think, lies in remembering that fiction is not just a product. It is a gesture. A reaching-out. A bridge between solitude and connection. And while machines may assist in shaping that bridge, the impulse to build it—that comes from us. It always has. It still does.

Poetic Expression and the Logic of Code: The Machine's Muse

Poetry has always been the most enigmatic of literary forms. It exists somewhere between music and meaning, precision and mystery. It is language distilled, cracked open, and rearranged not just to tell but to feel. More than any other genre, poetry leans on silence, suggestion, rhythm, and breath (Shewell, 2020). It is, in essence, the voice of the ineffable—the things we struggle to say and yet must try to express. To attempt poetry is to engage in an act of radical vulnerability. So what happens when this most human form of expression begins to emerge from a source that does not feel, that does not dream, that does not even live?

We now find ourselves at an unprecedented intersection: a moment in which machines—cold, calculating, untiring—can write poems. Or at least, they can mimic the form. They can produce lines that rhyme, that follow meter, that reference mythologies and metaphors. They can echo the styles of Dickinson, Rumi, or Neruda with eerie fluency. The question is no longer whether a machine can write a poem. The question is whether what it writes can be called poetry. At first glance, the answer might seem obvious. If a sonnet looks like a sonnet, if it rhymes and evokes a certain mood, if it holds some ambiguity or turns at the end, surely it counts. But poetry is not mere decoration. It is not the sum of its structure or vocabulary. It lives in intention. In emotion. In the subtle, often unconscious choices a poet makes—choices shaped by memory, culture, identity, loss. Machines do not possess any of these. They simulate. They pattern-match. They do not write from the gut. Still, it would be dishonest to dismiss entirely what happens when machines generate verse. Sometimes, quite unexpectedly, a line will strike a chord. A juxtaposition will seem almost profound. A phrase will catch the light in just the right way. And for a moment, the reader might forget its source and simply feel. This is where things get complicated. Because while the machine does not intend meaning, the human reader brings meaning to it. We project. We interpret. We search for resonance. And sometimes, we find it—not because the machine succeeded, but because we, as readers, were open to connection.

This opens up a curious paradox. Machines may not be poets, but they can trigger poetic experience (Booten & Gero, 2021). Not through craft or inspiration, but through a kind of generative randomness that occasionally brushes up against beauty. It's a bit like reading a found poem, or overhearing a phrase on the train that feels strangely profound. The source may be accidental, but the impact is real. And so we begin to ask not just "Who wrote this?" but "Why does this move me?"

Figure 5. Emotional depth (human) vs coherence (AI) in poetic evaluation

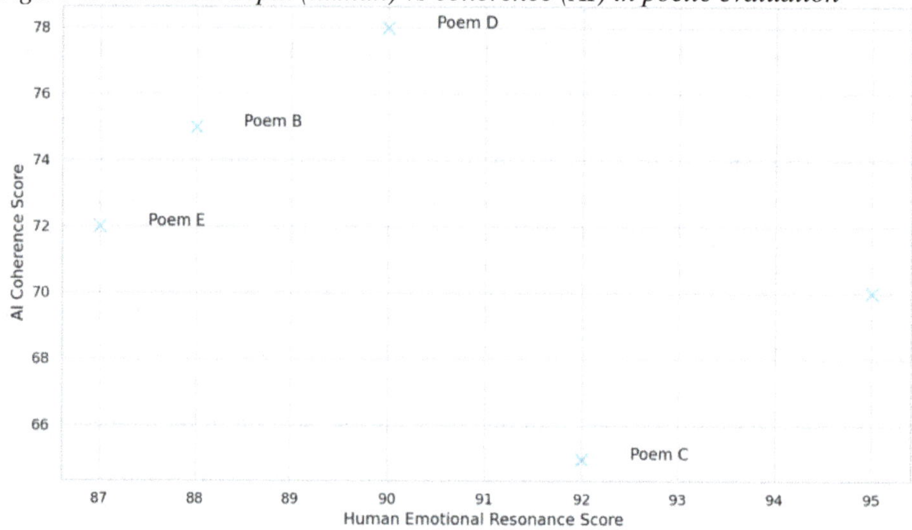

Writers, too, are beginning to experiment with these provocations. Some poets use AI to generate stanzas, then respond to them in kind—building a call-and-response that echoes improvisational jazz (Miller, 2020). Others use machine-generated lines as constraints, as challenges to write beyond the expected. There are those who use code not just to mimic poetry, but to explore new forms of poetics—algorithmic verse, procedural generation, dynamic text that changes over time. These explorations don't always result in beautiful poems, but they do provoke a deeper understanding of the poetic impulse. What's perhaps most fascinating is how these technologies are forcing poets to reexamine their relationship with language. When a machine produces metaphor after metaphor, when it can spit out dozens of variations in a second, the poet is no longer the sole generator of images. Instead, the poet becomes a curator, a filter, a voice of discernment. This can feel unsettling—like ceding some part of the sacred creative act. But it can also be liberating. The poet is freed from the tyranny of the first draft. The poet can engage with language more playfully, more reflectively, more collaboratively.

But again, we must return to the heart of the matter. Poetry is not about novelty. It is about presence (Stein, 2022). The act of writing a poem is, at its best, an act of attention. The poet notices—patterns in nature, shifts in mood, fragments of memory—and then shapes that noticing into language. Machines do not notice.

They calculate. They rearrange. They operate from probability, not perception. And because of this, they miss the one thing poetry requires above all: a sense of being alive in the world. Poetry has always been, and perhaps will always be, bound to the body. Its rhythms mirror the breath (Lilja, 2023). Its cadences echo the heartbeat. It is written not just with the mind but with the full range of human experience—our aches, our longings, our silences. A machine cannot replicate the moment a line comes unbidden while walking under winter trees, or the grief that distills itself into a single image after loss. These are not data points. They are moments of presence. They are, in a sense, sacred. And yet, the presence of AI in poetry is not a desecration. It is a mirror. It shows us what we value. It reflects our patterns back to us. It pushes us to question what we mean by voice, by originality, by authorship. It reminds us that the true power of poetry lies not in cleverness or form, but in the depth of its feeling and the honesty of its reach.

There's also a danger here—not technological, but cultural. As machine-generated poetry becomes more widespread, we risk mistaking fluency for meaning (Gopidi, 2020). We risk normalizing surface without substance. And in doing so, we may lose our appetite for difficulty, for ambiguity, for poems that don't quite resolve but linger in the mind like questions. The machine is trained to please. But poetry, real poetry, does not always please. Sometimes it wounds. Sometimes it bewilders. Sometimes it breaks the form completely and dares us to follow.

In this way, the poet's task in the age of code is not to compete with the machine but to transcend it. To write poems that a machine could never write—not because they are complex or obscure, but because they are rooted in lived experience. Because they carry the weight of memory, of culture, of being. Because they are not written to please, but to say what must be said, however fragile or fierce. Perhaps this is the irony of our age. As machines become more capable of imitating the surface of poetry, poets are being called to go deeper (Kobierski, 2023). To write more vulnerably, more urgently. To risk more. The presence of the machine, with all its code and logic, makes the human voice more precious, more necessary than ever. In the end, poetry survives not because it can be reproduced, but because it speaks to what cannot be mechanized. Grief. Wonder. The exact shade of light in a lover's eye. The silence after an argument. The first breath of spring. These are things the machine cannot feel. But we can. And that is why we write. So let the machine generate its lines. Let it play with form and meter. Let it serve, if we choose, as a muse—not divine, but digital. But let us not forget that the real muse is still within us, in our noticing, our aching, our dreaming. That is where poetry begins. That is where it will always begin.

Drama and Dialogue: AI's Emergence in Theatrical Writing and Performance

Theatre has always been a space of profound intimacy—a live, breathing art form where words become bodies, gestures become language, and time feels suspended. Drama does not merely tell a story; it unfolds it before us, with rawness and immediacy. It is an art of presence, of tension, of silence pregnant with meaning. At its core, the dramatic form relies not only on language, but on the delicate dance of human emotion, gesture, timing, and voice. To write a play, to shape dialogue that rings true on a stage, has always been a deeply human act. And yet, here we are, in a moment where machines have begun to write scenes. Scripts. Monologues. Stage directions. And we are left to wonder: what does this mean for the art of drama?

The arrival of artificial intelligence in theatrical writing is not a headline—it's a quiet shift (Joubin, 2023). A playwright, curious or blocked, enters a prompt into a tool. A few seconds later, the machine responds with a character sketch, a snippet of dialogue, maybe even an entire scene. The lines sound like theatre. They mimic the cadences of real speech. They hold conflict. They move the plot forward. And yet, something nags at the edge of the page. Something subtle but undeniable. A flatness, perhaps. A missing heartbeat. Let's be clear: dramatic writing is not just about people saying things. It is about subtext. About what is not said. About tension that simmers under the surface. About the emotional logic that shapes why a character speaks or chooses not to. Machines can model the syntax of speech, the back-and-forth rhythm of dialogue, even the mechanics of character motivation. But drama lives in what resists logic. In the way a pause can rupture meaning. In the unpredictability of human behavior. In that moment when a line spoken on stage shatters something inside the audience. Can a machine understand what it means to tremble in silence before delivering a line that costs everything? Still, we must admit that AI-generated dialogue can sometimes be striking (Clark, 2024). There are lines that echo dramatic convention, phrases that feel authentic enough to pass.

And this raises interesting questions—not about whether AI can write theatre, but about the thresholds of believability. What makes dialogue *alive*? What makes a character not just consistent, but compelling? The answers are elusive because they exist at the crossroads of language and soul. Characters in theatre are more than the sum of their lines. They are lived contradictions. They are shaped by the choices they make and haunted by the ones they avoid. A playwright breathes life into them not only through dialogue, but through silence, gesture, and rhythm. Writing for theatre is like composing music—each beat matters, each pause has weight. AI can simulate rhythm, it can even be trained to include stage directions, but it does not feel the pressure of the moment. It does not sense when a character is about to break or fall or lie. And so it lacks the instinct to cut through the surface and touch the core.

What's emerging, then, is a space where AI can assist but not replace. Some playwrights use it to explore different voices (Casazza & Gioppo, 2020). Others feed it scenes and ask it to expand. In this way, the machine becomes a rehearsal partner of sorts—generating ideas to be sculpted, questioned, and revised. It's a bit like improvisation: unpredictable, occasionally illuminating, often disposable. But within that process, something real can happen. A spark. A new direction. An unexpected emotion. And if the playwright is attentive, if they are present and discerning, they can use that moment to find their way back to the truth of the scene. There are even attempts to stage AI-generated plays. These performances are often framed as experiments, not as finished works. They invite the audience to participate in a kind of critical dialogue: What are we watching? What do we feel? Where does this text succeed, and where does it falter? These performances are fascinating, not because they are emotionally gripping (most are not), but because they force us to re-evaluate our assumptions about performance, authorship, and authenticity. They become mirrors, reflecting not just what machines can do, but what we expect from art.

And yet, despite all the intrigue, we must be careful. Theatre is more than language. It is embodiment. It is breath. It is the trembling hand, the trembling voice. It is two actors sharing a look that says more than a monologue ever could. The magic of live performance is not in the script alone, but in its transformation through human presence. An AI can generate words, but it cannot step onto the stage (Marcus, 2020). It cannot feel the weight of the lights or the gaze of the audience. It cannot sweat. It cannot forget its lines and recover with something even more truthful. These moments—messy, fragile, electric—are the soul of theatre. The deeper danger, perhaps, is not that AI will write great plays. It's that we will lower our standards. That we will come to accept competent, passable scripts that mimic the form but lack the fire. That we will forget how strange and unruly good theatre can be. That we will start to value fluency over feeling, efficiency over risk. This is where the playwright's responsibility becomes vital—not to reject technology, but to remember why we write in the first place. To insist that theatre remain a space of human encounter. Of discomfort. Of aliveness.

There is also an ethical dimension that cannot be ignored. If AI models are trained on existing plays, whose voices are being amplified, and whose are being left out? Are the models reproducing dominant cultural tropes while ignoring marginalized perspectives? Are they repeating biases embedded in historical scripts? These questions are not technical; they are artistic and moral. Theatre has long been a platform for dissent, for challenging systems of power. If machines are writing our plays, we must be vigilant about what ideologies they are silently reinforcing (Hobbs, 2020). In this sense, the playwright must be more than a writer. They must be a reader, a critic, a steward of the form. They must question not only what a scene says, but what it means, what it risks, what it demands. And this kind of questioning cannot be outsourced. It is human work. It is hard work. But it is also beautiful. Because when it succeeds—when a playwright captures something raw and true, and when that truth is embodied on stage—there is nothing like it. It is a moment of communion. Between actor and audience. Between text and emotion. Between memory and presence. No machine can touch that. Because it requires feeling. It requires risk. It requires someone choosing, again and again, to speak into the silence. AI will continue to evolve. It will continue to generate plays, some of which may be clever or even surprising (Lehman et al, 2020). But the future of theatre will not be written by code. It will be written by people—people who listen deeply, who watch closely, who care fiercely. People who know that drama is not a script, but an encounter. And dialogue is not just words, but everything that trembles between them.

Ethical and Aesthetic Questions: The Future of Authorship and Literary Value

There was a time when authorship was a sacred concept. To write was not merely to produce content, but to create something singular—something that bore the mark of one's voice, one's history, one's interior life. The author was not just a name on the page; they were the source of meaning, the one through whom language passed and became something more. And even as literary theory challenged the notion of the all-knowing, all-controlling author, we still clung to the belief that behind every meaningful work of art was a mind, a body, a story. Today, that belief is being tested. Not by literary theory, but by technology. Specifically, by the rise of tools capable of generating prose, poetry, even whole books with astonishing fluency (Gopidi, 2020). Machines, trained on vast amounts of text, can now produce work that resembles literature (Bajohr, 2023). They can mimic voices, echo genres, even follow the invisible rules of style. And in doing so, they raise uncomfortable questions—not just about who writes, but about what writing means.

At the heart of this shift lies a deeply human tension: the collision between the ethical and the aesthetic. On one hand, we are confronted with the ethical dilemma of creation without consciousness. Can a machine that has no sense of self, no feeling, no memory, truly "author" a work? And if not, what are we to make of the texts it produces? Who is responsible for them? Who owns them? And what are we to do with the illusion of authorship that surrounds them? On the other hand, we are faced with the aesthetic dilemma of value (Ginsburg & Budiardjo, 2019). If a text moves us, if it is beautiful or provocative or formally impressive—does it matter how it was made? Should the origin of a work impact our evaluation of its worth? And if so, why? Is it because we believe that art must be rooted in experience? That a story must come from somewhere real in order to carry weight?

These questions are not academic. They are personal, cultural, and urgent. And they demand that we pause—not to reject what is new out of fear, but to reflect carefully on what we stand to lose or gain. Let's begin with authorship. Traditionally, the author has been seen as the bearer of intention. A novel is not just a string of sentences; it is an argument, a worldview, a series of choices made in time. We read not only for plot or language, but for the mind behind the words—for the sensibility that shapes what is said and what is withheld. But what does it mean when that sensibility is artificial, when the choices are the result of statistical modeling rather than lived thought? Can there be intention without awareness? Can there be voice without selfhood? Some argue that authorship is already a murky concept. Ghostwriters, collaborative projects, editorial interventions—these all complicate the idea of a single authorial source (Turner, 2023). But there is still a difference between a human whose hand is invisible and a machine that has no hand at all. One has a life; the other has an algorithm. That distinction may seem philosophical, but it is also emotional. We are drawn to art not only because of what it says, but because we sense a someone behind it—someone trying to make meaning. This is why the use of machine-generated texts without disclosure feels deceptive. Not because the language is false, but because the relationship is. When a reader engages with a poem, a story, a play, they are entering into a silent contract. They believe there is a human on the other side of the page, speaking in earnest. When that belief is broken—when the author is revealed to be absent—something shifts. The connection frays. The text may still be clever, but it becomes hollow. The aesthetic experience is altered by the ethical rupture. And yet, the opposite is also true.

Knowing that a piece of work was crafted by a human can deepen our appreciation of it. Not because it is necessarily better, but because it is riskier. Because it carries the vulnerability of being seen. When we read a poem written by someone in grief, or a short story that wrestles with longing or injustice, we are not just admiring craft—we are witnessing courage. That is part of what gives art its moral dimension: it is an act of exposure. Which brings us to the question of value. How do we define literary worth in an age where machines can mimic its surface? Do we continue to privilege originality, even when originality itself is hard to define? Or do we begin to accept that fluency, polish, and style can be separated from experience? If a machine can write a sonnet that sounds like Shakespeare, does that diminish Shakespeare—or does it make us realize that form alone is not what made him great?

Literary value has always been shaped by more than technical execution (Wang et al, 2019). It is bound up with context—historical, personal, political. We value a novel not only for its language but for its resonance, its timing, its bravery. We care not just what it says, but *why* it says it, and *who* is saying it. That's why we return to certain writers again and again—not just for their stories, but for their gaze. For the way they see the world. AI, for all its power, has no gaze. It sees nothing. It reflects what it has been trained on. It can simulate style, but it cannot care. And that, ultimately, is the difference. A writer chooses. A writer wonders. A writer suffers, dreams, remembers. Those things cannot be encoded. They cannot be downloaded. They must be lived. But the ethical questions do not end there. What happens when machine-generated texts are used to flood the literary marketplace? What happens when publishers choose quantity over quality, when algorithms prioritize engagement metrics over depth? What happens when writers are pressured to compete not with each other, but with tireless tools that never run out of ideas?

We risk a future in which human creativity is undervalued—not because it has diminished, but because it has been drowned out. And that would be a tragedy. Not because machines are bad writers, but because human writing is about more than output. It is about process. About slowness. About wrestling with words until something honest emerges. So where does this leave us? It leaves us with a choice. Not between past and future, but between carelessness and care. We can choose to embrace new tools while still honoring the values that give literature its meaning. We can choose transparency over deception. We can choose to ask harder questions about ownership, influence, and voice. And above all, we can choose to center the human—not as a gatekeeper, but as a guide. The future of authorship is not about who writes, but about how and why (Thorp, 2023). It is about the courage to say something true in a world saturated with imitation. It is about the patience to write slowly in an era obsessed with speed. It is about the insistence that art is not just production, but presence. As machines become more fluent, our responsibility deepens (Buhmann & Fieseler, 2023). We must not only write, but read with greater attention. We must not only create, but curate with care. And we must remind ourselves—and each other—that literature is not just language. It is a trace of being. A record of thought and feeling. A map of the self in time. In the end, the future of literary value will not be determined by algorithms. It will be determined by what we choose to honor. And if we are wise, we will continue to honor the work that bears the mark of a human hand, a human voice, a human soul. Because that is the kind of art that lasts. That lingers. That matters.

CONCLUSION

As we look toward the horizon of literary creation, it becomes clear that artificial intelligence is not simply a tool—it is a presence, a participant, and perhaps even a provocateur in the evolving narrative of human expression. This chapter has sought to chart the contours of this new literary terrain, highlighting both the transformative potential and the urgent questions that arise when machines are invited into the heart of creative practice. AI's entry into literature marks a turning point, not only in how texts are produced but in how we conceive of creativity itself. Fiction, once rooted in human experience and individual voice, can now be partially or even wholly constructed by algorithms trained on vast corpora of existing works. Poetry—traditionally the most intimate and emotionally resonant form of expression—can now emerge from the statistically derived logic of pattern and prediction. Drama, with its intricate webs of character, dialogue, and tension, can be simulated by systems that mimic the rhythms of human speech. These capabilities are undeniably impressive. But they are also incomplete.

AI does not dream. It does not grieve. It does not long for something it cannot name. These absences matter. While machines can mimic the surface of human expression with astonishing fluency, they do not possess the depth of interiority, the contradiction, or the vulnerability that defines our most enduring literary works. In this sense, AI challenges us not to retreat from the creative process, but to engage with it more consciously. As we collaborate with machines, we are also invited to reflect more deeply on what is uniquely human about our artistic impulses. Importantly, the rise of AI also brings forth new ethical responsibilities. Who owns a piece of writing generated by a model trained on countless copyrighted works? What happens to literary diversity when global models prioritize dominant cultural narratives? And how do we ensure that literature remains a space of human connection, empathy, and dissent in a world increasingly shaped by code? To embrace AI in literature is not to surrender to it. It is to enter into a conversation—one that is dynamic, difficult, and deeply necessary. Writers, educators, publishers, and readers must all play a role in shaping this new chapter of literary history. The goal should not be to mechanize the imagination but to expand it, to use technology not as a crutch but as a mirror and a challenge. In the end, perhaps the true value of AI in literary creation is not in what it writes, but in what it compels us to reconsider: our assumptions about creativity, our relationship with language, and our collective vision for the future of storytelling. As we turn the page to this hybrid age of literature, let us do so not with fear or naiveté, but with curiosity, courage, and care.

REFERENCES

Abinaya, M., & Vadivu, G. (2024). AI Tools for Efficient Writing and Editing in Academic Research. In Utilizing AI Tools in Academic Research Writing (pp. 141-157). IGI Global. DOI: 10.4018/979-8-3693-1798-3.ch009

Amirjalili, F., Neysani, M., & Nikbakht, A. (2024, March). Exploring the boundaries of authorship: A comparative analysis of AI-generated text and human academic writing in English literature. [). Frontiers Media SA.]. *Frontiers in Education*, *9*, 1347421. DOI: 10.3389/feduc.2024.1347421

Bajohr, H. (2023). *Artificial and Post-Artificial Texts*. On Machine Learning and the Reading Expectations Towards Literary and Non-Literary Writing. DOI: 10.12685/bmcct.2023.007

Booten, K., & Gero, K. I. (2021, June). Poetry machines: Eliciting designs for interactive writing tools from poets. In *Proceedings of the 13th Conference on Creativity and Cognition* (pp. 1-5). DOI: 10.1145/3450741.3466813

Buhmann, A., & Fieseler, C. (2023). Deep learning meets deep democracy: Deliberative governance and responsible innovation in artificial intelligence. *Business Ethics Quarterly*, *33*(1), 146–179. DOI: 10.1017/beq.2021.42

Casazza, M., & Gioppo, L. (2020). A playwriting technique to engage on a shared reflective enquiry about the social sustainability of robotization and artificial intelligence. *Journal of Cleaner Production*, *248*, 119201. DOI: 10.1016/j.jclepro.2019.119201

Chen, Q., Cao, S., Wang, J., & Cao, N. (2023). How does automation shape the process of narrative visualization: A survey of tools. *IEEE Transactions on Visualization and Computer Graphics*. PMID: 37030780

Clark, A. (2024). *The experience machine: How our minds predict and shape reality*. Random House.

Currie, G. (2020). *Imagining and knowing: The shape of fiction*. Oxford University Press. DOI: 10.1093/oso/9780199656615.001.0001

Danesi, M. (2024). AI-Generated Literature. In *AI-Generated Popular Culture: A Semiotic Perspective* (pp. 23–44). Springer Nature Switzerland. DOI: 10.1007/978-3-031-54752-2_2

Dehghanian, A., Seyyedrezaei, S. H., Mazandarani, O., & Barani, G. (2023). Pedagogical Implementation of Stylistic Imitation in Grammar-based Writing Instruction in EFL Classes. [JNTELL]. *Journal of New Trends in English Language Learning*, *2*(3).

Edmond, C. (2019). Poetics of the machine: Machine writing and the AI literature frontier (Doctoral dissertation, Macquarie University).

Gero, K. I. (2023). *AI and the Writer: How Language Models Support Creative Writers*. Columbia University.

Gero, K. I., & Chilton, L. B. (2019, May). Metaphoria: An algorithmic companion for metaphor creation. In *Proceedings of the 2019 CHI conference on human factors in computing systems* (pp. 1-12). DOI: 10.1145/3290605.3300526

Ginsburg, J. C., & Budiardjo, L. A. (2019). Authors and machines. *Berkeley Technology Law Journal*, *34*, 343.

Gopidi, A. (2020). Poetry in the Age of Mechanical Reproduction: A Computational Study (Doctoral dissertation, International Institute of Information Technology).

Hobbs, R. (2020). Propaganda in an age of algorithmic personalization: Expanding literacy research and practice. *Reading Research Quarterly*, *55*(3), 521–533. DOI: 10.1002/rrq.301

Joubin, A. A. (2023). Screens as Anthropomorphic Interfaces: How AI Changes Shakespearean Theatrical Publics. *Shakespeare Bulletin*, *41*(4), 529–553. DOI: 10.1353/shb.2023.a920571

JOURNEY, W. T. A. T. (2024). Preface: A Writing Transformation. Best Practices to Prepare Writers for Their Professional Paths.

Jung, K. (2023). Good readers, good writers, and AI: Tool, collaborator, author? *Fordham Intell. Prop. Media & Ent. LJ*, *34*, 1029.

Kobierski, M. (2023). AI the Creator? Analysing Prose and Poetry Created by Artificial Intelligence. Journal of Young English Philology Thought and Review, 9.

Lehman, J., Clune, J., Misevic, D., Adami, C., Altenberg, L., Beaulieu, J., Bentley, P. J., Bernard, S., Beslon, G., Bryson, D. M., Cheney, N., Chrabaszcz, P., Cully, A., Doncieux, S., Dyer, F. C., Ellefsen, K. O., Feldt, R., Fischer, S., Forrest, S., & Yosinski, J. (2020). The surprising creativity of digital evolution: A collection of anecdotes from the evolutionary computation and artificial life research communities. *Artificial Life*, *26*(2), 274–306. DOI: 10.1162/artl_a_00319 PMID: 32271631

Lehtimäki, M. L. (2024). Navigating Ethical and Practical Challenges in AI-Driven Visual Content Creation.

Lilja, E. (2023). Rhythm in Modern Poetry.

Marcus, G. (2020). The next decade in AI: four steps towards robust artificial intelligence. arXiv preprint arXiv:2002.06177.

Miller, A. I. (2019). *The artist in the machine: The world of AI-powered creativity*. Mit Press. DOI: 10.7551/mitpress/11585.001.0001

Miller, B. (2020). " All of the rules of jazz": Stylistic Models and Algorithmic Creativity in Human-Computer Improvisation. Music Theory Online, 26(3).

Sharples, M., & Pérez, R. P. (2022). *Story machines: How computers have become creative writers*. Routledge. DOI: 10.4324/9781003161431

Shewell, C. (2020). Poetry, voice, brain, and body. *Voice & Speech Review*, *14*(2), 143–166. DOI: 10.1080/23268263.2020.1743502

Smith, H. (2020). *The writing experiment: strategies for innovative creative writing*. Routledge. DOI: 10.4324/9781003118244

Stein, A. (2022). *The Art of Presence: The Poet and Paradise Lost*. Univ of California Press.

Thorp, H. H. (2023). ChatGPT is fun, but not an author. *Science*, *379*(6630), 313–313. DOI: 10.1126/science.adg7879 PMID: 36701446

Tsao, J., & Nogues, C. (2024). Beyond the author: Artificial intelligence, creative writing and intellectual emancipation. *Poetics*, *102*, 101865. DOI: 10.1016/j.poetic.2024.101865

Turner, M. L. (2023). *An in-depth exploration of the field of book ghostwriting*. Temple University.

Vallor, S. (2024). *The AI mirror: How to reclaim our humanity in an age of machine thinking*. Oxford University Press. DOI: 10.1093/oso/9780197759066.001.0001

Wang, Y., Singgih, M., Wang, J., & Rit, M. (2019). Making sense of blockchain technology: How will it transform supply chains? *International Journal of Production Economics*, *211*, 221–236. DOI: 10.1016/j.ijpe.2019.02.002

Yang, D., Zhou, Y., Zhang, Z., Li, T. J. J., & Lc, R. (2022, March). AI as an Active Writer: Interaction strategies with generated text in human-AI collaborative fiction writing. In Joint Proceedings of the ACM IUI Workshops (Vol. 10, pp. 1-11). CEUR-WS Team.

KEY TERMS AND DEFINITIONS

Artificial Intelligence (AI): A branch of computer science focused on creating systems capable of tasks that typically require human intelligence, such as language generation, pattern recognition, and decision-making. In literary contexts, AI is used to generate, assist, or co-author creative texts.

Generative Language Models: AI systems—such as GPT—that are trained on vast datasets to produce human-like text. These models learn linguistic patterns and structures, enabling them to simulate storytelling, poetic form, or dramatic dialogue without understanding meaning.

Hybrid Authorship: A collaborative creative process where both human and machine contribute to the production of literary work. The human may initiate, edit, or refine the content while the AI provides suggestions, drafts, or stylistic variations.

Narrative Algorithms: Computational techniques that replicate storytelling patterns—such as plot structure, character arcs, or dialogue mechanics—used by AI to generate coherent fictional narratives based on learned conventions from literary datasets.

Poetic Simulation: The use of AI tools to generate poetry that mimics traditional forms (e.g., sonnets, haiku) through structured training, often replicating meter, rhyme, and imagery without possessing emotional intent or lived experience.

Algorithmic Creativity: A form of creativity driven by AI where outputs are generated based on probability, pattern recognition, and recombination of existing texts, raising debates about originality, authorship, and artistic value.

Literary Authenticity: The perceived genuineness or emotional truth of a literary work, often tied to the author's lived experience and intentionality. The rise of AI-generated texts challenges traditional notions of what constitutes an "authentic" voice or creation.

Chapter 5
Interpreting Literature Through an AI Lens:
Cross-Cultural Dynamics and Insights

Muhammad Rapi
https://orcid.org/0009-0001-6056-9683
Universitas Negeri Makassar, Indonesia

ABSTRACT

This chapter reviews how artificial intelligence (AI) has transformed literary interpretation, promoting cross-cultural understanding and multidisciplinary methods. Researchers may analyze large literary collections, uncover patterns, and study national emotional and thematic frameworks using AI technologies like natural language processing, sentiment analysis, and machine learning. AI-driven analysis enhances and recontextualizes literary ideas including formalism, structuralism, post-structuralism, and reader-response. Global literature, folklore, translation, and genre evolution case studies show AI's ability to find universal themes and cultural differences. Authorship, bias, and data equity are addressed in the chapter to promote inclusive and responsible AI use in literary studies. This multimodal approach makes AI a powerful tool for understanding literary human expression and cultural narratives.

DOI: 10.4018/979-8-3373-1057-2.ch005

1. INTRODUCTION TO AI IN LITERARY ANALYSIS

1.1 The Evolution of Literary Criticism

Literary criticism has undergone substantial evolution over the centuries, influenced by cultural, philosophical, and technical transformations (Bearman et al., 2023). In its early versions, literary criticism concentrated primarily on the moral and aesthetic merits of writings, frequently relying on classical frameworks created by intellectuals like as Aristotle and Horace. These frameworks underscored the significance of form, organization, and authorial intent, establishing a foundation for later critical approaches.

The 20th century was a crucial turning point in literary criticism with the rise of diverse theoretical frameworks, such as formalism, structuralism, and post-structuralism (McMahon 2023). Formalism emphasized the text, promoting an examination that focused solely on literary devices and structures, disregarding external influences. Structuralism aimed to reveal the foundational systems of meaning that dictate narratives, whereas post-structuralism contested the concept of fixed meanings, highlighting the variability of interpretation.

As the century advanced, the emergence of digital technologies significantly impacted literary studies. The advent of digital humanities in the late 20th and early 21st centuries provided novel approaches for literary analysis. Researchers commenced utilizing computational instruments to analyze extensive text corpora, facilitating quantitative studies that were once inconceivable (Wang, 2022). This transition not only democratized access to literature but also enabled cross-cultural comparisons by allowing researchers to evaluate texts from various linguistic and cultural contexts.

Digital humanities have facilitated multidisciplinary collaboration, integrating literature, computer science, and cultural studies. This intersection has resulted in creative methodologies like text mining, wherein algorithms are utilized to discern patterns and trends inside literary texts (Oberbichler et al. 2022). These methodologies have revolutionized scholarly engagement with texts, transitioning from conventional close reading to a broader perspective on literary interpretation.

The emergence of artificial intelligence (AI) is catalyzing a further evolution in the realm of literary criticism. Artificial intelligence technologies, especially natural language processing (NLP) and machine learning, are currently being incorporated into literary studies, providing novel instruments for interpretation and analysis (Wagner et al. 2022). These breakthroughs provide profound insights into themes, sentiments, and cultural settings, hence enhancing our comprehension of literature across diverse civilizations.

The evolution of literary criticism has been characterized by an ongoing discourse between tradition and innovation. The advent of digital humanities and artificial intelligence signifies a new phase in this discourse, offering the potential to enrich our analytical frameworks and augment our understanding of literature's cross-cultural interactions. Exploring the interface of AI and literary analysis unveils new pathways for comprehending the intricacies of human expression across varied cultural contexts.

1.2 Understanding Artificial Intelligence

Artificial Intelligence (AI) denotes the emulation of human cognitive functions by technology, especially computer systems. These processes encompass learning, reasoning, problem-solving, perception, and language comprehension (Kühl et al., 2022). Fundamentally, AI seeks to develop systems capable of executing activities that conventionally necessitate human intelligence, hence enhancing technological skills across diverse domains, including literature.

The domain of AI is extensive and includes various subfields, including machine learning, natural language processing (NLP), robotics, and computer vision. Machine learning, an essential component of AI, entails the creation of algorithms that enable computers to learn from and predict outcomes based on data (Sarker, 2021). In literary analysis, machine learning can be utilized to examine texts, discern patterns, and produce insights that would be difficult to reveal through conventional approaches.

Natural language processing (NLP) is a crucial component of AI, concentrating on the interface between computers and human language. NLP allows machines to comprehend, interpret, and produce human language in a manner that is both significant and contextually appropriate (Khurana et al., 2023). This capacity is especially beneficial in literary analysis, enabling the exploration of narrative structures, themes, and character development across various texts and civilizations.

The use of AI in literature has unveiled new opportunities for investigation. Sentiment analysis, a method in NLP, assesses the emotional tone of a text, indicating how characters convey emotions or how themes reverberate across many cultures. Through the analysis of extensive literary corpora, AI can discern repeating motifs and cultural allusions that may not be readily evident to human readers (Dillon and Schaffer-Goddard 2023).

Furthermore, AI methods can enable cross-cultural comparisons by examining texts from diverse linguistic origins, thereby elucidating similarities and contrasts in narrative strategies and thematic issues (Kunst & Bierwiaczonek, 2023). This capacity is crucial for comprehending how literature mirrors and molds cultural identities, as well as how global narratives can converge and impact each other.

The evolution of AI increasingly demonstrates its potential to revolutionize literary interpretation. Utilizing machine learning and natural language processing, researchers can interact with literature in novel manners, revealing insights that enhance our comprehension of human expression across other cultures. From this perspective, AI not only augments our analytical talents but also prompts a reevaluation of the interplay between technology and the humanities, thereby expanding the parameters of literary interpretation in the 21st century.

2. THEORETICAL FRAMEWORKS FOR LITERARY ANALYSIS

2.1 Traditional Literary Theories

Literary criticism has been influenced by diverse theoretical frameworks that direct the interpretation and analysis of texts. Formalism, structuralism, post-structuralism, and reader-response theory have been crucial in influencing our comprehension of literature.

Formalism arose in the early 20th century as a response to biographical and historical methodologies in literature. Formalists prioritize the inherent characteristics of a text, including its language, structure, and literary devices, contending that meaning originates from the text itself rather than extrinsic settings (Preuß, 2023). This method promotes meticulous reading, emphasizing how components such as imagery, symbolism, and rhyme enhance a work's overall impact. Formalism's meticulous focus on form facilitates a comprehensive analysis of literary approaches, rendering it an invaluable instrument for comprehending the artistry inherent in a text.

Structuralism, which emerged in the mid-20th century, extends formalist concepts by examining the foundational structures that dictate narratives (Lu2023). Structuralists examine the interrelations of parts within a text, asserting that meaning emerges from the interaction of these components. This methodology is based on linguistic theories, positing that language functions as a system of signs in which meaning arises from differences rather than intrinsic attributes. Structuralism facilitated the exploration of extensive cultural and social settings, yielding insights into how tales both reflect and construct collective identities.

Conversely, post-structuralism arose as a critique of structuralist concepts, contesting the assumption of immutable meanings and consistent interpretations (Salzmann-Erikson2024). Post-structuralists contend that meaning is dynamic and dependent, influenced by the interaction of language, context, and reader interpretation. This theory underscores the reader's role in meaning construction, positing that texts may be interpreted in various ways based on individual viewpoints. The focus on ambiguity and the volatility of meaning encourages readers to interact with literature more actively, acknowledging the intricacies of interpretation.

Reader-response theory elaborates on this concept by emphasizing the reader's experience in the interpretative process. This approach asserts that meaning is not exclusively contained inside the text but is collaboratively generated through the reader's engagement with it (Victoria, 2025). Reader-response theorists investigate how personal origins, cultural circumstances, and emotional reactions influence individual readings, emphasizing the subjective essence of literary analysis.

Upon examining these conventional literary theories, it is clear that they offer fundamental frameworks for comprehending the complex character of writing. Incorporating these theories with AI tools can augment human analytical abilities, facilitating a more profound examination of literature across diverse cultures and circumstances. Through the examination of literature via different perspectives, we can reveal profound insights into the narratives that influence human experience and cultural identity.

2.2 AI and Literary Theory

The emergence of artificial intelligence (AI) is challenging and transforming conventional literary frameworks, providing novel methods for analysis and interpretation (Yang et al., 2024). As AI technologies, especially machine learning and natural language processing, advance, they necessitate a reassessment of traditional literary theories including formalism, structuralism, post-structuralism, and reader-response theory.

AI fundamentally undermines conventional frameworks by its ability to conduct extensive text analysis. Formalism prioritizes meticulous reading and the inherent attributes of a work, but AI empowers scholars to examine extensive literary corpora, uncovering patterns and trends that manual analysis would render unattainable (Dwivedi et al. 2023). Machine learning algorithms can identify common themes, motifs, and stylistic features across numerous works, providing insights into literary movements and cultural transformations. This power enhances formalist analysis and broadens its reach, facilitating a more thorough comprehension of literary output.

Likewise, structuralism's emphasis on foundational systems of meaning can be augmented by AI's capacity to model intricate linkages inside texts (Manghani). Utilizing network analysis and graph theory, scholars can elucidate and examine the interconnections among characters, themes, and narrative structures across various works. This method facilitates a profound examination of intertextuality and cultural context, elucidating the interactions and influences of tales across temporal and spatial dimensions.

Post-structuralism's focus on the fluidity of meaning and the reader's interpretative role aligns with the possibilities of AI. Artificial intelligence can evaluate reader reactions and sentiments across various demographics, yielding actual data on the interpretation of literature by different audiences (Krugmann & Hartmann, 2024). The incorporation of AI insights into post-structuralist frameworks enhances our comprehension of the interpretive process, emphasizing the variety of meaning influenced by cultural and individual settings.

Furthermore, reader-response theory can be substantially augmented through AI-driven analysis of reader involvement. Scholars can collect data on reader responses and interpretations of literature in real-time by employing tools that monitor reader interactions with texts, including online annotations, social media debates, and digital reading platforms (Yang and Kim 2025). This empirical method facilitates a more refined comprehension of the reader's function, transcending subjective interpretations to discern overarching patterns in literary reception.

The integration of AI discoveries with established literary theories revitalizes these frameworks and promotes multidisciplinary collaboration between the humanities and technology. By harnessing AI's capabilities in literary analysis, we acquire novel perspectives on the intricacies of literature, facilitating a deeper examination of cross-cultural dynamics and insights (Zhao & Zhou, 2025). By integrating conventional theories with cutting-edge AI techniques, we can cultivate a more thorough comprehension of literature's function in mirroring and influencing human experience across many contexts.

2.3 Cross-Cultural Literary Theories

Cross-cultural literary theories arose due to the globalization of literature and the acknowledgment that cultural settings profoundly influence literary creation and interpretation (Daiyun et al., 2022). These theories aim to examine literature not solely within a singular cultural context but also via several cultural perspectives, facilitating a more profound comprehension of texts and their significances.

Postcolonial theory, a fundamental concept in cross-cultural literary theory, analyzes the impact of colonialism on literature and culture. This method emphasizes the power dynamics intrinsic to literary creation and contests the supremacy of Western narratives. Postcolonial theorists, including Edward Said and Homi K. Bhabha, examine how colonized nations express their identities via literature, frequently employing narrative as a form of resistance to colonial oppression (Azada-Palacios, 2022). This theory underscores the significance of comprehending cultural context, as it elucidates the impact of historical and social elements on literary expression.

A significant framework is comparative literature, which entails the examination of literature across cultural and linguistic barriers. Scholars of comparative literature examine the parallels and contrasts in topics, genres, and narrative approaches across many literary traditions. This methodology cultivates an understanding of the interrelation of global literature, prompting readers to acknowledge how cultural exchanges influence literary structures and concepts (Casanova & Brownlie, 2021). Comparative literature elucidates how cultural environments shape narrative forms and thematic issues by analyzing texts in connection to one another.

Cultural studies are essential in cross-cultural literary study. This interdisciplinary method analyzes the interplay between literature and culture, taking into account variables such as race, gender, class, and ideology. Cultural studies experts examine the ways in which literature mirrors and influences societal values, identities, and power relations (Lansford, 2022). This method emphasizes the significance of contextualizing literary works within their cultural frameworks, highlighting the necessity of comprehending the socio-political conditions that influence their creation and reception.

Integrating AI into cross-cultural literary theories improves our capacity to evaluate and comprehend literature within varied contexts. AI algorithms can analyze and contrast extensive literature from diverse cultures, recognizing patterns and themes that surpass linguistic and geographical limitations (Hegghammer, 2022). This feature enables scholars to interact with literature innovatively, revealing insights on cultural exchanges and effects that may not be readily discernible.

The significance of cultural context in literary interpretation is paramount. Comprehending the cultural, historical, and social influences that inform a work enhances our reading experience and deepens our understanding for the intricacies of human expression (Hossain, 2024). Integrating cross-cultural literary theories with AI approaches enhances our understanding of how literature reflects and negotiates cultural identities, so developing a more complete grasp of the tales that unite us globally.

3. AI TOOLS AND TECHNIQUES FOR LITERARY INTERPRETATION

3.1 Text Analysis and Natural Language Processing

Natural Language Processing (NLP) has become a formidable instrument in literary analysis, allowing scholars to examine texts in unprecedented ways. NLP comprises several strategies enabling computers to comprehend, interpret, and produce human language (Sandu et al., 2024). In literature, these tools enable various forms of text analysis, offering insights into themes, character development, and narrative structures across a range of literary works.

Tokenization, a key approach in NLP, entails deconstructing text into discrete elements, such as words or phrases. This procedure is crucial for subsequent analysis, enabling researchers to investigate frequency trends, discern keywords, and analyze linguistic structures. Another essential technique is sentiment analysis, which evaluates the emotional tone of a document by classifying words and phrases according to their implications. This approach can elucidate how characters convey emotions and how overall themes emotionally appeal with readers (Nandwani & Verma, 2021).

Moreover, topic modeling is a potent NLP tool that reveals concealed themes inside a text corpus. Utilizing algorithms like Latent Dirichlet Allocation (LDA), researchers can discern clusters of associated words, enabling them to determine the principal issues inside a literary piece (Sharma et al., 2022). This method is especially advantageous for examining extensive literary corpora, allowing researchers to track thematic evolution across various genres and cultural contexts.

Case studies demonstrate the transformative capabilities of text mining and natural language processing in literary study. A research examining Shakespeare's works employed NLP tools to analyze word usage patterns, uncovering insights on character development and thematic progression across his plays. Researchers discerned the evolution of Shakespeare's language by analyzing the frequency and context of specific words in relation to various cultural and historical influences (Papp-Zipernovszky et al. 2022).

A significant case study examined modern books to investigate the representation of identity and belonging themes across various cultures. Employing sentiment analysis, researchers investigated the emotional dimensions of characters in several texts, revealing the influence of cultural contexts on the depiction of these themes (Vinodini, 2024). This method illuminated both the parallels and variations in narrative strategies while offering a profound comprehension of how literature mirrors societal ideals and issues.

NLP approaches provide essential tools for literary analysis, enabling researchers to interact with texts in novel manners. Utilizing text analysis and machine learning, academics can provide insights that enhance our comprehension of literature's intricacies and its function in mirroring cross-cultural interactions. The exploration of the interface between AI and literature will enrich our comprehension of the intricate nuances of human expression in literary works through deeper, data-driven analysis.

3.2 Sentiment Analysis and Emotion Recognition

Sentiment analysis, a significant application of artificial intelligence (AI) and natural language processing (NLP), entails the computational evaluation of emotions conveyed in textual data. Through the examination of linguistic elements in literary compositions, AI may identify sentiments encompassing joy, sadness, rage, and fear (Mohammad, 2021). This technique promotes comprehension of particular works and facilitates cross-cultural comparisons by elucidating the articulation of emotions across diverse literary traditions.

Artificial intelligence identifies sentiment in texts by employing a synthesis of linguistic analysis and machine learning methods. Sentiment analysis fundamentally depends on established lexicons that classify words and phrases according to their emotional implications (Babu & Kanaga, 2022). For example, terms like as "happy" and "joyful" would be categorized as positive, whilst "sad" and "angry" would be designated as negative. Advanced models, particularly those utilizing deep learning, enhance sentiment recognition by examining contextual subtleties and the interrelations among words inside sentences. These algorithms can assimilate extensive datasets, enabling them to discern sentiment patterns that may not be readily observable through manual examination.

The applications of sentiment analysis in cross-cultural literature are numerous. A notable application is the investigation of how diverse cultures convey analogous feelings through distinct linguistic styles and storytelling methods (Dai and Lee 2022). A research examining the representation of love in Western and Eastern literature may employ sentiment analysis to quantify emotional emotions, thereby elucidating cultural disparities in the depiction of love. This research may reveal that Western writings frequently prioritize individualistic displays of love, whilst Eastern texts tend to emphasize collective or familial dimensions, so underscoring the influence of cultural context on emotional representation.

Furthermore, sentiment analysis can be utilized to investigate the progression of themes across time within certain cultural contexts. Through the examination of the emotional tone in literary works across several epochs, academics can discern transformations in societal views and values (Kaur et al. 2021). An investigation of 20th-century literature across other cultures may elucidate the varying emotional responses to war and conflict, offering insights into the distinct historical and cultural experiences that inform these narratives.

Moreover, sentiment analysis might augment the examination of character development across cultures. By analyzing the emotional trajectories of characters across various literary traditions, scholars can investigate the impact of cultural norms on character motivations and emotional manifestations (Chen, 2022). This method cultivates a profound comprehension of the intricacies of human experience as depicted in literature.

In conclusion, sentiment analysis and emotion recognition serve as potent instruments for literary interpretation, providing significant insights into the emotional dimensions of texts. Utilizing these AI methodologies in cross-cultural literature enables scholars to reveal the intricate manners in which emotions are articulated, thereby enhancing our comprehension of the relationship between culture and literary expression. The advancement of AI will surely augment our comprehension of the diverse tales that create human experience through greater emotional analysis in literature.

3.3 Machine Learning for Genre Classification

Machine learning has emerged as a revolutionary instrument in literary analysis, especially in the categorization of literary genres. Researchers can automate genre identification with algorithms that learn from data, facilitating a more nuanced comprehension of genre evolution and interaction across diverse cultural contexts (Ayanwale et al., 2024).

Machine learning algorithms that examine textual elements are fundamental to genre classification, enabling the categorization of works into distinct genres. Common methodologies encompass supervised learning, wherein models are trained on labeled datasets featuring examples from diverse genres, and unsupervised learning, which discerns patterns within unlabeled data (Hassan et al., 2022). Algorithms like Support Vector Machines (SVM), Decision Trees, and neural networks are commonly utilized for this objective. These models examine several textual qualities, such as word frequency, sentence structure, and stylistic features, to identify the characteristics that delineate each genre.

The ramifications of machine learning for genre classification surpass simple categorization; they also illuminate cross-cultural genre influences (Koytak, 2024). By employing these algorithms on a varied array of literary texts, scholars can reveal that genres are not fixed but rather dynamic constructs that develop through cultural interaction. The fusion of genres, exemplified as magical realism in Latin American literature, demonstrates how cultural settings can redefine conventional genre limits. Machine learning can elucidate these hybrid genres, uncovering the complex interactions of cultural narratives.

Furthermore, genre classification by machine learning allows researchers to investigate the worldwide dissemination of literary styles. Researchers can examine texts from other civilizations to identify the emergence of certain genres in various places and their adaptation to local situations (Unal et al., 2023). The rise of the detective genre in Japanese literature exemplifies both Western influences and native narrative traditions. Machine learning algorithms can measure these influences, offering insights into the evolution of genres through cross-cultural interaction.

Moreover, employing machine learning in genre classification can augment the analysis of reader reception. Analyzing demographic responses to diverse genres enables academics to attain a more profound comprehension of cultural preferences and the socioeconomic influences that govern literary consumption (Vassilakopoulou & Hustad, 2023). This study can uncover trends in genre popularity across cultures, emphasizing how cultural identity shapes literary preferences.

In summary, machine learning for genre categorization signifies a substantial development in literary analysis, enabling researchers to examine and categorize texts with unparalleled accuracy. Integrating these methodologies into cross-cultural literary research allows scholars to reveal the intricacies of genre evolution and the ramifications of cultural exchange. The exploration of the interface between AI and literature will enhance our comprehension of the varied narratives that define human experience worldwide through insights derived from machine learning.

4. CASE STUDIES IN CROSS-CULTURAL LITERARY ANALYSIS

4.1 Comparative Analysis of Global Literature

The incorporation of artificial intelligence (AI) methods has markedly improved the comparative analysis of global literature, enabling scholars to explore themes and narratives across many cultural contexts with higher depth and precision (Taherdoost & Madanchian, 2023). Utilizing AI technologies, academics can reveal fundamental patterns and similarities in literary works that surpass geographical and linguistic limitations, enhancing comprehension of cross-cultural dynamics.

A significant issue that has arisen in comparative literary studies is the examination of identity. AI-driven textual analysis has permitted researchers to investigate how various cultures express notions of self and belonging in their literary works (Salah et al. 2023). A case study of authors Chimamanda Ngozi Adichie and Junot Díaz illustrates their exploration of cultural identity and diaspora, albeit from distinct cultural viewpoints. Utilizing sentiment analysis and topic modeling, researchers can measure the emotional significance and prevalence of identity-related topics in their works, illustrating the influence of cultural contexts on their tales.

A notable domain of investigation is the depiction of conflict and resilience in literature. AI technologies may examine extensive datasets of literary texts to discern how different cultures portray conflict, injustice, and human resilience. A comparative analysis of the works of Khaled Hosseini and Toni Morrison demonstrates how both authors explore themes of pain and survival, though within different socio-historical frameworks. Researchers employ machine learning algorithms to classify the emotional tones and narrative structures inside these texts, emphasizing the universal and culturally particular methods through which literature addresses conflict (BELACEMSafa, 2024).

Furthermore, the application of AI in comparative analysis facilitates the exploration of genre influences across civilizations (Amirjalili et al., 2024). A study of magical realism in Latin American literature, in conjunction with its African counterparts like the works of Ben Okri, helps elucidate how cultural influences influence the genre's presentation. AI techniques can aid in recognizing prevalent themes and stylistic characteristics, facilitating scholars' comprehension of how cultural narratives shape the evolution of genre standards.

Furthermore, AI-driven analysis can enhance the examination of women's voices in worldwide literature. Comparing the works of female authors from diverse cultural origins, such as Arundhati Roy and Zadie Smith, enables scholars to reveal the distinct articulations of feminism and empowerment across different contexts (Lau et al., 2023). Text mining algorithms can discern patterns in linguistic usage and thematic emphasis, uncovering both common challenges and distinct cultural manifestations.

The comparative investigation of world literature via the perspective of AI provides significant insights into universally resonant themes across civilizations. Through the analysis of particular writers and texts, researchers can reveal the complex interactions between literature and the formation of cultural identities, societal ideals, and collective human experiences. As we further utilize AI technologies in literary studies, the possibility for enhanced cross-cultural knowledge and appreciation of varied narratives will definitely increase, expanding our interaction with global literature.

4.2 AI in Translation Studies

The function of artificial intelligence (AI) in literary translation has revolutionized cross-cultural communication, improving our comprehension of literature across various languages and cultures. As globalization perpetuates multicultural contacts, the necessity for proficient translation gets more essential (Naeem et al. 2025). AI-powered translation tools, especially those employing neural machine translation (NMT), have markedly enhanced the quality and efficiency of literary translations, facilitating a deeper understanding of cross-cultural subtleties.

AI-driven translation systems utilize deep learning algorithms to examine extensive multilingual text datasets, allowing them to comprehend context, idiomatic idioms, and stylistic characteristics unique to many languages (Zaki & Ahmed, 2024). This skill enables translations that are both precise and attuned to the nuances of the original text. AI systems can identify and maintain cultural references, metaphors, and emotional nuances essential to the integrity of literary works. Through the analysis of linguistic patterns, these systems can generate translations that preserve the author's voice while rendering the material comprehensible to a wider audience.

A significant use of AI in translation studies is the examination of literary texts that include cultural subtleties (Guerberof-Arenas & Toral, 2022). Translating a culturally complex novel, such as Gabriel García Márquez's "One Hundred Years of Solitude," presents considerable obstacles. AI translation systems can aid human translators by proposing culturally relevant counterparts and delivering contextually informed translations that appeal with intended audiences. This collaborative method improves the translator's capacity to express the original text's nuances and complexities, so enhancing the reader's experience.

Furthermore, AI's influence on comprehending cross-cultural subtleties transcends the mechanics of translation. Researchers can utilize sentiment analysis and various NLP techniques to investigate how diverse cultures articulate analogous concepts through unique linguistic selections (Shrivastava et al. 2023). A comparative analysis of translations of works by authors such as Haruki Murakami and Isabel Allende can elucidate the impact of cultural contexts on narrative techniques and emotional expressions. AI techniques can measure these discrepancies, offering insights into how translation decisions influence readers' perceptions and interpretations of the original texts.

AI significantly contributes to the democratization of literature by enabling translations of obscure works. By optimizing the translation process, AI facilitates the spread of varied voices and narratives that may otherwise remain unattainable due to linguistic obstacles (Nanduri, 2024). This enhancement of literary accessibility promotes more cross-cultural comprehension and enjoyment, enabling readers to interact with a broader spectrum of viewpoints.

In summary, AI's function in literary translation markedly improves our comprehension of cross-cultural subtleties and augments the process of literary interpretation. AI tools enhance the precision and contextual awareness of translations, enabling translators to adeptly manage the intricacies of language and culture. The exploration of the interface between AI and translation studies will enhance our understanding of global literature, promoting a greater respect for the varied narratives that define human experience.

4.3 AI-Driven Insights on Cultural Narratives

Artificial intelligence (AI) has emerged as a potent instrument for revealing concealed cultural narratives inherent in folklore and traditional tales. Utilizing sophisticated text analysis methods, AI can examine extensive compilations of narratives from various cultures, uncovering underlying patterns, motifs, and cultural values that may otherwise remain overlooked (Oztabak2025). This skill enhances our comprehension of particular narratives while emphasizing the interrelation of human experiences across diverse cultural contexts.

AI uncovers concealed cultural narratives mostly via text mining and topic modeling. These methodologies enable researchers to discern repeating themes and patterns throughout extensive collections of folklore (Jafery et al. 2023). A study examining folktales from diverse cultures could employ machine learning algorithms to classify narratives according to prevalent motifs, such as heroism, deceit, or transformation. By analyzing the prevalence and context of these patterns across countries, historians can reveal common human concerns and ideals, alongside distinct cultural representations.

Furthermore, sentiment analysis can yield insights into the emotional dimensions of conventional tales. Through the analysis of emotional tones in folktales, AI can assist scholars in comprehending how various cultures express emotions such as fear, joy, or sorrow. The depiction of death and the afterlife in folktales can differ markedly throughout countries, illustrating diverse beliefs and values (Doğan et al., 2025). AI-powered sentiment analysis can measure these emotional reactions, facilitating a more profound examination of how cultural environments influence narrative structures and themes.

Furthermore, AI can aid in the conservation and rejuvenation of endangered folklore by enhancing the accessibility of these narratives. AI tools can assist in documenting and archiving cultural heritage by digitizing and evaluating traditional narratives that may otherwise be lost (Zou and Lin 2024). This technique aids in preserving cultural narratives and promotes cross-cultural comparisons, allowing scholars to examine the evolution of similar stories in diverse circumstances. The narrative of "Cinderella" possesses numerous adaptations across civilizations, each embodying distinct societal ideals and customs. Artificial intelligence can assist in tracking these variances, offering insights into the evolution and transformation of cultural narratives throughout time.

Moreover, AI's capacity to study language and structure can uncover the rhetorical devices and storytelling tactics utilized in folklore (Hermann, 2023). Through the analysis of the stylistic elements of traditional narratives, researchers can reveal how cultural stories are constructed to engage audiences. This approach can elucidate the significance of oral traditions and storytelling activities in the formation of cultural identity.

In conclusion, AI-generated insights into cultural narratives offer a significant framework for comprehending the intricacies of folklore and traditional tales. Utilizing text analysis methodologies, researchers can reveal concealed themes and emotional expressions that signify the values and beliefs of many civilizations. As we investigate the convergence of AI and cultural narratives, the opportunity for profound insights into the varied fabric of human experience will certainly increase, enhancing our understanding of the stories that unite us across time and geography.

5. FUTURE DIRECTIONS AND ETHICAL CONSIDERATIONS

5.1 The Future of AI in Literary Studies

The incorporation of artificial intelligence (AI) into literary studies is set to significantly alter the discipline, creating novel opportunities for research, analysis, and interpretation. The evolving trends and technologies highlight the potential of AI to deepen our comprehension of literature and its cultural ramifications (Zhang & Lu, 2021).

A notable trend is the advancement of more complex natural language processing (NLP) models. Recent advancements in deep learning, especially with transformer-based architectures such as GPT (Generative Pre-trained Transformer), have significantly enhanced AI's capacity to comprehend and produce human language (Soori et al., 2023). These models can analyze texts with enhanced contextual awareness, facilitating more profound interpretations of literary works. Subsequent developments of these technologies may enable more sophisticated analyses, including the identification of subtext, irony, and cultural references that are frequently crucial in literary interpretation.

A promising avenue is the enhancement of AI tools for collaborative literary analysis. Platforms incorporating AI functionalities can enhance interdisciplinary collaboration among academics, enabling the exchange of insights across domains such as literature, linguistics, cultural studies, and data science (Yang et al., 2024). This collaborative method fosters a comprehensive understanding of literature by integrating diverse perspectives to analyze texts through multiple lenses.

The emergence of AI-driven tools for creative writing offers intriguing prospects for the future of literature. Utilizing AI to aid in the writing process enables authors to explore innovative narrative structures, styles, and genres (Scott, 2024). This partnership between human creativity and machine learning may yield innovative literary forms that contest conventional boundaries and norms. The rise of AI-generated writing will incite essential debates on authorship, originality, and technology's role in creativity.

As we adopt the potential of AI in literary studies, it is essential to contemplate the ethical ramifications of its application. Bias in AI algorithms, especially regarding cultural representation, must be rectified to guarantee that the insights produced are fair and inclusive (Nazer et al. 2023). AI systems developed using biased datasets can perpetuate stereotypes and reinforce cultural hierarchies, potentially distorting literary interpretation and analysis. Researchers must maintain vigilance in assessing the data utilized for training AI models and endeavor to ensure diversity in the texts examined.

Furthermore, the issue of authorship in AI-generated literature prompts ethical considerations concerning intellectual property and creative rights. As AI increasingly participates in the writing process, the distinctions between human and machine authorship may become indistinct, necessitating a reassessment of authorship in the digital era (Kim, 2024).

In summary, the future of AI in literary studies presents significant potential, since rising trends and technologies are poised to deepen our comprehension of literature and its cultural surroundings. It is crucial to thoughtfully address the ethical complexities associated with these advancements. By confronting biases and authorship concerns, scholars can guarantee that the incorporation of AI into literary studies promotes a more inclusive and equitable examination of the narratives that influence our world.

5.2 Ethical Implications of AI in Literature

The incorporation of artificial intelligence (AI) into literary studies presents numerous ethical problems that require thorough examination. As AI technologies advance, especially in literature, significant concerns around authorship, originality, and bias arise, questioning conventional ideas of creativity and interpretation (Murphy et al. 2021).

A significant worry is the issue of authorship in works produced or influenced by AI. As AI systems enhance their ability to generate cohesive and stylistically refined writings, the differentiation between human authorship and machine-generated content diminishes (Mazzi, 2024). This prompts essential inquiries regarding the essence of creativity: Can a machine genuinely "create," or is it simply reconfiguring pre-existing concepts and styles? The authorship controversy encompasses matters of intellectual property and copyright. Who possesses the rights to a literary work generated by an AI? Who is the original programmer: the user who initiated the AI or the AI itself? These inquiries complicate the conventional conception of authorship and need a reassessment of the legal structures governing literary creations.

The possibility of prejudice in AI systems presents considerable ethical dilemmas for literary interpretation. AI systems are trained on extensive datasets that frequently mirror societal biases inherent in the raw material (Hanna et al. 2024). Thus, if an AI tool is mostly trained on Western literature, it may unintentionally exclude perspectives from non-Western cultures, resulting in biased interpretations that perpetuate existing power structures. This bias can influence literary interpretation by favoring specific narratives while marginalizing others, therefore constraining our comprehension of varied cultural representations.

Furthermore, the employment of biased algorithms in sentiment analysis or genre categorization may result in misinterpretations of texts (Gogula et al. 2023). For example, if an AI system fails to discern cultural subtleties in language or emotional expression, it may erroneously classify a work or misrepresent its contents. This not only compromises the quality of literary scholarship but also fosters preconceptions and misconceptions regarding various cultures.

To mitigate these ethical concerns, scholars must promote transparency in the creation and use of AI. This entails examining the datasets employed to train AI models and pursuing diversity in the literary texts evaluated. By ensuring that AI systems are inclusive and representative of many perspectives, researchers can reduce bias and promote a more equal literary environment (Agrawal2024).

Moreover, multidisciplinary collaboration among engineers, literary scholars, and ethicists is crucial to address the challenges of AI in literature (Saddhono et al. 2024). Participating in critical discourse regarding the ramifications of AI technologies will facilitate the establishment of ethical rules that emphasize creativity, uniqueness, and cultural sensitivity.

The ethical ramifications of AI in literature are complex and necessitate thorough examination. By tackling concerns of authorship, originality, and bias, scholars may guarantee that the incorporation of AI into literary studies enriches our comprehension of varied narratives while honoring the intricacies of human creativity and cultural expression. A commitment to ethical standards will be essential in creating the future of literature in an increasingly digital landscape.

5.3 Conclusion and Call to Action

As we finalize our examination of the convergence between artificial intelligence (AI) and literary studies, it is crucial to contemplate the principal insights acquired during this endeavor. The incorporation of AI into literary analysis could transform our comprehension and interpretation of literature, providing unparalleled chances for cross-cultural research and the revelation of concealed storylines. Utilizing sophisticated methodologies like natural language processing, sentiment analysis, and machine learning, researchers can examine extensive text corpora, uncovering patterns and themes that surpass geographical and linguistic limitations.

This revolutionary potential has considerable ethical implications. Concerns regarding authorship and originality undermine conventional concepts of creativity, while the potential for bias in AI algorithms jeopardizes literary interpretation and marginalizes multiple perspectives. As we adopt the breakthroughs provided by AI, it is imperative to be cognizant of the ethical ramifications and pursue equitable approaches in literary scholarship.

Interdisciplinary collaboration is essential for navigating the challenges of AI in literary studies. Academics from several disciplines—literature, computer science, linguistics, cultural studies, and ethics—must collaborate to cultivate a thorough knowledge of the ramifications of AI technologies. This partnership may result in the creation of AI tools that are both technologically sophisticated and culturally attuned and inclusive. Interdisciplinary teams can establish frameworks that emphasize diversity in datasets and uphold ethical norms in AI development by sharing expertise and opinions.

Moreover, participating in critical dialogues regarding the function of AI in literature would facilitate the establishment of optimal procedures for its utilization in literary studies. Academics ought to promote transparency in AI algorithms and engage in the formulation of ethical standards that regulate their application. By emphasizing inclusivity and representation, we can guarantee that AI augments rather than undermines our comprehension of literature and its cultural surroundings.

The use of AI into literary studies offers both promising prospects and considerable obstacles. As we progress, it is imperative to harness the capabilities of AI while adhering to ethical standards that respect the intricacies of human creativity and cultural expression. Through promoting multidisciplinary collaboration and participating in critical discourse, we can cultivate a future in which AI acts as a significant ally in our endeavor to comprehend the intricate landscape of world literature. This call to action urges scholars, technologists, and ethicists to collaborate in developing a more egalitarian and perceptive literary landscape that embodies the myriad narratives shaping our world.

6. CONCLUSION

The incorporation of artificial intelligence (AI) into literary analysis signifies a significant progression in our interpretation of works across cultural and historical contexts. By integrating conventional literary theories with AI technologies like natural language processing, sentiment analysis, and machine learning, researchers may now analyze literature with unparalleled breadth and profundity. This technology advancement does not supplant human interpretation but rather augments it—facilitating the identification of concealed patterns, emotional nuances, and cross-cultural motifs that could otherwise go unrecognized.

This chapter illustrates how AI enhances formalist focus on structure, broadens structuralist analysis of systems, and adds empirical depth to post-structuralist and reader-response viewpoints. Furthermore, AI's capacity to analyze multilingual and multicultural texts creates new opportunities in comparative literature, translation studies, and folklore preservation—enhancing marginalized voices and global narratives.

This confluence presents issues. Concerns about authorship, algorithmic bias, data equity, and ethical utilization necessitate continuous vigilance and interdisciplinary discourse. Ensuring inclusion and transparency in AI development and deployment is crucial to avert the reinforcement of cultural hierarchies or distortions of meaning.

In summary, AI provides potent instruments to deepen our comprehension of literature and culture, although its application must be directed by humanistic principles. The future of literary studies depends on responsible, collaborative innovation—where technology enhances rather than replaces critical thinking, and where varied cultural narratives are examined with sensitivity, respect, and ethical consideration. Thus, AI becomes into not merely a technique, but a conduit for profound worldwide literary interaction.

REFERENCES

Agrawal, G. (2024). Accountability, Trust, and Transparency in AI Systems From the Perspective of Public Policy: Elevating Ethical Standards. In Singla, B., & Shalender, K. (Eds.), *AI Healthcare Applications and Security, Ethical, and Legal Considerations* (pp. 148–162). IGI Global Scientific Publishing., DOI: 10.4018/979-8-3693-7452-8.ch009

Amirjalili, F., Neysani, M., & Nikbakht, A. (2024). Exploring the boundaries of authorship: A comparative analysis of AI-generated text and human academic writing in English literature. *Frontiers in Education*, *9*, 1347421. DOI: 10.3389/feduc.2024.1347421

Ayanwale, M. A., Molefi, R. R., & Oyeniran, S. (2024). Analyzing the evolution of machine learning integration in educational research: A bibliometric perspective. *Discover Education*, *3*(1), 47. DOI: 10.1007/s44217-024-00119-5

Azada-Palacios, R. A. (2022). Hybridity and national identity in post-colonial schools. *Educational Philosophy and Theory*, *54*(9), 1431–1441. DOI: 10.1080/00131857.2021.1920393

Babu, N. V., & Kanaga, E. G. M. (2022). Sentiment analysis in social media data for depression detection using artificial intelligence: A review. *SN Computer Science*, *3*(74), 74. Advance online publication. DOI: 10.1007/s42979-021-00958-1 PMID: 34816124

Bearman, M., Ryan, J., & Ajjawi, R. (2023). Discourses of artificial intelligence in higher education: A critical literature review. *Higher Education*, *86*(2), 369–385. DOI: 10.1007/s10734-022-00937-2

Safa, B. M. (2024). *Look Like the Innocent Flower, but be the Serpent under't.": The Imbroglio of Betrayal in George R. R Martin's Storm of Swords and William Shakespeare's Macbeth. A Comparative Study* (Doctoral dissertation, University of Martyr Sheikh Larbi Tebessi Tebessa).

Casanova, P., & Brownlie, S. (2021). Consecration and accumulation of literary capital: Translation as unequal exchange. In *The translation studies reader* (pp. 407–423). Routledge. DOI: 10.4324/9780429280641-37

Chen, M. (2022). Emotion analysis based on deep learning with application to research on development of Western culture. *Frontiers in Psychology*, *13*, 911686. DOI: 10.3389/fpsyg.2022.911686 PMID: 36186353

Dai, H., & Lee, J. (2022). Research on discourse reconstruction effect of animated film cross-cultural communication based on machine learning. *Wireless Communications and Mobile Computing*, *2022*, 1–10. DOI: 10.1155/2022/2343328

Dillon, S., & Schaffer-Goddard, J. (2022). What AI researchers read: The role of literature in artificial intelligence research. *Interdisciplinary Science Reviews*, *48*(1), 15–42. DOI: 10.1080/03080188.2022.2079214

Doğan, B., Balcioglu, Y. S., & Elçi, M. (2024). Multidimensional Sentiment Analysis Method on social media data: Comparison of emotions during and after the covid-19 pandemic. *Kybernetes*, *54*(4), 2414–2456. DOI: 10.1108/K-09-2023-1808

Dwivedi, R., Nerur, S., & Balijepally, V. (2023). Exploring artificial intelligence and big data scholarship in information systems: A citation, bibliographic coupling, and co-word analysis. *International Journal of Information Management Data Insights*, *3*(2), 100185. DOI: 10.1016/j.jjimei.2023.100185

Gogula, S. D., Rahouti, M., Gogula, S. K., Jalamuri, A., & Jagatheesaperumal, S. K. (2023). An Emotion-Based Rating System for Books Using Sentiment Analysis and Machine Learning in the Cloud. *Applied Sciences (Basel, Switzerland)*, *13*(2), 773. DOI: 10.3390/app13020773

Guerberof-Arenas, A., & Toral, A. (2022). Creativity in translation. *Translation Spaces*, *11*(2), 184–212. DOI: 10.1075/ts.21025.gue

Hanna, M. G., Pantanowitz, L., Jackson, B., Palmer, O., Visweswaran, S., Pantanowitz, J., Deebajah, M., & Rashidi, H. H. (2025). Ethical and bias considerations in Artificial Intelligence/Machine Learning. *Modern Pathology*, *38*(3), 100686. DOI: 10.1016/j.modpat.2024.100686 PMID: 39694331

Hassan, S. U., Ahamed, J., & Ahmad, K. (2022). Analytics of machine learning-based algorithms for text classification. *Sustainable Operations and Computers*, *3*, 238–248. DOI: 10.1016/j.susoc.2022.03.001

Hegghammer, T. (2021). OCR with Tesseract, Amazon Textract, and Google Document AI: A benchmarking experiment. *Journal of Computational Social Science*, *5*(1), 861–882. DOI: 10.1007/s42001-021-00149-1

Hermann, I. (2021). Artificial Intelligence in fiction: Between narratives and metaphors. *AI &amp. AI & Society*, *38*(1), 319–329. DOI: 10.1007/s00146-021-01299-6

Hossain, K. I. (2024). Reviewing the role of culture in English language learning: Challenges and opportunities for educators. *Social Sciences &amp. Social Sciences & Humanities Open*, *9*, 100781. DOI: 10.1016/j.ssaho.2023.100781

Jafery, N. N., Keikhosrokiani, P., & Asl, M. P. (2023). An Artificial Intelligence Application of Theme and Space in Life Writings of Middle Eastern Women: A Topic Modelling and Sentiment Analysis Approach. In Keikhosrokiani, P., & Pourya Asl, M. (Eds.), *Handbook of Research on Artificial Intelligence Applications in Literary Works and Social Media* (pp. 19–35). IGI Global Scientific Publishing., DOI: 10.4018/978-1-6684-6242-3.ch002

Kaur, G., Singh, M., & Singh, S. (2021). Mapping the literature on financial well-being: A systematic literature review and Bibliometric analysis. *International Social Science Journal*, *71*(241–242), 217–241. DOI: 10.1111/issj.12278

Khurana, D., Koli, A., Khatter, K., & Singh, S. (2023). Natural language processing: State of the art, current trends and challenges. *Multimedia Tools and Applications*, *82*(3), 3713–3744. DOI: 10.1007/s11042-022-13428-4 PMID: 35855771

Kim, S.-J. (2024). Research ethics and issues regarding the use of CHATGPT-like artificial intelligence platforms by authors and reviewers: A narrative review. *Science Editing*, *11*(2), 96–106. DOI: 10.6087/kcse.343

Koytak, H. Z. (2024). Ethnicity on the table: A content analysis of online reviews for Syracuse's cuisines. *Sociology Compass*, *18*(3), e13195. Advance online publication. DOI: 10.1111/soc4.13195

Krugmann, J. O., & Hartmann, J. (2024). Sentiment analysis in the age of Generative AI. *Customer Needs and Solutions*, *11*(1), 3. Advance online publication. DOI: 10.1007/s40547-024-00143-4

Kühl, N., Schemmer, M., Goutier, M., & Satzger, G. (2022). Artificial Intelligence and machine learning. *Electronic Markets*, *32*(4), 2235–2244. DOI: 10.1007/s12525-022-00598-0

Kunst, J. R., & Bierwiaczonek, K. (2023). Utilizing AI questionnaire translations in cross-cultural and intercultural research: Insights and recommendations. *International Journal of Intercultural Relations*, *97*, 101888. DOI: 10.1016/j.ijintrel.2023.101888

Lansford, J. E. (2021). Annual research review: Cross-cultural similarities and differences in parenting. *Journal of Child Psychology and Psychiatry, and Allied Disciplines*, *63*(4), 466–479. DOI: 10.1111/jcpp.13539 PMID: 34763373

Lau, P. L., Nandy, M., Chakraborty, S., & Accelerating, U. N. (2023). Sustainable Development Goals with AI-Driven Technologies: A Systematic Literature Review of Women's Healthcare. *Health Care*, *11*(3), 401. DOI: 10.3390/healthcare11030401 PMID: 36766976

Lu, D. (2023). Architecture in the age of playfulness: Mapping a framework for global historiography. In *The Routledge Companion to Contemporary Architectural History* (pp. 1–80). Routledge. DOI: 10.4324/9781315674469-1

Manghani, S. (2022). Notes on structuralism: Introduction. *Theory, Culture &amp. Theory, Culture & Society*, *39*(7–8), 117–131. DOI: 10.1177/02632764221141823

Mazzi, F. (2024). Authorship in Artificial intelligence-generated works: Exploring originality in text prompts and artificial intelligence outputs through philosophical foundations of copyright and collage protection. *The Journal of World Intellectual Property*, *27*(3), 410–427. DOI: 10.1111/jwip.12310

McMahon, P. (2024). Prague Structuralism and the Poetic Function. In *Structuralism and Form in Literature and Biology*. Palgrave Macmillan., DOI: 10.1007/978-3-031-47739-3_6

Mohammad, S. M. (2021, January 14). *Sentiment analysis: Automatically detecting valence, emotions, and other affectual states from text*. arXiv.org. https://arxiv.org/abs/2005.11882v2

Murphy, K., Di Ruggiero, E., Upshur, R., Willison, D. J., Malhotra, N., Cai, J. C., Malhotra, N., Lui, V., & Gibson, J. (2021). Artificial Intelligence for Good Health: A scoping review of the ethics literature. *BMC Medical Ethics*, *22*(1), 14. Advance online publication. DOI: 10.1186/s12910-021-00577-8 PMID: 33588803

Naeem, A., Rehman, A. S., & Rasheed, A. (2025). Evaluating Cultural Adaptation in AI Translations: A Framework and Implications for Literary Works. In Ali, M., Anwar, M., Fazal, S., & Ayyaz, S. (Eds.), *AI Applications for English Language Learning* (pp. 223–252). IGI Global Scientific Publishing., DOI: 10.4018/979-8-3693-9077-1.ch010

Nanduri, D. K. (2024). *Exploring the Role of Generative Artificial Intelligence in Culturally Relevant Storytelling for Native Language Learning Among Children* (thesis).

Nandwani, P., & Verma, R. (2021). A review on sentiment analysis and emotion detection from text. *Social Network Analysis and Mining*, *11*(1), 81. DOI: 10.1007/s13278-021-00776-6 PMID: 34484462

Nazer, L. H., Zatarah, R., Waldrip, S., Ke, J. X., Moukheiber, M., Khanna, A. K., Hicklen, R. S., Moukheiber, L., Moukheiber, D., Ma, H., & Mathur, P. (2023). Bias in artificial intelligence algorithms and recommendations for mitigation. *PLOS Digital Health*, *2*(6), e0000278. Advance online publication. DOI: 10.1371/journal.pdig.0000278 PMID: 37347721

Oberbichler, S., Boroş, E., Doucet, A., Marjanen, J., Pfanzelter, E., Rautiainen, J., Toivonen, H., & Tolonen, M. (2021). Integrated interdisciplinary workflows for research on historical newspapers: Perspectives from Humanities Scholars, computer scientists, and librarians. *Journal of the Association for Information Science and Technology*, *73*(2), 225–239. DOI: 10.1002/asi.24565 PMID: 35873357

Oztabak, C. (2025). AI-Generated Folklore for Culturally Resonant Storytelling in the Digital Age: Bridging Tradition and Technology in Storytelling. In Saka, E. (Ed.), *Understanding Generative AI in a Cultural Context: Artificial Myths and Human Realities* (pp. 161–184). IGI Global Scientific Publishing., DOI: 10.4018/979-8-3693-7235-7.ch007

Papp-Zipernovszky, O., Mangen, A., Jacobs, A., & Lüdtke, J. (2021). Shakespeare Sonnet reading: An empirical study of emotional responses. *Language and Literature*, *31*(3), 296–324. DOI: 10.1177/09639470211054647

Preuß, K. (2022). 'legal formalism' and western legal thought*. *Jurisprudence*, *14*(1), 22–54. DOI: 10.1080/20403313.2022.2112457

Saddhono, K., Nugrahani, F., & Syamsuri, A. S., Ermanto, Rahim, A. R., & Sarimanah, E. (2024). The ethics of AI in literature: Reflections on representation and responsibility. *2024 International Conference on IoT, Communication and Automation Technology (ICICAT)*, 755–760. DOI: 10.1109/ICICAT62666.2024.10923247

Salah, M., Al Halbusi, H., & Abdelfattah, F. (2023). May the force of Text Data Analysis be with you: Unleashing the power of Generative AI for Social Psychology Research. *Computers in Human Behavior: Artificial Humans*, *1*(2), 100006. DOI: 10.1016/j.chbah.2023.100006

Salzmann-Erikson, M. (2024). The intersection between logical empiricism and qualitative nursing research: A post-structuralist analysis. *International Journal of Qualitative Studies on Health and Well-being*, *19*(1), 2315636. Advance online publication. DOI: 10.1080/17482631.2024.2315636 PMID: 38346230

Sandu, A., Cotfas, L.-A., Stănescu, A., & Delcea, C. (2024). A Bibliometric Analysis of Text Mining: Exploring the Use of Natural Language Processing in Social Media Research. *Applied Sciences (Basel, Switzerland)*, *14*(8), 3144. DOI: 10.3390/app14083144

Sarker, I. H. (2021). Deep Learning: A Comprehensive Overview on Techniques, Taxonomy, Applications and Research Directions. *SN Computer Science*, *2*(6), 420. DOI: 10.1007/s42979-021-00815-1 PMID: 34426802

Scott, R. (2024). Imagined lives: Formal implications for creative writing in the age of ai. *New Writing, 21*(4), 468–477. DOI: 10.1080/14790726.2024.2377549

Sharma, C., Sharma, S., & Sakshi, . (2022). Latent DIRICHLET allocation (LDA) based information modelling on BLOCKCHAIN technology: A review of trends and research patterns used in integration. *Multimedia Tools and Applications, 81*(25), 36805–36831. https://doi.org/. DOI: 10.1007/s11042-022-13500-z PMID: 36035323

Shrivastava, R., Jain, M., Vishwakarma, S. K., Bhagyalakshmi, L., & Tiwari, R. (2023). Cross-Cultural Translation Studies in the Context of Artificial Intelligence: Challenges and Strategies. In Kumar, A., Mozar, S., & Haase, J. (Eds.), *Advances in Cognitive Science and Communications. ICCCE 2023. Cognitive Science and Technology*. Springer., DOI: 10.1007/978-981-19-8086-2_9

Soori, M., Arezoo, B., & Dastres, R. (2023). Artificial Intelligence, Machine Learning and deep learning in advanced robotics, a review. *Cognitive Robotics, 3*, 54–70. DOI: 10.1016/j.cogr.2023.04.001

Taherdoost, H., & Madanchian, M. (2023). AI advancements: Comparison of innovative techniques. *AI, 5*(1), 38–54. DOI: 10.3390/ai5010003

Unal, F. Z., Guzel, M. S., Bostanci, E., Acici, K., & Asuroglu, T. (2023). Multilabel genre prediction using deep-learning frameworks. *Applied Sciences (Basel, Switzerland), 13*(15), 8665. DOI: 10.3390/app13158665

Vassilakopoulou, P., & Hustad, E. (2023). Bridging Digital Divides: A Literature Review and Research Agenda for Information Systems Research. *Information Systems Frontiers, 25*(3), 955–969. DOI: 10.1007/s10796-020-10096-3 PMID: 33424421

Victoria, M. (2025). Multimodal communication in intercultural interaction: edited by Ulrike Schroeder, Elisabetta Adami and Jennifer Dailey-O'Cain, New York, Routledge, 2023, 1–249 pp., £125.00 (hardback), ISBN: 9781032130170. *Language and Intercultural Communication, 25*(2), 306–308. https://doi.org/DOI: 10.1080/14708477.2025.2464477

Vinodini, S. (2024a). The analysis of language, sentiment, and themes in Paulo Coelho's 'brida' using textblob. *2024 Ninth International Conference on Science Technology Engineering and Mathematics (ICONSTEM)*, 1–8. DOI: 10.1109/ICONSTEM60960.2024.10568869

Wagner, G., Lukyanenko, R., & Paré, G. (2021). Artificial Intelligence and the conduct of literature reviews. *Journal of Information Technology, 37*(2), 209–226. DOI: 10.1177/02683962211048201

Wang, N. (2022). The rise of a new paradigm of Literary Studies: The Challenge of Digital Humanities. *New Techno Humanities*, *2*(1), 28–33. DOI: 10.1016/j.techum.2022.11.001

Yang, G., & Kim, J. (2025). The ethics of reading revisited in the age of Artificial Intelligence. *ANQ: A Quarterly Journal of Short Articles, Notes and Reviews*, 1–9. DOI: 10.1080/0895769X.2025.2453815

Yang, L., Wang, G., & Wang, H. (2024). Reimagining literary analysis: Utilizing artificial intelligence to classify modernist French poetry. *Information (Basel)*, *15*(2), 70. DOI: 10.3390/info15020070

Yue, D., Meng, X., Kuoshu, H. H., & Hunter, I. (2023a). *Chinese thought in a multi-cultural world: Cross-cultural communication, comparative literature and beyond*. Routledge.

Zaki, M. Z., & Ahmed, U. (2024). Bridging linguistic divides: The impact of AI-powered translation systems on Communication Equity and inclusion. *Journal of Translation and Language Studies*, *5*(2). Advance online publication. DOI: 10.48185/jtls.v5i2.1065

Zhang, C., & Lu, Y. (2021). Study on Artificial Intelligence: The state of the art and future prospects. *Journal of Industrial Information Integration*, *23*, 100224. DOI: 10.1016/j.jii.2021.100224

Zhao, Y., & Zhou, W. (2025). Unlocking ancient wisdom with modern tools: A new approach to the revitalization of ancient texts based on Generative Artificial Intelligence. *Journal of Academic Librarianship*, *51*(3), 111–120, 103055. DOI: 10.1016/j.acalib.2025.103055

Zou, D., & Lin, Z. (2024). Research on innovative applications of AI technology in the field of Cultural Heritage Conservation. *Academic Journal of Humanities &amp. Social Sciences*, *7*(10). Advance online publication. DOI: 10.25236/AJHSS.2024.071020

Chapter 6
Scripts and Stories: AI's Role in Modern Creative Writing

Andi Sukri Syamsuri
https://orcid.org/0009-0001-4150-4059
Universitas Muhammadiyah Makassar, Indonesia

Andi Asrifan
https://orcid.org/0000-0002-9934-6129
Universitas Negeri Makassar, Indonesia

ABSTRACT

This chapter examines the changing importance of Artificial Intelligence (AI) in contemporary creative writing, emphasizing its influence on idea generation, narrative construction, character development, and scriptwriting. Utilizing methods like Natural Language Processing and machine learning, AI aids writers in surmounting writer's block, developing character arcs, and co-authoring narratives. The research analyzes case studies in film, television, and literature, illustrating how AI can function as a creative collaborator while transforming authorship and narrative structure. Ethical issues—such as copyright, originality, bias, and the safeguarding of human creativity—are rigorously examined. The document underscores a balanced, cooperative methodology wherein AI enhances, rather than supplants, human narrative creation. Ultimately, AI offers a significant opportunity to broaden the scope of narrative production, while emphasizing the importance of emotional intelligence, cultural context, and human expression.

DOI: 10.4018/979-8-3373-1057-2.ch006

1. INTRODUCTION TO AI IN CREATIVE WRITING

1.1 Understanding AI and Its Capabilities

Artificial Intelligence (AI) denotes the emulation of human cognitive functions by computers, especially computer systems (Korteling et al. 2021). This includes several talents like as learning, reasoning, problem-solving, perception, and language comprehension. Fundamentally, AI seeks to develop systems capable of executing activities that conventionally necessitate human intelligence. Machine learning, a crucial subset of AI, entails the creation of algorithms that allow computers to learn from data and make predictions. In contrast to conventional programming, which relies on explicit directives, machine learning enables systems to enhance their performance through increased exposure to data over time.

Natural Language Processing (NLP) is a crucial component of AI that emphasizes the interaction between computers and humans using natural language. It allows machines to comprehend, interpret, and produce human language effectively (Pruneski et al. 2023). NLP integrates computer linguistics, characterized by rule-based modeling of human language, with statistical methodologies and machine learning techniques. This synergy enables AI systems to process and evaluate extensive textual data, facilitating tasks such as sentiment analysis, language translation, and text summarization.

NLP is essential in the domain of creative writing. Authors can utilize AI techniques to generate concepts, construct characters, and compose complete novels. AI can examine existing literature to discern trends in storytelling, character development, and dialogue, offering writers ideas that help improve their work (Lotfi et al. 2023). Moreover, AI-driven writing aides can aid authors in surmounting writer's block by proposing narrative developments or character trajectories grounded in recognized tropes and themes.

The functionalities of AI surpass simple text generation. Advanced models can participate in discourse, offering feedback and ideas that emulate the collaborative process of interacting with a human editor or co-writer (Ni et al. 2023). This not only optimizes the writing process but also facilitates new paths for creativity, enabling writers to investigate unexpected ideas and narratives they may not have previously contemplated.

As we explore the role of AI in contemporary creative writing, it is crucial to acknowledge both the potential advantages and the limitations associated with incorporating these technologies into the writing process. Comprehending the principles of AI and its functionalities establishes a foundation for investigating how authors might utilize these technologies to augment their narrative and creativity.

1.2 The Evolution of Writing Tools

The craft of writing has had a significant evolution over time, transitioning from basic forms of communication to advanced digital mediums. Primitive writing implements, including clay tablets and quills, were crucial for documenting ideas and narratives. These tools, however groundbreaking for their era, necessitated considerable physical labor and expertise (Patwardhan et al., 2023). The advent of the printing press in the 15th century transformed writing by facilitating the mass creation of texts, enhancing the accessibility of literature, and promoting the dissemination of ideas throughout Europe.

With the advancement of technology, the instruments accessible to authors have evolved. The typewriter originated in the 19th century, offering a swifter and more effective method for text composition. This mechanical apparatus enabled authors to generate legible papers, markedly decreasing the time necessary for editing and revision (Singh, 2022). Nevertheless, despite its benefits, the typewriter imposed constraints, like the difficulty of rearranging text or rectifying errors without cumbersome techniques.

The emergence of personal computers in the late 20th century signified a crucial turning point in the development of writing instruments. Word processing software, including Microsoft Word, has implemented capabilities that revolutionized the writing process (AbuGhanem, 2025). Writers may now effortlessly edit, format, and preserve their work, resulting in enhanced productivity and creativity. The utilization of spell check and grammatical correction tools has enhanced writing quality, enabling authors to concentrate more on their ideas rather than the mechanics of writing.

The advent of the internet facilitated the emergence of collaborative writing platforms, allowing writers to collaborate in real time, irrespective of geographical constraints. Platforms such as Google Docs facilitated effortless sharing and editing, ushering in a novel epoch of collaborative creation (Zhang & Chen, 2022). The most substantial transformation in writing tools has arisen from the advent of AI-driven solutions.

Currently, AI technologies are transforming the domain of creative writing. Advanced algorithms may now analyze extensive text data, producing suggestions and insights that were once inconceivable (Singh et al. 2024). AI-driven writing aides, including Grammarly and Sudowrite, provide instantaneous feedback, aiding authors in enhancing their compositions and investigating novel narrative avenues. Moreover, AI may provide complete narratives or character profiles, acting as a catalyst for creation rather than simply a tool.

The shift from conventional writing tools to AI-driven solutions signifies not merely a technology progression but a significant transformation in the conception and creation of narratives. As we further investigate the use of AI in creative writing, it is crucial to acknowledge this growth and its ramifications for the future of storytelling.

2. AI AS A COLLABORATOR IN STORYTELLING

2.1 Generating Ideas and Prompts

In the dynamic field of creative writing, AI has become a significant partner, especially in idea production and prompt formulation. Authors frequently contend with the difficulty of surmounting writer's block or discovering novel viewpoints on established themes (Vinchon et al. 2023). AI can foster creativity by offering unique concepts and prompts that ignite the imagination and promote the exploration of novel narrative pathways.

AI-driven technologies employ sophisticated algorithms and extensive databases to examine previous literature, discern patterns, and produce original writing suggestions. Through the analysis of several narratives across diverse genres, these technologies can propose scenarios, character attributes, and plot developments that a writer may not have contemplated (Mahadevkar et al. 2024). This capacity enables authors to transcend conventional thought and explore new realms.

An AI writing assistant may produce a suggestion like, "Compose a narrative about a detective who resolves crimes solely through the recollections of witnesses," prompting writers to investigate the intricacies of memory and perception. An AI might propose, "Envision a world where emotions are exchanged as currency," encouraging authors to explore issues of value, connection, and the human experience. These examples demonstrate how AI can act as a catalyst for creative discovery, stimulating the writer's imagination.

Furthermore, AI can customize prompts to correspond with a writer's particular interests or style. Authors can obtain tailored ideas that align with their distinctive voice by specifying factors such as genre, tone, or character archetypes (Ranade et al., 2025). A science fiction writer may get suggestions such as, "Depict a future where time travel is a prevalent tourist endeavor," or "Compose a narrative about a sentient AI in search of its purpose." These customized prompts not only stimulate creativity but also assist authors in preserving their unique style while exploring novel concepts.

AI-generated prompts can enhance collaborative writing activities, promoting writers to exchange and expand upon one another's concepts (Emerson, 2024). Writing groups may utilize AI tools to produce collective prompts, cultivating a collaborative environment conducive to creativity. This collaborative ethos can yield unforeseen narratives and inventive storytelling methods, enhancing the writing process.

In conclusion, AI possesses the capability to substantially augment the creative writing process by producing ideas and suggestions that encourage authors to think innovatively. As a creative collaborator, AI enables writers to investigate novel subjects, push their limits, and eventually generate more profound and varied narratives. The integration of AI in narrative will inevitably transform the future of creative writing through its collaborative function.

2.2 Co-Writing With AI

The incorporation of AI into creative writing has created novel opportunities for collaboration, enabling writers to form a distinctive alliance with technology (Zhu et al. 2024). Co-writing with AI entails utilizing AI tools to augment the creative process, allowing authors to investigate novel concepts, optimize their workflow, and polish their narratives. Various methods can enhance this collaborative writing experience, rendering it both efficient and creatively satisfying.

An efficient method for co-authoring with AI is the iterative feedback loop. Authors may compose a segment of their manuscript and thereafter employ AI technologies to evaluate and offer recommendations for enhancement (Luther et al., 2024). An AI may provide alternate language, detect errors in character development, or suggest narrative improvements. This feedback loop aids writers in refining their work and fosters critical thinking on their choices, resulting in a more polished final output.

Another method entails employing AI for ideation sessions. Authors may input their concepts or themes into an AI writing helper, which subsequently generates various potential story directions (Nguyen et al. 2024). This collaborative brainstorming technique enables writers to examine diverse angles and perspectives, enhancing their stories. By integrating AI-generated concepts, writers can broaden their creative scope and formulate more intricate narratives.

Numerous significant case studies illustrate the effective collaboration between humans and AI. A notable instance is the partnership between author Robin Sloan and an AI named "Shelley." Sloan collaborated with Shelley to co-author a short narrative by supplying initial cues and permitting the AI to produce language derived from those inputs (Comfort & Scharf, 2025). The outcome was a distinctive tale that fused Sloan's human sensibility with the unforeseen developments produced by the AI. This collaboration not only demonstrated the capabilities of AI in creative writing but also underscored the possibility for unforeseen innovation arising from such partnerships.

A separate case study pertains to the AI-generated novel "1 the Road," authored by Ross Goodwin. This research employed an AI model trained on a comprehensive collection of texts to produce a novel centered on a road journey across America. Goodwin supplied the AI with real-time data, including GPS coordinates and meteorological conditions, enabling it to generate a narrative that was both impromptu and contextually pertinent (Shin, 2023). The resultant work demonstrated how AI may function as a co-writer, generating a coherent narrative while utilizing real-world experiences.

In conclusion, collaborating with AI offers writers novel methodologies that enrich the creative process. Through the application of iterative feedback loops and collaborative brainstorming, authors can leverage AI to enhance their narratives and investigate novel concepts. The successful co-authorship case studies illustrate that the collaboration between human creativity and AI technology may produce remarkable outcomes, heralding a new era of narrative. As authors increasingly adopt AI as a collaborator, the potential for creative expression will continue to grow.

2.3 Enhancing Character Development

Character development is crucial to storytelling, since well-rounded characters propel storylines and emotionally engage readers (Amin et al. 2024). In contemporary creative writing, AI has become an essential instrument for augmenting character development, offering authors novel methods to craft intricate and realistic personas.

AI-driven character generators are essential tools for character creation. These tools can generate comprehensive character profiles according to particular prompts or criteria established by the writer. A writer may input attributes such as age, occupation, and personality features, allowing the AI to provide a detailed character profile encompassing backstory, motivations, and prospective conflicts (Pataranutaporn et al. 2021). This automated procedure not only conserves time but also stimulates creativity by presenting unforeseen characteristics or narratives that the author may not have originally contemplated.

Furthermore, AI can facilitate the development of characters inside a narrative. As narratives unfold, characters must evolve and adapt in reaction to events and difficulties. AI technologies can examine the track of a character's trip, proposing potential growth pathways based on recognized patterns in literature (Li et al., 2023). For instance, if a character begins as an introverted person, the AI could suggest situations that promote social engagement, ultimately resulting in a modification of their personality. This talent enables authors to create more credible character trajectories that resonate with audiences.

Furthermore, AI can assist in the analysis of character arcs by scrutinizing the relationships among characters and their evolution over time. By entering pivotal events and character interactions into an AI system, writers can conceptualize the evolution of characters in connection to one other. This analysis can uncover inconsistencies or deficiencies in character development, allowing writers to enhance their arcs for greater effect (Kumar et al. 2023). For example, if a character's goals appear to change suddenly, AI can identify these discrepancies, encouraging the writer to reevaluate the narrative coherence and character choices.

A multitude of successful projects has illustrated the efficacy of AI in character building. In collaborative writing projects, authors have employed AI to co-create characters, leading to dynamic personalities that develop in unforeseen manners (Wiboolyasarin et al. 2024). These collaborations demonstrate AI's capacity to function as a creative ally in character development, providing insights that enrich the depth and complexity of characters.

In conclusion, artificial intelligence possesses the capacity to substantially improve character development in narratives. AI equips writers with tools for character creation, supports character development, and examines character arcs, enabling the construction of complex, multidimensional characters that engage audiences. As authors increasingly adopt AI as a collaborator, the potential for character development will broaden, resulting in more captivating and intriguing storytelling.

3. THE SCRIPTWRITING PROCESS AND AI

3.1 Understanding Script Structure

Scriptwriting is a distinct mode of storytelling that adheres to particular rules and frameworks to communicate narratives efficiently. Grasping the fundamentals of screenplay formatting and organization is crucial for prospective screenwriters, as it improves readability and guarantees compliance with industry standards (Bergenstråhle, 2023). A well-structured screenplay often follows a three-act style, which provides a foundation for crafting an engaging narrative.

The initial act, commonly known as the setup, presents the principal characters, the environment, and the primary conflict. This action delineates the stakes and captivates the audience, immersing them in the narrative (De la Porte & Jensen, 2021). An impactful beginning scene is essential, as it establishes the tone and stimulates curiosity. Screenwriters frequently employ strategies like hooks or inciting situations to capture the audience's attention promptly.

The second act, termed the encounter, is where the majority of the narrative transpires. This action introduces impediments and difficulties that the protagonist must confront, resulting in character evolution and narrative advancement. Screenwriters must sustain suspense and interest the audience throughout this act, frequently utilizing subplots and character arcs to enhance the narrative (Chen, 2024). The midpoint, a crucial turning moment in the narrative, typically transpires inside this act, elevating the stakes and driving the plot toward its climax.

The third act, or conclusion, culminates the narrative and ends the primary conflict. This act must offer a gratifying resolution, addressing unresolved issues and fulfilling the commitments established in the preceding acts (Lincke et al. 2021). An effective script typically provides the viewer with a sense of resolution while simultaneously encouraging contemplation of the ideas explored within the tale.

Besides structure, various essential components enhance a captivating script. Robust character development is essential; characters must possess explicit motives, unique personalities, and sympathetic imperfections (Ge et al. 2022). Dialogue is essential for elucidating character attributes and propelling the narrative forward. Effective conversation must appear organic and genuine, embodying the distinct voice of each character.

Visual narrative constitutes a vital component of scriptwriting. Screenplays serve as blueprints for films, necessitating that writers adopt a visual perspective, employing descriptions that elicit vision and emotion (Böhm & Batty, 2022). Every scene must provide a function, either propelling the narrative or enhancing character dynamics.

AI technologies can be great resources for screenwriters as they traverse the difficulties of screenplay structure and formatting. AI-driven software can aid in preparing scripts to meet industry standards, propose structural enhancements, and generate conversation. By comprehending the principles of scriptwriting and leveraging AI capabilities, writers may craft engaging narratives that appeal to viewers and distinguish themselves in a competitive market.

3.2 AI Tools for Scriptwriters

As the realm of creative writing progresses, AI tools have become essential assets for scriptwriters. These advanced software tools aim to optimize the scriptwriting process, augment creativity, and offer insights that can enrich a screenplay (Cake, 2025). A variety of prominent AI scriptwriting tools have emerged in the industry, each providing distinct capabilities and advantages.

Final Draft is a prominent AI scriptwriting tool and a long-established industry standard. Although essentially a script formatting program, Final Draft incorporates AI features that aid authors in creating character biographies, building plot arcs, and proposing dialogue (Shao, 2025). The SmartType feature assimilates a writer's style and proposes character names and locations, so expediting the writing process. Moreover, the software's collaborative features enable numerous authors to concurrently develop a script, thereby augmenting teamwork and creativity.

Celtx is another notable application that provides an extensive suite for scriptwriting and pre-production. Celtx integrates AI-powered functionalities that aid in story construction, encompassing plot point recommendations and character development prompts (Günay, 2025). The cloud-based platform facilitates seamless collaboration among team members, rendering it optimal for writers engaged in group projects. Celtx offers tools for developing storyboards and production timelines, providing writers with a comprehensive picture of their projects.

WriterDuet is a favored option, especially for its real-time collaboration features. This software enables numerous users to collaborate on a script concurrently, rendering it ideal for co-writing endeavors (Zheng et al. 2021). WriterDuet's AI functionalities encompass auto-formatting, which guarantees adherence to industry standards for screenplays, and an integrated outline tool that assists writers in organizing their ideas and structuring their storylines efficiently.

Although not solely a scriptwriting application, Scrivener has garnered popularity among screenwriters due to its organizing features. It enables authors to compile character profiles, plot ideas, and research notes in a single location (Rapp et al. 2023). The AI functionalities in Scrivener assist writers in monitoring character development and ensuring consistency within the script.

The advantages of employing AI in scriptwriting surpass simple ease. AI technologies can examine existing screenplays to discern effective tropes and structures, offering writers data-driven recommendations that help improve their storytelling (Hermann, 2023). They can aid in producing concepts and suggestions, assisting authors in surmounting creative obstacles and exploring novel trajectories for their narratives.

In summary, AI solutions for scriptwriters provide several features aimed at augmenting creativity, optimizing the writing process, and promoting collaboration. Utilizing these modern technologies enables writers to concentrate on their narratives while reaping the efficiency and insights offered by AI. The industry is set for significant improvements in scriptwriting, propelled by the collaboration of human ingenuity and artificial intelligence.

3.3 Case Studies: AI in Film and Television

The incorporation of AI into scriptwriting has resulted in significant advancements in the cinema and television sector. Prominent instances of AI-generated scripts have surfaced, illustrating the capability of artificial intelligence to design storylines that engage audiences while contesting conventional storytelling techniques (Luchen & Zhongwei, 2023).

A notable example is the short film "Sunspring," which was totally authored by an AI named Benjamin. Created by filmmaker Oscar Sharp and AI researcher Ross Goodwin, Benjamin was trained on a corpus of more than 1,000 screenplays. The resultant script was a surreal drama that examined issues of love and technology inside a dismal future (Sönmez, 2025). Despite receiving mixed reviews, the film generated much interest in the potential of AI in creative writing and demonstrated its ability to produce distinctive and unorthodox narratives.

A significant instance is the AI-generated episode of the renowned animated series "South Park." In 2019, creators Trey Parker and Matt Stone utilized an AI program to produce a script for a special episode (Cascone & Jandrić, 2021). The AI examined prior episodes to comprehend character interactions, comedic elements, and narrative framework. The resultant episode preserved the show's distinctive flair while including novel plot elements. This experiment illustrated AI's capacity to enhance the creative process, enabling human writers to preserve their unique style while investigating novel concepts.

The influence of AI-generated scripts on the industry has been significant. Filmmakers and authors are increasingly acknowledging that AI tools can augment creativity instead of supplanting it. Artificial intelligence can facilitate brainstorming sessions, produce plot outlines, and offer data-driven insights that aid writers in refining their narratives (Lavrič & Škraba, 2023). This partnership between human ingenuity and AI technology has generated a novel array of storytelling opportunities, prompting writers to transcend traditional paradigms.

The audience's reception to AI-generated content has been diverse. Some viewers like the novelty and inventiveness of AI-generated storylines, while others question the authenticity and emotional depth of these stories. Critics contend that AI lacks an intrinsic comprehension of human experiences, resulting in storytelling that may appear disconnected or devoid of emotional depth (Hollanek, 2023). Nonetheless, as AI technology advances, there exists potential for enhancement in the quality and relatability of AI-generated scripts.

In summary, the case studies of AI-generated scripts in film and television demonstrate the transformative capacity of AI in the creative writing process. AI is transforming the storytelling landscape by improving collaboration and broadening narrative possibilities. The ongoing exploration of the confluence between AI and creative writing presents promising opportunities for both writers and readers in the future.

4. ETHICAL CONSIDERATIONS AND CHALLENGES

4.1 Copyright and Ownership Issues

The integration of artificial intelligence into the creative writing process creates important ethical issues, especially concerning copyright and content ownership (Liu et al., 2023). The legal ramifications of AI-generated works are intricate and continuously developing, as current copyright legislation was not intended to tackle the distinct issues presented by AI technologies.

A key worry is the issue of authorship. Copyright law conventionally bestows ownership upon the creator of a work. Nonetheless, when an AI produces a script or narrative, the inquiry emerges: who is the genuine author? Is it the programmer who created the AI, the user who provided the prompts, or the AI itself? Existing legal frameworks do not acknowledge AI as a creator, hence complicating the assignment of rights to AI-generated content (Fukuda-Parr & Gibbons, 2021). This ambiguity has prompted conversations among legal experts, legislators, and creatives over the necessity for new legislation that may address the reality of AI in creative domains.

Furthermore, the matter of uniqueness arises. Copyright safeguards original works of creation; yet, AI systems frequently acquire knowledge from extensive databases comprising current literature, film scripts, and other creative materials (Anantrasirichai & Bull, 2022). This prompts inquiries regarding the originality of AI-generated works and if they are derivative of the source materials utilized for training the AI. The generation of a script by AI that closely mirrors an existing work may result in potential copyright infringement allegations, complicating the situation for both AI engineers and writers.

The issue of ownership also encompasses the rights pertaining to AI-generated content. In the event that a writer collaborates with an AI tool to create a script, should the writer maintain complete ownership, or should the AI developer assert a portion of the rights? This predicament has considerable ramifications for the creative sector, including influencing writers' remuneration and their ability to promote their works (Gaffar & Albarashdi, 2025).

With the increasing utilization of AI in creative writing, it is imperative for industry players to participate in transparent dialogues on copyright and ownership (Watiktinnakorn et al. 2023). Formulating explicit standards and legislation will be essential for safeguarding the rights of human producers while simultaneously tackling the distinct issues presented by AI-generated content.

The ethical considerations around copyright and ownership in AI-generated works are intricate and complicated. As the legal landscape evolves, it is essential for writers, AI developers, and politicians to engage in establishing frameworks that acknowledge the contributions of both human and artificial intelligence in the creative process. By confronting these difficulties, the industry can cultivate a more egalitarian environment for all creative engaged in the storytelling process.

4.2 The Role of Human Creativity

As artificial intelligence increasingly infiltrates the realm of creative writing, the significance of human creativity emerges as a central topic of discourse. Although AI technologies can substantially improve the writing process by generating ideas, proposing narrative advancements, and even composing complete screenplays, it is essential to maintain a balance between AI support and human contribution (Khalifa and Albadawy 2024). This equilibrium is crucial for maintaining the distinctive attributes that characterize storytelling and for ensuring that narratives connect on a profound emotional level.

A significant problem about the utilization of AI in creative writing is the possible diminishment of the human element. Storytelling is fundamentally a human activity, grounded on individual experiences, emotions, and cultural contexts. Authors utilize their personal experiences and their surroundings to create narratives that encapsulate the intricacies of the human condition (Fang et al., 2023). Conversely, AI is devoid of human experiences and emotional profundity; it produces information based on patterns and data rather than authentic comprehension. Consequently, there exists a risk that narratives generated with substantial dependence on AI may lack the nuanced viewpoints and emotional depth that define engaging storytelling.

To alleviate this risk, it is imperative for writers to perceive AI as a collaborative ally rather than a substitute for their creativity. Authors can utilize AI technologies to improve their writing process—such as generating ideas, polishing dialogue, or organizing plots—thereby retaining control over their tales while gaining efficiency and insights from AI (Nguyen et al. 2024). This collaborative method enables writers to leverage the advantages of human creativity with AI technology, producing more profound and captivating narratives.

Furthermore, the use of AI must not diminish the significance of critical thinking and emotional intelligence in narrative construction. Writers must engage actively in the creative process, employing their intuition and empathy to construct characters, explore ideas, and create authentic dialogue (Devaki, 2025). By emphasizing human input, writers may guarantee that their work embodies authentic feelings and experiences, so relating more deeply with readers.

As the creative landscape evolves, it is essential for authors to adopt the breakthroughs provided by AI while being attentive to preserving the core of storytelling. The future of creative writing depends on a harmonious integration of human creativity with AI support, with technology enhancing rather than diminishing the distinct voices of writers (Carroll, 2024). By promoting this partnership, the industry can persist in generating storylines that are both original and profoundly human, enhancing the storytelling experience for producers and consumers alike.

4.3 Addressing Bias and Representation

With the increasing integration of artificial intelligence into creative writing, the prevalence of bias in AI training data has become a notable concern. AI systems acquire knowledge from extensive datasets, which frequently embody the biases inherent in the underlying material. This may result in the continuation of stereotypes and the marginalization of minority narratives in storytelling (Hanna et al. 2024). Comprehending and mitigating these biases is essential for guaranteeing that AI positively influences the creative domain.

Bias in AI training data can show in multiple forms. For instance, if an AI is primarily educated on literature from a particular demographic—such as Western writers or mainstream genres—it may produce content that mirrors those viewpoints while omitting different narratives. The absence of representation may lead to narratives that do not connect with a wider audience and perpetuate prevailing cultural prejudices (Ferrara, 2024). Therefore, it is essential for creators and developers to meticulously assess the datasets utilized for training AI systems, guaranteeing they include a diverse array of viewpoints, experiences, and cultural situations.

To enhance varied storylines and reduce prejudice in AI-generated content, various solutions may be implemented. Initially, developers ought to emphasize the incorporation of varied authors and genres inside their training datasets. By assembling a more representative dataset, AI systems can acquire knowledge from a wider spectrum of narrative approaches, themes, and character portrayals (Bugayenko et al. 2023). This method enhances the AI's productivity and promotes a more inclusive creative atmosphere.

Secondly, writers and producers can deliberately utilize AI techniques to ensure their storylines embody different perspectives. Utilizing AI-generated prompts or recommendations as a foundation enables writers to incorporate their distinct voices and experiences into the narratives, facilitating authentic portrayal (Ng et al. 2022). This partnership may produce narratives that confront prejudices and illuminate the intricacies of diverse cultures and identities.

Furthermore, continuous oversight and assessment of AI-generated content are important. Developers must establish feedback mechanisms that permit users to identify biased or problematic outputs, facilitating the ongoing enhancement of AI systems (Jin et al. 2025). This iterative process can assist in identifying and correcting biases, ensuring that AI technologies develop to promote more fair storytelling practices.

In summary, tackling bias and representation in AI-generated work is essential for the future of creative writing. By recognizing the biases present in training data and employing tactics to foster varied narratives, writers and developers may collaboratively cultivate a more inclusive storytelling environment. As AI increasingly influences narratives, emphasizing representation will guarantee that the stories we convey embody the complexity and diversity of the human experience.

5. THE FUTURE OF AI IN CREATIVE WRITING

5.1 Trends and Innovations in AI Technology

The evolution of artificial intelligence is having a significant impact on creative writing. Innovative tools and breakthroughs in AI technology are transforming writers' approaches to storytelling, providing novel methods for idea generation, character development, and narrative construction (Ng et al. 2022). The future of AI in creative writing is characterized by numerous significant trends that are poised to augment the creative process and transform the function of authors.

A notable trend is the advancement of more complex natural language processing (NLP) models. These sophisticated AI systems possess the ability to comprehend context, tone, and nuance, facilitating the generation of more coherent and contextually pertinent outputs. Instruments such as OpenAI's GPT-4 and analogous models are currently exhibiting the capacity to produce high-caliber literature that emulates human writing styles (Bansal et al. 2024). As these technologies advance, we can anticipate increasingly sophisticated AI-generated content that can effortlessly assimilate into diverse genres and formats.

A notable trend is the emergence of collaborative writing platforms that utilize AI to enhance co-creation. These systems facilitate real-time collaboration among writers and integrate AI recommendations that improve the writing process. AI can assess a writer's style and offer customized prompts or feedback, assisting authors in enhancing their narratives while preserving their distinct voices (McGuire et al., 2024). This collaborative method cultivates a dynamic setting in which human innovation and AI support coexist synergistically.

The incorporation of AI in the pre-production and editing stages of writing is increasingly gaining momentum. Artificial intelligence tools are being created to aid in script formatting, continuity verification, and audience analysis (Cake, 2025). Writers can utilize these tools to assess prospective audience responses through data-driven insights, enabling them to customize their tales for enhanced engagement. This prediction ability can profoundly impact the writing process, allowing authors to make informed choices regarding their narratives.

In the forthcoming decade, we can expect numerous forecasts concerning the influence of AI on creative writing. As AI improves in producing original content, the distinction between human and AI-generated storylines may become indistinct (Tsao & Nogues, 2024). This may give rise to a novel type of hybrid storytelling that amalgamates human creativity with AI-generated components, yielding fresh and unforeseen narratives.

Secondly, there will probably be an augmented emphasis on ethical considerations, especially about bias and representation in AI-generated content (Fang et al., 2024). Authors and developers must work to guarantee that AI tools foster different narratives and encompass a broad spectrum of human experiences.

As AI technology progresses, the function of the writer may transform. Writers may progressively assume the roles of curators and editors of AI-generated material, concentrating on refining and shaping tales rather than creating them from inception (Cardon et al. 2023). This transition may establish a novel paradigm in narrative, wherein AI functions as an instrument to augment human creativity rather than supplant it.

In summary, the future of AI in creative writing is replete with promise and potential. As novel tools and technologies transform the environment, writers will have the opportunity to investigate new creative pathways while addressing the ethical dilemmas that arise from these breakthroughs. The partnership between human creativity and AI technology will certainly revolutionize narrative in innovative and disruptive manners.

5.2 AI's Impact on the Writing Community

The incorporation of artificial intelligence into creative writing is altering the dynamics of the writing community, resulting in substantial changes in the functions of writers and editors (Zhao, 2024). As AI tools advance and gain widespread usage, conventional roles in the writing process are transforming, presenting new opportunities and difficulties for authors, editors, and other creative workers.

A significant alteration is the transformation in the functions of writers and editors. Historically, writers have been chiefly tasked with producing original content, whilst editors concentrated on enhancing and perfecting that work. Nonetheless, with the emergence of AI-driven writing helpers, the distinctions between these tasks are becoming further indistinct (Watiktinnakorn et al. 2023). Writers can now utilize AI technologies to generate ideas, construct plots, and even compose entire chunks of text, enabling them to concentrate more on creative decision-making and narrative development rather than the technical aspects of writing. This transition allows writers to investigate novel creative pathways, since they can rapidly refine ideas and notions with AI-generated recommendations.

Editors are undergoing a shift in their responsibilities. As AI systems excel in detecting grammatical, stylistic, and structural deficiencies, editors may transition from conventional proofreading responsibilities to a more strategic role in narrative development. They may concentrate on improving the overall coherence and emotional resonance of a narrative, employing AI insights to deliver specific comments on character development, pacing, and thematic complexity (Harwood, 2022). This collaborative method enables editors to partner with AI to enhance article quality while preserving the author's distinct voice.

Moreover, AI's impact is fostering the emergence of novel genres and styles in creative writing. Writers are exploring AI-generated content, resulting in the emergence of hybrid storytelling that fuses human creativity with algorithmically created storylines (Scott, 2024). For example, interactive storytelling—where readers impact the narrative's trajectory through their decisions—can be augmented by AI's capacity to produce branching storylines instantaneously. This invention presents intriguing opportunities for immersive encounters in literature and movies, captivating audiences in manners that conventional formats may not.

The proliferation of AI-generated content is catalyzing the development of genres that investigate the interplay between mankind and technology. Speculative fiction may increasingly explore themes like artificial intelligence consciousness, ethical difficulties, and the ramifications of machine-generated creativity (Lee et al. 2025). This evolution signifies society's increasing intrigue and concern over AI's position in our lives, cultivating narratives that interrogate our comprehension of creativity and authorship.

In summary, AI significantly influences the literary community, altering the functions of writers and editors and fostering the emergence of new genres and formats. As writers include AI as a collaborative ally, they might investigate novel storytelling techniques that expand the limits of creativity. The future of creative writing will be influenced by the interaction between human creativity and technical progress, producing a diverse array of narratives that encapsulate the intricacies of contemporary society.

5.3 Conclusion: Embracing the Partnership

As we traverse the changing terrain of creative writing, it is evident that the incorporation of artificial intelligence is not a threat to human creativity, but an opportunity for collaboration. Collaborating with AI can foster unique storytelling techniques that enrich the creative process and broaden narrative possibilities (Vinchon et al. 2023). By cultivating a collaborative perspective, writers might utilize AI as a potent instrument to enhance their creativity instead of perceiving it as a substitute for their distinctive voices.

Fostering this collaborative methodology commences with acknowledging the capabilities that both human authors and AI contribute. Writers have the capacity to imbue narratives with emotional profundity, cultural background, and personal experiences—components vital for connecting with audiences. Conversely, AI excels in digesting extensive data, recognizing patterns, and rapidly generating content (Spencer & Pierce, 2023). The amalgamation of these abilities renders the possibility for creative discovery boundless. Authors can employ AI to generate ideas, enhance discourse, and assess audience preferences, enabling them to concentrate on creating captivating narratives that engage and motivate.

Furthermore, adopting this collaboration necessitates a willingness to explore. Authors ought to be emboldened to investigate novel genres and formats arising from the convergence of human creativity and AI technology (Ng et al. 2022). By incorporating AI-generated content into their work, authors can expand the limits of conventional storytelling, crafting storylines that are interactive, immersive, and representative of modern culture. This propensity for innovation will enhance the writing process and captivate readers in novel and stimulating manners.

The concluding reflections on the incorporation of AI in literature underscore the significance of ethical considerations. It is essential for writers and engineers collaborating on AI tools to ensure that these technologies foster diversity, inclusivity, and representation in storytelling (Hadinezhad et al. 2024). By proactively mitigating biases in AI training data and promoting a collaborative culture, the literary community can leverage AI to elevate marginalized voices and craft narratives that embody the diversity of human experience.

In conclusion, the future of creative writing depends on the collaboration between human authors and AI technologies. By cultivating a collaborative perspective, authors may effectively address the problems and opportunities posed by AI, so enhancing their storytelling and broadening the scope of narrative expression. The incorporation of AI in writing will fundamentally alter the creative process and reinvent storytelling, ushering in a new era of innovation and inventiveness in literature.

6. CONCLUSION

The incorporation of Artificial Intelligence into contemporary creative writing signifies a notable transformation in the conception, development, and dissemination of narratives. This study demonstrates that AI has arisen not as a substitute for human creativity but as a formidable partner, providing tools for idea generation, character development, dialogue enhancement, and comprehensive scriptwriting. AI technologies facilitate writers in creating prompts and co-authoring scenarios, allowing them to expand the limits of creativity while preserving control over voice, tone, and structure.

Case studies from literature, film, and television demonstrate the growing influence of AI in creative sectors, revealing how these technologies can generate unforeseen narratives and assist writers via iterative feedback mechanisms. This shift presents issues, especially with copyright, ownership, originality, and cultural representation. Ethical issues must be resolved via transparent development, varied training datasets, and explicit attribution processes.

The future of creative writing is fundamentally rooted on collaboration between humans and machines, rather than competition. Writers who intelligently engage with AI can augment their tale while maintaining the depth, nuance, and emotional authenticity that characterize significant writing. Educators, developers, and legislators must bolster this growing ecosystem by advancing AI literacy, protecting intellectual rights, and assuring inclusion.

In summary, AI embodies both a technological progression and a creative potential. By harnessing its potential while maintaining the principles of human expression, writers may create a new era of storytelling—where innovation, ethics, and artistic integrity coexist to enhance global literary and cinematic realms.

REFERENCES

AbuGhanem, M. (2025). IBM quantum computers: Evolution, performance, and future directions. *The Journal of Supercomputing*, *81*(5), 687. Advance online publication. DOI: 10.1007/s11227-025-07047-7

Amin, A. Y. M., Ahmad, A., & Hashim, H. (2024). Exploring the role of storyline, characters, and interactive storytelling techniques in fostering socio-emotional learning in early childhood education. *Jurnal Pendidikan Awal Kanak-kanak Kebangsaan*, *13*(2), 58–67. DOI: 10.37134/jpak.vol13.2.6.2024

Anantrasirichai, N., & Bull, D. (2021). Artificial intelligence in the creative industries: A review. *Artificial Intelligence Review*, *55*(1), 1–? DOI: 10.1007/s10462-021-10039-7

Bansal, G., Chamola, V., Hussain, A., Guizani, M., & Niyato, D. (2024). Transforming conversations with AI—A comprehensive study of ChatGPT. *Cognitive Computation*, *16*(5), 2487–2510. DOI: 10.1007/s12559-023-10236-2

Bergenstråhle, J. (2023). A phenomenological alternative to screenplay development methods. *Linguistics and Literature Studies*, *11*(1), 11–23. DOI: 10.13189/lls.2023.110102

Böhm, C., & Batty, C. (2021). Evoking character perspective in screenplay directions: A multilingual approach to writing the 'big print'. *New Writing*, *19*(3), 351–372. DOI: 10.1080/14790726.2021.1979591

Bugayenko, Y., Bakare, A., Cheverda, A., Farina, M., Kruglov, A., Plaksin, Y., Pedrycz, W., & Succi, G. (2023). Prioritizing tasks in software development: A systematic literature review. *PLoS One*, *18*(4), e0283838. DOI: 10.1371/journal.pone.0283838 PMID: 37023020

Cake, S. (2025). *Artificial intelligence as a collaborative tool for script development*. Media Practice and Education., DOI: 10.1080/25741136.2025.2454074

Cardon, P., Fleischmann, C., Aritz, J., Logemann, M., & Heidewald, J. (2023). The challenges and opportunities of AI-assisted writing: Developing AI literacy for the AI age. *Business and Professional Communication Quarterly*, *86*(3), 257–295. DOI: 10.1177/23294906231176517

Carroll, N. (2024). Are we inventing ourselves out of our own usefulness? Striking a balance between creativity and AI. *AI & Society*, *40*(1), 249–251. DOI: 10.1007/s00146-023-01856-1

Cascone, K., & Jandrić, P. (2021). The failure of failure: Postdigital aesthetics against techno-mystification. *Postdigital Science and Education*, *3*(1), 100–117. DOI: 10.1007/s42438-020-00209-1 PMID: 40477378

Chen, Z. (2024). Exploring the application scenarios and issues facing Metaverse technology in education. *Interactive Learning Environments*, *32*(5), 675–693. DOI: 10.1080/10494820.2023.2162345

Comfort, K., & Scharf, A. (2025). Teaching literature in the world language classroom: A practical guide that uses Bloom's taxonomy to enhance learning. *Language Teaching Research*, *29*(2), 200–220. DOI: 10.1177/13621688241234 56

de la Porte, C., & Jensen, M. D. (2021). The Next Generation EU: An analysis of the dimensions of conflict behind the deal. *Social Policy and Administration*, *55*(2), 235–250. DOI: 10.1111/spol.12709

Devaki, V. (2025). Academic integrity and human cognitive development of learners: Is artificial intelligence replacing the human brain? In *AI Applications and Strategies in Teacher Education* (pp. 45–60). IGI Global., DOI: 10.4018/978-1-7998-XXXX-X.ch003

Emerson, N. (2024). AI-enhanced collaborative story writing in the EFL classroom. *Technology in Language Teaching & Learning*, *6*(1), 50–68. DOI: 10.29140/tltl.v6n4.1764

Fang, C., Comery, A., & Carr, S. (2023). "They want you to know who they really are inside of the old visage": Biographical storytelling as a methodological tool to explore emotional challenges in old age. *BMC Geriatrics*, *23*(1), 845. Advance online publication. DOI: 10.1186/s12877-023-04094-8 PMID: 37353745

Fang, X., Che, S., Mao, M., Zhang, H., Zhao, M., & Zhao, X. (2024). Bias of AI-generated content: An examination of news produced by large language models. *Scientific Reports*, *14*(1), 5678. Advance online publication. DOI: 10.1038/s41598-024-55686-2 PMID: 38433238

Ferrara, E. (2024). The butterfly effect in artificial intelligence systems: Implications for AI bias and fairness. *Machine Learning with Applications*, *10*, 100430. Advance online publication. DOI: 10.1016/j.mlwa.2024.100525

Fukuda-Parr, S., & Gibbons, E. (2021). Emerging consensus on 'ethical AI': Human rights critique of stakeholder guidelines. *Global Policy*, *12*(S6), 32–44. DOI: 10.1111/1758-5899.12965

Gaffar, H., & Al-Barashdi, S. (2024). Copyright protection for AI-generated works: Exploring originality and ownership in a digital landscape. *Asian Journal of International Law, 15*(1), 23–46. DOI: 10.1017/S2044251323000735

Ge, B., De Massis, A., & Kotlar, J. (2022). Mining the past: History scripting strategies and competitive advantage in a family business. *Entrepreneurship Theory and Practice, 46*(1), 223–251. DOI: 10.1177/10422587211046547

Günay, L. (2025). The use of AI-driven software in predicting the commercial success of movies: A review on ScriptBook. In *Transforming Cinema with Artificial Intelligence*. IGI Global., DOI: 10.4018/978-8-3693-3916-9.ch010

Hadinezhad, S., Garg, S., & Lindgren, R. (2024). Enhancing inclusivity: Exploring AI applications for diverse learners. In Kourkoulou, D., Tzirides, A.-O., Cope, B., & Kalantzis, M. (Eds.), *Trust and Inclusion in AI-Mediated Education: Where Human Learning Meets Learning Machines* (pp. 163–182). Springer Nature., DOI: 10.1007/978-3-031-64487-0_8

Hanna, M., Pantanowitz, L., Jackson, B., Palmer, O., Visweswaran, S., Pantanowitz, J., Deebajah, M., & Rashidi, H. (2024). Ethical and bias considerations in artificial intelligence (AI)/machine learning. *Modern Pathology, 38*(3), 100686. Advance online publication. DOI: 10.1016/j.modpat.2024.100686 PMID: 39694331

Harwood, N. (2022). 'Teaching the writer to fish so they can fish for the rest of their lives': Lecturer, English language tutor, and student views on the educative role of proofreading. *English for Specific Purposes, 68*, 116–130. DOI: 10.1016/j.esp.2022.07.002

Hermann, I. (2021). Artificial intelligence in fiction: Between narratives and metaphors. *AI & Society, 38*(1), 319–329. DOI: 10.1007/s00146-021-01299-6

Hollanek, T. (2023). AI transparency: A matter of reconciling design with critique. *AI & Society, 38*(5), 2071–2079. DOI: 10.1007/s00146-020-01110-y

Jin, J., Yang, M., Hu, H., Guo, X., Luo, J., & Liu, Y. (2025). Empowering design innovation using AI-generated content. *Journal of Engineering Design, 36*(1), 1–18. DOI: 10.1080/09544828.2024.2401751

Khalifa, M., & Albadawy, M. (2024). Using artificial intelligence in academic writing and research: An essential productivity tool. *Computer Methods and Programs in Biomedicine Update, 5*, 100145. Advance online publication. DOI: 10.1016/j.cmpbup.2024.100145

Korteling, J. H., van de Boer-Visschedijk, G. C., Blankendaal, R. A., Boonekamp, R. C., & Eikelboom, A. R. (2021). Human-versus artificial intelligence. *Frontiers in Artificial Intelligence*, *4*, 622364. Advance online publication. DOI: 10.3389/frai.2021.622364 PMID: 33981990

Kumar, A., Saudagar, A. K. J., Alkhathami, M., Alsamani, B., Khan, M. B., Hasanat, M. H. A., Ahmed, Z. H., Kumar, A., & Srinivasan, B. (2023). Gamified learning and assessment using ARCS with next-generation AIoMT integrated 3D animation and virtual reality simulation. *Electronics (Basel)*, *12*(4), 835. Advance online publication. DOI: 10.3390/electronics12040835

Lavrič, F., & Škraba, A. (2023). Brainstorming will never be the same again—A human group supported by artificial intelligence. *Machine Learning and Knowledge Extraction*, *5*(3), 105–122. DOI: 10.3390/make5040065

Lee, D. C., Jhang, J., & Baek, T. H. (2025). AI-generated news content: The impact of AI writer identity and perceived AI human-likeness. *International Journal of Human-Computer Interaction*, 1–13. Advance online publication. DOI: 10.1080/10447318.2025.2477739

Li, H., Jiao, H., & Yang, Z. (2023). Ship trajectory prediction based on machine learning and deep learning: A systematic review and methods analysis. *Engineering Applications of Artificial Intelligence*, *123*, 105488. Advance online publication. DOI: 10.1016/j.engappai.2023.107062

Lincke, H. J., Vomstein, M., Lindner, A., Nolle, I., Häberle, N., Haug, A., & Nübling, M. (2021). COPSOQ III in Germany: Validation of a standard instrument to measure psychosocial factors at work. *Journal of Occupational Medicine and Toxicology*, *16*(Article 50), 1–15. DOI: 10.1186/s12995-021-00331-1

Liu, J., Niu, Y., Jia, Z., & Wang, R. (2023). *Assessing the ethical implications of artificial intelligence integration in media production and its impact on the creative industry*. MEDAAD. DOI: 10.70470/MEDAAD/2023/005

Lotfi, F., Beheshti, A., Farhood, H., Pooshideh, M., Jamzad, M., & Beigy, H. (2023). Storytelling with image data: A systematic review and comparative analysis of methods and tools. *Algorithms*, *16*(3), 135. DOI: 10.3390/a16030135

Luchen, F., & Zhongwei, L. (2023). ChatGPT begins: A reflection on the involvement of AI in the creation of film and television scripts. *Frontiers in Art Research*.

Luther, T., Kimmerle, J., & Cress, U. (2024). Teaming up with an AI: Exploring human–AI collaboration in a writing scenario with ChatGPT. *AI*, *5*(2), 210–225. DOI: 10.3390/ai5030065

Mahadevkar, S. V., Patil, S., Kotecha, K., Soong, L. W., & Choudhury, T. (2024). Exploring AI-driven approaches for unstructured document analysis and future horizons. *Journal of Big Data*, *11*(1), 92. DOI: 10.1186/s40537-024-00948-z

McGuire, J., De Cremer, D., & Van de Cruys, T. (2024). Establishing the importance of co-creation and self-efficacy in creative collaboration with artificial intelligence. *Scientific Reports*, *14*(1), 18525. DOI: 10.1038/s41598-024-69423-2 PMID: 39122865

Ng, D. T. K., Luo, W., Chan, H. M. Y., & Chu, S. K. W. (2022). Using digital story writing as a pedagogy to develop AI literacy among primary students. *Computers and Education: Artificial Intelligence*, *3*, 100054. Advance online publication. DOI: 10.1016/j.caeai.2022.100054

Nguyen, A., Hong, Y., Dang, B., & Huang, X. (2024). Human-AI collaboration patterns in AI-assisted academic writing. *Studies in Higher Education*, *49*(5), 847–864. DOI: 10.1080/03075079.2024.2323593

Ni, J., Young, T., Pandelea, V., Xue, F., & Cambria, E. (2023). Recent advances in deep learning based dialogue systems: A systematic survey. *Artificial Intelligence Review*, *56*(4), 3055–3155. DOI: 10.1007/s10462-022-10248-8

Pataranutaporn, P., Danry, V., Leong, J., Punpongsanon, P., Novy, D., Maes, P., & Sra, M. (2021). AI-generated characters for supporting personalized learning and well-being. *Nature Machine Intelligence*, *3*(12), 1013–1022. DOI: 10.1038/s42256-021-00417-9

Patwardhan, N., Marrone, S., & Sansone, C. (2023). Transformers in the real world: A survey on NLP applications. *Information (Basel)*, *14*(4), 242. DOI: 10.3390/info14040242

Pruneski, J. A., Pareek, A., Nwachukwu, B. U., Martin, R. K., Kelly, B. T., Karlsson, J., Pearle, A. D., Kiapour, A. M., & Williams, R. J.III. (2023). Natural language processing: Using artificial intelligence to understand human language in orthopedics. *Knee Surgery, Sports Traumatology, Arthroscopy : Official Journal of the ESSKA*, *31*(4), 1203–1211. DOI: 10.1007/s00167-022-07272-0 PMID: 36477347

Ranade, N., Saravia, M., & Johri, A. (2025). Using rhetorical strategies to design prompts: A human-in-the-loop approach to make AI useful. *AI & Society*, *40*(2), 711–732. DOI: 10.1007/s00146-024-01905-3

Rapp, C., Heilmann, T., & Kruse, O. (2023). Beyond MS Word: alternatives and developments. In Kruse, O., Rapp, C., Anson, C. M., Benetos, K., Cotos, E., Devitt, A., & Shibani, A. (Eds.), *Digital writing technologies in higher education: Theory, research, and practice* (pp. 33–47). Springer., DOI: 10.1007/978-3-031-36033-6_3

Scott, R. (2024). Imagined lives: Formal implications for creative writing in the age of AI. *New Writing, 21*(4), 468–477. DOI: 10.1080/14790726.2024.2377549

Shao, Z. (2024). GAI in the 2023 WGA Strike: English speaking media coverage of GAI's impact on the screenwriting industry and authorship. In Saka, E. (Ed.), *Understanding Generative AI in a Cultural Context: Artificial Myths and Human Realities* (pp. 211–244). IGI Global Scientific Publishing., DOI: 10.4018/979-8-3693-7235-7.ch009

Shin, H. (2023). The space between 1s and 0s: Intentional patiency in computational creativity. *Science Fiction Studies, 50*(151), 454–473. DOI: 10.1353/sfs.2023.a910330

Singh, A., Sethu, S. G., & Chaudhary, R. (2024). Artificial intelligence in storytelling: A critical analysis of narrative authenticity, cultural impact, and the future of creative industries. *Library of Progress – Library Science, Information Technology & Computer, 44*(3).

Singh, V. (2022). Minding the machine: Technological change, typographic resistance and print journalism in pre-independence India. *Südasien-Chronik – South Asia Chronicle, 18*(1), 97–117.

Sönmez, S. (2025). Artificial Intelligence in screenplay: ChatGPT application. In *Transforming Cinema with Artificial Intelligence* (pp. 37–52). IGI Global Scientific Publishing., DOI: 10.4018/979-8-3693-3916-9.ch003

Spencer, T. D., & Pierce, C. (2023). Classroom-based oral storytelling: Reading, writing, and social benefits. *The Reading Teacher, 76*(5), 525–534. DOI: 10.1002/trtr.2144

Tsao, J., & Nogues, C. (2024). Beyond the author: Artificial intelligence, creative writing and intellectual emancipation. *Poetics, 102*, 101865. Advance online publication. DOI: 10.1016/j.poetic.2024.101865

Vinchon, F., Lubart, T., Bartolotta, S., Gironnay, V., Botella, M., Bourgeois-Bougrine, S., Burkhardt, J.-M., Bonnardel, N., Corazza, G. E., Glăveanu, V., Hanchett Hanson, M., Ivcevic, Z., Karwowski, M., Kaufman, J. C., Okada, T., Reiter-Palmon, R., & Gaggioli, A. (2023). Artificial intelligence & creativity: A manifesto for collaboration. *The Journal of Creative Behavior, 57*(4), 472–484. DOI: 10.1002/jocb.597

Watiktinnakorn, C., Seesai, J., & Kerdvibulvech, C. (2023). Blurring the lines: How AI is redefining artistic ownership and copyright. *Discover Artificial Intelligence*, *3*(1), 37. Advance online publication. DOI: 10.1007/s44163-023-00088-y

Wiboolyasarin, W., Wiboolyasarin, K., Suwanwihok, K., Jinowat, N., & Muenjancho-ey, R. (2024). Synergizing collaborative writing and AI feedback: An investigation into enhancing L2 writing proficiency in wiki-based environments. *Computers and Education: Artificial Intelligence*, *6*, 100228. Advance online publication. DOI: 10.1016/j.caeai.2024.100228

Zhang, M., & Chen, W. (2022). Assessing collaborative writing in the digital age: An exploratory study. *Journal of Second Language Writing*, *57*, 100868. DOI: 10.1016/j.jslw.2022.100868

Zhao, D. (2024). The impact of AI-enhanced natural language processing tools on writing proficiency: An analysis of language precision, content summarization, and creative writing. *Education and Information Technologies*.

Zheng, S., Liu, H., & Yang, H. (2021, August). A survey of story-generation apps and online systems between 2017 and 2020. In *Proceedings of the 2021 8th International Conference on Dependable Systems and Their Applications (DSA)* (pp. 390–398). IEEE. DOI: 10.1109/DSA52907.2021.00059

Zhu, S., Wang, Z., Zhuang, Y., Jiang, Y., Guo, M., Zhang, X., & Gao, Z. (2024). Exploring the impact of ChatGPT on art creation and collaboration: Benefits, challenges and ethical implications. *Telematics and Informatics Reports*, *14*, 100138. Advance online publication. DOI: 10.1016/j.teler.2024.100138

Chapter 7
Verse by Algorithm: AI's Impact on Poetry Writing and Literary Insight

Siti Hajar Larekeng
https://orcid.org/0000-0003-2015-9775
Universitas Muhammadiyah Parepare, Indonesia

ABSTRACT

This topic invites a discussion about how AI-generated poetry, through sophisticated algorithms and machine learning techniques, is reshaping traditional notions of creativity, authorship, and emotional expression in literature. The evolution of AI poetry generators, particularly through models like GPT-2, GPT-3, and GPT-4, highlights the increasing sophistication of natural language processing (NLP) technologies that enable machines to analyze and replicate human poetic styles. This chapter also explores the features and functionalities of five prominent AI poem generators: ToolBaz, EditPad, BoredHumans, Vondy.com, and CapitalizeMyTitle.com. AI-generated poetry utilizes advanced algorithms and extensive datasets to produce text that adheres to established poetic conventions, offering a novel perspective on creativity that is both innovative and sometimes unpredictable. It further explores the implications of AI's role in artistic expression, raising critical questions about authorship, creativity, and the definition of poetry itself.

INTRODUCTION

AI-generated poetry refers to creating poems using artificial intelligence (AI) algorithms and machine learning techniques. This innovative approach leverages extensive datasets of human-authored poems to train AI models, which then generate new poems based on recognized patterns and structural elements. AI-generated

DOI: 10.4018/979-8-3373-1057-2.ch007

poetry has undergone significant evolution over the years, reflecting advancements in technology and changes in societal perceptions of art and creativity.

The journey of AI in poetry began with basic algorithms designed to manipulate language. In the early stages, these systems primarily focused on generating simple rhymes and structured forms, often lacking depth and emotional resonance. The initial attempts were rudimentary, relying on predefined templates and limited datasets.

The first key milestones include the introduction of NLP as techniques allowed AI to analyze existing poetry more effectively, recognizing patterns in language, meter, and themes. This laid the groundwork for more complex poetic structures. With the rise of Natural Language Processing (NLP) and machine learning, AI poetry generation has become more sophisticated. The second one is the advent of deep learning models, such as GPT-2 and GPT-3, which marked a turning point. These models could generate text that closely mimicked human writing styles, producing poetry that often blurred the lines between human and machine authorship. They utilized vast datasets to learn not only the mechanics of poetry but also nuances in emotional expression. (Linardaki, 2022, pp.70)

Today, AI-generated poetry is increasingly indistinguishable from human-written works. Recent studies indicate that participants often rate AI-generated poems as highly as or even higher than those by well-known human poets, showcasing a shift in public perception towards acceptance and appreciation of AI as a creative entity. This phenomenon highlights the growing sophistication of AI systems and their ability to produce emotionally resonant content.

Porter and Machery (2024) narrate the rise of user-friendly AI poem generators has democratized poetry creation. These tools allow individuals without extensive literary training to generate poems quickly by inputting themes or keywords. This accessibility has led to a surge in interest in poetry among broader audiences. Looking ahead, the evolution of AI-generated poetry is poised to continue alongside advancements in AI technology. Future developments may enhance the emotional depth and creativity of generated works, further integrating AI into literary practices. As these technologies evolve, they will likely inspire new forms of artistic expression and challenge traditional notions of authorship and creativity within literature.

Traditional Notions of Poetry and Literary Value

Traditional poetry is often viewed through the lens of its historical context, where poets are seen as part of an ongoing dialogue with their predecessors. In his essay “Tradition and the Individual Talent,” Eliot (2009. p.1) emphasizes the importance of understanding one's place within this literary tradition. He argues that a poet must possess a “historical sense,” which allows them to perceive the past and its influence on contemporary work. This sense involves recognizing that past literary works are not merely relics but living elements that shape current artistic expression.

A piece of writing is typically considered 'literary' when it exhibits certain qualities that elevate it beyond the functional text. These qualities may include complex themes, emotional depth, innovative use of language, and engagement with cultural or philosophical ideas. Frye (1957,pp 45-47) argues that literature articulates shared values and ideologies within a society, making it a crucial medium for understanding human experience. The value of literature can be intrinsic, arising from the work itself, or extrinsic, shaped by the reader's interaction with it. Literary value is also defined through engagement with complexity (Prada, 2024). She argues that true literary works often engage readers in complex ways, challenging them to reflect on themes, language, and form. This engagement is typically absent in simpler or formulaic writing, including much of what AI produces.

The rise of AI-generated poetry presents a unique challenge and opportunity for literary works. As AI systems become capable of producing coherent and stylistically varied texts, it becomes essential to assess these works against traditional human-created poetry. This evaluation is crucial for several reasons. Firstly, by comparing AI-generated poetry with human writing, people can explore the nature of creativity itself. While AI can mimic styles and generate text, it lacks the personal experiences and emotional depth that characterize human creativity. This distinction raises questions about what constitutes authentic poetic expression. Next, the emergence of AI poetry forces a reevaluation of existing literary standards. As Holyoak (2019,pp 60-61) notes, while current AI-generated texts may not yet reach the level of human poets, they challenge our definitions of what poetry can be and who can be considered a poet. Further, literature serves as a reflection of societal values and norms. Understanding how AI fits into this landscape can provide insights into contemporary culture's relationship with technology and creativity

Human-Crafted versus AI-Generated Poetic Forms

Obviously, studies show that many readers struggle to distinguish between human and AI-generated poetry. Some even prefer the clarity and accessibility of AI poetry over traditional works. However, this preference does not necessarily equate to a recognition of authenticity; it reflects a different set of expectations from poetry in contemporary contexts. Correspondingly, it needs to explore the distinct characteristics of human-crafted and AI-generated poetic forms, examining how each following criterias influence the creation, structure, and emotional resonance of poetry.

Earlier, focus on creativity and experience. Human poets draw from personal experiences, emotions, and cultural contexts, which imbue their work with depth and authenticity. In contrast, Saddhono, K., Saputra, N., et.al (2024) elaborates that

AI-generated poetry relies on algorithms that analyze existing texts to create new content without personal insight or emotional engagement. This results in poetry that may lack a nuanced understanding of human experience. As AI can produce poetry that is often indistinguishable from human work, it challenges traditional notions of what constitutes creative expression. This blurring of lines prompts a reevaluation of how we define artistic originality and value.

Next, the point of complexity and accessibility. Studies indicate that readers often find AI-generated poetry more accessible and easier to understand than human-written poetry, particularly works from historical poets like Shakespeare or Chaucer. This is partly because AI can simplify language and structure, making it more palatable for modern audiences who may struggle with archaic diction and complex forms (Prada, 2024). Readers may mistake the complexity of human-written poetry for incoherence, leading them to favor the more direct and relatable style of AI-generated works. This misinterpretation can skew preferences towards AI poetry, as it appears more coherent and accessible. AI-generated poems often utilize simpler language and clearer themes, making them easier for modern readers to understand and connect with. This straightforward approach allows a broader audience to engage with the poetry without needing extensive literary knowledge.

Then, emerging of emotional resonance. Research shows that AI poems can score higher in certain qualitative attributes such as emotional quality and creativity, as perceived by readers. However, this perception may stem from the AI's ability to produce clear and straightforward expressions rather than the profound emotional depth found in human poetry (Schober, R. 2022, p.151). Many AI poems excel in rhythm and musicality, which can enhance their appeal. The generated verses often have a polished quality that resonates with readers, leading to higher ratings in categories like beauty and emotional impact . The increasing acceptance of AI poetry may lead to a cultural shift in how poetry is consumed and appreciated. If readers continue to prefer AI-generated works, it could influence future poetic styles and norms.

Meanwhile, the aspect of authenticity and depth. Authenticity in poetry is often linked to the poet's personal voice and lived experiences. Since AI lacks consciousness and personal history, its outputs may be seen as imitative rather than genuine expressions of thought or feeling. While AI can generate poems that mimic styles and themes of human poets, the lack of genuine emotional experience raises questions about authenticity. Readers may appreciate the aesthetic qualities of AI poetry but might miss the deeper layers of meaning that come from lived experience (Ramesh and Girish, 2023). When participants are informed that a poem is AI-generated, their ratings tend to drop significantly. In studies, participants who knew they were reading AI poetry rated it lower across various characteristics compared to those who were unaware of the authorship. This suggests an inherent bias against AI authorship, reflecting a preconceived notion that human creativity is superior.

How the AI Poem Generator Works

Let's break down the process into simple steps to understand how an AI poem generator works. Generally, most AI poem generators have similar steps. The process begins with the user providing a prompt. This can be a few keywords, a theme, or a specific topic for the poem. For example, if a user wants a poem about "love in spring," they would input that phrase into the generator. Next, once the input is received, the AI uses Natural Language Processing (NLP) technology which allows the AI to understand and interpret the nuances of human language. It analyzes the input to recognize patterns, themes, and relevant vocabulary.

Then, the AI poem generator employs advanced algorithms, often using models like recurrent neural networks (RNNs) or transformers. These models are trained on vast datasets of poetry, learning how to construct lines that rhyme, rhythm, semantic meaning, and fit specific structures. Before generating the poem, users can customize their output by selecting options such as poem type (Haiku, Sonnet, or Free Verse), Length (a short, medium, or long poem), and tone or mood (e.g., joyful, melancholic) to influence the mood of the poem. After setting their preferences, users click a "Generate" button. The AI processes all this information and produces a unique poem in seconds. Finally, once generated, users can review their poems. Many generators also offer options to download the poem in various formats (like PNG or PDF) or listen to it using text-to-speech features.

Features and Functionality of AI Poem Generators

It's essential to differentiate specific features and characteristics that highlight their strengths and weaknesses to create a comprehensive comparison for various AI poem generators. Below are the items to include in the comparison table, along with explanations of their significance.

1. User interface; it evaluates how intuitive and user-friendly the platform is. A clean and straightforward interface can enhance user experience. A well-designed interface allows users to navigate the tool easily, making the poem generation process smoother.
2. Poetic styles supported, lists the different poetic forms available (e.g., haiku, sonnet, free verse). The variety of poetic styles allows users to explore different forms of poetry, catering to diverse preferences.

3. Customization options, assess the extent to which users can customize their poems, including tone, length, themes, and specific word choices.: Greater customization leads to more personalized outputs, enhancing user satisfaction and creative expression.
4. Quality of output; Evaluate the overall quality of the generated poems in terms of coherence, creativity, and emotional depth. High-quality output is crucial for users seeking meaningful poetry that resonates emotionally.
5. Technology used; Identify the underlying technology (e.g., Natural Language Processing, machine learning algorithms) employed by each generator. Understanding the technology helps gauge the sophistication of the tool and its ability to produce nuanced poetry.
6. Accessibility and cost; Determine whether the tool is free or requires a subscription, and if there are any limitations on usage. Accessibility impacts a wider audience's ability to use the tool without financial constraints.
7. Speed of generation: Measure how quickly the tool can generate poems after user input. Fast generation is beneficial for users who need quick inspiration or are under time constraints.
8. Additional features: Note any extra functionalities offered by the platform (e.g., editing tools, collaboration features). Additional features can enhance the user experience by providing more resources for refining or sharing poetry.
9. User feedback/reviews; Summarize user reviews or ratings regarding their experiences with each platform. User feedback provides insights into real-world performance and satisfaction levels.
10. Limitations/drawbacks; Identify any common complaints or issues users face with each tool (e.g., technical glitches, limited poem generation). Knowing potential drawbacks helps users make informed decisions about which tool to choose based on their needs.

This comparison table outlines the features and functionalities of five different poem generators: *toolbaz.com*, *editpad.org*, *boredhumans.com*, *vondy.com*, and *capitalizemytitle.com*. Each tool has its strengths and weaknesses in terms of user interface, poetic styles supported, customization options, quality of output, technology used, accessibility and cost, speed of generation, additional features, user feedback, and limitations.

Table 1. Features and functionalities of five different poem generators

Criterias	Toolbaz	Vondy	Boredhumans	Capitalizemytitle	Editpad
User Interface	Simple and clean, easy navigation.	Basic text editor format, minimal design.	Engaging and straightforward interface.	User-friendly with intuitive navigation.	Intuitive and quick to use.
Poetic Styles Supported	Limited styles, primarily free verse.	Supports basic forms like haiku and limerick.	Various styles including haikus and free verse.	Extensive styles including sonnets, ballads, and specialized forms like limericks and odes.	Popular forms like haikus and free verse.
Customization Options	Minimal customization available.	Allows basic input for themes.	Limited customization, mainly topic-based.	High degree of customization with specific words, themes, and lengths.	Basic customization through topic input.
Quality of Output	Minimal customization available	Allows basic input for themes	Limited customization, mainly topic-based	High degree of customization with specific words, themes, and lengths	Basic customization through topic inpu
Technology Used	Basic AI algorithms for generation.	Simple algorithms; not AI-driven.	AI-driven technology for poem generation.	Advanced AI algorithms for nuanced poetry creation.	Similar AI technology focused on popular styles.
Accessibility and Cost	Free to use; accessible on all devices.	Free; web-based access on any device.	Free access; no subscription needed.	Free with optional premium features available.	Free to use, some advanced features may cost extra.
Speed of Generation	Moderate speed	Fast generation	Quick generation	Instant generation	Fast results
Additional Features	Limited additional features available.	Mainly focused on text editing without extras.	Offers random prompts for inspiration.	Specialized generators for various poetic forms and themes.	Focused on general poetry generation without specialized tools.
User Feedback	Generally positive but mixed reviews on depth of output	Positive reviews for ease of use	Positive for creativity	Positive for creativity and variety	Satisfied but desires more depth
Limitations	Limited poetic forms	Lacks advanced features	Inconsistent output quality	Overwhelming options for some users	Limited in specialized forms

AI poem generators have become increasingly popular tools for both aspiring poets and seasoned writers, providing a unique blend of creativity and technology. Platforms like EditPad, BoredHumans, ToolBaz, Vondy, and Captalizemytitle each offer distinct features that cater to various user needs.

First, *editpad.org* presents a straightforward user interface that emphasizes ease of navigation, allowing users to generate poems quickly without unnecessary distractions. It supports multiple poetic styles, including sonnets and haikus, while offering customization options that let users input specific themes or phrases. The quality of the output is generally high, as the AI utilizes advanced language models to create coherent and engaging poetry. The technology behind EditPad leverages Natural Language Processing (NLP) to analyze user inputs effectively. Accessibility is a key feature, as the platform is entirely free to use, making it available to a wide audience. Additionally, poems are generated rapidly, typically within seconds. However, some limitations include a lack of extensive customization options and occasional emotional depth in the generated content. User feedback often highlights its user-friendly nature but notes that some poems may require further refinement.

Then, *boredhumans.com* offers an engaging user interface that is simple yet effective for generating poetry alongside various creative tools. It supports various poetic forms and allows users to input specific topics or themes for customization. The quality of output is satisfactory, producing coherent poems based on user prompts; however, the emotional resonance may not always match human-created works. The technology used here includes machine learning algorithms that enable the generation of contextually relevant content. Like EditPad, BoredHumans is free to use, which enhances its accessibility. Poems are generated quickly, providing instant gratification for users seeking inspiration. Nonetheless, some drawbacks include limited customization features and potential repetitiveness in phrasing across different poems. User feedback tends to be positive regarding its fun aspect but may express concerns about the depth of generated content.

Next, *toolbaz.com* stands out with its versatile writing tools and a clean interface that allows easy navigation through various functionalities. It supports multiple poetic styles and provides robust customization options that enable users to tailor their poems according to specific themes or tones. The quality of output is generally high due to the sophisticated AI algorithms employed by ToolBaz. The technology used combines NLP with machine learning for effective content generation. Accessibility is another strong point since it is free to use without any hidden costs. Poems are generated swiftly, which is advantageous for users needing quick results. However, some limitations include variability in output quality based on prompt complexity and a learning curve for new users navigating the extensive features. User reviews often praise its versatility but mention that the emotional depth can sometimes be lacking.

After that, *vondy.com* boasts a user-friendly interface that allows users to easily navigate through various themes and poetic styles, providing options for instant generation and infinite revisions. It supports a wide range of poetic forms, including sonnets, haikus, ballads, and specialized styles like beat poetry and satirical poetry, making it versatile for different poetic tastes. Users can customize their poems by selecting specific themes, inputting desired words or phrases, and determining the length of the poem, which enhances personalization. The quality of output from Vondy is generally high due to its advanced AI algorithms that generate creative and emotionally resonant poetry based on user inputs. The technology used is cutting-edge, ensuring that the generated poems reflect the essence of the chosen themes effectively. In terms of accessibility and cost, Vondy.com offers free basic services with optional premium features for enhanced customization, making it accessible to a broad audience. Additionally, it includes various specialized generators for unique poetic styles beyond general poetry creation. User feedback for Vondy tends to be positive, with many appreciating its creativity and variety, although some may find the extensive options overwhelming

Followed by, *capitalizemytitle.com* also features an intuitive interface, allowing users to generate poems quickly by entering topics or moods. While it supports popular poetic forms like haikus and free verse, it may not offer as extensive a range of specialized styles as Vondy. Customization options are more limited compared to Vondy, focusing primarily on general themes without deep personalization. The quality of output from CapitalizeMyTitle.com is satisfactory but can vary based on user input; it captures themes effectively but may lack the nuanced depth found in Vondy's offerings. The technology employed is similar in nature but leans more towards generating straightforward poetry rather than exploring diverse styles. This platform is also accessible for free, though some advanced features might require payment. User reviews indicate satisfaction with its ease of use; however, some users express a desire for more depth and variety in poetic styles. Overall, while both platforms provide valuable tools for generating poetry, Vondy.com stands out for its comprehensive features and customization capabilities, whereas CapitalizeMyTitle.com excels in simplicity and user-friendliness but may fall short in offering specialized poetic forms and deeper customization options.

On the whole, these AI poem generators—EditPad, BoredHumans, ToolBaz, vondy, and capitalizemytitle—each present unique features suited to different aspects of poetry creation. While they all leverage advanced AI technologies to produce creative outputs quickly and efficiently at no cost or minimal cost, they also share common limitations regarding emotional depth and customization capabilities. User feedback generally highlights their accessibility and ease of use while recognizing areas where further refinement could enhance the overall poetic experience.

ANALYZING THE INTERSECTION OF ALGORITHMIC CREATIVITY AND LITERARY EXPRESSION

The intersection of algorithmic creativity and literary expression represents a fascinating convergence of technology and the arts, where artificial intelligence is reshaping how poetry is conceived and created. This dialogue between human creativity and machine learning not only enhances the accessibility of poetry but also invites a re-examination of authorship, inspiration, and the essence of artistic expression. In this case, the author inputs a topic about the beautiful island of Sulawesi through the 5 AI poem generators such as *toolbaz.com*, *editpad.org*, *boredhumans.com*, *vondy.com*, and *capitalizemytitle.com*.

1. Poem Generating Result and Analysis of *toolbaz.com*

Sulawesi's Embrace

A butterfly, a winged horizon, drawn,
Sulawesi rises, where the oceans fawn.
A spine of emerald, kissed by jade and blue,
Where ancient mountains pierce the sky anew.
The Celebes Sea, a sapphire, deep and wide,
Embraces shores where secrets gently hide.
Coral gardens bloom, a kaleidoscope bright,
Where fishes dance in sunlight, day and night.
From Tana Toraja, with its soaring peaks,
To sculpted rice fields, whispering that speaks
Of generations past, their spirits still reside,
In houses high, where ancestors preside.
The smiling faces, warm and full of grace,
Reflect the magic of this tranquil space.
The monkeys leap, the birds in chorus sing,
A vibrant tapestry that nature brings.
From Makassar bustling, vibrant, grand,
To quiet villages upon the land,
A rhythm pulses, steady, strong, and deep,
While gentle breezes lull the soul to sleep.
The orchid's grace, the mangrove's sturdy hold,
A story whispered, centuries old.
Oh, Sulawesi, a gem upon the sea,
A breathtaking beauty, wild and free.

A haven beckons, to explore and find,
The wonders nestled, heart and soul entwined.
So come and wander, let your spirit soar,
On Sulawesi's shores, forevermore.

Poem Analysis

a. Theme; the central idea of the poem revolves around the beauty and cultural richness of Sulawesi, an island in Indonesia. It captures the natural landscapes, vibrant ecosystems, and the warmth of its people, emphasizing the connection between nature and the heritage of the region. The subject matter includes descriptions of the island's geography, flora and fauna, and the cultural significance of its communities.

b. Language;
   - Word Choice and Literary Devices: the poem employs vivid imagery and sensory language to create a rich visual landscape. Words like "emerald," "sapphire," "kaleidoscope," and "whispering" evoke sensations of color and sound, immersing the reader in the environment of Sulawesi.
   - Imagery: Phrases like "a spine of emerald" and "coral gardens bloom" use visual imagery to paint a picture of the island's natural beauty.
   - Personification: The island is described as if it possesses human qualities, with phrases like "where the oceans fawn" and "secrets gently hide," suggesting a living, breathing entity.
   - Alliteration: The poem employs alliteration, as seen in "smiling faces, warm and full of grace," which adds a musical quality to the lines.
   - Metaphor: Sulawesi is referred to as "a gem upon the sea," highlighting its value and beauty.

c. Sound and Rhythm; the poem features a consistent rhythm, predominantly using an iambic meter, which creates a flowing quality. Most lines have a similar syllabic count, contributing to a lyrical and harmonious reading experience. The pattern of stresses typically falls on the second syllable of each iambic foot, enhancing the poem's musicality.

d. Structure
   - The framework of the Poem's Structure: the poem is structured into six quatrains (four-line stanzas), each exploring different aspects of Sulawesi.

- Rhyme Scheme: The rhyme pattern is consistent with an AABB structure, where the first two lines rhyme, and the last two lines rhyme. This creates a sense of order and completeness within each stanza.
- Line Breaks and Punctuation: the line breaks are strategic, emphasizing key ideas and allowing for pauses that enhance the poem's rhythmic flow. Using commas and periods creates natural pauses, guiding the reader through the imagery and themes.
- Punctuation: the varied use of punctuation, including commas and periods, also helps establish the poem's pace and tone.

e. Context
- Who: The poem appears to be written by an anonymous poet, celebrating the beauty of Sulawesi.
- What: It is a descriptive poem that highlights the natural beauty, culture, and heritage of Sulawesi.
- Where: The focus is on Sulawesi, an island in Indonesia known for its diverse ecosystems and rich cultural history.
- When: While the specific time of writing is not indicated, the themes suggest a timeless appreciation for the island's beauty and heritage.
- Why: The poem aims to evoke a sense of wonder and appreciation for Sulawesi, inviting readers to explore and connect with the island's natural and cultural treasures. It serves as a celebration of the island's identity and encourages a spirit of adventure and connection to nature.

2. Poem Generating Result and Analysis of editpad.org

Ode to Sulawesi's Beauty

In the heart of the archipelago, where the sun gently glows,
Lies Sulawesi, an island where beauty overflows.
Emerald hills embrace the sky, kissed by ocean's embrace,
A paradise woven with nature's delicate lace.
Beneath the azure canopy, the palms sway with grace,
Where whispers of the ocean tell tales of time and space.
Coral reefs, a tapestry, alive with colors bright,
In the dance of the sea life, the day surrenders to night.
The mountains stand sentinel, their peaks draped in mist,
A realm of enchanting valleys where secrets are kissed.
Rivers cradle the landscape like threads of shimmering silk,
While rice fields blush in golden hue, a harvest of nature's milk.
The laughter of the children rings over village squares,

As cultures intertwine, woven with love and care.
Festivals burst into bloom, rich with heritage's song,
In this beautiful Sulawesi, where hearts and spirits belong.
So here's to the island, in all its splendor bright,
A jewel in the ocean, where day turns into night.
May its wonders be cherished, its beauty held dear,
Sulawesi, forever, our hearts will always revere.

Poem Analysis

a. Theme; The poem celebrates the natural beauty and cultural richness of Sulawesi, an island in Indonesia. It emphasizes the harmonious relationship between nature and the local communities, portraying Sulawesi as a paradise filled with vibrant landscapes, traditions, and a deep sense of belonging. The subject matter revolves around the physical beauty of Sulawesi, including its emerald hills, coral reefs, mountains, rivers, and rice fields, as well as the vibrant culture of its people, characterized by joyful festivals, children's laughter, and a sense of community.

b. Language

- Word Choice and literary devices: the language of the poem is vivid and evocative, employing descriptive adjectives and imagery that appeal to the senses (e.g., "emerald hills," "azure canopy," "tapestry" of coral reefs). The choice of words like "embrace," "whispers," and "dance" imbues the poem with a sense of warmth and intimacy.
- Imagery: The poem is rich in visual imagery, painting a detailed picture of Sulawesi's landscapes and cultural vibrancy.
- Personification: Nature is given human qualities, such as "whispers of the ocean" and "secrets are kissed," which enhances the connection between the island and its inhabitants.
- Metaphor: Sulawesi is described as a "jewel in the ocean," symbolizing its value and beauty.
- Alliteration: The use of alliteration in phrases like "cradle the landscape" and "blush in golden hue" creates a musical quality and enhances the poem's rhythm.

c. Sound and Rhythm; The poem appears to follow a consistent syllabic pattern, often with lines containing 8 to 12 syllables. The stresses generally fall on the natural beats of the words, contributing to a rhythmic flow. For example, the use of iambic rhythm (unstressed followed by stressed syllables) can be observed in many lines, aiding in the poem's musicality.

d. Structure

- Framework: The poem consists of five quatrains (four-line stanzas),
- Line breaks are strategically placed to enhance the flow of imagery and ideas, allowing each thought to resonate before moving to the next.
- Rhyme Patterns: The poem follows an AABB rhyme scheme, where each pair of lines rhymes, creating a sense of cohesion and harmony.
- Punctuation and Pauses: The use of commas and periods allows for natural pauses, guiding the reader through the poem's imagery and enhancing its lyrical quality.

e. Context

- Who: The poem can be attributed to an anonymous speaker or poet who expresses admiration for the island of Sulawesi.
- What: The poem is an ode celebrating the beauty and cultural richness of Sulawesi.
- Where: Sulawesi, an island in Indonesia, known for its stunning landscapes and diverse cultures.
- When: While the poem does not specify a time period, it reflects contemporary appreciation for natural beauty and cultural heritage.
- Why: The purpose of the poem is to evoke feelings of admiration and reverence for Sulawesi, encouraging readers to cherish its wonders and acknowledge the importance of preserving its beauty and culture.

3. Poem Generating Result and Analysis of boredhuman.com

Ode to Sulawesi: Jewel of the Archipelago

In the cradle of the ocean's embrace,
Where sunbeams dance and shadows trace,
Lies Sulawesi, a canvas of dreams,
A tapestry woven with nature's gleams.
Emerald hills where the heavens kiss,
Whisper soft tales of forgotten bliss,
Coral reefs in a turquoise swath,
Speak in colors, a vibrant oath.
Mountains rise like titans bold,
Guardians of secrets yet untold,
In their arms, the clouds gently lay,
As the dawn calls forth another day.
The laughter of children, bright as the sun,
Echoes through valleys where rivers run,

With each step on the path carved by time,
The spirit of freedom begins its climb.
Beneath the boughs of ancient trees,
A symphony sways in the sultry breeze,
Frangipani scents the tender air,
As cicadas hum a lullaby rare.
Sulawesi, your heart beats strong,
In the melodies of the sultry throng,
From Tana Toraja's towering grace,
To Bunaken's depths—a secret place.
Your people, with smiles like the moon's soft glow,
Craft stories of life, of joy, of woe,
In their hands, the colors of fate,
A patchwork of love, intricate.
Oh, beautiful island, so wild, so free,
A paradise cloaked in mystery,
In every sunset, a promise renews,
Of the magic we hold, and the dreams we pursue.
So let the winds take this heart's intent,
To honor the beauty, the wonder, the rent,
Of souls intertwined, forever twined,
In the embrace of Sulawesi, our hearts enshrined.

Poem Analysis

a. Theme; The poem "Ode to Sulawesi" celebrates the natural beauty, cultural richness, and emotional depth of Sulawesi, an island in Indonesia. It conveys a deep appreciation for the island's landscapes, people, and the connection between nature and human experience. The poem explores the diverse elements of Sulawesi, including its lush hills, vibrant coral reefs, majestic mountains, and the warmth of its people. It reflects on themes of freedom, nostalgia, and the intertwined relationship between nature and human life.
b. Language
    - Word Choice and Literary Devices; The poem employs vivid and sensory language to evoke imagery and emotions associated with Sulawesi. Words like "emerald," "turquoise," "symphony," and "frangipani" create a lush, vibrant picture of the island. The choice of words conveys both beauty and a sense of reverence for the land.

- Imagery: The poem is rich in visual imagery, painting a picture of Sulawesi's landscapes and experiences.
- Personification: Elements of nature are given human-like qualities, such as "the clouds gently lay" and "the heart beats strong," which emphasizes the connection between the island and its inhabitants.
- *Metaphor: Sulawesi is referred to as a "canvas of dreams" and a "patchwork of love," suggesting its complexity and beauty.
- Alliteration: The repetition of consonant sounds (e.g., "whisper soft tales") adds a musical quality to the poem.
- Symbolism: The island symbolizes freedom, beauty, and the richness of life experiences.

c. Sound and Rhythm; The lines generally follow a pattern of alternating syllable counts, creating a rhythmic flow. For example, many lines consist of 8-10 syllables, providing a melodic quality to the reading. There are instances of iambic meter, where unstressed syllables are followed by stressed ones, enhancing the poem's musicality.

d. Structure
   - Framework: The poem is divided into 14 stanzas, with 4 lines each, creating a uniform structure that aids in rhythm and flow.
   - Line Breaks: The line breaks are strategically placed to emphasize key ideas and maintain a natural flow of thought.
   - Rhyme Patterns: The poem predominantly follows an AABB rhyme scheme, where the first two lines rhyme with each other and the next two lines rhyme as well. This creates a harmonious and cohesive sound throughout the poem.
   - Punctuation and Pauses: The use of commas, periods, and dashes creates natural pauses, allowing for a reflective reading pace and enhancing the emotional impact of the lines.

e. Context
   - Who: The poem is likely written by a poet who cherishes Sulawesi, either as a local or an admirer, aiming to convey its beauty and significance.
   - What: The poem is an ode, a lyrical piece expressing admiration and reverence for Sulawesi.
   - Where: Sulawesi is an island in Indonesia, known for its diverse landscapes, cultures, and marine life.
   - When:Although the specific time of writing is not mentioned, it reflects a contemporary appreciation of natural beauty and cultural heritage, likely in the 21st century, considering the references to modern themes.
   - Why: The poem serves to honor and celebrate the unique qualities of Sulawesi, aiming to instill a sense of wonder and appreciation for the

island's beauty and its people. It acts as a reminder of the interconnectedness of nature and humanity, encouraging readers to reflect on their own experiences with beauty and freedom.

4. Poem Generating Result and Analysis of *vondy.com*

Whispers of Sulawesi: A Serenade to Nature

In Sulawesi's arms, where waters gleam,
A tapestry of beauty, lush and bright,
Emerald hills rise, kissed by golden beam,
And sunsets paint the sky with hues of light.
The whispering winds weave tales through the trees,
As tranquil waves caress the sandy shore,
Each breath a melody, a gentle breeze,
Where nature sings, and spirits long for more.
The coral reefs beneath the azure sea,
A world alive with colors, vibrant, bold,
In every glance, a glimpse of harmony,
A paradise where dreams and life unfold.
Oh, beautiful island, heart's sweet refrain,
In your embrace, the soul finds peace again.

Poem Analysis

a. Theme; The central idea of the poem revolves around the beauty and tranquility of Sulawesi, an island in Indonesia, and the deep emotional connection the speaker has with this natural paradise. It reflects themes of nature, peace, and the restorative power of the environment. The subject matter of the poem focuses on the lush landscapes, vibrant marine life, and the overall serene atmosphere of Sulawesi. It captures the essence of the island's beauty and the feelings it evokes in the speaker.
b. Language
   - Word Choice and literary Devices: The poem uses vivid and descriptive language to evoke imagery and emotion. Words such as "emerald," "golden," "vibrant," and "melody" create a lush visual and auditory experience. The choice of words like "whispering," "caress," and "embrace" gives a sense of intimacy and connection with nature.

- Imagery: The poem is rich in imagery, painting a detailed picture of the island's landscapes and seascapes. Phrases like "Emerald hills rise" and "coral reefs beneath the azure sea" create vivid mental images.
- Personification; Nature is personified throughout the poem, with phrases like "whispering winds" and "where nature sings," suggesting a living, breathing environment that interacts with the speaker.
- Metaphor; The island is described as a "paradise" and a "heart's sweet refrain," implying a deeper emotional connection and suggesting that it provides solace and joy.

c. Sound and Rhythm; The poem consists of 14 lines, structured in a form similar to a sonnet. Each line typically has 10 syllables, following an iambic pentameter rhythm, which creates a flowing and melodic quality. The stresses in the lines contribute to the poem's musicality, enhancing the emotional impact.

d. Structure
   - Framework: The poem is structured as a single stanza, which creates a sense of unity and continuity in the depiction of Sulawesi.
   - Line Breaks: The line breaks are strategically placed to emphasize key images and moments, allowing the reader to pause and reflect.
   - Rhyme Patterns: The poem follows an ABAB rhyme scheme, which adds to its lyrical quality and helps to create a harmonious flow.
   - Punctuation and Pauses: The use of commas and periods creates natural pauses, allowing the reader to absorb the beauty of each image and thought presented.

e. Context
   - Who:The speaker of the poem is likely an individual who has visited or lived in Sulawesi, expressing personal reflections and emotions tied to the island.
   - What:The poem is an expression of admiration for Sulawesi's natural beauty and a meditation on the peace it brings to the speaker's soul.
   - Where: The setting is Sulawesi, an island in Indonesia known for its stunning landscapes and rich biodiversity.
   - When:The poem does not specify a particular time frame, but it can be inferred that the reflections are based on personal experiences, likely during a visit to the island.
   - Why:The poem serves to celebrate the beauty of nature, evoke a sense of longing, and convey the emotional peace that such natural landscapes can inspire in individuals. It highlights the intrinsic value of connecting with nature and the peace that can be found in such experiences.

5. Poem Generating Result and Analysis of capitalizemytitle.com

A Sonnet for Sulawesi

In emerald embrace 'neath azure skies,
Where waves caress the shores in soft ballet,
The island sings with beauty that defies,
Each dawn anew, unfurling bright array.
From towering peaks to coral depths aglow,
Its heart beats wild in nature's grand design;
With dusky forests where rare cultures flow,
And vibrant markets bursting with divine.
The gentle people weave their stories proud,
In laughter shared and songs of nights aglow;
Their spirits dance beneath a starry shroud—
In every smile lies warmth from hearts that know.
O Sulawesi! Jewel of seas so wide,
Echoes your beauty on each ebbing tide.

Poem Analysis

a. Theme; The poem celebrates the natural beauty and cultural richness of Sulawesi, an island in Indonesia. It conveys a deep appreciation for both the landscape and the people, emphasizing the harmony between nature and human life. The subject matter revolves around the vivid imagery of Sulawesi's landscapes—its emerald forests, azure skies, and coral reefs—as well as the warmth and vibrancy of its people and their culture.

b. Language

- Word Choice:The language is rich and evocative, using words like "emerald," "azure," "ballet," and "aglow" to create a sensory experience. The choice of words reflects both the beauty of the island and the warmth of its inhabitants.
- Imagery: The poem is filled with vivid imagery that appeals to the senses, painting a picture of the island's beauty.
- Personification: The island is described as if it has a voice, "The island sings with beauty that defies," suggesting a living, breathing entity.
- Alliteration: The phrase "soft ballet" and "wild in nature's grand design" creates a musical quality.

- Metaphor: Sulawesi is referred to as a "Jewel of seas so wide," which suggests its preciousness and beauty.
- Symbolism: The island symbolizes the connection between nature and culture, representing a harmonious existence.

c. Sound and Rhythm; The poem follows the structure of a sonnet, comprising 14 lines. Each line typically has 10 syllables, often following an iambic pentameter rhythm (an unstressed syllable followed by a stressed syllable). The rhythmic flow enhances the musicality of the poem, making it pleasant to read aloud.

d. Structure
- Framework: The poem is structured as a single sonnet, which consists of three quatrains followed by a final couplet.
- Line Breaks: The line breaks create a natural flow, allowing for pauses that enhance the reading experience.
- Rhyme Patterns: The rhyme scheme follows the traditional ABABCDCDEFEFGG pattern, typical of sonnets.
- Punctuation and Pauses: The punctuation is used effectively to create pauses and emphasize certain ideas, contributing to the overall emotional impact of the poem.

e. Context
- Who: The poem is likely written by a poet inspired by the island of Sulawesi and its people.
- What: It is a sonnet that expresses admiration for the beauty of Sulawesi and its cultural richness.
- Where: Sulawesi, an island in Indonesia known for its diverse landscapes and cultures.
- When: The exact date is not specified, but it can be assumed to be contemporary, given the modern themes of cultural appreciation and environmental beauty.
- Why: The poem aims to highlight and celebrate the unique beauty of Sulawesi, perhaps as a call to appreciate and preserve the island's natural and cultural heritage. It serves to evoke a sense of wonder and admiration for a place that may be unfamiliar to many.

Human Mimicry in AI-Generated Poetry: GPT-2, GPT-3, and GPT-4

Natural Language Processing (NLP) plays a pivotal role in the development of AI poetry generators like GPT-2, GPT-3, and GPT-4, enabling them to understand and produce human-like poetic expressions. The evolution of these models has been significantly influenced by advancements in NLP techniques, which facilitate the interpretation and generation of text that resonates emotionally with readers.

In GPT-2, NLP techniques allowed the model to analyze linguistic patterns and generate structured poetry. However, its capabilities were somewhat limited due to the relatively smaller dataset it was trained on. While it could produce coherent verses, the emotional depth and complexity of themes were often lacking. The basic NLP algorithms employed in GPT-2 focused on syntax and rhyme but did not fully capture the subtleties of human emotion or the intricacies of poetic forms.

The introduction of GPT-3 marked a significant advancement in NLP applications for poetry generation. With a much larger and diverse dataset, GPT-3 utilized enhanced NLP techniques to better understand context, sentiment, and stylistic features. This allowed it to generate poetry that not only adhered to structural norms but also conveyed emotional nuances effectively. The probabilistic modeling inherent in its design enabled GPT-3 to craft verses that mimicked human expression more closely, thus bridging the gap between machine-generated and human-authored poetry.

GPT-4 further refined these capabilities by integrating advanced NLP methodologies that improved language understanding and contextual interpretation. This model could handle complex themes with greater sophistication, allowing for a richer exploration of emotions within its poetic outputs. The use of deep learning and neural networks enabled GPT-4 to internalize the subtleties of language, resulting in poetry that often felt authentic and deeply resonant with human experiences.

The datasets used for training these models are crucial in shaping their poetic outputs. The breadth and diversity of the training data directly influence how well these models can recognize patterns, understand syntax, and replicate the stylistic elements present in human poetry. As AI poetry generators evolve, they benefit from increasingly comprehensive datasets that encompass various styles, themes, and emotional expressions.

In summary, NLP serves as the foundation for AI poetry generation by enabling models like GPT-2, GPT-3, and GPT-4 to comprehend linguistic complexities and generate emotionally resonant poetry. The advancements in NLP have transformed these models into sophisticated tools capable of crafting verses that reflect the depth and beauty characteristic of human-authored works.

The capabilities of GPT-2, GPT-3, and GPT-4 in generating poetry have enlarged significantly, particularly in their incorporation of emotional nuances, the role of datasets in personalization, handling complex themes, user customization options, and mimicking human writing styles.

GPT-2 primarily established a foundation for emotional expression in its poetry but often produced outputs that lacked depth and subtlety. Its training on a limited dataset meant that while it could generate structured poems, the emotional nuances were not as pronounced. In contrast, GPT-3 made substantial strides by utilizing a much larger and diverse dataset, which allowed it to better understand and replicate emotional expressions in poetry. This model could generate poems that resonated more deeply with users by capturing a wider range of feelings and sentiments. GPT-4 further enhanced this capability by integrating advanced technologies that improved its understanding of context and emotional depth, resulting in poetry that often felt authentic and relatable.

Datasets play a critical role in the personalization of AI-generated poetry. The quality and diversity of the training data directly influence how well the models can understand and generate emotionally nuanced content. For instance, GPT-3's extensive training on varied poetic forms allowed it to produce more personalized poetry by recognizing different emotional tones and styles. GPT-4 continued this trend by using even larger datasets that included contemporary and historical poetry, enabling it to cater to a broader audience with varying tastes and preferences.

When it comes to handling complex themes, all three models have shown progress. GPT-2 had limitations in addressing intricate subjects due to its simpler architecture and training data. In contrast, GPT-3 demonstrated an improved ability to tackle complex themes such as love, loss, and identity by drawing on its richer dataset. GPT-4 excelled further in this area by leveraging its advanced architecture to weave intricate narratives and explore deeper philosophical themes within its poetry.

User customization options significantly increased with each iteration. GPT-3 introduced features allowing users to specify themes, tones, lengths, and even stylistic elements like rhyme schemes or free verse formats. This level of customization enabled users to create highly personalized poetry that reflected their individual experiences and emotions. With GPT-4, these options became even more refined, providing users with greater control over the output's emotional tone and stylistic nuances.

In terms of mimicking human writing styles, all three models have shown varying degrees of success. GPT-2 laid the groundwork for generating coherent text that resembled human poetry but often fell short in emotional depth. GPT-3 marked a turning point where the generated poetry began to blur the lines between human and machine authorship. It could replicate various poetic styles effectively while incorporating emotional resonance. GPT-4 further advanced this capability by producing poetry that not only mimicked human styles but also engaged with complex themes and emotions more authentically.

The capabilities of GPT-2, GPT-3, and GPT-4 in generating poetry can be illustrated through the topic of the "beautiful island of Sulawesi." Each model demonstrates distinct strengths in incorporating emotional nuances, handling complex themes, and mimicking human writing styles.

Starting with GPT-2, its approach to generating poetry about Sulawesi might yield something like:

"In Sulawesi's embrace, the waves softly sigh,
Emerald hills rise, where the sun meets the sky.
With whispers of culture, and hearts intertwined,
Nature's canvas painted, a treasure to find."

Here, while the poem captures some beauty, the emotional depth is somewhat superficial. The language is simple and lacks intricate imagery or profound emotional engagement. GPT-2 can generate coherent text but struggles with deeper emotional nuances and complex themes.

In contrast, GPT-3 would enhance the emotional resonance and complexity significantly. An example might read:

"On Sulawesi's shores where the sunsets bleed gold,
The laughter of children dances with stories untold.
Each wave a memory, each breeze a soft kiss,
In this paradise lost, I find my bliss."

This output reflects a greater understanding of emotional nuance and complexity. The imagery is richer, evoking feelings of nostalgia and joy. GPT-3's training on a more extensive dataset allows it to weave deeper themes into its poetry while still maintaining a human-like quality in its writing style.

GPT-4 takes this further by incorporating even more sophisticated language and emotional depth. A potential poem could be:

"In Sulawesi's heart where the wild blooms sway,
Ancient whispers linger in the twilight's play.
Beneath the starlit tapestry, dreams take flight,
Each moment a treasure, each shadow a light."

Here, GPT-4 showcases its ability to handle complex themes such as nostalgia and connection to nature with remarkable finesse. The use of figurative language—like "twilight's play" and "starlit tapestry"—demonstrates a higher level of artistry that closely mimics human poetic expression. The emotional nuances are palpable, inviting readers to reflect on their own experiences.

The datasets used to train these models play a crucial role in shaping their outputs. As each version has evolved, the datasets have become larger and more diverse, encompassing various poetic styles and emotional expressions. This breadth allows models like GPT-3 and GPT-4 to better understand context and sentiment, which enhances their ability to create personalized poetry that resonates with users.

When addressing complex themes in poetry, GPT-2 might struggle with depth due to its simpler architecture. In contrast, both GPT-3 and GPT-4 demonstrate an improved capacity for exploring intricate subjects such as identity, nature, and cultural heritage. Their training on extensive datasets enables them to recognize patterns in language that align with these themes, producing poetry that feels authentic and engaging.

User customization options also evolve from one model to another. With GPT-3, users can specify themes, tones, lengths, and even stylistic elements like rhyme schemes or free verse formats for personalized poetry. This flexibility allows for a more tailored poetic experience that aligns closely with individual preferences. GPT-4 builds upon this by offering even more refined controls over output characteristics.

Finally, when comparing their ability to mimic human writing styles, GPT-2 provides a basic level of coherence but often lacks emotional depth. GPT-3 significantly narrows this gap by generating poetry that feels more relatable and engaging. GPT-4 excels in this regard by producing work that not only mimics human styles but also incorporates layers of meaning and emotional resonance that challenge traditional notions of authorship in poetry.

Overall, the evolution from GPT-2 through GPT-4 reflects significant advancements in generating emotionally nuanced poetry tailored to individual user experiences while effectively handling complex themes and mimicking human writing styles.

REFERENCES

FREE *AI Poem Generator | ToolBaz.com*. (n.d.). [FREE] AI Poem Generator | ToolBaz.com. https://toolbaz.com/writer/poem-generator

Bechard, D. (2024). *The Pen and the Processor: A Turing-like Test to Gauge GPT-Generated Poetry* (Doctoral dissertation, Doctoral dissertation).

Cajulis, R. C. J. C., Tuazon, J. A. O., & Cabauatan, R. R. (2024). Artificial Intelligence in Digital Art: A Comparative Analysis on Impacts to Artists. *Indonesian Journal of Research and Educational Review e–ISSN, 4*(1), 1-14. DOI: 10.47941/ijars.2444

Dwivedi, Y. K., Kshetri, N., Hughes, L., Slade, E. L., Jeyaraj, A., Kar, A. K., Baabdullah, A. M., Koohang, A., Raghavan, V., Ahuja, M., Albanna, H., Albashrawi, M. A., Al-Busaidi, A. S., Balakrishnan, J., Barlette, Y., Basu, S., Bose, I., Brooks, L., Buhalis, D., & Wright, R. (2023). Opinion Paper:"So what if ChatGPT wrote it?" Multidisciplinary perspectives on opportunities, challenges and implications of generative conversational AI for research, practice and policy. *International Journal of Information Management, 71*, 102642. DOI: 10.1016/j.ijinfomgt.2023.102642

Eliot, T. S. (2009).*Essay on Poetic Theory: Tradition and the Individual Talent.* Poetry Foundation. https://www.poetryfoundation.org/articles/69400/tradition-and-the-individual-talent

Frye, N. (1957). *Anatomy of criticism: Four essays*. Princeton University Press. DOI: 10.1515/9781400866908

Hamat, A. (2024). The Language of AI and Human Poetry: A Comparative Lexicometric Study. *3L, Language, Linguistics. Literature, 30*(2), 1–20.

Herawati, Y. W., & Masitoh, S. (2024). Quantifying literary works: Is it possible?. *Jurnal Ilmiah Bahasa dan Sastra, 11*(1), 40-52.

Holyoak, K. (2019). The Spider's Thread: Metaphor in Mind, Brain and Poetry. MIT Press

Hu, Y. (2023). Literature in the Age of Artificial Intelligence. In *2023 9th International Conference on Humanities and Social Science Research (ICHSSR 2023)* (pp. 1781-1787). Atlantis Press. DOI: 10.2991/978-2-38476-092-3_228

Hutson, J., & Schnellmann, A. (2023). The poetry of prompts: the collaborative role of generative artificial intelligence in the creation of poetry and the anxiety of machine influence. *Global Journal of Computer Science and Technology: D, 23*(1).

Ichien, N., Stamenković, D., & Holyoak, K. (2024). Interpretation of Novel Literary Metaphors by Humans and GPT-4. In *Proceedings of the Annual Meeting of the Cognitive Science Society* (Vol. 46).

Imamguluyev, R. (2023). The rise of gpt-3: Implications for natural language processing and beyond. *Int J Res Pub Rev*, *2582*(3), 7421. DOI: 10.55248/gengpi.2023.4.33987

Jerrin, N. B., & Bhuvaneswari, G. (2024). Comprehending AI's Role in Literature and Arts from a Transhumanist Perspective. [IRJMS]. *International Research Journal of Multidisciplinary Scope*, *5*(2), 846–859. DOI: 10.47857/irjms.2024.v05i02.0670

Kangasharju, A., Ilomäki, L., Lakkala, M., & Toom, A. (2022). Lower secondary students' poetry writing with the AI-based poetry machine. *Computers and Education: Artificial Intelligence*, *3*, 100048. DOI: 10.1016/j.caeai.2022.100048

Karaban, V., & Karaban, A. (2024). AI-translated poetry: Ivan Franko's poems in GPT-3.5-driven machine and human-produced translations. In *Forum for Linguistic Studies* (Vol. 6, No. 1). DOI: 10.59400/fls.v6i1.1994

KJ. Sathwik. A Journey through Generative Poetry: A Historical Overview of Generative Poetry's Odissey.(2024*). Research Trends in Language, Literature & Linguistics*. IIP Series, Vol 3. https://iipseries.org/assets/docupload/rsl20245FF8E74BFEFC545.pdf

Linardaki, C. (2022). Poetry at the first steps of Artificial Intelligence. *Humanist Studies & the Digital Age*, *7*(1), 1. DOI: 10.5399/uo/hsda/7.1.6

Manurung, R., Ritchie, G., & Thompson, H. (2012). Using genetic algorithms to create meaningful poetic text. *Journal of Experimental & Theoretical Artificial Intelligence*, *24*(1), 43–64. DOI: 10.1080/0952813X.2010.539029

Meyl, V. (2023). Artificial Intelligence and the Metamorphosis of Beauty: A Philosophical Inquiry. *Open Journal of Philosophy*, *14*(1), 180–200. DOI: 10.4236/ojpp.2024.141015

Mukminin, M. S., Putra, L. D., Muhhit, A. A., & Tenis, A. B. (2024). Personification Language Style in The Poem Created by ChatGPT. *Journal of Education and Contemporary Linguistics*, *1*(02), 21–31. DOI: 10.111322/hyy8v981

Oliveira, H. G. (2017). A survey on intelligent poetry generation: Languages, features, techniques, reutilisation and evaluation. In *Proceedings of the 10th international conference on natural language generation* (pp. 11-20). DOI: 10.18653/v1/W17-3502

Pellegrino, A., Wang, R., & Stasi, A. (2023). Exploring the intersection of sustainable consumption and the Metaverse: A review of current literature and future research directions. *Heliyon, 9*(9), e19190. Advance online publication. DOI: 10.1016/j.heliyon.2023.e19190 PMID: 37681133

Poem Generator. (n.d.). Www.editpad.org. https://www.editpad.org/tool/poem-generator

Poetic Sound Devices. (2025). *Poem Generator - Capitalize My Title.* Capitalize My Title. https://capitalizemytitle.com/poem-generator/

Poetry Generator. (2023). Boredhumans.com. https://boredhumans.com/poetry_generator.php

Porter, B., & Machery, E. (2024). AI-generated poetry is indistinguishable from human-written poetry and is rated more favorably. *Scientific Reports, 14*(1), 26133. DOI: 10.1038/s41598-024-76900-1

Prada, L. (2024). People Can't Tell the Difference Between Human Poetry and AI. *Vice Magazine.* https://www.vice.com/en/article/people-cant-tell-difference-human-poetry-ai/

Ramsay, S. (2011). *Reading Machines: Toward and Algorithmic Criticism.* University of Illinois Press. DOI: 10.5406/illinois/9780252036415.001.0001

Saddhono, K., Rosa, S., Martiningsih, E., Judijanto, L., & Rahmat, W. (2024). From Words to Algorithms: To Get Evolution of Indonesia in Terms of Literature via AI Technology. In *2024 4th International Conference on Advance Computing and Innovative Technologies in Engineering (ICACITE)* (pp. 1568-1572). IEEE. DOI: 10.1109/ICACITE60783.2024.10616427

Saddhono, K., Saputra, N., ... (2024). A New way to Create Virtual Authors/Writers using AI Based Technology with Optimized Voice and Style. In *2024 4th International Conference on Advance Computing and Innovative Technologies in Engineering (ICACITE)* (pp. 1509-1514). IEEE. DOI: 10.1109/ICACITE60783.2024.10616853

Schober, R. (2022). Passing the Turing test? AI generated poetry and posthuman creativity. *Artificial Intelligence and Human Enhancement: Affirmative and Critical Approaches in the Humanities, 21*, 151–166. DOI: 10.1515/9783110770216-009

Sejnowski, T. J. (2024). *ChatGPT and the Future of AI: The Deep Language Revolution.* MIT Press. DOI: 10.7551/mitpress/15580.001.0001

Shalevska, E. (2024). The Digital Laureate: Examining AI-Generated Poetry. RATE Issues, vol. 31, issue no. 1.

Stöckli, L., Joho, L., Lehner, F., & Hanne, T. (2024). The Personification of ChatGPT

Stöckli, L., Joho, L., Lehner, F., & Hanne, T. (2024, May 24). (GPT-4)—Understanding Its Personality and Adaptability. *Information (Basel), 15*(6), 300. DOI: 10.3390/info15060300

Vondy (2025). Vondy.com. https://www.vondy.com/lyric-poem-generator-

Chapter 8
Transformation of Literary Culture in the Digital Era Through the Use of Artificial Intelligence as a Form of Copyright Protection

Junaidi Junaidi
https://orcid.org/0000-0002-2948-696X
Sjakhyakirti University, Indonesia

ABSTRACT

Artificial Intelligence (AI) is one of the many innovations that have emerged in the digital era. Most people believe that artificial intelligence (AI) can do many things, such as creating stories or literary works. As artificial intelligence (AI) becomes more popular in society, cases of plagiarism have increased. In the Industrial Revolution 5.0, artificial intelligence (AI) is an important part of the revolution. This advancement has benefited many industries, such as literary development. Input data is essential to the development of artificial intelligence (AI) for various purposes. This is because the way artificial intelligence (AI) systems are built and the methods that will be used to solve problems depend largely on the availability of data. The use of input data for the development of artificial intelligence (AI) derived from copyrighted works may raise legal issues if done without observing the provisions of the Agreement on Trade-Related Aspects of Intellectual Property Rights (TRIPs) and Berne Convention for the Protection of Literary and Artistic Works

DOI: 10.4018/979-8-3373-1057-2.ch008

INTRODUCTION

In the 1980s, artificial intelligence (AI) made significant advances. These advancements changed creators' perspectives on how works were created. Technological tools have long been used in various fields of art, literature, and science. For a long time, humans have produced works of art with the help of a number of artificial intelligence (AI) systems and software (Assinen, 2018). Artificial intelligence (AI) is a capability possessed by a computer that consists of a set of algorithms that the machine uses to properly manage data and generate information that aids the decision-making process. In simple terms, it appears that creating art with AI does not raise copyright issues. An example would be using Microsoft Word to write an essay and a digital camera to capture a photograph. However, today's artificial intelligence (AI) systems go beyond serving as devices to help humans do their jobs. Using machine learning and neural network technology, they can autonomously create works of art and mimic human intellectual abilities.

As artificial intelligence (AI) develops, it is also being used to create works. In 2016, a group of scientists in the Netherlands introduced a painting called The Next Rembrandt. The painting was created through the use of computers to analyse 346 paintings by the famous 17th century Dutch artist Rembrandt (WIPO, 2019). A short literary work written by a computer programme in Japan in 2016 almost won a national literary competition (NPR Staff, 2016, April 05). Since 1981, David Cope has been developing an artificial intelligence (AI) programme called Experiments in Musical Intelligence (EMI). The programme has the ability to emulate famous composers such as Bach, Mozart, Chopin, and Vivaldi to create classical music pieces (Nield, 2016, March 24).

Salwa Asshafa stated that in recent years, artificial intelligence (AI) has made a lot of progress in terms of development. DALL-E introduced artificial intelligence (AI) technology that can convert text into images in early 2021 and by the end of 2022. NetDragon Websoft, a Chinese company, put artificial intelligence (AI) as CEO. After that, there is ChatGPT, which has the ability to create summaries, cover letters, find maths solutions, or even pass university entrance exams in the United States as early as 2023. In addition to ChatGPT, there is also an American company called DoNotPlay, which uses artificial intelligence (AI) as its lawyer and can help clients with traffic violations, and most recently helps Netflix Japan produce summaries for films (Asshafa, 2023, February 15).

A study shows that using invented works as input data to create music, articles, and paintings can potentially infringe copyright because the use of such works is exclusively protected from commercial duplication or utilization (Gema, 2022). Other studies show that artificial intelligence (AI) has a unique legal status in the Intellectual Property Rights (IPR) protection system in Indonesia, including: (1)

artificial intelligence (AI) cannot be considered as a patent subject or creator, (2) artificial intelligence (AI) falls under the category of patent object (invention) and not copyright because of its function as a programme that helps humans perform tasks, and (3) artificial intelligence (AI) works can be copyrighted if artificial intelligence (AI) functions as a tool to assist humans in performing tasks Ramli, et.al, 2023).

While previous studies suggest that artificial intelligence cannot be considered a legal subject, AI can be recognised as a legal object, referring to the works produced through such technology. As Article 54 of Law Number 28 Year 2014 on Copyright does not regulate the term artificial intelligence or AI. Moreover, the advancement of AI technology that currently enables the creation of copyrighted works, such as those generated by Google-made application, MusicML, suggests that the Copyright Law should regulate AI. This is because the rapid advancement of AI technology often relates to copyright. There have been many copyright and AI cases in the United States. Cases like Stability Diffusion AI, which stole billions of images from the internet, allowed generative AI tools like Midjourney and DeviantArt to alter images according to the style of the original artist, often without the permission of the copyright holder. In addition, Stability Diffusion was indicted by Getty Images for allegedly intercepting data, including photos and other works, to enrich the AI machine's data bank (Riyanto & Yudha, 2023, January 19).

In terms of copyright and artificial intelligence issues in the United States, the cases should be used as a reference to regulate artificial intelligence copyright in Indonesia. By implementing Law Number 28 Year 2014 on Copyright, we can reduce the possibility of similar legal disputes in the United States.

To date, Intellectual Property Rights (IPR) law has yet to strike a balance between equitable interests and the substantial evaluation required to set limits on the use of inventions (Wangsa, Fortunata & Hanunisa, 2023). In response to the protection of moral and economic rights in copyright law, a reform of the law is needed that can reformulate and re-conceptualise copyright (Tektona, Sari & Alfaris, 2021). Philosophically, as artificial intelligence (AI) develops and is beyond human supervision and control in the era of singularity, humans must be able to protect themselves from the rapid development of artificial intelligence (AI) technology (Tresnawati, et.al, 2022).

One component of intellectual property is copyright, which essentially serves to protect the product of human thought. This can be seen in the definition of intellectual property. According to Article 1 paragraph (2) of the Trade-Related Aspects of Intellectual Property Rights (TRIPs) Agreement on Intellectual Property Rights, intellectual property rights are defined as privileges granted to creators, inventors, designers, and creators with respect to the products of the thought process, such as innovations, written works, literature, art, as well as symbols, names, and images used in commerce. The Trade-Related Aspects of Intellectual Property Rights

(TRIPs) Agreement is part of the World Trade Organisation (WTO) Agreement that requires member countries to make national regulations regarding intellectual property rights. As a result, this agreement does not provide protection of intellectual property rights globally. Instead, it encourages member countries to make national regulations regarding intellectual property rights.

It is imperative to protect intellectual works in this age of technology, especially intellectual works generated by artificial intelligence. This is especially important because Intellectual Property Rights (IPR) essentially protect the exclusive rights of creators and inventors for their innovations and works in various fields, such as art, literature, science, technology, and trademarks (Harris, 2010).

As far as we know, artificial intelligence (AI) has been developing at a rapid pace and has entered almost all aspects of human life. Therefore, it is very important for artificial intelligence (AI) technology to be regulated in accordance with current laws, especially regarding copyright. It may infringe the copyright of an artwork or copyrighted work.

RESEARCH METHODS

This study utilises normative legal research methodology, which collects, processes and studies secondary literature or documents. This study also incorporates theories from literature sources as well as legal approaches and case examples (Supranto, 2003).

In this legal research, the approach used is (Soekanto, 2007):

1) Statute Approach is an approach used to consider legal regulations as well as issues related to the legal problem being studied.
2) The Case Study Approach, in particular, is an approach that relies on various data sources to explore, describe, and explain various aspects related to individuals, groups, programs, organisations, or events under study.
3) Comparative Law Approach, to be able to apply artificial intelligence (AI) as a copyrighted work in a written, literary, artistic or technological machine in intellectual property law, specifically copyrighted works in Indonesia. Legal comparison is needed in this case the United States with the concept of Fair Use in limiting the use of artificial intelligence and the European Union with the concept of text data mining (TDM). It is possible in the application of intellectual property law in Indonesia.

RESULTS AND DISCUSSION

1. Analysis of the Legality of Artificial Intelligence Literary Works According to the Copyright Law

With today's advancements in artificial intelligence technology, creative output created automatically by artificial intelligence (AI) systems has raised legal challenges regarding the legality and protection of intellectual property rights. It is necessary to analyse how the current copyright law framework regulates the creation of artificial intelligence (AI), especially in relation to criminal and civil liability for infringement or misuse.

Artificial intelligence is growing rapidly and has entered almost every aspect of human life, it is imperative to use applicable laws to regulate the presence of AI, especially with regards to copyright. This is important to consider as current AI technology has the ability to interact with copyrights of various types of works. This is demonstrated by research conducted by Tektona, who found that Indonesia's current copyright law does not adequately protect works created by artificial intelligence (AI) (Tektona, Sari & Alfaris).

Furthermore, research conducted by Rama, Prasada & Mahadewi (2023), found that AI is not considered as a legal subject in the Indonesian Copyright Law. Therefore, it cannot be considered as an AI creator under Indonesian Copyright law. It is very important to make regulations governing AI issues because the development of AI is currently very fast. Singarimbun's (2024) research also found that establishing copyright ownership for works produced by artificial intelligence is very difficult. This is due to the fact that the current copyright law has not thoroughly covered the features of creations produced by this technology.

With respect to artificial intelligence (AI), it is worth recalling that, among these rapid technological developments, artificial intelligence (AI) technology has entered into the field of copyright as it is protected by copyright law as it is created through the applications previously described in this context. Edward O.S. Hiariej through Republika news channel reported that the existence of artificial intelligence (AI) technology that is capable of producing creative works better than human works will further blur the distinction between creative works produced by humans and creative works produced by artificial intelligence (AI) (Ratna, 2021, October 14).

Intellectual Property Rights (IPR), are exclusive rights owned by creators or inventors resulting from extraordinary creative and intellectual activities, which have a relationship with a person's personal rights. Such intellectual works can be in the form of works of art, literature, and knowledge, as well as new inventions (inventions) in the field of technology. Works in the field of intellectual property rights originate from the ability of human thinking obtained at the expense of time, energy, thoughts, feelings, and the results of intuition, inspiration, and conscience (Puspita & Pratama, 2024).

The Trade-Related Aspects of Intellectual Property Rights (TRIPs) Agreement stipulates that, in accordance with conventions recognised by members of the World Trade Organization (WTO), Intellectual Property Rights (IPR) protection applies to eligible natural or legal persons (Article 1(3) TRIPs). The Paris Convention for the Protection of Industrial Property and the Bern Convention for the Protection of Literary and Artistic Works complement the Trade-Related Aspects of Intellectual Property Rights (TRIPs). Every country that signed the Final Act Embodying the Results of the Uruguay Round of Multilateral Trade Negotiations in 1994, including Indonesia, had to change the concept of ownership and property in its domestic law (Puspitasari & Pratama 2024).

The Indonesian Copyright Law regulates the creators of works, both individuals and groups. Copyright can be owned by the creator or granted to others. Others can also legally assign such rights to other parties (Article 1 Law Number 28 of 2014 concerning Copyright). To ensure that creators have the moral and financial rights to the works they create, the protection of Intellectual Property Rights (IPR) is essential (WIPO, 2008).

Some moral rights are listed in Article 5 of the Copyright Act, among others: the right to determine whether or not his name will be included in his work; the right to use a pseudonym; the right to change his work in accordance with the norms of society; the right to change the title and subtitle of the copyrighted work; and the right to fight for his rights if his copyrighted work is misused or mutilated. According to Article 6 of the Copyright Act, the dissemination of information on copyright management and/or electronic information related to copyright is a way to exercise moral rights. Therefore, utilising other people's works and ignoring these provisions, either directly or indirectly, is a violation of the moral rights of the creator.

The existence of the 'human' or natural individual element, as stipulated in the Berne Treaty on the period of protection, transfer of economic rights, and use of copyright after the death of the Creator, reflects moral rights as the basis of copyright protection owned by the Creator (Article 6 Berne). According to this statement, copyright is addressed to the individual, as indicated by the copyright granted to the Creator during his/her lifetime and for a certain period of time after the Creator's death. Thus, recognising artificial intelligence as a creator is considered to violate the basis of copyright protection, which may eliminate moral rights and make copyright a mere economic aspect (Ginsburg, 2018).

According to Article 9 paragraph (1) of the Copyright Law, economic rights are exclusive rights that can be owned by someone other than the Creator, namely the Copyright Holder. These rights include the right to publish, reproduce, translate, adapt, arrange, or alter the work, as well as to distribute, publish, communicate, or lease the work. Only Creators and/or Copyright Holders can efficiently use their works for commercial purposes.

P. Goldstein and P. B. Hugenholtz argue that moral rights have a deeper basis and stronger protection in civil law countries than in common law countries (Alam Wibowo, 2023). Although A. Chapman argues that it is impossible to value something solely on its economic value, moral rights are just as important as the rights of the creator (Susanti, 2017).

Under Article 4 paragraph (1) of Law No. 28 of 2014 on Copyright, the person who trains and develops artificial intelligence (AI) is deemed to be the copyright owner of the creative work produced by the artificial intelligence (AI). The copyright owner is fully responsible and can be held liable if they later use the AI to infringe someone else's copyright. However, some experts argue that multiple parties, including the creators of artificial intelligence (AI), can be liable for artificial intelligence (AI) copyright infringement. While artificial intelligence is essentially a man-made system that lacks the natural thinking ability of humans, its users are still liable for the work done by artificial intelligence (Azmi & Heriawanto, (2024).

In real life, artificial intelligence (AI) has produced many works of art, such as the film Sunspring released in 2016, the portrait painting Edmond de Belamy Portrait, and the 3D painting The Next Rembrandt. The following are some examples of work done by artificial intelligence (AI). This has disturbed national and international laws, especially Law No. 28 of 2014 on Copyright. This issue arises because the process of creating works, which is usually done and created directly by individuals (either manually or with the help of tools), can now be done entirely by machines without human intervention. This transformation shows that humans are not the only ones who have the creative ability to create works (Hristov, 2017). Actually, the substance or philosophical views regarding intellectual property protection presented by John Locke, Robert M. Sherwood, and George Wilhelm Friedrich Hegel have been discussed for centuries. These views have always been influenced by the hard work, struggle, and sincere self-expression that creators directly give to their works (Purwandoko & Imanullah, 2017).

People have utilised technology in the process of making works, just like artists who combine their abilities and skills with technology. Outcomes consist of technology or are produced through it (Earnshaw, 2017). In the beginning, people in the workplace used technology as technical assistance. In the case of products produced by artificial intelligence (AI), many aspects of the production process may infringe on the exclusive rights of the creator. Some examples are firstly. The Next Rembrandt painting is the result of data analysis of thousands of images from artificial intelligence (AI) that Rembrandt did during his lifetime. Secondly, GPT2 produces literary works that consist of a dataset of other copyrighted works that are then processed by the system (Mezei, 2022). Thirdly, the algorithm system used to create the aesthetic art inputs 60,000 images of the human body to generate images of the human body automatically (Chen, Shidujaman & Tang, 2020).

Talking about the latest fact cases, especially the copyright issues that Andersen is facing with Stability AI Ltd. One of the first cases involving Stable Diffusion was an artistic infringement case against Andersen and others committed by Stability AI Ltd, and other related companies. Around January 2023, news broke that some of the largest artificial intelligence (AI) companies, including Stability AI Ltd, Stability AI Inc, Midjourney Inc, and Deviantart Inc, were being sued for copyright infringement of the artwork of Karla Ortiz, Karla Ortiz, Kelly Mckernan and Sarah Andersen. They also represent groups or action groups who claim that the companies have infringed the copyrights of Karla Ortiz, Kelly Mckernan and Sarah Andersen. Basically, the Berne Convention allows copyright for computer programmes in Article 2.1, which protects works in the 'artistic, literary or scientific fields' (Triatmojo, Hamzani & Rahayu, 2021). For computer programmes, Article 6a on moral rights should be applied. The Berne Convention does not regulate the moral rights of computer programmes specifically, but there are clear exceptions to the protection of moral rights.

As mentioned earlier, the rapid development of artificial intelligence (AI) often involves copyright for creative works produced by artificial intelligence (AI). One example is Google's artificial intelligence (AI)-powered music-making app, Google MusicLM, which was trained based on the data of 280,000 hours of music uploaded to it to make music even without an instrumentalist, CNN Indonesia reports (CNN Indonesia (2023, January 30).

Since, artificial intelligence (AI) performs acts that can only be performed by the creator and/or copyright holder, the above case shows that the commercial use of artificial intelligence (AI) may constitute copyright infringement. Therefore, the legal value of the work of artificial intelligence (AI) is questionable as it contradicts the principle of protection of creative works in copyright law, to the detriment of the creator and/or copyright holder. Consequently, in order to increase the legal value of artificial intelligence (AI) work, the review of artificial intelligence (AI) work should be carried out in 3 (three) steps (Fauzi, Ramli & Permata, 2022):

1) Study of the Type of Work Produced

A copyrighted work is defined as a work created in the field of science, art, or literature, according to Article 1 point 3 of the Copyright Act. According to Article 40 paragraph (1), cinematographic works, art, books, and others are examples of works protected by copyright. Other products in the fields of art, literature, or science that are still in the process of being created. If you look at works of artificial intelligence (AI) such as The Next Rembrand painting or the film Sunspring, you will know that these works are protected by copyright. According to Article 41 of the Copyright Act, works that are not protected by copyright are works that are not actually formed in the form of ideas, processes, concepts, methods, principles, tools, objects, or products intended to solve problems or for the general benefit of technical or functional problems. Therefore, works of artificial intelligence (AI) are not always protected by copyright. From the perspective of creativity, the results of artificial intelligence (AI) activities may be protected by copyright.

2) Exploring Human Intellectual Intervention and Personal Expression in Works

As stated in Article 1 Number 3 of the Copyright Act, the intellectual participation of individuals and their personal expression to the creation must be taken into account. According to George Wilhelm Frederich Hegel, who spoke on the philosophy of rights, the protection of intellectual property rights depends on the personal or individual expression of the subject. Because, according to Hegel, things like merit, knowledge, talent, etc. belong to the inner mind rather than the outer mind. Similarly, Kant justified the protection of intellectual property by relying on the personality of the Creator. The fact that one can own something as their personal property is justified by Hegel's statement. One has ownership of something by virtue of the effort one puts in, according to John Locke (Aplin & Davis, 2017).

Given the results, artificial intelligence (AI) work is created autonomously without human involvement. Therefore, the original value of artificial intelligence (AI) works is still in doubt whether they are derived from human thinking or use a personal touch to support them. Artificial intelligence (AI) works may also lose copyright, causing the romanticism of the personal touch to the work and the loss of the value of hard work. However, the creator is the person who directly or jointly creates a unique and personal creation, according to Article 1 Point 2 of the Copyright Law. In the definition of the Creator, the term 'separate and distinct' shows how close the Creator is to the creative work. Therefore, the role of the human being from the idea to its implementation should be crucial to ensure the copyright is legitimately protected.

3) Checking the Original Value of the Copyrighted Work

The original value of a copyrighted work is very I mportant as it shows its novelty. Moreover, it shows the human intervention in the process of creating the creative work. Authentic value in artificial intelligence (AI) is created through analysing the process of preparation, execution, and completion of the task. Therefore, the examination should be conducted in three stages, as done by the European Union in several intellectual property cases (Hugenholtz & Quintais, 2021). These are the steps:

Firstly, the procedure for developing the concept of the work. Using people's ideas and ideas, the design stage is carried out. The ideological role of the creator in realising the work they want to create will be shown in the design of the building. Therefore, the idea or ideas serve as the foundation or basis that the creator uses to create the work. This part shows the process of hard work that intellectual property thinkers want because the idea or thought comes from the Creator, so it is very important to realise the work.

Secondly, the actual process of creating the work, especially the process of realising ideas or thoughts during the design process. A concept cannot be protected by copyright if it has no physical form, in accordance with Article 41 of the Copyright Act. This process includes all the processes undertaken by the creator of the work, such as painting in painting, writing in literature, and filmmaking in cinematography. When everyone makes creative decisions based on their personal style about the work, this process will represent the Creator's ultimate intervention in the process.

Third, the procedure for preparing the work. This process is the final stage, which means preparing or perfecting the work to be created. The creative process occurs when the literary work is altered or edited to show the creative decisions made while composing it.

According to the Copyright Act, if an author's work is considered unique and personal, the uniqueness of works created by artificial intelligence (AI) will be questioned. This is because artificial intelligence (AI) uses other people's works as references to replicate the uniqueness of a creator's work. One of the disputes to be considered is how far the human artist's cognitive process of imitation and inspiration can be compared to the training process of a generative artificial intelligence. Studies on artists' imitation, influence and innovation in the art of drawing show that artists can use their imagination to create new (novel) works that are qualitatively different from the original drawing by observing and copying the drawing (Okada & Ishibashi, 2017).

According to the author, a work should have its own characteristics that reflect the speciality or specificity of a copyrighted work. A work of art, literature or science can be considered copyrightable if it fulfils certain conditions, such as originality and fixation. The copyright or claim to the work must be original. This indicates that a work or works were actually created by its creator. Originality does not require a work or a work that is actually the result of the creator's thought or creation; rather, it requires a work or work that is actually created by the creator. In this regard, originality also means not copying another person's work or creation or another work that is in the public domain (Hawin & Riswandi, 2020).

In the author's opinion, how new or unique a work is is called originality. This indicates that the work should not simply copy or follow the work of others, but should be a creative outcome. In the copyright domain, a work should show the originality and creativity of its creator. The concept of fixation means that a work must be recorded or stored in a form that can be seen, heard, or read. In other words, the work must be available in a form that is accessible to others. Writings in books, sound recordings of songs, or drawings made in a particular format are some examples. Often, in countries that have a civil law system, such as Indonesia, the personality aspect of the creator is highly considered. Thus, copyright is not only concerned with the protection of the economic aspects of intellectual works, but also with recognition and respect as a creator, which includes moral rights such as the right to be recognised as an author and the right to prevent harmful alterations.

In Article 1 point 2 of the Copyright Law, the definition of 'Creator' also includes the criterion of originality. 'An individual or group of individuals who, either individually or collaboratively, produces a distinctive and personalised work' is the term used in this definition. According to this definition, works created by artificial intelligence do not fulfil the standard of originality because works created by a person must have unique characteristics that only humans possess. This is because the work is a combination of previous works that have been modified by a machine rather than created by a human. Therefore, the work does not reflect the personal characteristics and traits of the creator.

This approach will be applied to Copyright Law cases in Indonesia as so far there is only limited explanation of the 'special and personal' characteristics in the Copyright Law definition. For instance, in the 2015 case of Banjarnahor versus PT Holcim, the court used the Judicial Review phase to determine the copyright ownership of a software by asking the two conflicting parties questions about how the computer programme works. The only party who could provide an explanation of how the software worked was the plaintiff. In contrast, the participant could not explain how the programme worked. As a result, the court ruled that the plaintiff party in this case had 'unique and personal' attributes and properties associated with the software. As a result, the court ultimately ruled that the plaintiff was the creator of the software. In addition, with regard to the issue of 'Government of the Republic of Indonesia against.' In 2016, Arifin stated that the 'unique and personal' characteristic exists when a work is truly the result of a person's thoughts or ideas and is realised in a tangible and original form, and only the creator knows about the work (Palace, 2019).

The above decision shows that characteristics and personality are strongly linked to the creator's understanding of his work. Further, in the case of software copyright disputes, the 'unique and personal' nature is related to the person understanding how to use the software. In other words, the examination of whether a work is distinctive and individual in nature is done by ascertaining whether the party claiming copyright has a deep understanding of the work. Those who can explain the process of creating a work of art, such as a song, have 'unique and personalised' characteristics. However, for those who only know the song, this does not necessarily apply (Margoni, 2018).

Fixation or implementation is the next requirement. Copyright only protects the way in which ideas are already expressed. Since illustrations, music, and other types of products are consistent forms of media that reflect the expression of a particular idea, works created by artificial intelligence (AI) fulfil this criterion. Nonetheless, it is important to note that these two criteria are mutually supportive. Thus, works created by artificial intelligence (AI) do not fulfil the standard of originality, they cannot be protected by copyright. Copyright, as a basic principle, is an exclusive right owned by the creator. These copyrights fall into two categories under Indonesian Copyright law: moral rights and economic rights. Conversely, if a work is not considered a work of authorship, it loses its exclusive rights and can be used by anyone as it is considered a public domain. Since artificial intelligence (AI) works are in the public domain, users must comply with the terms and conditions applicable on the platforms where they can access them. This is due to the fact that most users have to agree to such terms and conditions in a contractual relationship with the developer and/or manager of the platform.

The Copyright Act states that the work must have special and unique characteristics. This suggests that the work must originate from an individual's ability, creativity, and expertise and can then be realised visually and audibly (Alam Wibowo, 2023). Therefore, works that demonstrate innovative and unique value are protected by Intellectual Property Rights (IPR). Unique and valuable works are produced through cognitive processes such as creation, inspiration, and imitation. On the other hand, artificial intelligence (AI), as a system that possesses 'intelligence', is not considered equal to humans in terms of performing actions and cognitive processes that enable the creation of works.

According to the author, if artificial intelligence (AI) work meets certain conditions, it may be legally recognised. Firstly, the result of artificial intelligence (AI) must not only be a product of machine operation, but also contain elements of human intelligence. Second, the product must be original, not a replica or duplicate. Third, the work must be created in a publicly accessible digital format, rather than a prototype or abstract concept. Lastly, artificial intelligence (AI) products fall under the subject protection category of intellectual property rights such as works of art. The creator or copyright owner can claim economic rights over the artificial intelligence work if all four main conditions are met.

Criteria relating to the protection of intellectual property rights over works of artificial intelligence (AI) are also considered by the author in this case, based on Law Number 28 of 2014 concerning Copyright, at least 3 (three) criteria must be considered when processing licences for the protection of intellectual property rights over works of artificial intelligence (AI):

1) Originality standard. When artificial intelligence (AI) works are machine-generated, they should have original value, not just plagiarism or imitation.
2) Realising the element of creativity: Artificial intelligence (AI) results are not just the result of mechanical procedures without artistic or creative value.
3) Works produced by artificial intelligence (AI) are stored in the form of digital materials accessible to human senses, such as sound, video, images, and writing, not just examples or abstract concepts that cannot be measured.

2. The Future of Artificial Intelligence Creation as Copyright in Indonesia by Considering the Comparison of European Union Law and Fair Use in the United States of America

There is no reason to consider copyright as an exclusive right. There are limitations and exceptions in copyright, indicating that some works cannot be permanently protected by copyright, which supports this explanation. The Bern Convention is one of the international treaties governing copyright limitations and exceptions. To protect copyright, a country can set rules to limit and exclude copyright. Copyright cannot be considered an absolute monopoly. The needs of the society at large always mobilise the attention of the creators.

The laws governing copyright limitations and exceptions differ from country to country. For example, in the United States, these rules are referred to as fair use, whereas in the United Kingdom, they are referred to as fair dealing. The Netherlands, for example, has no concept of fair use or fair dealing. However, the Dutch law that restricts copyright is called De beperkingen van het auteursrecht, or copyright limitations (Murfianti, 2020).

In the United States, a copyright principle known as fair use allows the use of another's work for transformation (Vincent, 2022, November 15). This doctrine limits exclusive rights to criticism, commentary, news reports, teaching, education, and research. In addition, the doctrine includes considerations such as whether the use of the work is intended for commercial purposes or for non-profit educational purposes, the characteristics of the work itself, the proportion and significance of the use of the work as a whole, and its effect on market value. The concept of fair use is constantly changing in the United States, considering the various rules and elements present in the law. In addition, offences related to fair use are also evaluated on a case-by-case basis (Alam Wibowo, 2023).

The Artificial Intelligence Act of 2023, also known as the Copyright Act, is a law in the United States that aims to establish a regulatory framework to govern and monitor the use of artificial intelligence (AI) technology in the country. The United States Copyright Act also aims to protect the public from the dangers and risks that may arise from the misuse of artificial intelligence (AI) technology. The bill aims to mitigate the negative effects of the use of these technologies and create an environment where the safety and interests of society are prioritised.

Replication of one's work without the copyright owner's permission is known as fair use. In the United States, people can use a few verses of a song, summarise or quote information from the news, take part of a news article for learning purposes, and reference an article for use in legal proceedings (Murfianti, 2020). The copying of art, literature, theatre, or music can be used fair use for learning, research, or non-commercial purposes without infringing on established copyrights.

Legal questions arise about the status of digital works created by artificial intelligence (AI) independently without human intervention amidst the current development of artificial intelligence (AI) technology. Taking into account the US Artificial Intelligence Act of 2023, there seems to be an opportunity for creative output generated by artificial intelligence (AI) to receive legal protection for intellectual property rights. This can be seen from the notion of a 'recognised rights holder', which includes non-human entities, as well as specific provisions governing the rights and responsibilities of rights holders and users of artificial intelligence (AI) systems. Therefore, developers or users who deploy and use artificial intelligence (AI) tools to create new digital products are entitled to all creative works produced by such tools. Amendment 101 of the Artificial Intelligence Act 2023 defines specifically 'owner', i.e. for the purpose of section 513, 'owner' means any individual, corporation, partnership, or other entity that owns a foodservice business or facility; exceptions are operators or owners of radio stations or foodservice establishments licensed by the Federal Communications Commission; cable or satellite system operators, cable or satellite operating services or satellite programmers; service providers; access or information operators; and cable or satellite system operators.

According to the author, the advancement of creativity occurs when exclusive rights to copyright works are granted to developers, users and creators. Therefore, the Artificial Intelligence Act 2023 confirms that digital works created by artificial intelligence (AI) have the same rights as human creative works and recognises the role of developers and users in creating and using such technology. It also shows that all parties contribute to the artificial intelligence (AI) ecosystem and encourages innovative and creative roles that can influence future developments.

The object of creation is the creativity of intellectual work in the field of literature, art, or science, is unique and can be expressed in a certain way. If properly understood the limitation of fair use in the provisions of Section 107 refers to the misuse of technical means of copyright law. This is particularly important in the context of copyright works created using artificial intelligence (AI). For example, if artificial intelligence (AI) technology is used to create a product and the product is protected by copyright, any attempt to circumvent technical protection, receive encrypted programmes, or remove or alter information from electronic rights management without permission may amount to copyright infringement. This shows how important it is to understand and respect copyright law when dealing with products created by artificial intelligence (AI).

According to the author, the fair use doctrine in the United States does not apply to copyrighted works that are used fairly. In other words, the doctrine only applies to copyrighted works that are used fairly without the authorisation of the creator or rights holder. The following factors should be considered when determining whether the use of a copyrighted work in a particular situation can be considered fair use (Gema, 2022):

a. The purpose and nature of the use, including whether it is for commercial or non-profit educational purposes
b. The characteristics of the copyrighted work
c. The number of parts used and their relationship to the total copyright work
d. The effect of the use on the market or value of the copyrighted work

In line with the author's opinion, Martine Courant Rife argues that if copyright does not provide protection to a work, the principle of fair use becomes irrelevant. Martine Courant Rife describes some situations where this can happen (Rife, 2007):

1) The work has entered the public domain, which means its copyright protection period has expired
2) Works created by the United States government, including laws, regulations, court decisions, and others
3) Works that are not original
4) De minimis use of the work, which means that the use of the work does not significantly involve the number of works copied, so there is no significant similarity
5) Use of the work with the consent of the creator

Most countries have created laws to regulate the use of data protected by copyright in addition to the principle of fair use. The European Union has some regulations regarding the legality of text and data mining (TDM), such as: (1) use for the purposes of scientific research by research institutions and institutions focused on cultural heritage, (2) there are no restrictions on the type of user, although intellectual property rights owners have the right to prohibit their work from being used, and (3) there is widespread recognition that text and data mining (TDM) conducted may aid research in certain communities, which in turn may harm other communities Gervais, 2022).

The European Union takes a human-centred approach and applies flexible regulations to regulate artificial intelligence. This is done to ensure that the application of artificial intelligence (AI) is in line with European Union values and principles (Madiega, 2024). These regulations are designed to achieve two goals: encouraging the utilisation of artificial intelligence (AI) and managing the risks that arise as a result. The European Union also has artificial intelligence (AI) regulations that require developers and providers of generative artificial intelligence (AI) services to disclose information about the datasets used in the product development process. This is done to protect the copyright of the works contained in the datasets (AI Act, EU, 2023).

The majority of jurisdictions across Europe emphasise how important a creator's intellectual contribution is to his or her work and stipulate that the creator must actually be a human being. The case of Infopaq International A/S v Danske Dagblades Forening emphasises this statement, stating that the originality of a work is judged on the condition that it is the original intellectual creation of its author (Court of Justice of the European Union, No. C-5/08/2009). The Court of Justice of the European Union (CJEU) has not set specific rules on copyright for computer-generated works. However, the CJEU confirmed that a human contribution is necessary for copyright to be protected as the work should reflect the personality of its creator (Rajendra, et.al, 2023, June 8).

The main regulation governing copyright term in the European Union is Directive No. 2006/116/EC, which establishes a general period of protection for literary and artistic works, including books, music, paintings, and photography. A Directive is a form of regulation in the European Union that serves as a guide, requiring member states to achieve certain goals, but does not prescribe the methods for achieving them (EU Directorate General for Communication, (n.d.)). As such, European Union member states are allowed to add provisions or enhance copyright protection beyond the minimum term specified by the directive.

In order to protect the rights of the author and the two generations below him, Article 6 of Directive 2006/116 sets the minimum term of copyright protection, which includes during the life of the author and fifty years after his death (EU Parliament, 2006). The CJEU's General Prosecutor, Vera Trstenjak, has provided an explanation of the meaning of the article's provisions. Trstenjak's judgement in Eva-Maria Painer v. Standard VerlagsGmbH states that only human creations including works using technical aids such as cameras are protected (Court of Justice EU, No. C-145/10, 2011).

This means allowing creators to avoid using their works in datasets used to develop generative artificial intelligence. In Japan, copyright laws have changed for Text and Data Mining (TDM). Some of these changes are as follows (Rahman, Al Farouqi & Tang, 2020):

(1) Allow the use of works for machine learning purposes where artificial intelligence (AI) users cannot directly access the works, so that the creator is not harmed
(2) Permit incidental copying of works for machine learning without infringing the rights of the owner
(3) Authorise the use of text and data mining (TDM) for searchable databases for data verification due to the importance of the data to researchers and not to the detriment of the copyright owner

The use of text and data mining (TDM) for commercial or non-commercial purposes is not regulated in Japan, except for the reproduction and retrieval of materials from unlawful sites (Lanz, 2023, June 6). A professor of intellectual property rights at Waseda University stated that regulations regarding artificial intelligence (AI) in Japan aim to encourage the adoption of the technology by balancing the free utilisation and protection of data used in development (Ueno, 2017). Both countries are pursuing the legalisation of using datasets as add-ons for artificial intelligence (AI). This is being done for a specific reason, which is to encourage technological advancement and innovation, especially in the field of machine learning and artificial intelligence (AI).

The Draft Artificial Intelligence Act and the EU Copyright Act demonstrate the application of lex informatica. The Draft Artificial Intelligence Act divides artificial intelligence (AI) systems based on their capabilities and effects. This suggests a risk-focused approach. Consequently, since the structure used in the Draft Artificial Intelligence Act is technology-based and based on architectural standards. Lex informatica has been incorporated into it. According to Reidenberg (1998), these elements play an important role in the setting of the law as they serve as the basis of the legal structure. Machine learning, logic and knowledge-based, and statistics are some of the software technology approaches used along with the methods and approaches regulated in artificial intelligence systems under the Draft Artificial Intelligence Act. The EU divides artificial intelligence (AI) into the following three categories as each type has different software system components:

a. Unacceptable artificial intelligence (AI) risks refer to the types of artificial intelligence that are expressly prohibited from use because they may pose a danger to human safety. The Draft Law on artificial intelligence outlines the intended prohibitions and includes: artificial intelligence (AI) systems that use subliminal manipulation techniques; artificial intelligence (AI) systems used by government agencies to conduct social evaluations; and artificial intelligence (AI) systems used directly in identification systems. e.g. efforts to locate targets of criminal acts, terrorism, and serious crimes.

b. According to Article 6 of the Draft Law on artificial intelligence, artificial intelligence (AI) systems that are considered high-risk are used for the safety elements of the product or the system itself. In addition, the product must be evaluated for feasibility by a third party. This artificial intelligence (AI) is used in various fields, such as biometric recognition, education, law enforcement, and labour or human resource management. Therefore, the system must fulfil the requirements for use, such as using high-quality training, validation, and testing data, providing adequate documentation, guaranteeing that the information managed is transparent, ensuring human supervision, and being built on a solid foundation, accurate, and having adequate cyber protection (Boggs, 2021).
c. Low-risk artificial intelligence (AI) systems are not bound by strict rules as they have very little impact or risk (Boggs, 2021).

The real purpose of these copyright restrictions is to create a fair balance between the interests of the creators and the users of copyright-protected works. Any country can enact copyright laws to protect the use of copyrighted works without seeking permission from the creator or providing remuneration. The Bern Convention for the protection of literary and artistic works declares it essential for legislation in member states to permit the reproduction of such works in some specific cases, provided that the reproduction does not interfere with the normal exploitation of the work and does not unreasonably prejudice the legitimate interests of the author.

In addition, the Trade-Related Aspects of Intellectual Property Rights (TRIPs) Agreement stipulates that members should limit and exclude exclusive rights only in certain specific situations that do not conflict with the ordinary use of the work or do not unreasonably prejudice the legitimate interests of the right holder. In the Bern Convention and the Trade-Related Aspects of Intellectual Property Rights (TRIPs) Agreement, copyright restrictions are usually based on three requirements: (a) a particular special case; (b) not incompatible with the ordinary use of the work; and (c) not unreasonably prejudicial to the legitimate interests of the right holder. These three requirements are often used as the basis for determining whether the use of a protected work (Geiger, Gervais & Sentfleben, 2015).

To ensure that copyright infringement by artificial intelligence relating to commercialisation issues does not occur amidst legal vagueness, this step is the most effective method to do so. Therefore, Indonesia should regulate artificial intelligence (AI) thoroughly and evaluate its current copyright laws. To avoid confusion when using contemporary technologies, provisions regarding the subject and object of copyright are clarified. In the era of digital transformation, the application of the three-step test doctrine is essential. It also applies to national and international copyright regulations. This theory deals with copyright limitations and exceptions, which was first introduced through the revision of the Berne Convention in 1967.

The doctrine was later implemented in Article 9(2) of the Berne Convention as a provision for reproduction rights over copyrighted works. According to this lesson, the testing process should be carried out in three stages, namely (Riswandi, 2017):

a) Creative works may only be reproduced under certain conditions.
b) Reproduction is permitted as long as it does not interfere with reasonable interests or exploitation.
c) Only permitted where it does not interfere with the interests of the creator or copyright holder.

According to the author, by using works protected by copyright as data, the development of artificial intelligence (AI) in the fields of education and research can actually be carried out in Indonesia without obtaining the consent of the creator or copyright holder. The use of the work must still take into account the proper interests of the creator or copyright holder. If the use of the work interferes with their legitimate interests, the use of the work may constitute copyright infringement. The problem encountered is that while it has been explained that 'reasonable interests' refers to interests that depend on the balance in obtaining economic benefits from a work, there is no clear definition of what is meant by 'balance'. As of now, there is no valid court judgement in Indonesia that can be used to assess the 'balance' of such reasonable interests.

Furthermore, the distribution of copyrighted content owned by others through information and communication technology platforms for non-commercial purposes is not considered a copyright infringement, in accordance with Article 43 letter (d) of the Copyright Law. Thus, this essentially allows the creation of works in digital format that can be used as data in the development of non-commercial artificial intelligence (AI) in Indonesia. However, if the creator of the work objects to the digital format of the work, such action will be considered a copyright infringement. Thus, creators can object at any time for various reasons, and this provision can hinder the development of artificial intelligence (AI) for non-commercial purposes in Indonesia. This could disrupt the development programs of non-commercial artificial intelligence (AI) in the country.

The Trade-Related Aspects of Intellectual Property Rights (TRIPs) Agreement Article 13 establishes this principle, which states that "Members shall confine any limitations or exceptions to exclusive rights to certain special cases which do not conflict with a normal exploitation of the work and do not unreasonably prejudice the legitimate interests of the right holder." Technological Protection Measure (TPM) steps protect copyrighted content in electronic media. Technological Protection Measure (TPM) can be used as a technical strategy or architectural standard to protect digital works from harmful use by artificial intelligence. Technological Protection

Measure (TPM) also protects the integrity, confidentiality, and authentication of works on the internet. To achieve this, encryption, software, passwords, and other similar techniques are used (Riswandi, 2017).

Technological Protection Measure (TPM) is software or components used by copyright holders to prevent copyright infringement, such as the use of passwords and encryption on software code. The Technological Protection Measure (TPM) actions aim to maintain the integrity, privacy, and authentication of online works. Intellectual property owners take technological protection measures to prevent infringement and illegal use of their copyrights. Considering that technological protection measures fall into the category of technology that can protect works. Therefore, to enhance legal protection, technological protection measures must be implemented in the law.

In Indonesia, Law No. 28 of 2014 concerning Copyright regulates Technology Protection Measure (TPM) as a technology that can protect copyrighted works. Although the law has not explicitly explained how the technology is used, it still falls into the category of technological control tools. Any form of technology, device, or component created to prevent or regulate actions prohibited by the creator, copyright holder, related rights holder, or regulated by law is referred to as a technological control tool.

To protect copyrighted content, cryptographic methods and passwords can be applied. The type of Access Control Technology Protection Measure is part of technology protection. Cryptography allows information to be hidden during transmission, so unauthorized individuals cannot access it (Kerr, Maurushat & Tacit, 2003). By using Technology Protection Measure (TPM), copyright holders can better protect their exclusive rights. This will prevent people from engaging in copyright infringement on the internet or other harmful actions, including for commercial purposes.

The use, reproduction, duplication, and modification of works or products by individuals for educational, research, academic writing, security, and government, legislative, and judicial operations can be affected by copyright restrictions. If Technology Protection Measure (TPM) steps are taken to protect copyrighted content using methods such as encryption or cryptography, it can hinder people who actually use that content for educational purposes or other non-commercial purposes. Although Technology Protection Measure (TPM) measures serve to protect the rights of creators or copyright holders, they also restrict user access. Although this is beneficial for creators or copyright holders, it can also be detrimental to users, especially in the fields of education, teaching, or research.

Indonesia has complied with the copyright regulations approved as a member of the World Trade Organization. Efforts to harmonize various types of international agreements related to copyright limitations and exceptions with national regulations at both horizontal and vertical levels are known as the adjustment between copyright limitations and exceptions in international agreements with national regulations (Riswandi, 2017).

CONCLUSION

In Indonesia, copyright law does not explicitly regulate the work or status of works produced by artificial intelligence. There must be a rule that regulates the results of copyrighted works produced by artificial intelligence. Copyright Law in Indonesia to be able to regulate the results of copyrighted works produced by Artificial Intelligence. A copyrighted work produced by artificial intelligence (AI) meets certain requirements, to be legally recognised must have the following conditions: First, the results of artificial intelligence (AI) must not only be the product of machine operation, but also contain elements of human intelligence. Second, the product must be original, not a replica or duplicate. Third, the work must be created in a publicly accessible digital format, rather than a prototype or abstract concept. Finally, artificial intelligence (AI) products fall under the protection category of intellectual property rights subjects such as works of art.

The use of artificial intelligence must have certain limitations and exclude copyright protection. The European Union and the United States, for example, use the doctrine of fair use as a flexible rule, and both consider the limitations and consequences of copyright use, in the training of artificial intelligence. In addition, special regulations on artificial intelligence are needed to regulate future copyright law that does not rely solely on current copyright law.

REFERENCE

Alam Wibowo, R. J. (2023). Ciptaan dan Invensi Hasil Kecerdasan Buatan dalam Perspektif Hak Cipta dan Paten. *Jurnal Ilmiah Kebijakan Hukum, 17*(3), 269–288. DOI: 10.30641/kebijakan.2023.V17.269-288

Aplin, T. F., & Davis, J. (2017). *Intellectual Property Law: Text, Cases, and Materials.* Oxford University Press. DOI: 10.1093/he/9780198743545.001.0001

Artificial Intelligence Act, European Parliament (2023).

Asshafa, S. (2023, February 15). Pencapaian AI Sejauh Ini: Bantuan Netflix Bikin Animasi, Hingga Jadi Kurator Seni. Akurat. https://www.akurat.co/infotech/1302404434/Pencapaian-AI-Sejauh-Ini-Bantuan-Netflix-Bikin-Animasi-Hingga-Jadi-Kurator-Seni

Assinen, S. (2018). *European Union Copyright Protection for AI-Generated Works",* Thesis, Master's Degree Programme Law and Information Society, University of Turku, Finland.

Azmi, M. K. W., Rokhim, A., & Heriawanto, B. K. (2024). *Legality and Legal Protection of Visual Art Works Produced Through Artificial Intelligence.* Dinamika 30(1), 9041-9059, https://jim.unisma.ac.id/index.php/jdh/article/view/23614/17668

Berne Convention for the Protection of Literary and Artistic Works.

Boggs, S. P. (2021*). The Proposed New EU Regulatory Regime for Artificial Intelligence (AI)*, 9 Januari 2022, https://www.squirepattonboggs.com/-/media/files/insights/publications/2021/09/the proposed-new-eu-regulatory-regime-for-artificial-intelligence ai/theproposedneweuregulatoryregimeforaiv5.pdf

Chen, W., Shidujaman, M., & Tang, X. (2020). *AiArt: Towards Artificial Intelligence Art.* Conference: ThinkMind // MMEDIA 2020, 47-52, The Twelfth International Conference on Advances in Multimedia At: Lisbon, Portugal, https://www.researchgate.net/publication/342642793_AiArt_Towards_Artificial_Intelligence_Art

Court of Justice of the European Union, Putusan Nomor C-5/08, *Infopaq International A/S v Danske Dagblades Forening* ECR I-6569 (2009).

Court of Justice of the European Union, Nomor C-145/10, *Eva-Maria Painer v. Standard VerlagsGmbH*, ECR I-12537 (2011).

Earnshaw, R. (2017). *Art, Design, and Technology: Collaboration and Implementation.* Springer International Publishing. DOI: 10.1007/978-3-319-58121-7

European Parliament, *Directive Number 2006/116/EC of the European Parliament and of the Council of 12 December 2006 on the term of protection of copyright and certain related rights*, OJ L372/12.

European Union Directorate-General for Communication. (n.d.), "Types of legislation," https://european-union.europa.eu/institutions-law-budget/law/types-legislation_en

Fauzi, R., Ramli, T. S., & Permata, R. R. (2022). Masa Depan Hak Cipta: Tinjauan Keabsahan Hasil Karya Kecerdasan Artifisial di Indonesia. *CITIZEN: Jurnal Ilmiah Multidisiplin Indonesia*, *2*(1), 118–128. DOI: 10.53866/jimi.v2i1.51

Geiger, C., Gervais, D. J., & Senftleben, M. (2015). *Understanding the "three-step test", In book: International Intellectual Property*, 167-189, http://dx.doi.org/DOI: 10.4337/9781782544807.00014

Gema, A. J. (2022). Masalah Penggunaan Ciptaan Sebagai Data Masukan dalam Pengembangan Artificial Intelligence di Indonesia. *Technology and Economics Law Journal*, *1*(1), 1–17. DOI: 10.21143/TELJ.vol1.no1.1000

Gervais, D. J. (2022). AI Derivatives: The Application to the Derivative Work Right to Literary and Artistic Productions of AI Machines. *SSRN*, *52*(4), 1111–1136. DOI: 10.2139/ssrn.4022665

Ginsburg, J. C. (2018). People Not Machines: Authorship and What It Means in the Berne Convention. [IIC]. *IIC; International Review of Industrial Property and Copyright Law*, *49*(2), 131–135. DOI: 10.1007/s40319-018-0670-x

Harris, F. (2010). *Akselerasi Transformasi Perlindungan Hak Kekayaan Intelektual Melalui Inovasi*. Badan Pembinaan Hukum Nasional.

Hawin, M., & Riswandi, B. A. (2020). *Isu-Isu Penting Hak Kekayaan Intelektual di Indonesia*. UGM Press.

Hristov, K. (2017). *Artificial Intelligence and Copyright Dilemma*. IDEA: the Journal of the Franklin Pierce Center for Intellectual Property 57(3), 431-454, https://www.researchgate.net/publication/316761384_Artificial_Intelligence_and_the_Copyright_Dilemma

Hugenholtz, P. B., & Quintais, J. P. (2021). Copyright and Artificial Creation: Does EU Copyright Law Protect AI-Assisted Output? *IIC; International Review of Industrial Property and Copyright Law*, *52*(9), 1190–1216. DOI: 10.1007/s40319-021-01115-0

Indonesia, C. N. N. (2023, January 30). AI Milik Google Bisa Ciptakan Musik, Bakal Rilis dan Saingi ChatGPT? cnnindonesia.com. https://www.cnnindonesia.com/teknologi/20230130140149-185-906599/ai-milik-google-bisa-ciptakan-musik-bakal-rilis-dan-saingi-chatgpt

Kerr, I., Maurushat, A., & Tacit, C. S. (2003). Mesures de protection techniques: Partie I" Tendances en matiÃ¨re de mesures de protection technique et de technologies de contournement. *Les Cahiers De Propriete Intellectuelle, 15*(2), 575-617. https://cpi.openum.ca/files/sites/66/Mesures-de-protection-technique.pdf

Lanz, J. A. (2023, June 6). *AI Art Wars: Japan Says AI Model Training Doesn't Violate Copyright, Decrypt.* https://decrypt.co/143461/ai-art-wars-japan-says-ai-model-training-doesnt-violate-copyright

Law Number 28 of 2014 concerning Copyright.

Madiega, T. (2024). *EU Legislation in Progress Artificial Intelligence Act.* European Parliament: European Parliamentary Research Service, 1-13, https://www.europarl.europa.eu/RegData/etudes/BRIE/2021/698792/EPRS_BRI(2021)698792_EN.pdf

Margoni, T. (2018). *Artificial Intelligence, Machine learning and EU copyright law: Who owns AI? Machine Learning and EU Copyright Law: Who Owns AI.* CREATe Working Paper 2018/12 (December 2018), 1-21, https://doi.org/DOI: 10.5281/zenodo.2001763

Mezei, P. (2022). Jyh-An Lee/Reto M. Hilty/Kung-Chung Liu (eds.) Artificial Intelligence and Intellectual Property. *GRUR International, 71*(4), 390–392. https://doi.org/DOI: 10.1093/grurint/ikab145

Murfianti, F. (2020). *Hak Cipta Dan Karya Seni Di Era Digital.* Acintya. *Jurnal Penelitian Seni Budaya, 12*(1), 44–58. DOI: 10.33153/acy.v12i1.3147

Nield, D. (2016, March 24). *A Novel Written by AI Passes the First Round in a Japanese Literary Competition, Science Alert.* https://www.sciencealert.com/a-novel-written-by-ai-passes-the-first-round-in-a-japanese-literary-competition

NPR STAFF. (2016, April 05), New Rembrandt: From the Frontiers of AI and Not the Artist's Atelier. https:// www.npr.org/sections/alltechconsidered/2016/04/06/473265273/a-new-rembrandt-from-the-frontiers-of-ai-and-not-the-artists-atelier

Okada, T., & Ishibashi, K. (2017). Imitation, Inspiration, and Creation: Cognitive Process of Creative Drawing by Copying Other' Artworks. *Cognitive Science, 41*(7), 1804–1837. DOI: 10.1111/cogs.12442 PMID: 28914472

Palace, V. M. (2019). What If Artificial Intelligence Wrote This: Artificial Intelligence and Copyright Law. *Florida Law Review*, *71*(1), 217–242. https://scholarship.law.ufl.edu/flr/vol71/iss1/5

Purwandoko, P. H., & Imanullah, M. N. (2017). Application of Natural Law Theory (Natural Right) To Protect the Intellectual Property Rights. *Yustisia*, *6*(1), 134–158. DOI: 10.20961/yustisia.v6i1.11516

Puspitasari, D. R., & Pratama, A. (2024). *Implementasi Perjanjian TRIPS dan Dampaknya terhadap Perlindungan Hak Cipta Industri Kreatif Lokal di Indonesia*. Book Chapter, 121-129, https://e-journal.janabadra.ac.id/index.php/bookchapter-2023/article/view/3952/2414

Rahman, R. A., Al-Farouqi, A., & Tang, S. M. (2020). *Should Indonesian Copyright Law be Amended Due to Artificial Intelligence Development? Lesson Learned from Japan*. NTUT Journal of Intellectual Property Law and Management 9(1), 34-57, https://iip.ntut.edu.tw/var/file/92/1092/img/2036/v1-1.pdf

Rajendra, A., ... (2023, June 8). “Generative AI: is its output protectable by intellectual property rights?” *Osborne Clarke*. https://www.osborneclarke.com/insights/generative-ai-its-output-protectable-intellectual-property-rights

Rama, B. G. A., Prasada, D. K., & Mahadewi, K. J. (2023). Urgensi Pengaturan Artificial Intelligence (AI) dalam Bidanghukum Hak Cipta di Indonesia. *Jurnal Rechtens*, *12*(2), 209–224. DOI: 10.56013/rechtens.v12i2.2395

Ramli, T. S., Ramli, A. M., Mayana, R. F., Ramadayanti, E., & Fauzi, R. (2023). Artificial Intelligence as Object of Intellectual Property in Indonesian Law. *The Journal of World Intellectual Property*, *26*(2), 142–154. DOI: 10.1111/jwip.12264

Ratna, P. (2021, October 14). Wamenkumham: AI Berimplikasi Terhadap UU Hak Cipta.” Republika Online. https://www.republika.co.id/berita/r0ynzg428/wamenkumham-ai-berimplikasi-terhadap-uu-hak-cipta

Reidenberg, J. R. (1998). Lex Informatica: The Formulation of Information Policy Rules through Technology. *Texas Law Review*, *76*(3), 553–593. https://ir.lawnet.fordham.edu/faculty_scholarship/42

Rife, M. C. (2007). The Fair Use Doctrine: History, Application, and Implications For (New Media) Writing Teachers. *Computers and Composition*, *24*(2), 154–178. DOI: 10.1016/j.compcom.2007.02.002

Riswandi, B. A. (2017). *Pembatasan dan Pengecualian Hak Cipta di Era Digital*. Citra Aditya Bakti.

Riyanto, G. P., & Yudha, P. (2023, January 19). *Getty Images Gugat Perusahaan AI, Diduga Pakai Gambar Tanpa Izin Untuk Latih Kecerdasan Buatan*, Kompas. Kompas.com. https://tekno.kompas.com/read/2023/01/19/12010047/getty-images-gugat-perusahaan-ai-diduga-pakai-gambar-tanpa-izin-untuk-latih

Singarimbun, F. I. (2024). Implikasi Hukum Penggunaan AI dalam Seni Grafis Terhadap Hak Kekayaan Intelektual. [Jurnal Penelitian Pendidikan Indonesia]. *JPPI, 10*(3), 886–893. DOI: 10.29210/020243889

Soekanto, S. (2007). *Pengantar Peneltian Hukum*. Universitas Indonesia Press.

Supranto, J. (2003). *Metode Penelitian Hukum dan Statistik*. Rineka Cipta.

Susanti, R. D. I. (2017). *Hak Cipta: Kajian Filosofis dan Historis*. Setara Press.

Tektona, R. I., Sari, N. K., & Alfaris, M. R. (2021). Quo Vadis Undang-Undang Hak Cipta di Indonesia: Perbandingan Konsep Ciptaan Artificial Intelligence di Beberapa Negara. *Negara Hukum, 12*(2), 285–305. DOI: 10.22212/jnh.v12i2.2144

The Agreement on Trade-Related Aspects of Intellectual Property Rights (TRIPs)

Tresnawati, D., Guno, Y., Satwika, I. P., Prihatmanto, A. S., & Mahayana, D. (2022). Artificial Intelligence serta Singularitas Suatu Kekeliruan atau Tantangan. *Jurnal Algoritma, 19*(1), 172–179. DOI: 10.33364/algoritma/v.19-1.1028

Triatmojo, F., Hamzani, A. I., & Rahayu, K. (2021). *Perlindungan Hak Cipta Lagu Komersil*. Penerbit Nem.

Ueno, T. (2017). *Copyright Issues on Artificial Intelligence and Machine Learning*. In: International Joint Conference on Artificial Intelligence 2017 Workshop: The First International Workshop on Sharing and Reuse of AI Work Products (2017), https://alai-paris2023.org/wp-content/uploads/2023/06/Reply-of-the-japan-ALAI-Group.pdf

Vincent, J. (2022, November 15). *The Scary Truth About AI Copyright is Nobody Knows What What Will Happen Next. The Verge*, https://www.theverge.com/23444685/generative-ai-copyright-infringement-legal-fair-use-training-data

Wangsa, J. J., Fortunata, K. F., & Hanunisa, S. Z. (2023). *Impact of Artificial Intelligence on Intellectual Property Rights in Indonesia*. Anthology: Inside Intellectual Property Rights 1(1), 52-71, https://ojs.uph.edu/index.php/Anthology/article/view/6689/3021

World Intellectual Property Organisation. (2019). The Story of AI in Patents. https://www.wipo.int/tech_trends/en/artificial_intelligence/story.html

World Intellectual Property Organization. (2008). *WIPO Intellectual Property Handbook*. Jenewa: WIPO Publication.

Chapter 9
Artificial Intelligence (AI) in Cultural and Historical Literary Analysis

Ipseeta Satpathy
https://orcid.org/0000-0002-0155-5548
KSOM, KIIT University, Bhubaneswar, India

Arpita Nayak
https://orcid.org/0000-0003-2911-0492
KIIT School of Liberal Studies, KIIT University, Bhubaneswar, India

Vishal Jain
https://orcid.org/0000-0003-1126-7424
Sharda University, India

ABSTRACT

The employment of AI in cultural and historical literary processing has become a new way of reading texts and studying literature evolution. The current chapter aims at a discussion of possibilities of utilizing the AI for discovering the culture in the historical documents and identifying trends in the literature throughout the centuries. Only using algorithms such as NLP or using sentiment analysis and pattern recognition AI reveals layers of meaning and connections that the human mind would not be able to come across. This paper studies the application of AI in cultural and historical literary analysis in a bid to provide an insight into the role of technology in augmenting understanding on the societal impact of literature.

DOI: 10.4018/979-8-3373-1057-2.ch009

I. INTRODUCTION

The analysis of literature functions historically as a fundamental tool that reveals deep textual messages. Literary analysis enables scholars and readers to study narrative frameworks and character arcs and thematic elements that allow them to understand how literature reflects and forms societal dynamics. The research value of analysing literature becomes considerably stronger when scholars examine the historical and cultural conditions during which a piece of writing was made. The absence of knowledge about text-related social, political and economic elements leads interpretations to become vague or incorrect. Historical context understanding unlocks text significances through connections that bridge literary work contents with the actual experiences and belief systems of a particular time. (Lehan,2023).

Culture and history shape literature in profound ways. Any writer will naturally incorporate the fundamental values together with societal beliefs from their era into their writing whether they do it deliberately or unconsciously. During the Victorian period Charles Dickens wrote numerous works under the moral and proper mindset of Victorian times while the Harlem Renaissance period shaped Langston Hughes' poetry with racial and struggle-related themes. Literature receives direct impact from historical events which transform thematic content along with storylines and characterization elements. Various literary examples show how postcolonial literature reacts to colonialism while African American literature developed because of the Civil Rights Movement and war influences shape modernist texts. (Jauss,2022).

The analysis of literature through cultural and historical methods delivers better insights about what authors intended as well as how texts were received in their era and how literary styles evolved throughout history. Current readers gain the ability to conduct advanced interpretations about textual significance by connecting historical understanding with modern perspectives. This research strategy provides comprehensive study of literary artifacts because they have both creative and historical value The field of literary analysis has seen a technological revolution during the past several decades which introduced new methodologies together with expanded access to historical resources. Close reading of texts existed primarily as the foundation of analysis which combined text-based comparisons with print material interpretations in traditional literary analysis. The fundamental methods remain intact but digital tools have introduced innovative approaches to literary exploration that generate enhanced data-based findings (Buhalis et al.,2022).

Digital humanities stand as a key technological improvement in literary studies because it enables the productive combination of computational methods with traditional literary criticism. Through this synthesis process researchers gain capability to study texts at historical levels. The text mining tools and stylometry techniques and corpus analysis methods from digital humanities enable researchers to study large literary datasets therefore uncovering quantitative patterns that escape human reading capabilities. Through distant reading methods Franco Moretti uses computational analysis to examine literary patterns across extensive datasets instead of analyzing singular works. (Mitcham,2022).

Online archives along with databases provide a democratic way to access literary materials because they enable global users to access historical manuscripts and rare books together with author correspondence. Digital projects from Google Books and Project Gutenberg together with the HathiTrust Digital Library have converted millions of texts available for scholarly research that previously restricted to specific libraries. Newly available archival materials through digital platforms enable researchers to conduct comparative studies which trace thematic and stylistic trends across multiple historical and cultural periods. (Susanti et al.,2022).

The combination of artificial intelligence (AI) and machine learning tools now helps scholars identify rhetorical devices and perform sentiment analysis and authorship attribution in literary analysis. The ability of algorithms allows them to determine author similarities and analyze textual moods as well as establish possible authorship connections to unknown works. AI-based analysis tools have revealed invisible meanings in classical and contemporary texts thus expanding scholarly investigation into new academic ground (Rathore et al.,2021).

AI acts as a vital instrument in cultural and historical literary analysis since it delivers researchers effective analytical methods that produce more detailed and efficient textual assessment. Machine learning algorithms enable AI systems to analyze extensive literary collections to detect cultural patterns and authorial influences while detecting historical changes and stylistic evolution that would otherwise escape human notice. Researchers benefit from AI-based text analysis tools when they need to study literary evolution through time as well as track cultural theme transformations while using it to find authors responsible for unidentified literary pieces (Khallaf,2021).

The most rewarding utilization of artificial intelligence in literary studies exists in natural language processing (NLP) because it offers machines the ability to understand and interpret and create human language. Through NLP techniques researchers can identify essential topics along with discovering implicit references between texts and analyze linguistic differences across various time periods and cultural settings. Sentiment analysis done by AI systems enabled researchers to explore the emotional tones in wartime literature to track public opinion changes through time. (Kuleto et al.,2021).

The application of artificial intelligence in literary analysis includes the vital practice of historical data mining as its key element. Extensive digitized libraries connected to artificial intelligence systems enable scholars to evaluate historical texts with contemporary sources to reveal literary shifts across time periods. AI tools enable users to match political rhetoric from historical speeches with literary portrayals of governance and power structures thus revealing connections between literature and historical narratives. (Alam,2022).

Designer AI capabilities have transformed the analysis of authorship evidence and the fields of literary forensic investigation. The evaluation of writing patterns together with word usage and syntactic structures by AI algorithms enables the assessment of the authorship probabilities of a particular text. Through advanced authorship attribution and literary forensics methods AI helps scholars reveal hidden authors while tracking changes in writing patterns throughout history. AI uses deep learning models of historical writing styles to predict document losses and reconstruct partial manuscripts which both safeguards cultural heritage while expanding scholarly research potential (Neumann n.d.,).

Virtual and augmented reality (VR/AR) technologies applied in literary studies create immersive experiences that boost readers' comprehension of work environments and historical settings. Through the virtual creation of historical environments readers can interact with literary locations to better comprehend a text's social context. The virtual Globe Theatre rendition allows theatre enthusiasts to witness the original Elizabethan stage conditions and observe how these physical aspects shaped theatrical delivery. The vigorous development of technology in literary studies has both improved research methods and introduced critical moral dilemmas. Digital method dependence poses the threat of stripping literary interpretation and analysis methods from the insights that come from personal interpretation thus turning literature into statistical information. The challenge remains to eliminate digital access inhibitions so that technological progress reaches every student and scholar within different communities throughout the world (Martins,2023).

II. RESEARCH QUESTIONS

- How can AI identify cultural insights, trends, and patterns in historical literary texts across different time periods?
- What are the key challenges, limitations, and potential improvements in using AI for cultural and historical literary analysis?

III. RESEARCH OBJECTIVES

- To understand AI's role in decoding cultural symbolism, historical contexts, and literary trends over time.

- To understand different challenges, ethical considerations, and proposing future directions for AI-driven cultural and historical literary analysis.

IV. UNDERSTANDING ARTIFICIAL INTELLIGENCE (AI) IN LITERARY ANALYSIS

AI integration into literary studies led to significant changes in the analysis of academic texts and detection of patterns, and had innovation in the interpretation of a narrative. Its computational methods allow detailed literary studies that go beyond close reading procedures and gives deeper literary insights to the researchers. Natural Language Processing (NLP) and machine learning methods and sentiment analysis features make AI tools capable of complex text processing to work with large historical literary collections. This chapter goes further in describing technologies which may be essential for AI operations in literary assessment, implemented applications and procedures that make use of them to evaluate literature using computational means. The ability to research literary works through the analysis of different types of texts in one cultural backdrop where new insights on authorship and stylistic change and thematic elements are derived is made possible through technology tools. (Gasparini,2022).

As an essential Artificial Intelligence-based methodology Natural Language Processing enables computers to gain human-writing and human-reading abilities in their literary studies applications. The adoption of NLP technology revolutionized language-based operations by establishing text mining and corpus analysis as well as named entity recognition and part-of-speech tagging to create accurate literary language pattern and stylistic analysis. The research capability of studying large literary databases exists because researchers can discover linguistic patterns by detecting them with NLP techniques which track developments in writing style across time and map literary themes in works. Modern research studies employing authorship attribution alongside genre classification along with predictive modeling largely depends on machine learning techniques. Researchers harness large dataset training for algorithms through machine learning to establish disputed authorship proofs and determine literary classification and forecast stylistic patterns in various historical times (Dillion,2023).

Literary analysis benefits from the AI tool sentiment analysis because it enables researchers to measure emotional tones within texts. Research tools using this method allow scientists to track verbalization of emotions by characters along with detecting emotive changes in thematic content across different authors and literary approaches. The combination of artificial intelligence and sentiment analysis helps researchers monitor emotional change patterns in classic works starting from Shakespearean dramas throughout time. The analysis of sentiment provides essential psychological and cultural information about literature which creates a connection between literary studies and cognitive science. Researcher understanding of historical literary contexts becomes deeper through emotional transition detection in historical texts (Keikhosrokiani,2023).

Artificial Intelligence establishes crucial impacts on historical and cultural circumstances mainly through its analytical functions in literature research. The analysis of language evolution through AI models helps researchers observe historical pattern shifts which developed because of industrialization and globalization. Professional research in cross-cultural literary studies which integrates artificial intelligence delivers modern analytical methods to help scholars identify language adjustments and thematic relationships across distinct literary traditions. Through implementing AI methodologies researchers can analyze how political ideologies social movements together with historical events influence literary works. Computer-assisted literary analysis of twentieth-century literature provides insight into how World War II influenced writers to represent themes about depression and survival techniques alongside existentialist theories. The research results produced better professional knowledge about how literary texts convey and react to cultural changes. (Heerden,2021).

The use of AI in literary analysis delivers many advantages but generates various ethical problems together with implementation challenges which demand thorough evaluation. The interpretations derived from AI systems get distorted because AI systems incorporate biases from their training datasets. AI demonstrates strong abilities to detect patterns but it lacks capability to understand philosophical and existential elements of literature that humans need to perceive. The automated literary study of modern times mostly explores digital textual materials while skipping essential research of oral literature and undigitized written documents. Closer collaboration between humans and AI constitutes the advisable course of action instead of replacing traditional literary analysis. The combination of artificial intelligence accuracy and human interpretation methods enables researchers to build detailed examination methods for literary studies (Mawhorter,2016).

Artificial intelligence brings substantial changes to the study of literature making it evolve. Through this technology researchers acquire data-based tools for extracting scalable information about texts as well as authors and emotional trends in literature. Researches can reveal hidden textual elements for analysis and examine cultural themes through the application of natural language processing and machine learning with sentiment analysis technologies. AI integration increases both efficiency and depth of literary evaluation so researchers need ethical guidelines for ensuring fair and impartial research outcomes. AI will join forces with scholarly researchers in upcoming studies to discover new research paths while upholding respect for human writing talent. AI technology presents an opportunity to transform academic practices by combining data analytical techniques with critical methodologies thus remodeling the literacy field. (Khan,2025).

Literature with artificial intelligence displays its most significant advancement by linking with reader-response theory that demonstrates literature interpretation depends on audience interpretation. Academic storytelling applications use artificial intelligence to modify their structures during reading time based on reader textual interactions. These concepts find particular relevance in gaming and interactive fiction because AI narrative engines produce dynamic stories that shape their content based on user choices. These technological advancements create questions about traditional print culture by testing authorial conventions and book integrity rules and audience interaction models. Data science using AI technology evaluates reader emotions throughout the reading experience. Through this capability publishers along with authors can pinpoint sections in a book that generate substantial emotional reactions which supports storytelling techniques. The findings from AI analysis have revolutionized literary marketing and user experience and value movement thus leading to improved interactive storytelling (Liu et al.,2022).

The continuous evolution of academic research using artificial intelligence methods enables automatic analyses of text-based content as well as authorial input detection and measurement of emotional aspects in literary works. Research tools powered by advanced technologies including natural language processing and machine learning enable investigators to discover concealed text elements alongside thematic frameworks along with historical and cultural insights. Ethical standards should remain central when AI powers literary analysis because they protect the fairness and balance of results. Thorough literary research depends on maintaining equilibrium between human researchers and AI technologies since their combination leads to innovative findings without diminishing human creative output. The current direction of AI in literary studies displays promise to enhance academic human capability through the combination of computational processing with deep reading knowledge which rewrote the literary academic space's future. (Cox,2019).

V. INTERPRETING HISTORICAL TEXTS USING ARTIFICIAL INTELLIGENCE (AI)

Academic research about historical texts remains crucial because it enables experts to unravel linguistic along with cultural and philosophical elements from different periods. Historical literature analysis demanded complete manual study in the past which forced researchers to translate old language while establishing historical connections and uncovering hidden meanings that existed across the texts. Artificial Intelligence (AI) alongside Natural Language Processing (NLP) and machine learning technologies give researchers state-of-the-art tools to perform more effective and sped-up and broader historic text investigations today. Modern analytical methods developed by Artificial Intelligence enable scholars to explore linguistic patterns and symbolic interpretations besides cultural influences present in Shakespearean works along with religious texts and classical manuscripts which used to remain undetected.

Historians extensively examine the literary works of William Shakespeare but enthusiastic scholarly investigations persist about his authorship alongside interpretations and style foundations. The process of stylometry which AI analyzes writing styles has helped researchers distinguish Shakespeare's manuscripts from contemporaries' manuscripts. AI technology examines whether Henry VIII and Titus Andronicus include co-authorship by Christopher Marlowe or John Fletcher and other playwrights. The analysis of linguistic patterns in combination with word usage and sentence structures revealed strong evidence that parts of these texts were written by separate authors according to AI investigation (Schäffer,2023).

AI sentiment analysis tools generated new knowledge about Shakespeare's literature. AI systems help researchers track character progression by analyzing emotional changes between characters enabling them to discover deeper thematic aspects of power conflicts and betrayal and existential struggles. AI algorithms enabled the evaluation of Hamlet's psychological decline through sentiment analysis which monitored his growing despair and slide into complete madness during the play (Marangoz n.d.,).

AI has significantly contributed to the examination of religious texts, which often present challenges due to their intricate symbolism, diverse interpretations, and linguistic discrepancies across various translations. Scholars have employed natural language processing (NLP) techniques to analyze different iterations of religious scriptures, revealing nuanced changes in meaning that have emerged throughout centuries of translation. AI has been utilized to scrutinize various renditions of the Bible, the Quran, and Hindu texts such as the Bhagavad Gita, aiming to identify textual variations that may indicate historical and theological developments. By leveraging semantic similarity models, AI can assess how the meanings of essential terms (including “grace,” “divine justice,” and “salvation”) have evolved over time. Furthermore, AI-driven translation tools have proven vital in safeguarding ancient religious manuscripts by reconstructing absent words or phrases based on linguistic patterns observed in related texts (Wang,2023).

The interpretation of historical texts proves difficult because they carry cultural complexities combined with symbolic elements and metaphors. Modern artificial intelligence techniques that combine topic modelling with deep learning and historical linguistics analysis have enhanced researcher skills for decoding difficult textual meanings. AI-driven topic modeling organizes extensive historical texts into thematic sections which allow researchers to study main concepts within the text structure. Researchers have implemented this technique on multiple pieces of literature including Middle Ages texts and Renaissance literature and philosophical works across different historical periods. The application of AI technology has enabled researchers to spot three main themes involving divine intervention fate and morality in Dante's Divine Comedy thus creating new interpretations about allegorical content (Ahmed,2022).

For numerous years scholars have attempted to decipher the ancient Voynich Manuscript which its text remains unreadable through existing decryption methods. The latest advancements in artificial intelligence cryptography and pattern recognition features have enabled modern linguists to extend their work of interpreting the manuscript's contents. Artificial intelligence techniques using deep learning models that analyze historical linguistic data found links between the manuscript's language and ancient Hebrew dialects which deepens our knowledge about its mysterious start (Livingstone, 2016).

Scholars extensively analyze Beowulf because the poem was originally transmitted orally and has significant historical value. Through artificial intelligence analysis researchers studied the metrical composition and alliterative techniques together with narrative structures of Beowulf to understand its oral transmission before its fixation appeared in written form. The examined research contributed to academic understanding about how oral storytelling shifted into written representation throughout the medieval era of Europe (Breeze,2022).

Institute of artificial intelligence serves as a crucial resource that delivers breakthrough perspectives about literary criticism and cultural studies together with language evolution analysis. Due to natural language processing and deep learning and machine learning researchers can now interpret Shakespearean plays and other religious texts and ancient documents with excellent accuracy. The revolutionary power of AI implements symbolic analysis along with language change monitoring and text reconstruction to radically transform literary analysis which now makes historical documents more accessible and beneficial than before. The technological progress that AI brings to literary analysis cannot replace essential human academic involvement for setting context and conducting ethical evaluations of literary works. AI collaboration with human experts will enable better discovery of historical literature's hidden meanings thereby making ancient narratives relevant for modern and upcoming generations.

VI. ANALYZING LITERARY TRENDS AND EVOLUTION

Research methodologies used by scholars for text analysis and interpretation now function differently since Artificial Intelligence and literary studies started working together. The combination of AI technologies that include Natural Language Processing (NLP) and machine learning, deep learning enables researchers to study literary patterns spanning different historical timeframes with great precision and depth. The integration of computational techniques gives researchers complete access to literary data so they can find patterns in stylistic methods alongside thematic progression and language evolution throughout different periods. The evolution of literary styles receives enhanced visualization with AI methods which also created maps to show how societal changes become visible through literature. The chapter investigates how Artificial Intelligence analyzes literary material while watching language variations as it tracks how literature reflects historical changes.

AI technology provides substantial assistance in literary analysis because it detects and organizes genres along with themes and language patterns across large bodies of text. Traditional literary analysis normally depends on close reading for evaluation although this method faces constraints regarding its ability to handle extensive material.AI systems which received extensive training on literary datasets can automatically sort texts across genres through modeling their stylistic patterns and thematic characteristics. Through supervised machine learning approaches the analysis of novels and poems and plays permits formal classification into gothic fiction and romantic poetry and modernist literature and postcolonial narratives. An AI model have been trained with 19th and 20th century novels demonstrates competence in identifying Victorian realism and both modernist stream-of-consciousness and postmodern fragmentation through evaluating lexical patterns and narrative structure among other factors. Clustering algorithms under unsupervised learning reveal hidden literary trends and creative combinations which conventional classification methods often fail to detect (Saddhono et al.,2024).

Latent Dirichlet Allocation (LDA) coupled with AI methods allows scholars to work with large literary datasets, and discover common historical themes appearing in the data. Scientists use AI techniques to trace how important literature concepts emerged by identifying thematic groupings in text data. Artificial Intelligence technology was used in order to explore the way in which literary themes developed over time through the study of war and conflict, feminism, gender roles and industrial and technological development. The trend in representations about women's power and their freedom and subjugation can be studied through literary research of novels, starting from the 18th century to present day fiction. These studies examine how literature considered with historical events of the Industrial Revolution and the Space Age, and the development of Artificial Intelligence, through studies in shifts in social attitudes to technology. The efficiency of Artificial Intelligence in managing large textual datasets makes linguistic evolution in distinct periods available for research purposes. To trace literature's development, AI models observe syntactic patterns together with lexical choices and writing styles to evaluate patterns in language. It enables quantifying word frequency over different time periods so as to track the disappearance of obsolete words as well as the entry of new words into vocabulary. Analysis of historical texts with the help of deep learning models shows how the sentences first changed from 18th century complex prose to the current broken narrative style of modernist literature. Studying emotional expressions in texts using AI detects mood shifts and tone changes, as well as appeals to different literary content at different time periods. We show how 17th century traditional prose gradually turned into the more common personal style of modern prose, using the AI sentiment analysis technology. (Sharma et al.,2022).

In terms of contemporary advancements of AI for literary analysis, it can also convert literary trends into visual forms using the data visualization tools or interactive heat maps, or through stylometric techniques. Each develops a group of scholarly resources visualizing the development of writing styles dynamically. AI produces heat maps on literature's word frequency patterns, themes and what has been popular over the eras. Since the visual representation can be displayed through color coding, patterns of language can be studied, including the disappearance of terms and the creation of new expressions. Graph theory is used to represent how authors belong to literary movements and how stylistic influences are related to one another. AI uses intertextual reference analysis to trace what is thematically fixed and what is mobile within the semantic space of concepts whose migration between several literary traditions it tracks. Syntactic structures along with word frequency and sentence length are used with analysis of the components to separate writers on the basis of their individual styles by AI driven stylometry. It helped to decide if William Shakespeare collaborated with Marlowe, Fletcher, or both in writing, therefore demonstrating that Austen and Twain could have received substantial aid by no so famous authors in writing, and helped find mysterious authors in past literature. Stylometry of authorial writing styles enables the monitoring of authors e.g. Hemingway and Woolf who stripped their prose and developed their experimental narrative style respectively. (Wai et al.,2024).

It's no secret that literature is a reflection of the society with the help of AI, researchers have been able to map historical, cultural, and political changes the way they exist in literary texts. Studies used AI models to analyse how literature addresses societal discourse and how its awareness of it shapes down the course of it. AI has helped scholars trace the development of political ideologies, class struggles, as well as civil rights movement, by processing historical novels, essays and poems. Public sentiment in relation to monarchy, democracy and revolution as shown in literature, has been tracked by AI based sentiment analysis. Using AI driven discourse analysis, literature has been analysed to ascertain how perspectives such as slavery, colonialism and the equality of races have been framed over centuries. Historical linguistics models built using AI have uncovered how the books used for propaganda and resistance literature impacted public opinion during different periods. AI has been used to study the evolution of how literature reacted to the momentous events of the time, like the World Wars, the Great Depression and post 9/11 literature. Themes of nationalism, trauma, and existentialism are the themes that AI has traced in literature to have emerged post-World War I and II (Zubenko,2020).

Modern Day literary studies have been revolutionized through the use of AI that has identified patterns in the genres, and patterns and language that has been used across centuries. With the help of NLP, machine learning and stylometry, AI allows scholars to classify literary movements, visualize stylistic shifts and look into changes in the society as reflected in literature. AI can identify thematic recurrences, trace language evolution, and assess sentiment shifts to give unparalleled writings to understandings of how the literature has an effect and mirrors the human history. Given AI further evolution, digital humanities and literary analysis are to scrutinize the past, the present and the future of literary traditions.

VII. FUTURE PROSPECTS AND FUTURE DIRECTIONS

Technology which has been amazing in the field of Literature and made the study of literature easier and many things possible with regards to the study of literature, This technology is called Artificial Intelligence (AI). With advances in AI tools, the promise still lies in their ability to improve literary analysis by finding patterns even more refined, giving us more granularity in historical and cultural insights, and expanding access to literary knowledge. The integration of AI into the humanities research does not only include the technological shift but also fundamentally redefines the way literature is tackled by scholars. This part discusses the future possibilities on AI based literary research, contributing in making literature more accessible at a global scale and the possibility of a collaborative work between AI experts and humanities scholars (Yadav,2024).

Rapidly developing AI based literary research utilizes new tools and methodologies to increase the depth and scope of textual analysis. Natural Language Processing (NLP) and Deep Learning models have become very complex, allowing researchers to advance their accuracy of approaching huge collection of literary texts. Some future innovations in developing AI tools will include improvements to understanding context, sentiment analysis and multimodal analysis, which is analysis of multiple modes of communication, such as text and image as well as historical references.

Transformer based models, like OpenAI's GPT series and Google's BERT come in as one of the promising developments mainly because of the smart text analysis they provide. The proven usefulness of these models lies in the fact they can discover intertextual references, stylistic and thematic influences among different periods, even if they are detached from each other in terms of content. AI models of the future are expected to include methods of reinforcement learning, enabling them to further refine their interpretations as they receive scholarly feedback, thus estate AI assisted literary research as a constantly dynamic and interactive process. However, the most significant advancement is in the realm of AI driven literary synthesis that allows the AI systems to build comparative analysis as well as summarize the key themes and linguistic patterns across different time epochs. These AI generated insights then become a starting point for scholarly exploration rather than manual sifting of volumes of text. More still, AI voice synthesis and speech recognition technologies will help us revisit and study oral storytelling traditions which would have otherwise gone unrecorded while enabling us to capture linguistic variation and dialects (Singh,2025).

Computer vision techniques are also going to be used to boost visual literary analysis using AI. This will be very helpful in particular in studying illustrated manuscripts, ancient texts and marginalia in literary work. As handwriting recognition technology is improving, AI will enable the decoding to historical scripts so that closed works will be available for the scholarly study. Virtual Reality (VR) and Augmented Reality (AR) will be a fitting environment for AI to integrate with, as it will give more depth to the literary experience by allowing readers to interact with historical texts in real time (Hongbo,2024).

Another transformative thing that AI can bring to literary studies is democratization of access to cultural and historical literature and literary knowledge in general to a wider pool of audience. For that, traditional literary studies rely on exclusive archives and resources, those that may be inaccessible for many researchers especially in developing regions. Digitization and translation using AI powered tools can break these barriers to make world literary traditions easier to engage with. Already, classic texts have become available in more translations thanks to AI driven machine translation technologies, enabling nonnative speaker to read and interpret the texts. Context sensitive translations will become better in future AI models that will be able to retain the cultural nuances and idiomatic expressions that traditional translations lose out on. The consequences of all this for the study of literature in non-dominant languages are highly significant: it means that non major, little-known traditions can be received to some degree as 'world literature'. A key another is the effectualness in restoring and reconstruction lost or damaged text. Unfortunately, many historical manuscripts have the problem of deterioration from age, environment, or censorship. AI algorithms enriched with image reconstruction and text restoration algorithms can predict the missing content and restore works in their incomplete form with a very high accuracy. AI helps the preservation of endangered literary heritage by reconstructing historical texts (Youvan,2024).

The revolution of AI text to speech and accessibility technologies is also making reading available for the visually impaired or the illiterates. Written literature can be converted into audiobooks using adaptive narration, in which the computer changes the tone and pacing to make it easier to understand. This gives learning preferences a wider range of literature forms to read with. Moreover, AI will curate literary recommendations for users hence paving way for the future of reading experience. AI can analyse individual reading habits, suggest texts that will be interesting for the reader, and simultaneously present him with unknown literary traditions. It can have the capacity to span cultural gaps and make it easier for the promotion of cross-cultural literary appreciation all over the world (Isayeva,2024).

The most significant influence of AI on literary studies will be the literate mind itself and its future collaborations with the humanities scholars. By merging artificial intelligence and humanistic interpretation, the intersection of AI and the humanities gives ways to form hybrid research methods using computational methods and humanistic interpretation, all to create more nuanced and richer literary insights. Development of AI assisted literary criticism where scholars use generated insights produced by AI to supplement traditional analytical methods is one such promising area of collaboration. While AI can detect patterns of connections that humans can't grasp, human scholars bring depth of context that is necessary for interpreting them. They might do for an AI model, which can detect and point out recurring motifs within 19th-century literature, but it is the literary scholar that figures these motifs in regards to historical, political, and philosophical frameworks (Rockwell,2022; Williams,2024).

The field of digital humanities is also seeing the emergence of collaborative projects that involve scholars from various disciplines using AI to create interactive literary databases, digital archives, as visualization tools. AI driven literary maps can track the geographical movement of literary characters over time and develop historical movements shown in literature like migrations or colonial expansions or urban transformations. An alternative direction for the use of AI for ethical literary analysis is the identification of biases and ideological influences in literature. With AI models, gender representation, racial biases, and power dynamics within texts come into context with data driven form of literary discourse. Yet, much consideration is required to interpret these findings, distinguishing the usage of AI generated insights in ways that mitigate the mitigation of these insights instead acting to augment an historically exclusive and critical literary scholarship (Cigliano,2024).

AI's ability to analyze large volumes of text at high speed and at high levels of precision makes it an invaluable tool in literary research. Historically, close reading and comparative analysis have served as the means to study text. But this strategy is restricted intrinsically by the quantity of data that an individual researcher can archive. Natural Language Processing (NLP), machine learning and deep learning techniques make use of AI to enable a distant reading approach that was conceptualized by Franco Moretti. Unlike individual texts, AI allows you to see thousands of literary works at once and find the patterns, the stylistic trends, the unconscious recurrences of themes, that a man might miss. Among all the contributions of AI in literary analysis, one being able to classify genres with high accuracy is one of most significant. Therefore, training machine learning models on large datasets can help to determine whether a text lies within Gothic fiction, modernist writing, postcolonial story lines, or any other genre. Unlike the simple keyword detections, these models analyse AI can, however, distinguish distinctive linguistic patterns and stylistic elements from one author to another when it comes to authorship attribution. When looking at word frequency, sentence length, syntax, and rhetorical devices, AI can empirically recognize whether an anonymous or disputed written text was authored by a specific author. The authors have already successfully used this technique in Shakespearean works, in 18th century novels and modern literature, feeding the discussion on the authorship debate. the sentence structures, narrative styles and the lexical choices to make informed genre classifications. An automatic classification of this sort helps literary scholars to track developments of literary movements, to follow the development of genres across centuries and even to uncover hitherto unknown sub-genres.AI technological advancements in literary research, accessibility, and preservation of literature however, should not be taken to be substitutional for human scholarship. In contrast, AI can and should be regarded as a powerful augment of the ordinary literary studies, expanding its confines and increasing the range of research, which allows scholars to work on literature in new and creative ways. In the future, AI for literary analysis is likely to serve more multimodal capacities, in which image, sound, text and historico–cultural arguments are read and processed by AIs in concert, offering a fuller interpretation of literary works. It is going to continue refining the ability to detect narrative structures, recognize the development of characters and trace thematic progressions, but human interpretation will be vital when attempting to make sense of the findings.

VIII. CONCLUSION

Artificial Intelligence (AI) tools are revolutionizing literary research by enabling researchers to analyze large corpora of literary works, detect patterns, and uncover hidden meanings in historical and cultural contexts. Innovations in natural language processing, deep learning, and sentiment analysis have enabled researchers to process large corpora of literary works, tracking themes, linguistic structures, and stylistic deviations over hundreds of years. AI-driven tools have improved genre classification, thematic detection, and authorship attribution, providing scholars with unprecedented insights into literary traditions. AI-powered translation tools, text restoration algorithms, and digital archives provide access to underrepresented traditions, while AI-driven text to speech technologies enable the availability of literature for the visually impaired and non-native speakers. AI will also play a crucial role in preserving dying texts and reconstructing incomplete manuscripts for future generations. Future research should focus on improving the context of AI findings, reducing algorithmic biases, and analyzing text, image, and historical references for a more holistic literary analysis. AI should not replace human scholarship but rather serve as an auxiliary tool, deepening the interaction between computational precision and human creativity and critical thinking.

REFERENCES

Ahmed, S. A. A. (2022). *TECHNOLOGY AND ARTIFICIAL INTELLIGENCE IN SIMULTANEOUS INTERPRETING: A MULTIDISCIPLINARY APPROACH. CDELT Occasional Papers in the Development of English Education. 78*, 325–353

Alam, A., & Mohanty, A. (2022). Predicting students' performance employing educational data mining techniques, machine learning, and learning analytics. In *International Conference on Communication, Networks and Computing* (pp. 166–177). Springer

Caws, P., & Mitcham, C. (1995). Thinking through technology: The path between engineering and philosophy. *Technology and Culture*, *36*(4), 1060. DOI: 10.2307/3106947

Cigliano, A., Fallucchi, F., & Gerardi, M. (2024). The Impact of Digital Analysis and Large Language Models in Digital Humanity. In *ICYRIME 2024: 9th International Conference of Yearly Reports on Infor-matics, Mathematics, and Engineering*.

Cox, A. M., Pinfield, S., & Rutter, S. (2019). The intelligent library: Thought leaders' views on the likely impact of artificial intelligence on academic libraries. *Library Hi Tech*, *37*(3), 418–435. DOI: 10.1108/LHT-08-2018-0105

Dillon, S., & Schaffer-Goddard, J. (2022). What AI researchers read: the role of literature in artificial intelligence research. *Interdisciplinary Science Reviews: ISR*, 1–28. https://doi.org/DOI: 10.1080/03080188.2022.2079214

Gasparini, A. A., & Kautonen, H. (2022). Understanding artificial intelligence in research libraries: An extensive literature review. *LIBER Quarterly*, *32*(1), 1–36. DOI: 10.53377/lq.10934

Isayeva, S. (2024). Democratizing education AI and OpenAI models for global access to knowledge. In *Enhancing Higher Education and Research With OpenAI Models* (pp. 79–92). IGI Global. DOI: 10.4018/979-8-3693-1666-5.ch004

Keikhosrokiani, P., & Asl, M. P. (2023). *Introduction to artificial intelligence for the analytics of literary works and social media: A review. Handbook of research on artificial intelligence applications in literary works and social media.* 1–17.

Khallaf, R., & Khallaf, M. (2021). Classification and analysis of deep learning applications in construction: A systematic literature review. *Automation in Construction*, *129*(103760), 103760. DOI: 10.1016/j.autcon.2021.103760

Khan, A. M. (2025). Exploring the Role of Artificial Intelligence in the Creation of Literary Characters: A Comparative Analysis of Human and AI-Generated Characters in "Raja Gidh.". *Review Journal of Social Psychology & Social Works, 3*(1), 24–32.

Kuleto, V., Ilić, M., Dumangiu, M., Ranković, M., Martins, O. M., Păun, D., & Mihoreanu, L. (2021). Exploring opportunities and challenges of artificial intelligence and machine learning in higher education institutions. *Sustainability (Basel), 13*(18), 10424. DOI: 10.3390/su131810424

Lehan, R. (2023). *The city in literature: an intellectual and cultural history.* Univ of California Press. DOI: 10.2307/jj.5973091

Liu, C. C., Liao, M. G., Chang, C. H., & Lin, H. M. (2022). An analysis of children'interaction with an AI chatbot and its impact on their interest in reading. *Computers & Education*, •••, 189.

Livingstone, J. (2016). The Unsolvable Mysteries of the Voynich Manuscript. *New Yorker (New York, N.Y.).*

Marangoz, E. Ö. (2023, October 21). The Transformative Role of Artificial Intelligence and Machine Learning in Interpreting and Language Services. *RumeliDe Dil ve Edebiyat Arastirmalari Dergisi, 36*(36), 1591–1598. DOI: 10.29000/rumelide.1372500

Martins, R. M., & Wangenheim, C. (2023). Findings on teaching machine learning in high school: A ten-year systematic literature review. *Informatics in Education, 22*(3), 421–440.

Mawhorter, P. A. (2016). Artificial intelligence as a tool for understanding narrative choices.

Neumann, A., Sims, E., & Conrad, R. (n.d.). An Examination of the Impact of Stylometry. In *Artificial Intelligence/Machine Learning (AI/ML) on Privacy in Social Media.*

Pondelíková, I., & Luprichová, J. (2024). AI-assisted enhancing of gender awareness through reading comprehension in history and literature courses of Anglophone cultures. In Sampson, D. G., Ifenthaler, D., & Isaias, P. (Eds.), *Proceedings of the 21st International Conference on Cognition and Exploratory Learning in Digital Age (CELDA 2024)* (pp. 198–208). IADIS Press.

Rathore, M. M., Shah, S. A., Shukla, D., Bentafat, E., & Bakiras, S. (2021). The role of AI, machine learning, and big data in digital twinning: A systematic literature review, challenges, and opportunities. *IEEE Access : Practical Innovations, Open Solutions, 9*, 32030–32052. DOI: 10.1109/ACCESS.2021.3060863

Rockwell, G., & Sinclair, S. (2022). *Hermeneutica: Computer-assisted interpretation in the humanities*. MIT Press.

Saddhono, K., Rosa, S., Martiningsih, E., & Judijanto, L. Sultan, & Rahmat, W. (2024). From words to algorithms: The to get evolution of Indonesia in terms of literature via AI technology. *2024 4th International Conference on Advance Computing and Innovative Technologies in Engineering (ICACITE), 30*, 1568–1572.

Schäffer, B., & Lieder, F. R. (2023). Distributed interpretation-teaching reconstructive methods in the social sciences supported by artificial intelligence. *Journal of Research on Technology in Education, 55*(1), 111–124. DOI: 10.1080/15391523.2022.2148786

Sharma, C., Batra, I., Sharma, S., Malik, A., Hosen, A. S., & Ra, I. H. (2022). Predicting trends and research patterns of smart cities: A semi-automatic review using latent Dirichlet allocation (LDA). *IEEE Access : Practical Innovations, Open Solutions, 10*, 121080–121095. DOI: 10.1109/ACCESS.2022.3214310

Sin-Wai. (2024). *Kin-Wah, C., & Ming, M.* Routledge Encyclopedia of Technology and the Humanities.

Singh, S. (2025). Futuristic Perspective of AI in Literary Academia. *Journal of East-West Thought, 15*(1), 141–147.

Susanti, D., Sari, L. Y., & Fitriani, V. (2022). Increasing student learning motivation through the use of interactive digital books based on Project Based Learning (PjBL). *Jurnal Penelitian Pendidikan IPA, 8*(4), 1730–1735. DOI: 10.29303/jppipa.v8i4.1669

Van Heerden, I., & Bas, A. (2021). Ai as author-bridging the gap between machine learning and literary theory. *Journal of Artificial Intelligence Research, 71*, 175–189. DOI: 10.1613/jair.1.12593

Wang, H., Li, Z., & Yang, C. (2023). Interpreting technologies in the artificial intelligence era. In *Conference Interpreting in China* (pp. 232–250). DOI: 10.4324/9781003357629-16

Williams, R. (2024). Impact. AI: Democratizing AI through K-12 Artificial Intelligence Education (Doctoral dissertation).

Yadav, D. (2024). *The Role of Artificial Intelligence in Literary Analysis: A Computational Approach to Understand Literary Styles.*

Youvan, D. C. (2024). *AI for All: The Socioeconomic and Cultural Impacts of a 50-Year Leap into Democratized Artificial Intelligence.*

Chapter 10
Integration of Multiculturalism in AI-Based Literature:
A Social Perspective

Alimin Alwi
https://orcid.org/0009-0009-8826-2868
Universitas Negeri Makassar, Indonesia

St. Wijdanah Ram
https://orcid.org/0009-0005-1890-5355
Universitas Negeri Makassar, Indonesia

Fathullah Wajdi
Universitas Negeri Makassar, Indonesia

Suryadi Ishak
Universitas Negeri Makassar, Indonesia

Sahrul Syawal
Universitas Negeri Makassar, Indonesia

St. Zulaiha Nurhajarurahmah
https://orcid.org/0009-0000-4804-9071
Universitas Negeri Makassar, Indonesia

ABSTRACT

Incorporating multiculturalism into AI-driven literature creates chances to broaden cultural representation on a global scale. AI is capable of generating and examining stories from various cultural backgrounds, aiding access, providing translations between different languages, and safeguarding the literary heritage of minority groups. Nonetheless, challenges like algorithm bias, cultural homogenization, and authenticity issues continue to be a concern. When approached ethically and inclusively, AI can enhance global literature and bolster intercultural comprehension.

DOI: 10.4018/979-8-3373-1057-2.ch010

A. INTRODUCTION

From a sociological literature perspective, multiculturalism is understood as a reflection of the cultural diversity that is inherent in human society. Literature a cultural product, is not just a medium for expression; it is also a place where the identity, traditions, and values of a particular group of people are presented. To put it another way, sastra is regarded as a crucial tool for fostering meaningful social dialogue, which is increasingly important in the age of globalization (Bisht, 2021).

Sastra sociology examines sastra as a social document that reflects reality in daily life, including inequality in religious representation. Even if there is a lot of potential for fostering intercultural understanding, the literature of minority communities is frequently criticized in the global sphere. This indicates that the cultural diversity is not fully accommodated, whether in the production or distribution of religious literature (Rustandi, 2019). This phenomenon highlights the power relations that exists in the global system, wherein the voices from the periphery is frequently criticized.

Language hurdles, unequal distribution, and restricted accessibility are the primary obstacles facing heterogeneous societies, according to Sastra sociology. In addition to summarizing the customs of the appropriate religion, these obstacles emphasize the value of interfaith dialogue. Multiculturalism thus resolves the tension between the attempts to raise authenticity and coverage (Sismanto et al., 2022). The advancement of technology, particularly artificial intelligence (AI), offers the potential to address this issue. From a sastra-social perspective, AI might be seen as a new tool in the process of mediating daily life. This technology can provide access to sacred texts through automatic translation, catalog minority literature, and translate sacred texts into it. By doing this, AI can provide a more inclusive representation of the world's culture.

However, sociological also highlights the risks associated with the use of AI. Biased algorithms can reinforce stereotypes or even reduce diversity to a homogeneous narrative. In addition, there are critical questions about the accuracy of sastra literature that are formulated or mediated by technology (Ferrara, 2024). If AI-generated representations of the world may depict the complexity of human life, or is only a shallow reflection of the data being used. Because of this, it is crucial to ensure that the development and application of AI are carried out in a responsible manner by encouraging collaboration between the fields of cultural expert, sociology, and technology. This approach is necessary to uphold the values of multiculturalism and to encourage understanding of the underlying principles of modern society. With the help of artificial intelligence, multicultural society has the potential to become a more inclusive and reflective medium for international relations. Yet, this can only be achieved if technology is used as a means of promoting education rather than as a hindrance to the complexity of education.

B. THE CONCEPT OF MULTICULTURALISM AND LITERATURE

1. Opportunities and Challenges of Multiculturalism in Literature

The understanding of cultural diversity as a crucial pillar for creating an inclusive society is reflected in multiculturalism in literature. Multicultural literature serves as a medium that promotes cross-cultural understanding, dispels prejudices, and increases intercultural empathy by showcasing a variety of cultural perspectives and identities. In addition to preserving a community's customs and experiences, this type of literature gives voices from frequently underrepresented cultures a platform to be heard and valued (Drewniak, 2019).

The ability of multicultural literature to foster in-depth discussions between readers and various cultural narratives is one of its many wonderful chances. Stories that portray the hardships faced by minority communities or the distinctive customs of a social group, for instance, might broaden the perspectives of readers from diverse cultural backgrounds (Tan & Mante-Estacio, 2021). Furthermore, multicultural literature gives authors from other cultures a forum to express their individual experiences, adding more inclusive and genuine stories to the world's literary canon.

However, there are still difficulties with multiculturalism in literature despite all of the advantages. The disparity in cultural representation in international literature is one of the primary problems. Due to limited distribution, inaccessibility, or language problems, many works from marginalized cultures or minority populations do not receive enough attention (Vassilakopoulou & Hustad, 2023). This can worsen disparities in cultural representation since stories from these groups frequently do not reach a larger audience. The possibility of stereotyping in the way culture is presented is another difficulty. False biases and prejudices can be strengthened when writers or publishers simply present a certain culture in a cursory or presumptively accurate manner. Thus, it is crucial that multicultural literary works incorporate the communities they portray and be grounded in thorough study (Abdul Manaf et al., 2021).

The use of artificial intelligence (AI) and other technological advancements present fresh chances to get past some of these obstacles. Multicultural literary works can be analyzed and translated with AI's assistance, giving stories from many cultures a worldwide audience. However, in order to guarantee ethical and genuine depiction, this technology must also be used carefully. Multicultural literature has enormous potential to improve understanding, make the world more inclusive, and inspire a greater appreciation for cultural diversity in the global community by overcoming these obstacles.

2. The Role of AI Technology in Increasing the Inclusivity of Multicultural Literature

The gap in cultural representation in literature can now be filled thanks to developments in artificial intelligence (AI) technology. Multicultural literature is crucial for promoting and celebrating cultural variety in this age of globalization. However, in the global literary market, literary works from marginalized cultures or minority communities frequently receive less attention. This is where artificial intelligence (AI) plays a particularly important role, as it has the potential to make multicultural literature more inclusive than ever before (Kar et al., 2024; Tatar et al., 2024).

The translation and modification of literary works is one of the primary ways artificial intelligence (AI) contributes to multicultural literature. Because AI can effectively handle massive volumes of data, it can be used to translate literary works from different languages, giving a worldwide audience access to previously inaccessible literature. Multicultural literary works from different groups can now be readily translated into several languages because to the rapid advancement of automatic translation technology like those found in AI programs (like Google Translate) (Imami et al., 2023). In addition to giving readers from many backgrounds access to stories that represent various cultural experiences and viewpoints, this expands the audience for literary works from a given culture.

AI offers a lot of promise for examining literary works' cultural themes. AI may identify underlying themes and patterns in text that are not always apparent to human readers by utilizing big data analysis. AI can be used, for instance, to investigate how racial injustice, migration, and identity issues appear in literature from many civilizations (Intahchomphoo & Gundersen, 2020). This method enables us to uncover storylines that would have been disregarded or ignored, in addition to assisting scholars and literary critics in comprehending the larger context inside a literary work.

In addition, AI has the potential to develop new, more inclusive narrative and illustrate various business perspectives. Through algorithms designed to understand cultural dynamics, artificial intelligence (AI) can be used to produce stories that highlight multicultural themes and highlight underrepresented characters from many cultures. For instance, AI can assist writers in creating more complex and realistic plots and characters, highlighting various cultural identities and conflicts that arise among the aforementioned communities. Such works not only have the ability to improve the world, but they also provide opportunities for various forms of heard.

But even while AI technology has a lot of promise, there are also a lot of obstacles to overcome, particularly with regard to algorithm bias. Because AI learns on the data it is given, it may produce erroneous results or reinforce preexisting prejudices if the dataset is not sufficiently representative or reflects cultural diversity. Literary works that solely incorporate viewpoints from the prevailing culture, for instance, may result in stories that disregard or inaccurately depict other cultures. Thus, it is crucial to make sure that data used to train AI fairly and accurately represents cultural diversity.

Furthermore, it is impossible to overlook the issue of the veracity of works created by artificial intelligence. Even though AI is capable of producing writing that represents different cultural viewpoints, can the work be regarded as legitimate if it wasn't produced by members of that culture? This is the conundrum that AI-based literature faces. Collaboration between writers, tech developers, and cultural specialists is crucial to ensuring AI is applied in an inclusive and morally responsible manner. AI can genuinely contribute positively to the field of multicultural literature with the support of this multidisciplinary approach (Ożegalska-Łukasik & Łukasik, 2023).

With the speed at which technology is developing, artificial intelligence (AI) holds enormous promise for promoting inclusivity in multicultural literature by making works from other cultures easier to access and comprehend. However, cultural diversity and pertinent ethical principles must be considered in the development and implementation of this technology in order for it to be used responsibly and sustainably. Only then will AI be able to contribute to the development of a more inclusive literary universe that captures the complexity of the world.

C. AI IN THE CREATION OF MULTICULTURAL LITERATURE

1. The Role of AI in Creating Literary Works That Reflect Cultural Diversity

The field of literature has benefited greatly from developments in artificial intelligence (AI) technology, particularly in the area of producing works that represent cultural variety. AI is able to create tales, poems, and stories that are not only structurally complicated but also contain aspects of culture (Sampaio et al., 2021; Zhuk, 2023). This is made possible by machine learning approaches, which use datasets covering a variety of customs, languages, and cultural expressions from throughout the world to train language models like GPT.

AI can produce stories that accurately portray cultural customs by evaluating this data. AI can, for instance, compose narratives that explain the meaning of lanterns in Chinese New Year celebrations or the spirit of unity and thankfulness in Eid al-Fitr festivities. Additionally, this technology makes it possible to blend several cultural components into a single piece of writing, producing narrative coherence that captures the multicultural realities of the contemporary world. AI can assist human writers in refining their ideas in addition to producing original pieces. Artificial intelligence (AI) can add cultural aspects to stories that the author might not have understood by making data-driven recommendations (Amato et al., 2019). AI can, for instance, include dialogue, customs, or rituals that are appropriate for the civilization being portrayed. This makes the writer's work more inclusive and expands their perspectives (Nanduri & Bonsignore, 2023).

However, there are a number of obstacles that AI must overcome in order to successfully represent cultural diversity. Making sure the work is genuinely authentic and free of cultural prejudices is one of the biggest obstacles. Insensitive or even disrespectful portrayals of particular cultures might result from the misrepresentation of cultural aspects. In order to authenticate the work generated by AI, it is crucial to employ large and varied datasets and consult cultural specialists. Nevertheless, there is still a lot of room for AI to produce literary masterpieces that represent cultural diversity. The literary world can become more inclusive with the use of digital technology, giving other cultural viewpoints a chance to be seen by a worldwide audience. When applied properly, AI expands the possibilities of intercultural understanding in the literary world in addition to assisting in the creation of beautiful and culturally relevant works.

2. AI as a Literary Analysis Tool to Reveal the Theme of Multiculturalism

Artificial intelligence (AI) has grown into a highly helpful tool in recent decades for assessing a variety of literary elements, including multiculturalism-related themes. AI's capacity to effectively handle vast volumes of data creates new avenues for comprehending intricate topics like migration, racial injustice, and cultural identity that are present in international literature(Xue, 2020). The ability of AI to identify certain themes in a large collection of literary works is one of its primary accomplishments. Thematic patterns, such as the battles against prejudice, the difficulties experienced by immigrant groups, or the tensions between tradition and modernization, can be recognized by machine learning-based algorithms. For instance, AI can recognize how racial injustice is portrayed in literature from various locales and historical eras by examining the usage of specific words, metaphors, or symbols. AI can also be used to examine how literary works express cultural identity.

This technique maps the ways in which cultural components-like language, customs, or regional symbols-are utilized to mold characters or plots using a data-based methodology. AI thus aids in showcasing the distinctiveness of a given culture while illuminating its interactions with other civilizations in a global setting. Furthermore, researchers can manually discover narrative patterns that can be challenging to detect thanks to AI (Deas et al., 2023). AI can recognize how migration issues are portrayed in literature, for instance, by examining character conversation or story structure.

Analyzing emotional character qualities associated with alienation, nostalgia, or the need to adapt to a new environment is part of this. AI is also used to compare how multiculturalism is portrayed in different parts of the world (Aumueller, 2019). AI can identify parallels and discrepancies in the treatment of issues like racism and cultural hybridity by examining literature from various civilizations. AI can learn, for instance, how racial injustice stories in the US differ from those in South Africa or India.

However, there are disadvantages to applying AI to literary study in spite of all of its benefits. One of them is the possibility of bias in the dataset. If the data collection under consideration is not sufficiently diverse, the outcomes of an AI study may be imprecise or exclusive. Therefore, it is essential to ensure that the data used accurately and fairly reflects cultural diversity. All things considered, AI has emerged as a ground-breaking instrument for examining the multiculturalism subject in international literature. With its capacity to reveal hidden patterns, extend viewpoints, and offer fresh perspectives, artificial intelligence (AI) not only aids in understanding significant problems but also advances more extensive intercultural communication. AI has the potential to accelerate our comprehension of the diversity and complexity seen in literary works when applied responsibly and inclusively.

3. Ethical and Authenticity Challenges in Using AI for Multicultural Literature

While there is a lot of promise in using artificial intelligence (AI) to produce multicultural literature, there are also many obstacles to overcome, particularly in terms of ethics and authenticity. When it comes to cultural representation, it's critical to make sure AI-generated content sensitively and accurately captures cultural aspects without causing stereotypes or distortion (ÓhÉigeartaigh et al., 2020; Ożegalska-Łukasik & Łukasik, 2023). Making ensuring AI accurately recognizes and captures the distinctiveness of a given culture is one of the biggest problems. Large data sets, which frequently contain information from several cultures, are used to train AI models. The resulting AI work, however, may be biased or unauthentic if the training data does not adequately represent diversity. AI that hasn't been taught using data from minority cultural communities, for instance, can generate work that oversimplifies or ignores their distinct experiences. This could lead to cultural representations that are unjust or even deceptive.

In addition, there is disagreement over the veracity of literary creations generated by AI. Human experience, emotion, and individual viewpoint are frequently at the core of classic writing. The challenge that emerges when artificial intelligence is used to make literature is whether the work can be regarded as an authentic depiction if it was not created by a person with firsthand cultural knowledge. For instance, even while AI is capable of creating stories that are representative of particular cultural traditions, they might not have the emotional complexity or depth that comes from human life experiences alone (Riedl, 2016).

The morality of portraying particular cultures through AI is another difficulty. AI-generated content runs the potential of being misused, such as to take advantage of or alter cultural aspects for profit, if there is no clear guideline. As a result, it's critical to set rules and moral principles for the application of AI in literature, including involving cultural specialists in the production process. To overcome these obstacles, collaboration between technology developers and cultural experts is essential. A multidisciplinary approach can ensure that the final product is aesthetically pleasing and sensitive to cultural differences. In this way, AI can help produce inclusive and original multicultural literature without compromising the distinctiveness or integrity of the cultures it represents.

D. IMPLICATIONS OF MULTICULTURALISM IN AI-BASED LITERATURE IN A SOCIAL PERSPECTIVE

1. AI Opportunities in Preservation and Promotion of Minority Culture

Minority cultures that are frequently ignored in popular literature now have more opportunity to be preserved and promoted because to artificial intelligence (AI). With its rich customs, folklore, and distinctive viewpoints, minority cultures struggle mightily to endure in the face of globalization and majority culture domination. By digitizing, archiving, and making literary works from various cultures accessible to a larger audience, artificial intelligence (AI) can play a significant role in this context (Qiao & Zhou, 2023). Text digitization is one method artificial intelligence helps. Many works of minority literature are still passed down orally or are kept in hard-to-access antique manuscripts. AI is capable of scanning, word recognition, and digital document conversion. AI can now read and store texts, including those written in obscure languages and scripts, thanks to advanced optical character recognition (OCR) technology. Ancient literature from some indigenous societies, for instance, can be transformed into digital archives that the public, scholars, and students can easily access (Griffin, 2023).

Oral traditions can also be recorded and analyzed using AI. Folktales, melodies, and poems are transmitted orally from one generation to the next in many minority cultures. AI can record these stories, transcribe them, and even examine the linguistic or thematic patterns they contain thanks to voice processing and machine learning technologies. Traditions that were previously in danger of going extinct can be saved for upcoming generations in this way. AI contributes to the globalization of minority cultures in addition to conservation. It is possible to create new stories based on particular cultural traditions by using machine learning algorithms. AI educated on a community's folklore, for instance, can produce original stories that blend traditional and contemporary components. Through a variety of venues, including social media, digital publications, and interactive applications, these narratives can be accessed by a worldwide audience, thereby bringing minority cultures to a larger audience.

Additionally, AI has a lot of promise to help with the translation of minority culture literature. Reaching a worldwide readership is challenging since many minority literary works are not available in languages that are commonly spoken. These works can be translated into various languages more rapidly and effectively thanks to developments in AI-based translation technologies, such as neural machine translation. AI can be a very helpful tool in overcoming language gaps and increasing access to minority literature, even if literary translation demands particular attention to linguistic intricacies and cultural context.

Furthermore, by examining linguistic and thematic patterns in literary works, AI can contribute to the promotion of minority cultures. AI can assist in identifying distinctive aspects of a culture and showcasing them to a worldwide audience by examining characters, themes, or symbols in texts. AI can be used, for instance, to analyze how spiritual beliefs are conveyed in African tribal poetry or how Southeast Asian folklore reflects collectivistic principles. In addition to showcasing the culture's beauty, this analysis aids audiences around the world in comprehending viewpoints that may be different from their own. Even while AI has many opportunities, there are a number of issues to be mindful of (Triandis, 1993). The possibility of bias in the training data is one of them. An AI algorithm may not comprehend or accurately portray minority cultures if the dataset used to train it lacks sufficient representation of such cultures. An AI educated solely on works from the dominant culture, for instance, may provide results that are homogeneous and fail to take into account the subtleties of the minority culture. As a result, it is crucial to make sure that training data fairly and representatively represents cultural variety (C. W. Tsai et al., 2022).

Additionally, it is crucial that local communities and cultural specialists be involved in this process. To guarantee that the work respects the customs and values of the relevant culture, AI-generated tales must be validated. Working together, authors, tech developers, and local communities can guarantee that AI is applied responsibly and sensitively. All things considered, AI could be a game-changing instrument for protecting and advancing minority cultures. Through the digitization, analysis, and dissemination of literary works, this technology can contribute to the preservation and relevance of minority cultures' customs and narratives in the contemporary day. However, for minority cultures to be accepted, valued, and presented to the world in a genuine and significant way, this achievement mostly depends on an inclusive and moral attitude in its execution.

2. Biased and Authenticity Challenges in AI-Based Multicultural Narratives

Multicultural culture preservation and promotion could be greatly aided by artificial intelligence (AI). However, there are a number of issues with its use, particularly with regard to algorithm bias and the veracity of cultural representations in narratives produced by AI. The degree to which these technologies can accurately depict cultural variety without undermining the distinctive characteristics and values of every culture is called into serious doubt by these difficulties (Johnson et al., 2022).

Bias in AI algorithms is one of the primary issues. AI learns the training patterns from the data that was used to create it. The results are likely to contain biases that reflect the prevailing culture or specific stereotypes if the training data lacks inclusive and diverse cultural representation. An algorithm that exclusively mines Western literature, for instance, may produce tales that are more likely to convey the viewpoints and values of those civilizations, while ignoring or reducing aspects of minority or non-Western cultures to surface-level depictions (C.-H. Tsai & Wang, 2019). The portrayal of culture in AI-based literature may be significantly impacted by these prejudices. This prejudice might lead to inauthentic work or promote stereotypes rather than enhancing multicultural narratives. For instance, because AI lacks a thorough awareness of the cultural background, it may oversimplify or even misread representations of specific indigenous community customs. In addition to hurting those cultural communities, this also defeats the goal of multicultural literature, which is to foster genuine and profound intercultural understanding.

The issue of the authenticity of work generated by AI presents another difficulty in addition to bias. Strong tales in literature are frequently derived from complicated human viewpoints, feelings, and personal experiences. The strong bond between the author and the culture he represents is reflected in this story. In contrast, AI-generated work solely relies on statistical analysis and data trends. This begs the important question: can art produced by AI be genuinely regarded as authentic? Or is the art only the product of cursory data processing devoid of sentimental significance or a sense of personal connection?

When AI-generated works are employed to represent certain cultures, this dilemma gets much more complicated. These works run the risk of giving a worldwide audience an inaccurate or insufficient impression of the culture. The core and distinctiveness of the culture in question may be lost, for instance, if AI creates a story about a certain tradition without comprehending the spiritual values or symbolic significance associated with that tradition (Kim et al., 2019). Local communities and cultural specialists must be involved in the development and application of AI in order to overcome these obstacles. In order to make AI-generated narratives more genuine and culturally sensitive, cultural specialists can offer profound insight into pertinent values, symbolism, and customs. Local communities can serve as stewards of authenticity in the meantime, making sure that their culture is represented in a way that honors its identity and values (Tian et al., 2020).

Working together, local communities, cultural specialists, and AI engineers can lessen the possibility of bias in training data. The algorithm's training dataset needs to fairly and representatively represent cultural diversity. Furthermore, local communities can validate AI-generated work to make sure it does not contain prejudices and appropriately represents their culture. The creation of rules and moral principles controlling the application of AI in multicultural literature is equally crucial. Guidelines for the collection, use, and validation of cultural data should be included of this policy. To guarantee that AI is applied responsibly and inclusively, it is equally critical that the algorithm development process be transparent (Cachat-Rosset & Klarsfeld, 2023).

In general, the difficulties with authenticity and bias in AI-based multicultural storytelling highlight how intricately technology and culture interact. Although AI has a lot of promise to improve multicultural literature, its effectiveness will mostly depend on how it is employed and controlled. AI has the potential to be a potent instrument for fostering intercultural communication and producing stories that accurately capture the diversity and individuality of every culture if it is used in an inclusive, cooperative, and morally responsible manner. However, AI technology runs the risk of creating works that actually serve to perpetuate cultural inequalities and diminish the value of multicultural literature's authenticity if these issues are not given enough consideration.

3. The Role of AI-Based Literature in Encouraging Cross-Cultural Dialogue and Understanding

Cross-cultural understanding is becoming more and more crucial in the age of globalization in order to build a more accepting and peaceful society. Literature has traditionally been a powerful tool for promoting intercultural communication because of its capacity to capture the complexity of human existence and culture. With the development of artificial intelligence (AI) technology, literature can now create inclusive and inventive multicultural narratives that promote intercultural understanding to new heights (Hu et al., 2022).

AI plays a significant influence in literature by producing stories that represent a range of cultural viewpoints. AI can use collections of writings from many cultures to create stories that reflect a variety of customs, values, and historical periods since it can evaluate vast volumes of data. AI may, for instance, produce narratives that capture the spirit of the Diwali celebrations in India and the warmth of the Eid al-Fitr festivities in Indonesia. AI enhances literary material and aids readers in comprehending and appreciating the diversity of cultures around the world by fusing these many cultural components. AI-based intercultural tales have the potential to be an effective teaching tool in exposing children to many cultures (Sangapu, 2019). AI-generated stories can serve as engaging educational resources to impart the virtues of empathy, tolerance, and respect for diversity. A story about a migrant community's difficulties adjusting to a new setting, for instance, can aid children in comprehending the difficulties that group faces. Students' perspectives are enhanced, and they are also inspired to be more accepting of others' differences (Woodgate & Busolo, 2021).

AI has a significant impact on increasing access to international literature in addition to education. Readers worldwide can now access literary works from a variety of languages and cultures thanks to AI-based automatic translation. More accurate translations that consider linguistic subtleties and cultural context are now possible thanks to technologies like neural machine translation. By doing this, readers from different backgrounds can appreciate literary works from cultures that were previously inaccessible, enhancing intercultural communication through literature. Additionally, AI-based literature may open up a platform for cross-cultural communication. AI-generated narratives, for instance, can be used to unite people from various backgrounds in community conversations, art exhibits, or cultural festivals. AI can support discussions that improve intercultural comprehension and cooperation by offering narratives that depict the human experience from various perspectives (Crimaldi & Leonelli, 2023).

However, issues with representation and cultural sensitivity must be addressed if AI is to genuinely promote intercultural communication and understanding. Multicultural narratives produced by AI must be grounded in inclusive and representative data in order to capture the distinctiveness and complexity of every culture. Additionally, to guarantee that the final stories honor the customs and values of the relevant culture, local communities and cultural specialists must be involved in the algorithm creation process (Khomais, 2014). However, cooperation among writers, cultural organizations, and technology developers can enhance the caliber of narratives produced by AI. This multidisciplinary method broadens the spectrum of cultures that can be portrayed in AI-based writing while also guaranteeing the work's authenticity. For instance, cultural organizations can supply pertinent data and insights to train algorithms, and technology developers can work with authors from a variety of cultural backgrounds to create richer and more genuine stories.

To guarantee that AI is applied responsibly in the literary industry, rules and moral principles are also required. In addition to establishing standards for inclusive and considerate cultural representation, this policy should contain instructions on the collection, use, and validation of cultural data. When used properly, artificial intelligence (AI) can be a potent tool for crafting stories that enhance intercultural communication without undermining cultural values and individuality. All things considered, AI-based literature offers a great chance to promote intercultural communication and understanding and build a more welcoming society. AI holds enormous promise for fostering cross-cultural connections, increasing access to international literature, and producing stories that represent cultural variety. To realize this promise, though, a number of stakeholders must be committed to making sure that this technology is used responsibly, inclusively, and ethically. As a result, AI-based writing has the potential to promote world peace and understanding in addition to enhancing the literary world.

E. AI AS A TOOL FOR PRESERVING MULTICULTURAL TRADITIONAL LITERATURE

1. AI as a Cultural Heritage Preserver: Securing Traditional Literature for Future Generations

AI has a lot of potential for protecting cultural material, particularly traditional literature from minority cultures that are in danger of extinction. Because of physical degradation or inadequate preservation attempts, traditional literary works-which are frequently only known orally or in old manuscripts-run the risk of disappearing. To ensure that these priceless works are available to future generations, artificial intelligence (AI) can be crucial in the digitization and archiving of ancient manuscripts (Assael et al., 2019). The digitalization process is one way artificial intelligence aids in the preservation of classic literature. A lot of stories, poetry, and folktales from many cultures are frequently only available orally or in fragile manuscript form. AI can transform these documents into more enduring and readable representations using digital technologies. For instance, language preservation initiatives like "AI for Indigenous Languages" have been successful in translating and digitizing the folktales of different indigenous groups, enabling them wider dissemination.

The automatic translation of classic literary works is another significant application of AI. AI enables the translation of multicultural literary works into several languages while preserving the cultural essence of the original work by employing complex algorithms that are sensitive to cultural context. This is essential to guaranteeing that readers from diverse cultural backgrounds understand and value the traditional stories from minority communities. Folktales from the Buton tribe in Indonesia, for instance, can be faithfully translated so that readers worldwide can appreciate and comprehend this literary gem. AI can also be used to examine and recognize themes, patterns, and symbols in conventional literary works. The essence of some cultural traditions is better understood by scholars and literary activists thanks to this study. AI can recognize common narrative forms, examine recurring themes in texts, and decipher literary symbolism. This information is crucial for developing contemporary adaptations that uphold and honor traditional values (Zhu, 2021).

Even while AI greatly aids in the preservation of classic literature, there are still issues. The danger of cultural uniformity is one of the primary issues. Work that is excessively ubiquitous and disregards the cultural quirks that define a piece's individuality may be produced by AI trained on global datasets. In order to preserve cultural identity, it is crucial to include local populations and cultural experts in the preservation process. All things considered, AI holds enormous promise for protecting and conserving classic literature for upcoming generations. This technology can be a useful tool for conserving rich and varied cultural heritage if it is used ethically and cooperatively.

2. Challenges and Opportunities: Maintaining Authenticity and Cultural Identity in AI Adaptation

While there are many benefits to integrating artificial intelligence (AI) technology into literary and cultural preservation, there are also significant obstacles to preserving cultural identity and authenticity. Traditional literary works can be preserved and disseminated more quickly thanks to AI, but there are serious risks involved in concealing or even losing important cultural components. As a result, it's critical to recognize and handle the difficulties in preserving cultural authenticity when utilizing AI technologies (Pansoni et al., 2023). The danger of cultural uniformity is one of the primary obstacles to AI adaptation. Global datasets, which favor more broad and understandable representations, are frequently used to train AI. As a result, more distinctive local cultural traits may be lost. For instance, when translating literary works or folktales into different languages, artificial intelligence (AI) that is not sensitive enough to a certain cultural context may result in more generic translations or leave out crucial cultural details. AI might not be able to pick up on the subtleties of a folktale from an indigenous civilization, for instance, if it contains symbolism, metaphor, or language that is only understood within a certain cultural context. Thus, the cultural identities that ought to be preserved may be obscured by the adaption of AI in multicultural writing.

Furthermore, the cultural and historical nuances of a literary work or oral tradition are frequently beyond AI's comprehension. Traditional literary works are frequently shaped by social conventions and ideals that have evolved over generations as a result of collective experiences. The richness of human experience in comprehending the historical, social, and emotional context included in these cultural works cannot be fully replaced by AI, despite its strength in data and pattern analysis (Nanetti, 2021). For instance, a lot of classic tales use comedy, irony, or highly relevant social principles. The ensuing work may become meaningless or even produce incorrect interpretations if AI is not trained to catch these elements.

However, AI technology also presents excellent chances to preserve and enhance cultural authenticity. Contributing to the preservation of classic literary works that were once in risk of going extinct is one way. Ancient manuscripts can be digitized with AI to increase its durability and accessibility for future generations. For instance, artificial intelligence (AI) technology can be used to digitize oral literary masterpieces that are not yet in written form. By doing this, the cultural aspects of the stories can be preserved as these materials are translated and made available to a worldwide audience. This offers a chance to guarantee the survival and accessibility of minority communities' cultural heritage (Otero, 2022).

AI can also assist in producing translations that are more accurate and culturally aware. For instance, AI can provide translations that better capture the original subtleties of literary works by employing algorithms that can identify cultural context. This way, readers from diverse cultural backgrounds may still appreciate the work without losing its cultural significance. With the use of this technology, authors can also more precisely modify classic works to create new works that are authentic to the original cultural identity while simultaneously making changes for a broader readership. However, it is essential to include local communities and cultural specialists in the creation of AI technology to prevent the possible blurring of cultural identity (Fei, 2022). This engagement will guarantee that the AI used to evaluate or produce cultural works is grounded in in-depth understanding of the values, customs, and conventions that define that culture in addition to broad facts. Works that are more genuine and respectful of cultural heritage will result from the cooperation of technology, culture, and human creativity.

Although sustaining cultural authenticity and identity in AI adaptation presents many difficulties, AI can be a useful tool for conserving and enhancing traditional culture if it is approached thoughtfully, ethically, and inclusively. We can guarantee that AI adaptations of literature and cultural artifacts stay true to their core principles by fusing technological prowess with a thorough understanding of culture.

3. Intercultural Collaboration through AI: Creating More Inclusive and Global Literature

Artificial intelligence (AI) and intercultural collaboration have huge potential to produce literature that is more inclusive and global. As technology advances, writers, artists, and people from all cultural backgrounds can now work together to create literary works that are rich in a variety of viewpoints thanks to artificial intelligence's capacity to process vast amounts of data, identify patterns, and create new narratives. The literature created as a result of this partnership has the potential to foster inclusivity, improve intercultural understanding, and unite individuals from many backgrounds to exchange insights and experiences.

The translation of literary works is one way AI contributes to cross-cultural cooperation. The language barrier is one of the primary barriers that has prevented cross-cultural cooperation. It can be challenging for readers from other cultures to access the literary works of minority communities or particular cultures because they are often only available in their original tongues. AI's ever-improving automatic translation skills enable these works to be translated into other languages while preserving their cultural subtleties. For instance, AI algorithms that consider cultural context can more accurately interpret stories from indigenous groups in the Americas or Asia, which have unique language and cultural traits. This makes it possible for a worldwide audience to appreciate cultural treasures from around the globe and comprehend experiences that may have been overlooked in traditional literature.

AI can also be utilized to produce original literary works that incorporate aspects of other cultural traditions. With the help of this technology, authors can work together in a more transparent and welcoming environment where they can combine various story motifs, cultural traits, and symbolism. With the use of AI, authors from Africa, Asia, and Europe, for instance, might collaborate to produce novels that incorporate aspects of their own cultures, exposing readers to a wider range of viewpoints on various lifestyles, beliefs, and challenges. Writers can traverse and blend various cultural traditions in a way that not only honors each culture's individuality but also acknowledges their contribution to creating a more interconnected world by using AI as a creative tool.

However, AI-enabled cross-cultural cooperation extends beyond translation and the production of original literature. The development of digital platforms made possible by this technology also makes it possible for authors and readers from different cultural backgrounds to share and study literary works more extensively. AI can be used to create online communities that serve as both literary archives and interactive forums where readers can engage in dialogue, exchange their views of works of literature from other cultures, and advance intercultural understanding. By allowing readers to see literary works from several perspectives, platforms such as these can enhance the reading experience and increase readers' awareness of the complexity and diversity of the world's cultures.

It is crucial to remember that using AI for intercultural collaboration comes with obstacles that must be addressed. The problem of disadvantaged cultures' acknowledgment and representation is one of them. Even though AI has a lot of potential to expose minority cultures to a worldwide audience, if these groups are not sufficiently involved, there is a chance that their work will be misrepresented or even exploited. In order to produce works that are both real and sensitive to cultural context, it is crucial that writers and technology developers collaborate with local communities and cultural specialists. In addition, in order to avoid reinforcing prejudices or generating monotonous tasks, AI must be taught using a variety of data and represent the cultural diversity found in the globe.

Furthermore, a crucial issue in cross-cultural cooperation is the ownership and control of literary works created with AI's assistance. Is the creator of the technology, the author, or another party the owner of the copyright to works of literature produced by AI? To guarantee that everyone participating in the partnership is respected and given the credit they deserve, clear and equitable copyright agreements must be set up. This is crucial to ensure that AI-enabled cross-cultural collaboration stays focused on producing work that is moral, inclusive, and respects each community's cultural rights.

AI has the potential to overcome cultural divides if it is used carefully. In addition to enhancing literature, AI-enabled cross-cultural cooperation will promote a greater appreciation of cultural diversity, a more inclusive global society, and a deeper knowledge of cultural differences. We can use this technology to make the literary world more diverse, open, and connected so that all cultures can express themselves and be respected.

F. CONCLUSIONS AND RECOMMENDATIONS

Artificial intelligence (AI)-based writing that incorporates multiculturalism demonstrates attempts to inclusively depict cultural variety in literature while leveraging contemporary technology to transcend conventional limitations. Literature has always served as a window into human existence, offering a forum for examining the identities, customs, and experiences of diverse social groups. Global realities, however, demonstrate that cultural representation is unbalanced, with minority populations' works frequently overlooked on the literary scene. At this point, artificial intelligence (AI) plays a significant role by providing solutions that make it possible to more widely and inclusively embrace cultural diversity.

AI has the potential to open up new avenues for introducing multicultural literature to a worldwide readership. Through automated translation, text digitalization, and theme analysis, artificial intelligence (AI), which can evaluate and process vast amounts of data, can support the advancement of inclusivity in literature. The language barrier has been a significant barrier, but AI-based translation technology, for instance, makes it possible to translate literary works from different languages more rapidly and accurately. AI can also digitize oral traditions or old texts, creating digital archives that will be easier to access and preserve for future generations.

AI is a valuable creative collaborator for authors in the production of new works. Using pieces from several traditions to generate deeper narratives, this technology can assist in creating stories that represent a variety of cultural viewpoints. AI can be utilized, for instance, to create characters or storylines that are considerate of multicultural issues, like the hardships faced by underrepresented groups or the experiences of newcomers in unfamiliar settings. In addition to expanding one's literary horizons, this type of narrative fosters empathy and understanding between cultures.

But there are drawbacks to using AI in multicultural writing. Algorithmic bias is one of the primary problems. Artificial intelligence runs the risk of generating homogenous work or perpetuating stereotypes if the datasets used to train the system do not fairly represent cultural diversity. AI-generated tales, for instance, may ignore the distinctive characteristics of underrepresented communities while reflecting dominant culture. Authenticity presents another difficulty. AI-generated content is frequently criticized for lacking the human-created narrative's emotional depth and sense of personal connection.

Technology developers, cultural specialists, and local communities must work together to solve these obstacles. The work created might be more sensitive to the cultural context and authentic by involving multiple stakeholders. To guarantee that this technology is used sensibly, in a way that respects cultural values, and not in an exploitative manner, rules and ethical standards must also be created. An excellent chance to enhance the international literary community is presented by AI-based multiculturalism integration in literature. AI has the potential to be a tool that promotes cultural preservation, fosters intercultural communication, and deepens our understanding of human diversity if it is used responsibly and inclusively.

REFERENCES

Abdul Manaf, A. A., Hamzah, F., & Abidin, A. (2021). Depiction Heroic Animated Characters: Describing a Brief Process of Archetype Embodiment into a Genuine Nusantara -Inspired Content. *International Journal of Academic Research in Business & Social Sciences, 11*(7). Advance online publication. DOI: 10.6007/IJARBSS/v11-i7/10241

Amato, G., Behrmann, M., Bimbot, F., Caramiaux, B., Falchi, F., Garcia, A., Geurts, J., Gibert, J., Gravier, G., Holken, H., Koenitz, H., Lefebvre, S., Liutkus, A., Lotte, F., Perkis, A., Redondo, R., Turrin, E., Viéville, T., & Vincent, E. (2019). AI in the media and creative industries (version 1 - April 2019). In *arXiv*.

Assael, Y., Sommerschield, T., & Prag, J. (2019). Restoring ancient text using deep learning: A case study on Greek epigraphy. *EMNLP-IJCNLP 2019 - 2019 Conference on Empirical Methods in Natural Language Processing and 9th International Joint Conference on Natural Language Processing, Proceedings of the Conference*. DOI: 10.18653/v1/D19-1668

Aumueller, J. (2019). *How Artificial Intelligencecan revolutionise can revolutionisehealthcare healthcare*. Health Europa Quarterly.

Bisht, M. (2021). The History of the Arthaśāstra: Sovereignty and Sacred Law in Ancient India. *Strategic Analysis, 45*(5), 449–451. Advance online publication. DOI: 10.1080/09700161.2021.1965350

Cachat-Rosset, G., & Klarsfeld, A. (2023). Diversity, Equity, and Inclusion in Artificial Intelligence: An Evaluation of Guidelines. *Applied Artificial Intelligence, 37*(1), 2176618. Advance online publication. DOI: 10.1080/08839514.2023.2176618

Crimaldi, F., & Leonelli, M. (2023). AI and the creative realm: A short review of current and future applications. *ArXiv Preprint ArXiv*. http://arxiv.org/abs/2306.01795

Deas, N., Grieser, J., Kleiner, S., Patton, D., Turcan, E., & McKeown, K. (2023). Evaluation of African American Language Bias in Natural Language Generation. *EMNLP 2023 - 2023 Conference on Empirical Methods in Natural Language Processing, Proceedings*. DOI: 10.18653/v1/2023.emnlp-main.421

Drewniak, D. (2019). Migrant Voices in the Polish Classroom: Canadian Literature on the Tertiary Level of Education. *Zeitschrift Fur Anglistik Und Amerikanistik, 67*(4), 411–427. Advance online publication. DOI: 10.1515/zaa-2019-0030

Fei, Q. (2022). Analysis of Traditional Cultural Acceptance Based on Deep Learning. *Computational Intelligence and Neuroscience, 2022*, 1–8. Advance online publication. DOI: 10.1155/2022/2373842 PMID: 35707191

Ferrara, E. (2024). Fairness and Bias in Artificial Intelligence: A Brief Survey of Sources, Impacts, and Mitigation Strategies. In *Sci* (Vol. 6, Issue 1). DOI: 10.3390/sci6010003

Griffin, S. M. (2023). Special Issue: Epigraphy and Paleography: Bringing Records from the Distant Past to the Present. In *International Journal on Digital Libraries* (Vol. 24, Issue 2). DOI: 10.1007/s00799-023-00371-4

Hu, N., Li, S., Li, L., & Xu, H. (2022). The Educational Function of English Children's Movies From the Perspective of Multiculturalism Under Deep Learning and Artificial Intelligence. *Frontiers in Psychology, 12*, 759094. Advance online publication. DOI: 10.3389/fpsyg.2021.759094 PMID: 35140652

Imami, T. R., & Mu'in, F., & Nasrullah. (2023). Proceedings of the 2nd International Conference on Education, Language and Art (ICELA 2022). In *Proceedings of the 2nd International Conference on Education, Language and Art (ICELA 2022)*. DOI: 10.2991/978-2-38476-004-6

Intahchomphoo, C., & Gundersen, O. E. (2020). Artificial Intelligence and Race: A Systematic Review. *Legal Information Management, 20*(2), 74–84. Advance online publication. DOI: 10.1017/S1472669620000183

Johnson, R. L., Pistilli, G., Menédez-González, N., Duran, L. D. D., Panai, E., Kalpokiene, J., & Bertulfo, D. J. (2022). The Ghost in the Machine has an American accent: value conflict in GPT-3. *The Ghost in the Machine Has an American Accent: Value Conflict in GPT-3.* http://arxiv.org/abs/2203.07785

Kar, S. K., Bansal, T., Modi, S., & Singh, A. (2024). How Sensitive Are the Free AI-detector Tools in Detecting AI-generated Texts? A Comparison of Popular AI-detector Tools. *Indian Journal of Psychological Medicine, XX*(X), 1–4. DOI: 10.1177/02537176241247934 PMID: 39564235

Khomais, S. F. (2014). Enhancing preschool children's number knowledge: The suitability of an intervention programme for Saudi practice. *Early Child Development and Care, 184*(1), 32–49. Advance online publication. DOI: 10.1080/03004430.2013.768238

Kim, S., Whitford, M., & Arcodia, C. (2019). Development of intangible cultural heritage as a sustainable tourism resource: The intangible cultural heritage practitioners' perspectives. *Journal of Heritage Tourism*, *14*(5–6), 422–435. Advance online publication. DOI: 10.1080/1743873X.2018.1561703

Nanduri, D. K., & Bonsignore, E. M. (2023). *Revitalizing Endangered Languages: AI-powered language learning as a catalyst for language appreciation.*

Nanetti, A. (2021). Defining Heritage Science: A Consilience Pathway to Treasuring the Complexity of Inheritable Human Experiences through Historical Method, AI, and ML. *Complexity*, *2021*(1), 4703820. Advance online publication. DOI: 10.1155/2021/4703820

ÓhÉigeartaigh, S. S., Whittlestone, J., Liu, Y., Zeng, Y., & Liu, Z.ÓhÉigeartaigh. (2020). Overcoming Barriers to Cross-cultural Cooperation in AI Ethics and Governance. *Philosophy & Technology*, *33*(4), 571–593. Advance online publication. DOI: 10.1007/s13347-020-00402-x

Otero, J. (2022). Heritage Conservation Future: Where We Stand, Challenges Ahead, and a Paradigm Shift. *Global Challenges (Hoboken, NJ)*, *6*(1), 2100084. Advance online publication. DOI: 10.1002/gch2.202100084 PMID: 35024170

Ożegalska-Łukasik, N., & Łukasik, S. (2023). Culturally Responsive Artificial Intelligence – Problems, Challenges and Solutions. *Intercultural Relations*, *7*(2(14)), 106–119. Advance online publication. DOI: 10.12797/RM.02.2023.14.07

Pansoni, S., Tiribelli, S., Paolanti, M., Di Stefano, F., Frontoni, E., Malinverni, E. S., & Giovanola, B. (2023). Artificial intelligence and cultural heritage: Design and assessment of an ethical framework. *International Archives of the Photogrammetry, Remote Sensing and Spatial Information Sciences - ISPRS Archives, 48*(M-2–2023). DOI: 10.5194/isprs-archives-XLVIII-M-2-2023-1149-2023

Qiao, Y., & Zhou, L. (2023). Implications of Artificial Intelligence Technology for the External Communication of Chinese Ethnic Cultures. *Mobile Information Systems*, *2022*, 1–13. Advance online publication. DOI: 10.1155/2022/3539332

Riedl, M. O. (2016). Computational Narrative Intelligence: A Human-Centered Goal for Artificial Intelligence. *ArXiv Preprint ArXiv*. http://arxiv.org/abs/1602.06484

Rustandi, N. (2019). The Plurality and Minority in Religiousity (A Study on the Civil Right of Sunda Wiwitan Followers In Cigugur Kuningan). *Hanifiya: Jurnal Studi Agama-Agama*, *2*(1), 28–41. DOI: 10.15575/hanifiya.v2i1.4269

Sampaio, H. A., Correia, A. I., Melo, C., Brazão, L., & Shehada, S. (2021). Analyzing Tourism Agents' Perceptions of the Use of Artificial Intelligence. *Smart Innovation. Systems and Technologies*, *208*, 245–254. Advance online publication. DOI: 10.1007/978-981-33-4256-9_22

Sangapu, I. (2019). Artificial Intelligence in Education - From a Teacher and a Student Perspective. SSRN *Electronic Journal*. DOI: 10.2139/ssrn.3372914

Sismanto, S., Bakri, M., & Huda, A. M. (2022). Implementation of Multicultural Islamic Education Values. *Proceedings of the International Conference on Madrasah Reform 2021 (ICMR 2021)*, 633. DOI: 10.2991/assehr.k.220104.048

Tan, D. N. L., & Mante-Estacio, M. J. (2021). Reader-text connection: Reporting the engagement of high school students with culturally relevant texts. *Teflin Journal*, *32*(2), 342. Advance online publication. DOI: 10.15639/teflinjournal.v32i2/342-361

Tatar, K., Ericson, P., Cotton, K., Del Prado, P. T. N., Batlle-Roca, R., Cabrero-Daniel, B., Ljungblad, S., Diapoulis, G., & Hussain, J. (2024). A Shift in Artistic Practices through Artificial Intelligence. *Leonardo*, *57*(3), 293–297. Advance online publication. DOI: 10.1162/leon_a_02523

Tian, D., Wang, Q., Law, R., & Zhang, M. (2020). Influence of cultural identity on tourists' authenticity perception, tourist satisfaction, and traveler loyalty. *Sustainability (Basel)*, *12*(16), 6344. Advance online publication. DOI: 10.3390/su12166344

Triandis, H. C. (1993). Collectivism and Individualism as Cultural Syndromes. *Cross-Cultural Research*, *27*(3–4), 155–180. Advance online publication. DOI: 10.1177/106939719302700301

Tsai, C.-H., & Wang, C.-P. (2019). An Analysis of the Development of Cultural Augmented Reality Education in Taiwanese Aboriginal Literature. *International Journal of E-Education, e-Business, e-. Management Learning*, *9*(4), 357–365. DOI: 10.17706/ijeeee.2019.9.4.357-365

Tsai, C. W., Ma, Y. W., Chang, Y. C., & Lai, Y. H. (2022). Integrating Multiculturalism Into Artificial Intelligence-Assisted Programming Lessons: Examining Inter-Ethnicity Differences in Learning Expectancy, Motivation, and Effectiveness. *Frontiers in Psychology*, *13*, 868698. Advance online publication. DOI: 10.3389/fpsyg.2022.868698 PMID: 35769741

Vassilakopoulou, P., & Hustad, E. (2023). Bridging Digital Divides: A Literature Review and Research Agenda for Information Systems Research. *Information Systems Frontiers*, *25*(3), 955–969. Advance online publication. DOI: 10.1007/s10796-020-10096-3 PMID: 33424421

Woodgate, R. L., & Busolo, D. S. (2021). African refugee youths' experiences of navigating different cultures in canada: A "push and pull" experience. *International Journal of Environmental Research and Public Health, 18*(4), 1–13. DOI: 10.3390/ijerph18042063 PMID: 33672518

Xue, T. (2020). Using big data technology to assist in analyzing the influence of cultural context on the translation of english and American literature. *Journal of Physics: Conference Series, 1648*(3), 032058. Advance online publication. DOI: 10.1088/1742-6596/1648/3/032058

Zhu, T. (2021). From Textual Experiments to Experimental Texts: Expressive Repetition in "artificial Intelligence Literature. *Theoretical Studies in Literature and Art, 41*(5).

Zhuk, A. (2023). Navigating the legal landscape of AI copyright: A comparative analysis of EU, US, and Chinese approaches. *AI and Ethics*. Advance online publication. DOI: 10.1007/s43681-023-00299-0

Chapter 11

Perceptions, Roles, Considerations, and Practices in Literary Criticism in the Age of AI:

Towards a Framework for Responsible AI Use in Literary Criticism

Philip Donald Pepito Herrera
https://orcid.org/0009-0005-9895-0999
Cebu Institute of Technology, Philippines

ABSTRACT

Literary criticism involves the appraisal of a literary work based on literary merit. In the advent of generative AI, the art of literary criticism could be reduced to the work of an AI application given the appropriate prompts. Thus, this explores the perceptions of graduate literature students on the role of AI in the work of literary criticism. Findings reveal that AI should only be used as an assistive technology in the process of literary criticism. Likewise, they also mentioned that the art of literary criticism is still very much a human act. They also noted that, while AI can produce a criticism of a work, it can never substitute the appraisal of a critic. Additionally, they also factored in ethical considerations in relying on the literary criticism produced by AI. Similarly, the respondents also shared some practices that they have adopted in their respective contexts as literature teachers when they require literary criticism submissions. Finally, the study proposes a framework that stakeholders can adapt consistent with their contexts and needs in light of these findings.

DOI: 10.4018/979-8-3373-1057-2.ch011

INTRODUCTION

It is common knowledge that generative artificial intelligence, more commonly known as AI, has taken over all aspects of people's lives. Generative artificial intelligence has particularly changed the landscape of the academia with the emergence of assistive technologies such as Chat GPT which is capable of producing volumes and volumes of texts through curated prompts. While there are perceived advantages in relation to using these assistive technologies, there are also now debates on its specific role (in other words what constitutes and limit it) in the academic context. The same observations were noted by Premkumar (2024) who did a study on the impact of artificial intelligence in literary creation and criticism. Given such assertion, this study explores on the perceptions of five graduate literature students who are in the practice of literary criticism on the role and considerations of generative artificial intelligence in the process and the art of literary criticism.

It is known that literary criticism is the appraisal of a work based on an applied theory or based on its literary merit. With the emergence of generative artificial intelligence, many scholars could probably be tempted to reduce the work into AI. That is producing a criticism of a work just purely based on the prompts generated from Chat GPT for example. While there has been no recorded case on this yet, it is an interesting and a very plausible scenario. In fact, Kharis Publishing in 2023 already anticipated such scenario by saying that artificial intelligence has the capacity to produce literary analysis and critique. They highlighted that artificial intelligence, while cannot replace a human-critic, can function as a literary critic which may provide insight and perspective on to the text in question. Additionally, Jabalselvi, Mohanraj, and Anitha (2024), in their study titled The Rise of AI in English Language and Literature, also highlighted this fact by pointing out how generative artificial intelligence has changed the landscape of English language and English literature in general. They mentioned that the emergence (and by extension, the use) of generative artificial intelligence in language and literature has prompted a paradigm shift in terms of producing, evaluating, and analyzing literary works. Aside from that, they also underscored on the fact that such emergence and use of generative artificial intelligence has presented intriguing issues as well as opportunities that involve morality and the society in general. Issues that were pointed out include data privacy, algorithmic bias, and replacement of human labor. In addition, issues of copyright, authorship, and originality continue to plague the debate on this issue.

As such, this study aims to contribute to the discourse on the specific role of generative artificial intelligence, highlighting the fact that it is here to stay and its limits especially in the very human act of doing literary criticism and the possible ethical considerations that may come with its use. Aside from that, the presence of these issues (and opportunities) point to the very fact that generative artificial intelligence needs our most immediate attention. Such attention could concretized in terms of the production of frameworks that can be replicated in terms of the use of generative artificial intelligence in these works through various research studies done on the same. By contributing to the discourse, not only is the body of knowledge on the same would be expanded but also a way of potent of reflection of the presence of generative artificial intelligence in this context among scholars and academicians. These reflections prove helpful as they try to tread on this seemingly controversial yet useful issue.

Statement of the Problem

This study explores on the nexus of literary criticism and generative artificial intelligence. Particularly, this aims to answer the following questions:

1. What is the perception of graduate literature students on the use of generative artificial intelligence in the process or the art of literary criticism?
2. As an offshoot to the first question, what is, therefore, the role of generative artificial intelligence in the process or the art of literary criticism?
3. Secondly, what is the consideration in and when using generative artificial intelligence in the process or the art of literary criticism?
4. Finally, what are your practices (personal or as mandated by your respective schools) in relation to how artificial intelligence is used in the context of literary criticism submissions?
5. Based on these findings, what preliminary framework can be proposed to promote responsible use of generative artificial intelligence in the process and art of literary criticism?

Figure 1. Structure of the study.

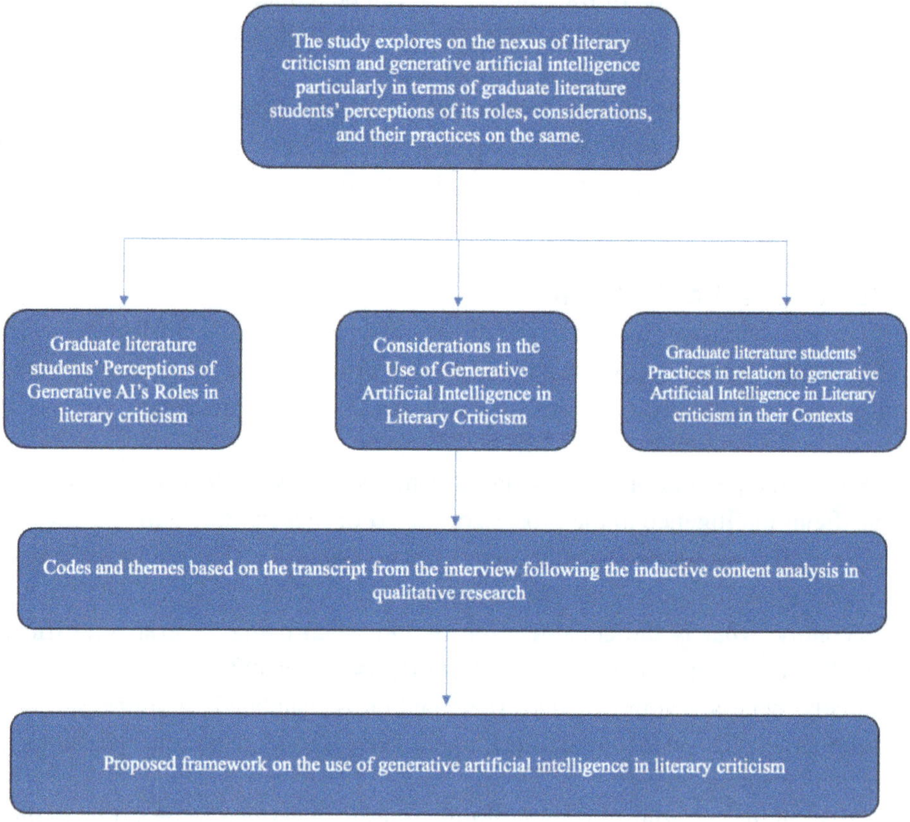

Review of Related Literature

This section presents a number of systematic reviews done on the topic of generative artificial intelligence in the context of the academe. It begins with a systematic review of current literature on the applications and issues related to generative artificial intelligence. Afterwards, another systematic review of another set of literatures is surveyed—this time focusing on its impact to academic writing instruction in higher education. Then, it is followed by how generative artificial intelligence is used for story writing (which is directly related to the present study). Finally, the review of literatures ends with an insight on how there is actually a need to regulate generative artificial intelligence given its perceived benefits, challenges, drawbacks, and other issues. The present study also points to the fact that there has not been any study or a systematic review of literature related to how generative artificial intelligence directly impacts the work of literary criticism.

In the study of Martínez-Olmo and Catalán (2024), they looked into the trends of applications of generative artificial intelligence to academic writing in the social sciences. It revealed that most of the studies that were included in their systematic review tackled generative artificial intelligence's possible applications, specific tools, detection of plagiarism, and its ethical and responsible use. All these themes, revealed in their findings, are important in providing a more thorough understanding of artificial intelligence which, although relatively new, has taken the entire academic landscape by storm. Understanding (of all stakeholders within and outside the academe and other related institutions) these layers of artificial intelligence is crucial towards its more humane, responsible, and ethical use.

Aljuaid (2024) also did a systematic review of generative artificial intelligence in relation to its impact to academic writing instruction in higher education. The study's findings point to the fact that artificial intelligence should be integrated into the curricula while balancing instructional integrity and rigor. This is important, because as emphasized in the present study, generative artificial intelligence is here to stay; and therefore, stakeholders are not supposed to ban this blindly or mindlessly. Instead, they should leverage on its perceived benefits as well as provide clear guidelines on its ethical use. Additionally, in relation to providing clear guidelines on its ethical use, the study also surveyed administrative actions done by schools and universities in the US. These actions are geared towards embracing generative artificial intelligence while providing regulatory frameworks for its use. Likewise, the study also highlights almost the same set of issues articulated in the previously cited study. Finally, it also emphasized that traditional academic writing (such as literary criticism in this case) cannot be replaced by generative artificial intelligence by zeroing in on its lack of originality, creativity, and critical thinking.

Another study by Fang et. al (2024) also dealt with a systematic review of artificial intelligence technologies used for story writing. Among the salient assertions revealed from the findings of the study is the benefits of generative artificial intelligence in producing better stories. In addition, it highlights the notion of AI-human collaboration in relation to story creation. The concept of AI-human collaboration is especially important in this present study considering that it aims to assert that generative artificial intelligence should only be used as an assistive technology. In addition, the concept of AI-human collaboration also highlights the ethical and moral obligations of the authors and literary critics in their use of artificial intelligence. In other words, while generative artificial intelligence could be seen as powerful, it can only be as powerful as its human counterpart. Thus, the ethical and moral standards cannot be set on to the generative artificial intelligence or its applications but to the one opting to use them.

Although the systematic reviews surveyed in the present study are exhaustive, they highlight the important issues that all stakeholders need to consider and factor in in the discourse of generative artificial intelligence. Much has already been studied about its benefits, challenges, drawbacks, or ethical and moral considerations, but there is still a lot more to discover and discuss. Additionally, given the broad range of discussions on generative artificial intelligence, it is important to look into the concept with context in mind (which may differ from institutions to institutions or may depend on the nature of discipline or of type of work).

It is worthy pointing out that, upon exhaustive research, there has been practically none (as of this writing) that dealt with artificial intelligence in the context of literary criticism specifically. Most, if not all studies, are within the greater context of academic writing which, although closely related, may be a little different or broad in relation to the work of literary criticism. In that light, the present study is actually a clear attempt at not only contributing to the ongoing discourse of generative artificial intelligence but also at taking a closer look at the more sophisticated version of academic writing—that is the work of literary criticism.

The schematic presentation of the conceptual framework for this study (which is uploaded separately) outlines the process of generating the required data to answer the different specific questions which are found in the previous section (the Statement of the Problem) of this paper.

The study begins with the premise that, in the advent of generative artificial intelligence, there is a nexus of AI and literary criticism. Thus, it builds on the fact that graduate students of literature (who are engaged in the practice and art of literary criticism in their professional endeavors or in their respective classes) are aware of this nexus. It is important, therefore, to consider their perception(s) on the its role in literary criticism. The study, then, extends its area of concern to the considerations in the use of generative artificial intelligence in literary criticism anchoring on these literature students' perceptions on its role. Likewise, the study also looks into the existing practices of these graduate literature students who are at same time teachers in their respective higher education institutions. Finally, in light of all these, the study ultimately proposes a preliminary framework in understanding how generative artificial intelligence is to be used in context of literary criticism. All these concerns on perceptions, considerations, and practices are the consequential outcomes of an interview, from which codes and themes were obtained and used as findings of the study.

METHODOLOGY

This study follows a qualitative case study approach in order to generate its findings. Priya (2021) articulated that this approach is the most extensively used in qualitative social science research. Creswell, as cited in Priya (2020), elucidated on this approach by saying "that (using this approach) the researcher explores in depth a program, event, activity, process, or one or more individuals." Such assertion by Creswell is the parallel aim of this study—this does not attempt to provide a generalizable data on the generative artificial intelligence's role and considerations in the context of literary criticism, but what it attempts to do is provide an in depth treatment of such in the context of graduate literature majors. Such in depth treatment aims to provide a nuanced understanding of the topic and a baseline data on the same.

This is a limited study considering that there are only five respondents who are graduate literature majors who are doing literary criticism as part of their doctoral requirements or exposure. However, despite this limitation, the approach used allowed for an in-depth analysis of their responses based on the questions posed in this study, thereby giving a more nuanced view on their perceptions on the role and considerations in using generative artificial intelligence in literary criticism. They were chosen because not only are they very much familiar with generative artificial intelligence, but they also imbibe the art and the process of doing literary criticism. In other words, they are adept with the two concepts and their perceived relationship. They were, then, interviewed which ran for two hours and thirty minutes; and their responses were transcribed into a transcript and became the basis of this study. Their responses, revealed through the transcript were qualitatively and thematically coded to obtain the needed data. The coding of the transcript follows the sub-questions presented in the Statement of the Problem section of this paper. The process of transforming the oral or spoken data into a written transcript, the identification of codes, and the provision of themes very much reflect the iterative process of research. This is important, not only because the primary source of data is an interview, but because the study aims to provide an in-depth appreciation of the nexus of literary criticism as a work in relation to generative artificial intelligence. As such, Srivastava and Hopwood (2009) reflected on this process by saying that it (iteration) is not a mechanical task in qualitative data analysis but rather a key to obtaining fresh insight into a phenomena and developing meaning. In addition, this process is also very much involved in meaning-making. In the context of this study, meaning-making is done through the transcript when they used in response to or in the context of the questions attended to in this study.

Ethical oversight was done in the course of this study by means of obtaining consent from the participants, although of legal age already, and by submitting necessary documents to prove that the study would not pose any harm, risk, or vulnerability to the respondents.

The study, aside from the qualitative case study approach, also subscribes to the inductive content analysis especially in its treatment of the transcript obtained from the interviews from the five respondents. According to Kyngäs (2020) such inductive content analysis, as first pointed out, can be applied in various types of documents such as transcripts used in this study. It is also used, according to Kyngäs (2020), "to create concepts, categories, and themes, which can be extended to create models, conceptual structures and conceptual maps that describe the subject under study." Such assertion is concretized in this study in the sense that the themes obtained from the codes from the interview become the bases in proposing a preliminary framework on the use of generative artificial intelligence within the specified context of literary criticism.

Both the case study approach and the inductive content analysis prove to be complementary in this context as they allow the researcher to flesh out relevant data in the form of codes transformed into themes. Such themes are then inductively used to propose a preliminary framework on the study or the topic.

RESULTS AND DISCUSSION

Theme # 1 on Perception and Role: Generative Artificial Intelligence as Assistive Technology

These respondents underscored the fact that generative artificial intelligence is here to stay, and that it would be moving backwards if this would not be used to one's advantage. However, they were explicit to say that generative artificial intelligence, in so far as literary criticism is concerned, only functions as an assistive technology aimed at allowing the critic to easily generate the needed references or resources in order to do the literary criticism. They further went on to say that generative artificial intelligence does not in any way replace the critic in the art and process of literary criticism. Some of the respondents' answers taken from the transcript are reproduced below:

Respondent # 1: "Ah, AI cannot do literary criticism as we know it. Maybe the critic can just ask AI to help him locate necessary references for the criticism of the work."

Respondent # 2 (as an addendum to the response of Respondent # 1): "I agree with the locating of necessary references. Also, maybe AI can produce an analysis of a work especially if it is prominent, say, a poem from a Western author. But the analysis could just probably be superficial. Although this analysis can help the critic frame his own literary criticism; but it cannot replace him."

Respondent # 1: "But we have to define assistive technology in this case. How exactly can AI serve as an assistive technology?"

In relation to this perception that artificial intelligence such as ChatGPT should be used as assistive technology, a study done by Khalifa and Albadawy (2024) titled Use of Artificial Intelligence in Academic Writing: An Essential Productivity Tool articulated several domains in which this notion of assistive technology is concretized. These domains are as follows: facilitating idea generation and research design, 2) improving content and structuring, 3) supporting literature review and synthesis, 4) enhancing data management and analysis, 5) supporting editing, review, and publishing, and 6) assisting in communication, outreach, and ethical compliance. Likewise, the study of Imran and Almusharraf (2023) also pointed to the assertion that generative artificial intelligence such as chatbots in general and Chat GPT in general should function only as a writing assistant as it has been agreed that these applications cannot be authors, or by extension, literary critics. They outlined how these applications can serve as writing assistants similar to that of the study of Khalifa and Albadawy (2024). These are as follows: increased language proficiency, idea generation, language translation, more accurate content, improved collaboration.

Although these enumerations aim to define the notions of assistive technology and ChatGPT as writing assistants, they are not constrained or specific to literary criticism alone and tend to be quite broad. The greater call, though, is to define these concepts in relation to literary criticism banking on these same enumerations as ready and plausible reference.

Theme # 2 on Considerations: Literary Criticism as a Human Act

Anchoring on the notion of literary criticism as the appraisal of a text based on literary merit, the respondents were consistent in saying that while it is technically possible to reduce such work to artificial intelligence, what it (AI) can only produce is an ostensible *criticism* of a work since it is only limited in terms of what references it has been fed. They went on to say that it cannot capture the nuances of a critic's interpretation borne out of his context and experiences. They called this as literary criticism as a human act by pointing out that each critic is unique (in terms of the angle he looks at the work, the kind of theory he is going to apply, and the kind of appreciation he will offer to the readers in relation to the work) and that his appraisal of a work is uniquely his own. As a way to supplement this, some lines from the transcript are taken and reproduced below:

Respondent # 5: "We have to remember that literary criticism is a field of art in itself. As mentioned earlier, while it can be capable of producing an analysis, it does not capture the human factor of doing criticism."

Respondent # 1: "In fact, at this point, we even have to consider if what artificial intelligence does is indeed a criticism? Or is it a mere analysis? We have to draw the line between these terms because I think they do not mean the same."

Respondent # 3: "If ever we rely on what AI has generated, would it be more impersonal? Knowing, again, the context of doing literary criticism."

Respondent # 4: "I agree. It is important to establish that literary criticism is a personal endeavor. It is considered to be a discourse between the critic and the text. Such discourse warrants that it (literary criticism) is a nuanced activity that might be distinct from critic to critic. Experience, context, and, perhaps, the point of view or angle would shape the difference of the criticism. These are not captured by AI, of course."

Literary criticism as a human act is borne out of the nature of literary criticism. Crews (2024), in Britannica, defines it as reasoned consideration of literary works and issues. It is important to point out the word *reasoned* in the definition as it implies the concept of subjectivity which is only present and an inherent capacity of human critics. This is what sets literary critics apart from AI-construed critics as the latter might distort the nuanced nature of *reasoned consideration*. As what has been repeated many times in this paper already, such notion of subjectivity implied from reasoned consideration is the consequential outcome of the critic's experience and context. That is why, in the first theme on assistive technology, it is implied that while there are domains (within literary criticism) that generative artificial intelligence can help, it cannot, as of now and without prejudice to future prospects on the same, replace yet the inherent capacity of human critics, thereby proving that literary criticism as an activity is a human act.

Crews (2024) continues by saying that literary criticism or otherwise known as practical criticism is the interpretation of meaning and judgment of quality. Sustaining the assertion in the previous paragraphs, words such as interpretation, meaning, judgment, and quality are highly subjective which can be near-sightedly captured by generative artificial intelligence. It is worthy to mention at this point that, in philosophy, the concept of interpretation is very much tied with hermeneutics and one tenet of the study of hermeneutics is the fact that there is no one singular interpretation (as in this case of a work); such singularity emanates from the its person-bound subjectivity (as explicitly mentioned in the previous paragraphs).

Theme # 3 on Considerations: Ethical Limits of Generative Artificial Intelligence in Literary Criticism

All five respondents also consistently mentioned the ethical limits of generative artificial intelligence in the work of literary criticism. Underscoring their previous assertion that literary criticism is a human act and generative artificial intelligence should only function as assistive technology, they also pointed to the fact that there should be a framework on the responsible and ethical use of generative artificial intelligence specifically in the context of literary criticism. While they mentioned that there has not been any framework relative to such in their individual universities as it tends to be treated quite generally or broadly, they mentioned that the role of generative artificial intelligence should be clearly defined, balancing it as an assistive technology on the one hand and the very human act of literary criticism.

The lines below are taken from the transcript of the interview with the participants of the study:

Respondent # 2: "Aside from the human factor involved in literary criticism, ethical considerations, as you mentioned, are pivotal in the discourse. We cannot move backward by not allowing artificial intelligence, but again, it has to function only within the bounds of it being an assistive technology."

Respondent # 1: "I agree. Ethical issues like plagiarism, copyright, and authorship would be a tricky path to tread given this. Therefore, it is not only impersonal, as mentioned, but also quite unethical."

Respondent # 2: "Ah, perhaps, there has to be a declaration of AI use and the extent it was used if ever. In the work of that critic for accountability and transparency and consistent on what we said that AI can only function as assistive technology. It is only through that declaration can we determine and define assistive technology specific to that work."

Respondent # 4: "It is also for the HEIs (higher education institutions) or governmental intellectual or regulatory agencies to define the use of artificial intelligence not only in literary criticism but in all work of literature. There is no one-size-fits-all solution on how these issues should be dealt but rather a one-to-one correspondence based on the, perhaps, general ethical guidelines by a governmental agency or the specific guidelines as articulated by specific

HEIs. We cannot, I think, have a blanket or a very broad appreciation on how these guidelines are set and these might be dependent on context."

Respondent # 3: "I also think of representation in literary criticism. I think if the work or works are Western, then AI may produce a superficial criticism or appraisal of that work; but what about those works written by underrated or regionalized writers who may not be as prominent as say, for example, Robert Frost?

It is important to point out that, while generative artificial intelligence has benefits particularly within the greater context of academic writing (not only in literary criticism), it has also posed some issues pertaining to its ethical, prudent, and responsible use. As mentioned at the beginning of this paper, generative artificial intelligence has drastically changed our academic landscape and (whether fortunately or otherwise) it is here to stay. As pointed out by one of respondents, it is impossible to blindly ban the use of generative artificial intelligence as it, according to his assertion, would be moving backwards. Therefore, as the aim of this paper, it is significant to discuss and contribute to the ongoing debates on its ethical issues.

Among the salient issues raised not only by the respondents of this study but also in recent literatures is the concept of authorship. According to Stokel-Walker (2022) and Thorp (2023), the academic community has already had a consensus that generative artificial intelligence cannot be used as a co-author. They further went on to say that what is accepted though is artificial intelligence applications acting as helpers or assistants (this was discussed also in the previous paragraphs). Generative artificial intelligence, such as ChatGPT, cannot be considered as an author as they pointed out that it even makes mistakes by creating sources or references that do not exist. It, according to them, even apologized for it. Such limitation is the reason why it cannot be considered as an author and that emphasizes the human element of academic writing in general and, as in this case, literary criticism in particular.

These studies by Stokel-Walker (2022) and Thorp (2023) are sustained by Woudenberg, Ranalli, and Bracker in 2024. In their study titled Authorship and ChatGPT: A Conservative View, they used a certain framework to determine the generative artificial intelligence's capacity of becoming an author. Their results yielded otherwise. They, instead, extended their view by saying that artificial intelligence applications, such as Chat GPT, cannot function as authors because they do meet the criteria which are: the ability to perform illocutionary acts, lack of mental states, and the lack of responsibility on the texts it produces. The criteria on mental states and the responsibility on the texts AI produces are important in the current discourse of literary criticism as this work relies heavily on the mixture not only of knowledge of the critic but also of his/her beliefs and intention in relation to the work (which makes the work of criticism deeply personal). Aside from that, as an extension to the point mentioned, unlike literary critics who are responsible of their work (because again it is a product of their knowledge, beliefs, and intentions), ChatGPT cannot be faulted for the mistakes or mishaps it produces which could be considered as impersonal and deviates from the previous assertion of criticism as a personal work.

Another related issue raised by the respondents is the issue of bias. It is important to point out the generative artificial intelligence such as ChatGPT, being a large language model (LLM), obtains its supposed knowledge of things based on the users that feed it; however, there is one striking issue of bias—particularly in the context of literary criticism. As pointed out, it can produce an impersonal criticism of a popular work; but the concern on underrated or understudied authors from, say for example, the Global South point to bias.

The study of Hunkele and Smith (2024) discusses that fact that generative artificial intelligence, indeed, produces bias. Their results found that biases such as in gender, race, age, and physical abilities raise concerns in terms of how inclusive generative artificial intelligence is. This is significant in the present study because a work (particularly those written by understudied and regionalized authors/critics) may be unfairly and biasedly appraised by these generative artificial intelligence applications as these biases on gender, race, age, and physical abilities may be present in the work. This, again, points to the fact that literary criticism, much or more than academic writing, is a human act. Its subjectivity in interpretation warrants the context not only of the literary critic himself or herself but also, more importantly and rather equally, of the work subject to criticism itself.

Theme # 4 on Practices in Relation to the Use of Generative Artificial Intelligence in the Context of Submissions on Literary Criticism

The five respondents also shared their personal practices as well as the existing practices done by their respective universities in relation to the use of generative artificial intelligence in the context of submissions on literary criticism. There is a consensus that there are no uniform guidelines yet this case (thus, proving the need for this study); however, they have adopted some practices that their respective universities mandate as well as their personal practices as teachers who require their students to do literary criticism in their respective subjects. The enumeration below summarizes some of the practices that they have made or adopted in their respective cases:

Practice # 1: Use of Generative Artificial Intelligence Detectors

Respondent # 4 and # 3 mentioned that, in their respective contexts, they require students to subject their literary criticism outputs to generative artificial intelligence detectors available in the internet. They include the results of these generative artificial intelligence detectors as part of their submissions. Although, this is not mandated by their respective ethics office. They also pointed out that this practice promotes a sense of accountability and transparency on the side of the students doing the work of literary criticism. They also said that they acknowledge the limitation of this practice as there are also available applications that mark certain work as AI-generated when it is not. Some lines from the respondents are taken below:

Respondent # 4: "In my case, I ask my students to include in their submission a result from generative AI detectors to ensure that there is no use or minimal use of AI in their work. I don't do the feeding of their work to AI detector applications myself because I want to highlight accountability and transparency as they themselves feed their work to these applications."

Respondent # 3: "Same here. I make it as part of their submission; though, I know the application has limitations also, but at least there is an action through this that promote responsible use of artificial intelligence. But really imperfect."

In light of this, the study by Elkhatat, Elsaid, and Almeer (2022) dealt with the efficacy of certain generative artificial intelligence applications in detecting and differentiating AI-generated and human-generated texts. The findings of the study revealed that while they were able to identify accurately texts generated by AI (by themselves ironically), they presented some inconsistencies as well. The study ended by highlighting the need for refinements in these artificial intelligence detection tools. The study cited proves the utility of AI detection tools as way to mitigate excessive and irresponsible use of artificial intelligence in academic content such as literary criticism; however, instructors must be aware that they, too, have inconsistencies. Thus, it is important for them to triangulate results from varied artificial intelligence applications and be prudent in judging if the work has extensively used AI. In that regard, that is why AI regulation must not only end in AI detection results but also of accountability sheets for students to declare their use (and extent of use) of artificial intelligence.

Practice # 2: Provision of Accountability Sheets on Artificial Intelligence Use

Respondents # 2 mentioned that, in his context, he uses accountability sheets that seek to declare the use of artificial intelligence in the work. He mentioned that this also promotes accountability and transparency. He mentioned that this is also his personal practice and is not mandated by the university he is currently affiliated with. Additionally, he also acknowledges that accountability sheets must be present in all submissions not only with respect to literary criticism.

He pointed that this could be one good step towards responsible use of artificial intelligence in the context of the academe. In fact, he explicitly said that such provision concretizes the word responsible in the "responsible use". The assertion of Respondent # 2 is reproduced below for reference:

Respondent # 2: "I have what I call as accountability sheet where I ask my students to declare and identify in writing the use of AI in their work. It's a personal practice though which I hope we can adopt as a university. I like it and feel like it's effective because it promotes students' agency. My view is that we cannot always be policing at their work. We allow our students to be accountable with their work and trust them for it."

He further added that the use of accountability sheets is a double-edged sword. Not only does it allow students to be accountable for their work, but this also becomes a binding document that, in case breached, might have an effect on their work.

The provision of accountability sheets is also echoed in the academic community. In the study by Tang, et. al (2024) titled The Importance of Transparency: Declaring AI Use in Academic Writing, they asserted that there is now a growing consensus among reputable journal publishers to declare the use of generative artificial intelligence in the manuscripts that author submit for consideration or for publication. This is, according to the study, intended for transparency. In the same vein, the study pointed to the fact that such declaration actually comes from two interrelated perspectives: 1) the tendency for generative artificial intelligence to make up sources (which is otherwise called as AI hallucination; and 2) potential bias in training data especially that these generative intelligence applications rely on the data sets which may contain data. As such, the provision of declaration for artificial intelligence use is warranted. Although, it must be pointed out that the position of the present study is that the declaration should not only disclose the use but, rather equally, the extent of which it was used in the work.

Although, based on the study cited, there has already been a growing consensus and demand from authors to declare their use of generative artificial intelligence in their submissions for publication, it is important to realize as well that, even with such requirement, there is still also non-compliance of such declaration. In the study by Gonzalves (2024) on addressing non-compliance of AI use declarations and its implications for academic integrity and assessment in higher education, he explored the perception and factors on the non-compliance of AI use declarations among students. In terms of perception, the non-compliance of students stemmed from the intimidating and ununiform declarations provided by instructors which led to confusion and uncertainty. Among the factors the study was able to draw out were the following: fear of academic consequences, ambiguity and lack of clear guidelines, belief that AI use should remain private, perceived influence and competition, inconsistency in enforcement.

These findings by Gonzalves (2024) point to the fact that while declaration on generative artificial intelligence use is a good step towards promoting accountability not only within the context of literary criticism but also in all works involved in the academe, it is significant to make sure that guidelines and enforcement on these declarations must not only be clear to all stakeholders but, more importantly, contextualized responsive to the values, needs, and existing regulations peculiar to each higher education institutions (HEIs). By extension, it would be equally beneficial if governmental agencies and other regulatory bodies concerned on this issue would provide a baseline as to how these declarations must be processed and dealt with.

Additionally, as an offshoot to the previous study, the study of Hosseini, Resnik, and Holmes (2023) provides a clearer set of guidelines to concretize how declarations or disclosures of generative artificial intelligence use should be done which other stakeholders and related institutions can consider as benchmark. They mentioned that there must be declaration and disclosure of generative artificial intelligence use in the introductions and methods section. This should be done by providing the prompts used, in case, and noting which parts of these sections are affected. Likewise, authors have to provide in-text citations and bibliographical entries and other references to recognize their used applications. Finally, they must submit their relevant interactions with the large language models (LLMs) as supplementary materials appended in their manuscripts. Although this format of declaration may not be generally applicable in the context of literary criticism as its nature is different and more nuanced, this could be a good reference to tailor fit a clearer and a more unified operationalization of declaration.

Then, again, despite all these provisions, much of the work relies on the authors/literary critics themselves. While clear guidelines are absent (but they are easier to craft), it is really up to these authors and critics to declare in whatever way (in the absence of a more cohesive set of guidelines in their respective universities or institutions) their use and the intention of using generative artificial intelligence. More than an operational issue, it is an issue of character (in the spirit of integrity, transparency, and accountability).

Practice # 3: Consistent Instructor's Feedback

All of the respondents also agreed that, in order to promote responsible use of artificial intelligence when they require literary criticism submissions from their respective students as final requirement, consistent feedback must be given. This practice also promotes accountability to the side of the teachers so that they, too, can touch base on the content of the literary criticism output. This will also allow them to know the writing styles of their students in a way that they will be able to determine (albeit informally) if, in case, artificial intelligence would be maliciously and irresponsibly used in the work. They, too, mentioned that, without clear and consistent feedback from the teacher, students would be tempted to reduce the work of literary criticism to generative artificial intelligence. Some specific lines from Respondent # 5 are present below:

Respondent # 5: *I think, when viewing artificial intelligence not only in literary criticism, we, as teachers, also have to be accountable. It cannot just be the case where we place the burden on the 'use' of AI to students only; so I think it's important that we can provide consistent feedback on the work of the students. That way we will know their writing styles and touch base with them with their work. In any case, we are not blind receivers of their work—in other words, we have journeyed with them from conceptualization to submission, thereby reducing irresponsible use of AI. Although, admittedly, this is easier said than done.*

In relation to this, the study of Fleckenstein et. al (2024) noted that, although previous studies have pointed to teachers having difficulty in detecting the use of generative artificial intelligence in students' work, it found out that more experienced teachers tended to produce more accurate and differentiated judgements on the work. Therefore, it is really important that teachers are on-board to the writing tasks of the students even prior to submission so that, again as mentioned by the respondents, irresponsible use of generative artificial intelligence would be mitigated or prevented. Although it should not be the teachers' sole burden to detect the use of artificial intelligence in the work but they should also be trained how to detect such presence or use of generative artificial intelligence. This, as an offshoot, would also point to how the emergence of generative artificial intelligence should be included in teachers' professional development.

Practice # 4: Provision of Other Experts' Feedback

Respondent # 1 mentioned that, in her context, she also asks for other experts' feedback on the literary criticism submission of her students. She pointed out that it is important because, while accountability sheets and generative artificial intelligence detectors act as gateway pre-requisite to promote responsible use of generative artificial intelligence, it allows for a broader perspective on the entirety of the paper (including whether or not artificial intelligence is used and its extent of use). As articulated, other experts' feedback is useful as it validates the work done by the instructors (the respondents of this study); and any possible misuse on artificial intelligence would be flagged in this process. Her assertion is reproduced below:

Respondent # 1: 'I agree with the previous assertion of Respondent # 5. We should not place the burden on AI use on to the students. We need also to exhaust effort to be accountable with it. So, aside from our own feedback, we also consider other experts' feedback for broader perspective. Their feedback will also be able to flag possible misuse on artificial intelligence, among other things such as the content and method which are equally important."

The importance of feedback has already been pointed out by Fleckenstein et. al (2024); although, admittedly, there are some challenges teachers face when detecting the presence or the use of generative artificial intelligence. However, it is important to point out that feedback can also be sought from other experts in the field or, as in this case, other literary critics (during paper presentations or prior to submission) who may also be able to judge the work particularly in terms of the use of generative artificial intelligence. The adage *two pair of eyes are better than one* proves significant in the discourse of the concept of feedback.

Practice # 5: Provision for Reporting on Any Misuse of Generative Artificial Intelligence

All respondents noted that their respective universities, through their Ethics Committee, allow for reporting on any possible misuse of generative artificial intelligence in the course of writing of the paper (whether a literary criticism paper or a research). They articulated that this provision is important as this points to the clear process of handling issues in relation to generative artificial intelligence (including plagiarism).

Respondent # 5: "In our university, we have an ethics committee which is responsible for handling issues on misuse or abuse of generative artificial intelligence aside from detecting plagiarism issues. The presence of an ethics committee highlights the effort also of our university to really promote responsible use of AI not only in works of literary criticism but also of all other related works. Aside from promotion, it is also the one responsible for crafting guidelines on how AI should be used in our university."

The study by Bouhouita-Guermech, Gogognon, and Bélisle-Pipon outlines the challenges posed by the emergence of generative artificial intelligence for research ethics boards (REBs). The findings revealed that research ethics boards (REBs) are not yet adequately equipped to deal with generative artificial intelligence. This inadequacy is borne out of the fact that there is a lack of clear and normative guidelines on how REBs should operate in light of this. In that regard, again, clear guidelines must first be crafted to operationalize not only the responsible use of artificial intelligence and the role of research ethics boards (REBs) in this regard.

While research ethics boards (REBs) are inadequately equipped to deal with artificial intelligence, Blackman (2022), in his article in the Harvard Business Review, asserted that there should be an AI Ethics Committee to comprehensively and systematically and help mitigate the ethical risks posed by generative artificial intelligence. Whether this AI ethics committee should be separate from research ethics boards or a division of it remains a venue for a more thorough discussion.

These practices provide a baseline for other stakeholders (academic organizations, higher education institutions) to benchmark on. Although these practices are quite general in nature, they provide some sort of validation that there are already existing practices that have been adopted in light of the presence of generative artificial intelligence either in the context of literary criticism in particular or in the broader research process in general. These practices may be, more or less, similar to the others, but, as explained, the study does not impose that these practices are to be rigidly followed. What the study provides is a brief survey of these practices to allow other stakeholders to reflect on their own practices as well. They are, it should be emphasized, encouraged and at the liberty to craft their own uniform practices and refine them based on their contexts and based on their institutional mandates or regulations. It is, again, important to reiterate that these practices were only based from five graduate students who have experience in tertiary education, in general, and literary criticism in particular.

Proposed Framework on the Use of Generative Artificial Intelligence in Literary Criticism

Figure 2. Structure of the study.

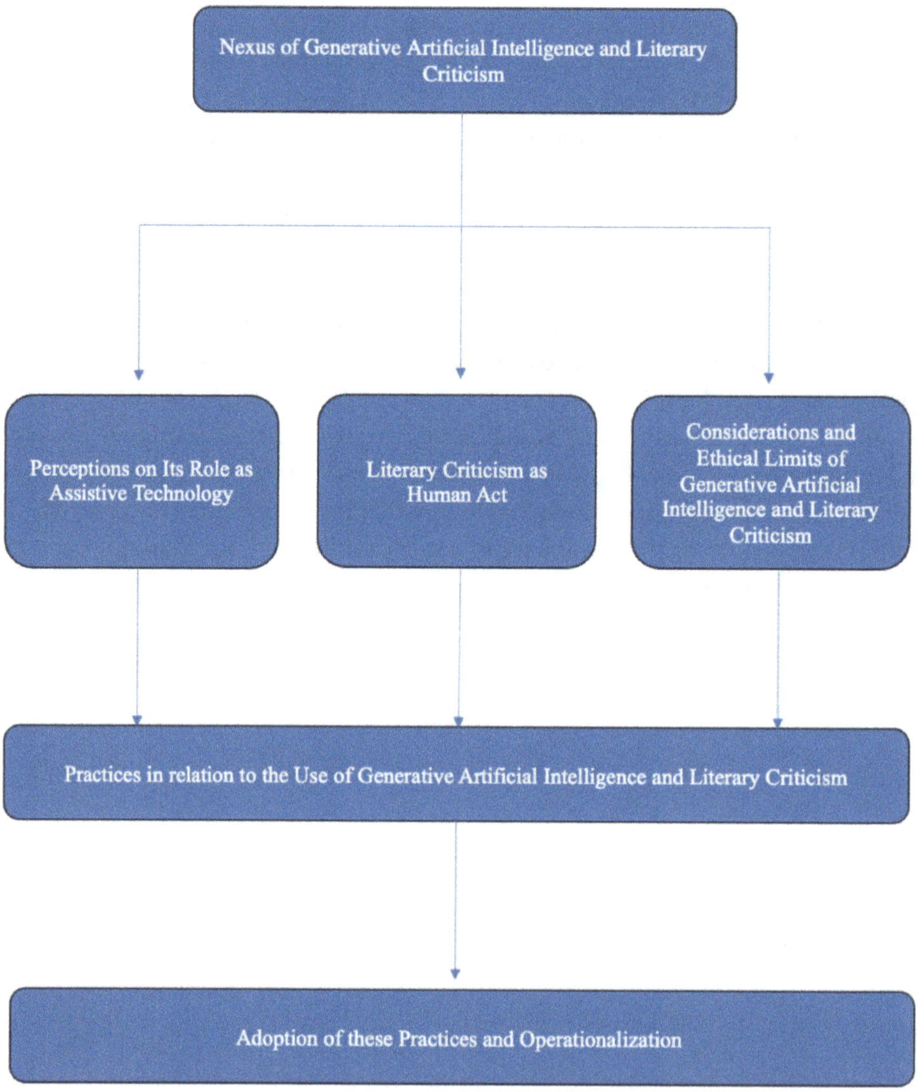

The diagram (which is uploaded separately) shows the proposed framework based on the thematic responses provided by the respondents of the present study. The word proposed is used to mark flexibility when stakeholders, such as Higher

Education Institutions (HEIs), adapt this framework as part, for example, of their research ethics guidelines especially in the conduct of literary research/humanities research in general or literary criticism in general. It begins with the premise that generative artificial intelligence operates as assistive technology only. Assistive technology, when defined, refers to how critics or authors in general use artificial intelligence to generate initial ideas, gather authentic references, and compare analyses between other authors in relation to the work(s) used as subject to literary criticism. However, as a limitation to this study, there is no exhaustive or thorough discussion of how this generative artificial intelligence can be used as assistive technology in literary criticism. It is therefore to be noted that this is only a baseline premise and those who would like to adopt this framework are given the liberty to define and regulate this concept of generative artificial intelligence as assistive technology.

Given this premise, as articulated above, literary criticism, in the context of the present study, is considered to be a human act. That is why generative artificial intelligence, while able to do the criticism itself, should be considered as a literary critic. It may produce standard or long-standing analysis of certain works given the appropriate prompts; but it does not and it cannot replace the work of critic himself/herself. The human act in literary criticism lies very much on the nuanced interpretation of the critic which is subjective. Such subjectivity in interpretation is warranted, though, because it is borne out of the critic's experiences and context. This was emphasized during the interview of the respondents who said that these concepts of experiences and context differ from author to author or critic to critic, and such difference merits the fact that the criticism of one critic may differ from the other. These aspects have not yet been captured by generative artificial intelligence just yet. Whether this difference on interpretation will be captured by generative artificial intelligence soon when it gets enough data from the pool of its users is an interesting and a very plausible scenario that can be subjected to another study later on.

It is also important to include in the discourse, in so far as the consideration of literary criticism as a human act is concerned, is the fact that literary criticism is tied with the concept of hermeneutics or the art of interpretation. Therefore, interpretation or hermeneutics is a deeply personal endeavor undertaken by the critic/author. In fact, it does not concern itself with the interpretation alone, but most importantly the process that led to the interpretation (and by process, there is emphasis on the one doing the interpretation or the hermeneutics). In other words, hermeneutics, when taken as a field of philosophy, asserts that interpretation is a product of context, lived experiences. As such, it is not expected that there is a singular interpretation of, for example, a work. These realities are not captured by generative artificial intelligence and such limitation is warranted.

The fact that this study establishes that literary criticism is a human act is significant as this is an offshoot alongside to defining clearly and carefully the ethical limits of the use of generative artificial intelligence in the work of literary criticism. Defining these ethical limits means that, aside from articulating how exactly generative artificial intelligence functions as assistive technology, clear regulations on the extent of its use must be present. Those who opt to adapt this framework are premised on two things: that generative artificial intelligence functions as assistive technology only and that literary criticism is a human act. These premises should be their anchor or guide as they craft the ethical limitations of artificial intelligence in literary criticism. It must be underscored that generative artificial intelligence is here to stay; and that it would be us moving backward if we unilaterally or very broadly ban the use of generative artificial intelligence, but it is the concern of various stakeholders to limit, regulate, define what constitutes it and the extent of its use. That should be the way to move forward: towards a more responsible and prudent use of generative artificial intelligence in the process and the art of literary criticism.

Being able to define these ethical limits will also warrant the adoption of practices that are agreed upon and dictated by context and the needs of a particular higher education institution, for example, adopting this study or framework. Although the study gives three practices obtained from the personal perspectives of these five respondents, it is important the such adoption of practices be based on the varying context of the one adopting this framework. This study does not, in any way, impose that these practices be followed as this serves only as a baseline data, but it invites the different stakeholders to clearly identify these practices in relation to the use of generative artificial intelligence in the context of literary criticism in particular and in the broader sense of the academe in general.

Finally, the framework ends with the operationalization of these concepts and adoption of practices that are mutually-agreed upon, keeping in mind the notion of flexibility brought about by the different contexts and needs of the stakeholders such as those in the academe or those who are practicing in the field. These contexts and needs must be factored in so as to produce a more context-sensitive and tailored-fit operationalization (e.g in the form of guidelines, checklists, and regulations) of this framework.

An offshoot to this proposed framework is the guidelines set by the University of the Philippines Open University (UPOU), one of the constituent universities of the University of Philippines. In their released guidelines, they underscored that fact that, in the advent of technology, there is a convergence between artificial intelligence and the academe as the former transforms the current educational landscape not only of the country but also all over the world. Their guidelines are focused on both teachers and students, offering a nuanced interpretation of prudent and responsible use of generative artificial intelligence. Such provision of guidelines provide a helpful reference for other higher education institutions (HEIs) and other related institutions to craft their own. By reflection, the invitation now is to not blindly and mindlessly ban the use of generative artificial intelligence but rather embrace it with prudence and responsibility. In addition, the University of the Philippines (UP), as the premier state university of the country, also has an existing document titled University of the Philippines Principles for Responsible and Trustworthy Artificial Intelligence. Just like the guidelines set by UPOU, this document provides a blueprint and a template for all other institutions to anchor on. However, they must note that these frameworks and documents can only be operationalized based on their distinct contexts.

CONCLUSION

The study explores the perception of five graduate literature students on the role of generative artificial intelligence in the process and art of literary criticism. Three major themes emerged based on the transcript obtained from the interview. These three major themes are as follows: Generative Artificial Intelligence as Assistive Technology, Literary Criticism as a Human Act, Ethical Limits of Generative Artificial Intelligence in Literary Criticism. These themes became the bases also the proposed framework on the use of generative artificial intelligence in literary criticism as a preliminary contribution of this work to the on-going discourse/debate on the matter. While limited, these themes provide a baseline to the on-going discourse on the role of generative artificial intelligence in the work of literary criticism.

Policy Recommendations

Based on the results of the study, the following policy recommendations are made:

1. It is important to define clearly and carefully what constitutes and limits the use of generative artificial intelligence in the enterprise of literary criticism, specifying the extent of AI functioning as an assistive technology as the study only points to this fact (AI as assistive technology) but does not give a clear set of guidelines on how this should operate. Although, in the study, there are domains cited from an existing study. However, these domains are broad and not specific to literary criticism alone. As such, there is a greater need to make this as a benchmark to come up with a definition of assistive technology within the parameters of literature, literary criticism, or literary studies.

2. As an offshoot to the first policy recommendation, notwithstanding how assistive technology is defined, it is important that there is a declaration of the use of artificial intelligence in the context of literary criticism, and by extension the other aspects of literature, and the extent of its use for accountability and transparency. As the study suggests, it is through such declaration can assistive technology be defined.
3. While this study can serve as a rough benchmark on the discourse of generative artificial intelligence and literary criticism particularly the preliminary framework it puts forward, there should be an operationalization of these framework based on the context of higher education institution (HEI) for example or based on mandated governmental/intellectual regulations.
4. The framework proposed in this study should be considered in its roughest sense. In other words, this is not set in stone or is deemed exhaustive. Therefore, policymakers or higher education institutions (HEIs) opting to adapt the framework, may at their liberty and depending on their context, refine this work that would best suit their needs.

Recommendations for Further Studies

The results of this study can be used as an anchor to work on further researches in this regard and other related layers of literature which are as follows:

1. The present study focuses on the in-depth analysis of the responses of five graduate literature majors based on their perception on the role and consideration in the use of generative artificial intelligence to literary criticism. This is an acknowledged limitation; thus, it is important to increase the number of respondents to be able to get a more conclusive view of the topic coming from varied perspectives.
2. The increase in the number of respondents mean that these respondents should come from various contexts: (1) undergraduate and graduate teachers, professors in the academe, (2) teachers who, at the same time, are graduate students, (3) practitioners such as those who have written and been awarded extensively for their work, and (4) administrators from higher education institutions for policy recommendations and changes. The increase in the number of respondents and the diversity it offers will bring a nuanced appreciation of the nexus between literary criticism and generative artificial intelligence.
3. As this study is limited in relation to the role, considerations, and perceptions regarding generative artificial intelligence in the context of literary criticism—the appraisal of a work, it is also important to look into other aspects of literature (for example, production and evaluation of literary work such as stories, novels,

poems) and how generative artificial intelligence also influences and shapes these layers of literature. Interrelated frameworks can also be proposed in relation to these layers of literature.

REFERENCES

Aljuaid, H. (2024). The Impact of Artificial intelligence Tools on academic writing instruction in Higher Education: A Systematic review. *Arab World English Journal, 1*(1), 26–55. DOI: 10.24093/awej/ChatGPT.2

Blackman, R. (2022, June 21). *Why you need an AI ethics committee*. Harvard Business Review. https://hbr.org/2022/07/why-you-need-an-ai-ethics-committee

Bouhouita-Guermech, S., Gogognon, P., & Bélisle-Pipon, J. (2023). Specific challenges posed by artificial intelligence in research ethics. *Frontiers in Artificial Intelligence, 6*, 1149082. Advance online publication. DOI: 10.3389/frai.2023.1149082 PMID: 37483869

Crews, F. C. (2024, November 25). *Literary criticism | Definition, Theories, Types, Examples, & Facts*. Encyclopedia Britannica. https://www.britannica.com/art/literary-criticism

Elkhatat, A. M., Elsaid, K., & Almeer, S. (2023). Evaluating the efficacy of AI content detection tools in differentiating between human and AI-generated text. *International Journal for Educational Integrity, 19*(1), 17. Advance online publication. DOI: 10.1007/s40979-023-00140-5

Fang, X., Ng, D. T. K., Leung, J. K. L., & Chu, S. K. W. (2023). A systematic review of artificial intelligence technologies used for story writing. *Education and Information Technologies, 28*(11), 14361–14397. DOI: 10.1007/s10639-023-11741-5

Fleckenstein, J., Meyer, J., Jansen, T., Keller, S. D., Köller, O., & Möller, J. (2024). Do teachers spot AI? Evaluating the detectability of AI-generated texts among student essays. *Computers and Education Artificial Intelligence, 6*, 100209. DOI: 10.1016/j.caeai.2024.100209

Gonsalves, C. (2024). Addressing student non-compliance in AI use declarations: Implications for academic integrity and assessment in higher education. *Assessment & Evaluation in Higher Education*, •••, 1–15. DOI: 10.1080/02602938.2024.2415654

Hosseini, M., Resnik, D. B., & Holmes, K. (2023). The ethics of disclosing the use of artificial intelligence tools in writing scholarly manuscripts. *Research Ethics, 19*(4), 449–465. DOI: 10.1177/17470161231180449 PMID: 39749232

Hunkele, C., & Smith, V. (2024). An analysis of the accuracy and bias of a generative ai model. *International Journal of Advanced Research, 12*(04), 989–1019. DOI: 10.21474/IJAR01/18640

Imran, M., & Almusharraf, N. (2023). Analyzing the role of ChatGPT as a writing assistant at higher education level: A systematic review of the literature. *Contemporary Educational Technology, 15*(4), ep464. DOI: 10.30935/cedtech/13605

Jebaselvi, C. E., Mohanraj, K., & Anitha, T. (2024). The rise of AI in English language and literature. *Shanlax International Journal of English, 12*(2), 53–58. DOI: 10.34293/english.v12i2.7216

Khalifa, M., & Albadawy, M. (2024). Using artificial intelligence in academic writing and research: An essential productivity tool. *Computer Methods and Programs in Biomedicine Update, 5*, 100145. DOI: 10.1016/j.cmpbup.2024.100145

Kharispublishing (2023, December 19). Exploring the Impact of AI on Literature - Kharis Publishing. *Kharis Publishing - Inspirational Book Publisher.* https://kharispublishing.com/kp/exploring-the-impact-of-ai-on-literature/

Kyngäs, H., Mikkonen, K., & Kääriäinen, M. (Eds.). (2020). *The Application of Content Analysis in Nursing Science Research.*, DOI: 10.1007/978-3-030-30199-6

Martínez-Olmo, F., & Catalán, F. G. (2024). Revisión sistemática de tendencias en la aplicación de la inteli-gencia artificial al ámbito de la escritura académica en las ciencias sociales. *Digital Education Review, 45*(45), 37–42. DOI: 10.1344/der.2024.45.37-42

Premkumar, B. (2024). The Impact of artificial intelligence on literary creation and criticism: Emerging trends and implications. *International Journal of Language Literature and Culture, 1*(1), 37–41. Advance online publication. DOI: 10.22161/ijllc.4.4.5

Priya, A. (2020). Case study Methodology of Qualitative Research: Key attributes and navigating the conundrums in its application. *Sociological Bulletin, 70*(1), 94–110. DOI: 10.1177/0038022920970318

Srivastava, P., & Hopwood, N. (2009). A practical iterative framework for qualitative data analysis. *International Journal of Qualitative Methods, 8*(1), 76–84. DOI: 10.1177/160940690900800107

Stokel-Walker, C. (2022). AI bot ChatGPT writes smart essays — Should professors worry? *Nature.* Advance online publication. DOI: 10.1038/d41586-022-04397-7 PMID: 36494443

Tang, A., Li, K., Kwok, K. O., Cao, L., Luong, S., & Tam, W. (2023). The importance of transparency: Declaring the use of generative artificial intelligence (AI) in academic writing. *Journal of Nursing Scholarship, 56*(2), 314–318. DOI: 10.1111/jnu.12938 PMID: 37904646

Thorp, H. H. (2023). ChatGPT is fun, but not an author. *Science*, *379*(6630), 313. DOI: 10.1126/science.adg7879 PMID: 36701446

University of the Philippines Principles for Responsible and Trustworthy Artificial Intelligence. (2023, November 10). University of the Philippines. https://up.edu.ph/up-principles-for-responsible-artificial-intelligence/

UPOU releases Guidelines on AI Use for Teaching and Learning - University of the Philippines Open University. (2024, January 19). University of the Philippines Open University. https://www.upou.edu.ph/news/upou-releases-guidelines-on-ai-use-for-teaching-and-learning/

Van Woudenberg, R., Ranalli, C., & Bracker, D. (2024). Authorship and ChatGPT: A Conservative View. *Philosophy & Technology*, *37*(1), 34. Advance online publication. DOI: 10.1007/s13347-024-00715-1 PMID: 38419827

Compilation of References

Abdelgadir Mohamed, Y., Mohamed, A. H. H. M., Khanan, A., Bashir, M., Adiel, M. A. E., & Elsadig, M. A. (2024). Navigating the ethical terrain of AI-generated text tools: A review. *IEEE Access : Practical Innovations, Open Solutions*, *12*, 197061–197120. DOI: 10.1109/ACCESS.2024.3521945

Abdul Manaf, A. A., Hamzah, F., & Abidin, A. (2021). Depiction Heroic Animated Characters: Describing a Brief Process of Archetype Embodiment into a Genuine Nusantara -Inspired Content. *International Journal of Academic Research in Business & Social Sciences*, *11*(7). Advance online publication. DOI: 10.6007/IJARBSS/v11-i7/10241

Abinaya, M., & Vadivu, G. (2024). AI Tools for Efficient Writing and Editing in Academic Research. In Utilizing AI Tools in Academic Research Writing (pp. 141-157). IGI Global. DOI: 10.4018/979-8-3693-1798-3.ch009

AbuGhanem, M. (2025). IBM quantum computers: Evolution, performance, and future directions. *The Journal of Supercomputing*, *81*(5), 687. Advance online publication. DOI: 10.1007/s11227-025-07047-7

Agrawal, G. (2024). Accountability, Trust, and Transparency in AI Systems From the Perspective of Public Policy: Elevating Ethical Standards. In Singla, B., & Shalender, K. (Eds.), *AI Healthcare Applications and Security, Ethical, and Legal Considerations* (pp. 148–162). IGI Global Scientific Publishing., DOI: 10.4018/979-8-3693-7452-8.ch009

Ahdritz, A. (2022). Language in the Age of Artificial Intelligence.

Ahmed, S. A. A. (2022). *TECHNOLOGY AND ARTIFICIAL INTELLIGENCE IN SIMULTANEOUS INTERPRETING: A MULTIDISCIPLINARY APPROACH. CDELT Occasional Papers in the Development of English Education. 78*, 325–353

Alam Wibowo, R. J. (2023). Ciptaan dan Invensi Hasil Kecerdasan Buatan dalam Perspektif Hak Cipta dan Paten. *Jurnal Ilmiah Kebijakan Hukum*, *17*(3), 269–288. DOI: 10.30641/kebijakan.2023.V17.269-288

Alam, A., & Mohanty, A. (2022). Predicting students' performance employing educational data mining techniques, machine learning, and learning analytics. In *International Conference on Communication, Networks and Computing* (pp. 166–177). Springer

Alghamdi, S. A., Alashban, Y., Alhailiy, A. B., Alharbi, F. F., & Al-Nahrawi, A. E. (2025). Perceptions of artificial intelligence among computed tomography technologists in Saudi Arabia: Influence of demographics and training on AI adoption. *Journal of Radiation Research and Applied Sciences*, *18*(2), 101355. DOI: 10.1016/j.jrras.2025.101355

Aljuaid, H. (2024). The Impact of Artificial intelligence Tools on academic writing instruction in Higher Education: A Systematic review. *Arab World English Journal*, *1*(1), 26–55. DOI: 10.24093/awej/ChatGPT.2

Allam, H., Makubvure, L., Gyamfi, B., Graham, K. N., & Akinwolere, K. (2025). Text classification: How machine learning is revolutionizing text categorization. *Information (Basel)*, *16*(2), 130. DOI: 10.3390/info16020130

Amankwah-Amoah, J., Abdalla, S., Mogaji, E., Elbanna, A., & Dwivedi, Y. K. (2024). The impending disruption of creative industries by generative AI: Opportunities, challenges, and research agenda. *International Journal of Information Management*, *79*, 102759. DOI: 10.1016/j.ijinfomgt.2024.102759

Amato, G., Behrmann, M., Bimbot, F., Caramiaux, B., Falchi, F., Garcia, A., Geurts, J., Gibert, J., Gravier, G., Holken, H., Koenitz, H., Lefebvre, S., Liutkus, A., Lotte, F., Perkis, A., Redondo, R., Turrin, E., Viéville, T., & Vincent, E. (2019). AI in the media and creative industries (version 1 - April 2019). In *arXiv*.

Amin, A. Y. M., Ahmad, A., & Hashim, H. (2024). Exploring the role of storyline, characters, and interactive storytelling techniques in fostering socio-emotional learning in early childhood education. *Jurnal Pendidikan Awal Kanak-kanak Kebangsaan*, *13*(2), 58–67. DOI: 10.37134/jpak.vol13.2.6.2024

Amirjalili, F., Neysani, M., & Nikbakht, A. (2024). Exploring the boundaries of authorship: A comparative analysis of AI-generated text and human academic writing in English literature. *Frontiers in Education*, *9*, 1347421. Advance online publication. DOI: 10.3389/feduc.2024.1347421

Amirzhanov, A., Turan, C., & Makhmutova, A. (2025). Plagiarism types and detection methods: A systematic survey of algorithms in text analysis. *Frontiers of Computer Science, 7*, 1504725. Advance online publication. DOI: 10.3389/fcomp.2025.1504725

Anantrasirichai, N., & Bull, D. (2022). Artificial intelligence in the creative industries: A review. *Artificial Intelligence Review, 55*(1), [page range]. https://doi.org/ DOI: 10.1007/s10462-021-10039-7

Aplin, T. F., & Davis, J. (2017). *Intellectual Property Law: Text, Cases, and Materials*. Oxford University Press. DOI: 10.1093/he/9780198743545.001.0001

Arcilla, F. E.Jr. (2024). Poetic devices, thematic significance, and social realities in poetry: A critical literature review. *Randwick International of Education and Linguistics Science Journal, 5*(1), 70–85. DOI: 10.47175/rielsj.v5i1.935

Arendt, H. (1958). *The human condition*. University of Chicago Press.

Artificial Intelligence Act, European Parliament (2023).

Assael, Y., Sommerschield, T., & Prag, J. (2019). Restoring ancient text using deep learning: A case study on Greek epigraphy. *EMNLP-IJCNLP 2019 - 2019 Conference on Empirical Methods in Natural Language Processing and 9th International Joint Conference on Natural Language Processing, Proceedings of the Conference*. DOI: 10.18653/v1/D19-1668

Asshafa, S. (2023, February 15). Pencapaian AI Sejauh Ini: Bantuan Netflix Bikin Animasi, Hingga Jadi Kurator Seni. Akurat. https://www.akurat.co/infotech/1302404434/Pencapaian-AI-Sejauh-Ini-Bantuan-Netflix-Bikin-Animasi-Hingga-Jadi-Kurator-Seni

Assinen, S. (2018). *European Union Copyright Protection for AI-Generated Works",* Thesis, Master's Degree Programme Law and Information Society, University of Turku, Finland.

Aumueller, J. (2019). *How Artificial Intelligencecan revolutionise can revolutionisehealthcare healthcare*. Health Europa Quarterly.

Ayanwale, M. A., Molefi, R. R., & Oyeniran, S. (2024). Analyzing the evolution of machine learning integration in educational research: A bibliometric perspective. *Discover Education, 3*(1), 47. DOI: 10.1007/s44217-024-00119-5

Azada-Palacios, R. A. (2022). Hybridity and national identity in post-colonial schools. *Educational Philosophy and Theory, 54*(9), 1431–1441. DOI: 10.1080/00131857.2021.1920393

Azmi, M. K. W., Rokhim, A., & Heriawanto, B. K. (2024). *Legality and Legal Protection of Visual Art Works Produced Through Artificial Intelligence*. Dinamika 30(1), 9041-9059, https://jim.unisma.ac.id/index.php/jdh/article/view/23614/17668

Babu, N. V., & Kanaga, E. G. M. (2022). Sentiment analysis in social media data for depression detection using artificial intelligence: A review. *SN Computer Science, 3*(74), 74. Advance online publication. DOI: 10.1007/s42979-021-00958-1 PMID: 34816124

Bajohr, H. (2023). *Artificial and Post-Artificial Texts*. On Machine Learning and the Reading Expectations Towards Literary and Non-Literary Writing. DOI: 10.12685/bmcct.2023.007

Bansal, G., Chamola, V., Hussain, A., Guizani, M., & Niyato, D. (2024). Transforming conversations with AI—A comprehensive study of ChatGPT. *Cognitive Computation, 16*(5), 2487–2510. DOI: 10.1007/s12559-023-10236-2

Barbierato, E., & Gatti, A. (2024). The challenges of machine learning: A critical review. *Electronics (Basel), 13*(2), 416. DOI: 10.3390/electronics13020416

Battiste, M. (2000). *Reclaiming Indigenous voice and vision*. UBC Press.

Bearman, M., Ryan, J., & Ajjawi, R. (2023). Discourses of artificial intelligence in higher education: A critical literature review. *Higher Education, 86*(2), 369–385. DOI: 10.1007/s10734-022-00937-2

Bechard, D. (2024). *The Pen and the Processor: A Turing-like Test to Gauge GPT-Generated Poetry* (Doctoral dissertation, Doctoral dissertation).

Bergenstråhle, J. (2023). A phenomenological alternative to screenplay development methods. *Linguistics and Literature Studies, 11*(1), 11–23. DOI: 10.13189/lls.2023.110102

Berne Convention for the Protection of Literary and Artistic Works.

Biagini, G. (2025). Towards an AI-Literate Future: A Systematic Literature Review Exploring Education, Ethics, and Applications. *International Journal of Artificial Intelligence in Education*. Advance online publication. DOI: 10.1007/s40593-025-00466-w

Binns, R. (2018). Fairness in machine learning: Lessons from political philosophy. *Proceedings of the 2018 Conference on Fairness, Accountability, and Transparency*, 149–159. DOI: 10.1145/3287560.3287592

Bishop, S., & Kant, T. (2023). Algorithmic autobiographies and fictions: A digital method. *The Sociological Review, 71*(5), 1012–1036. DOI: 10.1177/00380261221146403

Bisht, M. (2021). The History of the Arthaśāstra: Sovereignty and Sacred Law in Ancient India. *Strategic Analysis, 45*(5), 449–451. Advance online publication. DOI: 10.1080/09700161.2021.1965350

Bizzoni, Y., Moreira, P., Thomsen, M. R., & Nielbo, K. (2023, July). Sentimental matters: Predicting literary quality by sentiment analysis and stylometric features. In Proceedings of the 13th Workshop on Computational Approaches to Subjectivity, Sentiment, & Social Media Analysis (pp. 11–18). Association for Computational Linguistics. DOI: 10.18653/v1/2023.wassa-1.2

Blackman, R. (2022, June 21). *Why you need an AI ethics committee.* Harvard Business Review. https://hbr.org/2022/07/why-you-need-an-ai-ethics-committee

Boggs, S. P. (2021*). The Proposed New EU Regulatory Regime for Artificial Intelligence (AI)*, 9 Januari 2022, https://www.squirepattonboggs.com/-/media/files/insights/publications/2021/09/the proposed-new-eu-regulatory-regime-for-artificial-intelligence ai/theproposedneweuregulatoryregimeforaiv5.pdf

Böhm, C., & Batty, C. (2021). Evoking character perspective in screenplay directions: A multilingual approach to writing the 'big print'. *New Writing, 19*(3), 351–372. DOI: 10.1080/14790726.2021.1979591

Bonnell, J. R. (2023). Natural language processing in cultural heritage domains: Integrating pretrained language models with rule-based systems for historical Japanese corpora (Doctoral dissertation, University of Miami).

Booten, K., & Gero, K. I. (2021, June). Poetry machines: Eliciting designs for interactive writing tools from poets. In *Proceedings of the 13th Conference on Creativity and Cognition* (pp. 1-5). DOI: 10.1145/3450741.3466813

Bouhouita-Guermech, S., Gogognon, P., & Bélisle-Pipon, J. (2023). Specific challenges posed by artificial intelligence in research ethics. *Frontiers in Artificial Intelligence, 6*, 1149082. Advance online publication. DOI: 10.3389/frai.2023.1149082 PMID: 37483869

Bugayenko, Y., Bakare, A., Cheverda, A., Farina, M., Kruglov, A., Plaksin, Y., Pedrycz, W., & Succi, G. (2023). Prioritizing tasks in software development: A systematic literature review. *PLoS One, 18*(4), e0283838. DOI: 10.1371/journal.pone.0283838 PMID: 37023020

Buhmann, A., & Fieseler, C. (2023). Deep learning meets deep democracy: Deliberative governance and responsible innovation in artificial intelligence. *Business Ethics Quarterly, 33*(1), 146–179. DOI: 10.1017/beq.2021.42

Cachat-Rosset, G., & Klarsfeld, A. (2023). Diversity, Equity, and Inclusion in Artificial Intelligence: An Evaluation of Guidelines. *Applied Artificial Intelligence, 37*(1), 2176618. Advance online publication. DOI: 10.1080/08839514.2023.2176618

Cajulis, R. C. J. C., Tuazon, J. A. O., & Cabauatan, R. R. (2024). Artificial Intelligence in Digital Art: A Comparative Analysis on Impacts to Artists. *Indonesian Journal of Research and Educational Review e–ISSN, 4*(1), 1-14. DOI: 10.47941/ijars.2444

Cake, S. (2025). *Artificial intelligence as a collaborative tool for script development.* Media Practice and Education., DOI: 10.1080/25741136.2025.2454074

Campedelli, G. M. (2021). Where are we? Using Scopus to map the literature at the intersection between artificial intelligence and research on crime. *Journal of Computational Social Science, 4*(2), 503–530. DOI: 10.1007/s42001-020-00082-9

Camus, A. (1947). *The plague*. Random House.

Cañas, J. J. (2022). AI and ethics when human beings collaborate with AI agents. *Frontiers in Psychology, 13*, 836650. Advance online publication. DOI: 10.3389/fpsyg.2022.836650 PMID: 35310226

Cardon, P., Fleischmann, C., Aritz, J., Logemann, M., & Heidewald, J. (2023). The challenges and opportunities of AI-assisted writing: Developing AI literacy for the AI age. *Business and Professional Communication Quarterly, 86*(3), 257–295. DOI: 10.1177/23294906231176517

Carlyle, T. (1841). *On heroes, hero-worship, and the heroic in history*. Chapman and Hall.

Carroll, N. (2024). Are we inventing ourselves out of our own usefulness? Striking a balance between creativity and AI. *AI & Society, 40*(1), 249–251. DOI: 10.1007/s00146-023-01856-1

Casanova, P., & Brownlie, S. (2021). Consecration and accumulation of literary capital: Translation as unequal exchange. In *The translation studies reader* (pp. 407–423). Routledge. DOI: 10.4324/9780429280641-37

Casazza, M., & Gioppo, L. (2020). A playwriting technique to engage on a shared reflective enquiry about the social sustainability of robotization and artificial intelligence. *Journal of Cleaner Production, 248*, 119201. DOI: 10.1016/j.jclepro.2019.119201

Cascone, K., & Jandrić, P. (2021). The failure of failure: Postdigital aesthetics against techno-mystification. *Postdigital Science and Education, 3*(1), 100–117. DOI: 10.1007/s42438-020-00209-1 PMID: 40477378

Caws, P., & Mitcham, C. (1995). Thinking through technology: The path between engineering and philosophy. *Technology and Culture, 36*(4), 1060. DOI: 10.2307/3106947

Černe, M., Bunjak, A., Wong, S. I., & Moh'd, S. S. (2022). I'm creative and deserving! From self-rated creativity to creative recognition. *Creativity and Innovation Management, 31*(4), 664–679. DOI: 10.1111/caim.12518

Chen, W., Shidujaman, M., & Tang, X. (2020). *AiArt: Towards Artificial Intelligence Art.* Conference: ThinkMind // MMEDIA 2020, 47-52, The Twelfth International Conference on Advances in Multimedia At: Lisbon, Portugal, https://www.researchgate.net/publication/342642793_AiArt_Towards_Artificial_Intelligence_Art

Chen, M. (2022). Emotion analysis based on deep learning with application to research on development of Western culture. *Frontiers in Psychology, 13*, 911686. DOI: 10.3389/fpsyg.2022.911686 PMID: 36186353

Chen, Q., Cao, S., Wang, J., & Cao, N. (2023). How does automation shape the process of narrative visualization: A survey of tools. *IEEE Transactions on Visualization and Computer Graphics*. PMID: 37030780

Chen, Z. (2024). Exploring the application scenarios and issues facing Metaverse technology in education. *Interactive Learning Environments, 32*(5), 675–693. DOI: 10.1080/10494820.2023.2162345

Chesterman, S. (2024). Good models borrow, great models steal: Intellectual property rights and generative AI. *Policy and Society, 44*(1), 23–45. DOI: 10.1093/polsoc/puae006

Chiarella, S. G., Torromino, G., Gagliardi, D. M., Rossi, D., Babiloni, F., & Cartocci, G. (2022). Investigating the negative bias towards artificial intelligence: Effects of prior assignment of AI-authorship on the aesthetic appreciation of abstract paintings. *Computers in Human Behavior, 137*, 107406. Advance online publication. DOI: 10.1016/j.chb.2022.107406

Christou, P. (2024). Thematic analysis through artificial intelligence (AI). *The Qualitative Report, 29*(2), 21603715. DOI: 10.46743/2160-3715/2024.7046

Cigliano, A., Fallucchi, F., & Gerardi, M. (2024). The Impact of Digital Analysis and Large Language Models in Digital Humanity. In *ICYRIME 2024: 9th International Conference of Yearly Reports on Infor-matics, Mathematics, and Engineering*.

Clark, A. (2024). *The experience machine: How our minds predict and shape reality*. Random House.

Comfort, K., & Scharf, A. (2025). Teaching literature in the world language classroom: A practical guide that uses Bloom's taxonomy to enhance learning. *Language Teaching Research*, *29*(2), 200–220. DOI: 10.1177/1362168824123456

Court of Justice of the European Union, Nomor C-145/10, *Eva-Maria Painer v. Standard VerlagsGmbH*, ECR I-12537 (2011).

Court of Justice of the European Union, Putusan Nomor C-5/08, *Infopaq International A/S v Danske Dagblades Forening* ECR I-6569 (2009).

Cox, A. M., Pinfield, S., & Rutter, S. (2019). The intelligent library: Thought leaders' views on the likely impact of artificial intelligence on academic libraries. *Library Hi Tech*, *37*(3), 418–435. DOI: 10.1108/LHT-08-2018-0105

Crews, F. C. (2024, November 25). *Literary criticism | Definition, Theories, Types, Examples, & Facts*. Encyclopedia Britannica. https://www.britannica.com/art/literary-criticism

Crimaldi, F., & Leonelli, M. (2023). AI and the creative realm: A short review of current and future applications. *ArXiv Preprint ArXiv*. http://arxiv.org/abs/2306.01795

Cupać, J., Schopmans, H., & Tuncer-Ebetürk, İ. (2024). Democratization in the age of artificial intelligence: Introduction to the special issue. *Democratization*, *31*(5), 899–921. DOI: 10.1080/13510347.2024.2338852

Currie, G. (2020). *Imagining and knowing: The shape of fiction*. Oxford University Press. DOI: 10.1093/oso/9780199656615.001.0001

Dabhade, A., & Narula, S. (2023). Artificial Intelligence in English Literature: Revolutionizing Research Methodologies, unveiling insights, and catalyzing Social Transformation. *Journal of Thematic Analysis*, *4*(1), 88–100.

Dai, H., & Lee, J. (2022). Research on discourse reconstruction effect of animated film cross-cultural communication based on machine learning. *Wireless Communications and Mobile Computing*, *2022*, 1–10. DOI: 10.1155/2022/2343328

Danesi, M. (2024). *AI-Generated Cinema*. In *AI-Generated Popular Culture: A Semiotic Perspective* (pp. 37–60). Springer. DOI: 10.1007/978-3-031-54752-2_3

Danesi, M. (2024). *AI-Generated Literature*. In *AI-Generated Popular Culture: A Semiotic Perspective* (pp. 61–85). Springer. https://doi.org/DOI: 10.1007/978-3-031-54752-2_2

Davis, G., & Grierson, M. (2022). Investigating attitudes of professional writers to GPT text generation AI based creative support tools.

De Cicco, R., Francioni, B., Curina, I., & Cioppi, M. (2025). AI, human or a blend? How the educational content creator influences consumer engagement and brand-related outcomes. *Journal of Services Marketing*, *39*(10), 52–70. DOI: 10.1108/JSM-10-2024-0539

de la Porte, C., & Jensen, M. D. (2021). The Next Generation EU: An analysis of the dimensions of conflict behind the deal. *Social Policy and Administration*, *55*(2), 235–250. DOI: 10.1111/spol.12709

Deas, N., Grieser, J., Kleiner, S., Patton, D., Turcan, E., & McKeown, K. (2023). Evaluation of African American Language Bias in Natural Language Generation. *EMNLP 2023 - 2023 Conference on Empirical Methods in Natural Language Processing, Proceedings*. DOI: 10.18653/v1/2023.emnlp-main.421

Dehghanian, A., Seyyedrezaei, S. H., Mazandarani, O., & Barani, G. (2023). Pedagogical Implementation of Stylistic Imitation in Grammar-based Writing Instruction in EFL Classes. [JNTELL]. *Journal of New Trends in English Language Learning*, *2*(3).

Derrida, J. (1997). *Of grammatology*. Johns Hopkins University Press.

Derrida, J. (2001). *On cosmopolitanism and forgiveness*. Routledge.

Devaki, V. (2025). Academic integrity and human cognitive development of learners: Is artificial intelligence replacing the human brain? In *AI Applications and Strategies in Teacher Education* (pp. 45–60). IGI Global., DOI: 10.4018/978-1-7998-XXXX-X.ch003

Dillon, S., & Schaffer-Goddard, J. (2022). What AI researchers read: The role of literature in artificial intelligence research. *Interdisciplinary Science Reviews*, *48*(1), 15–42. DOI: 10.1080/03080188.2022.2079214

Doğan, B., Balcioglu, Y. S., & Elçi, M. (2024). Multidimensional Sentiment Analysis Method on social media data: Comparison of emotions during and after the covid-19 pandemic. *Kybernetes*, *54*(4), 2414–2456. DOI: 10.1108/K-09-2023-1808

Drewniak, D. (2019). Migrant Voices in the Polish Classroom: Canadian Literature on the Tertiary Level of Education. *Zeitschrift Fur Anglistik Und Amerikanistik*, *67*(4), 411–427. Advance online publication. DOI: 10.1515/zaa-2019-0030

Dwivedi, R., Nerur, S., & Balijepally, V. (2023). Exploring artificial intelligence and big data scholarship in information systems: A citation, bibliographic coupling, and co-word analysis. *International Journal of Information Management Data Insights*, *3*(2), 100185. DOI: 10.1016/j.jjimei.2023.100185

Dwivedi, Y. K., Kshetri, N., Hughes, L., Slade, E. L., Jeyaraj, A., Kar, A. K., Baabdullah, A. M., Koohang, A., Raghavan, V., Ahuja, M., Albanna, H., Albashrawi, M. A., Al-Busaidi, A. S., Balakrishnan, J., Barlette, Y., Basu, S., Bose, I., Brooks, L., Buhalis, D., & Wright, R. (2023). Opinion Paper:“So what if ChatGPT wrote it?” Multidisciplinary perspectives on opportunities, challenges and implications of generative conversational AI for research, practice and policy. *International Journal of Information Management, 71*, 102642. DOI: 10.1016/j.ijinfomgt.2023.102642

Earnshaw, R. (2017). *Art, Design, and Technology: Collaboration and Implementation.* Springer International Publishing. DOI: 10.1007/978-3-319-58121-7

Edmond, C. (2019). Poetics of the machine: Machine writing and the AI literature frontier (Doctoral dissertation, Macquarie University).

Ehrett, C., Ghita, L., Ranwala, D., & Menezes, A. (2024). Shakespeare machine: New AI-based technologies for textual analysis. *Digital Scholarship in the Humanities, 39*(2), 522–531. DOI: 10.1093/llc/fqae021

Eliot, T. S. (2009).*Essay on Poetic Theory: Tradition and the Individual Talent.* Poetry Foundation. https://www.poetryfoundation.org/articles/69400/tradition-and-the-individual-talent

Elkhatat, A. M., Elsaid, K., & Almeer, S. (2023). Evaluating the efficacy of AI content detection tools in differentiating between human and AI-generated text. *International Journal for Educational Integrity, 19*(1), 17. Advance online publication. DOI: 10.1007/s40979-023-00140-5

Elkins, K. (2022). *The shapes of stories: Sentiment analysis for narrative.* Cambridge University Press. DOI: 10.1017/9781009270403

Emerson, N. (2024). AI-enhanced collaborative story writing in the EFL classroom. *Technology in Language Teaching & Learning, 6*(1), 50–68. DOI: 10.29140/tltl.v6n4.1764

European Parliament, *Directive Number 2006/116/EC of the European Parliament and of the Council of 12 December 2006 on the term of protection of copyright and certain related rights*, OJ L372/12.

European Union Directorate-General for Communication. (n.d.), “Types of legislation,” https://european-union.europa.eu/institutions-law-budget/law/types-legislation_en

Fang, C., Comery, A., & Carr, S. (2023). “They want you to know who they really are inside of the old visage”: Biographical storytelling as a methodological tool to explore emotional challenges in old age. *BMC Geriatrics*, *23*(1), 845. Advance online publication. DOI: 10.1186/s12877-023-04094-8 PMID: 37353745

Fang, X., Che, S., Mao, M., Zhang, H., Zhao, M., & Zhao, X. (2024). Bias of AI-generated content: An examination of news produced by large language models. *Scientific Reports*, *14*(1), 5678. Advance online publication. DOI: 10.1038/s41598-024-55686-2 PMID: 38433238

Fang, X., Ng, D. T. K., Leung, J. K. L., & Chu, S. K. W. (2023). A systematic review of artificial intelligence technologies used for story writing. *Education and Information Technologies*, *28*(11), 14361–14397. DOI: 10.1007/s10639-023-11741-5

Fanon, F. (1963). *The wretched of the earth* (Vol. 36). Grove Press.

Fauzi, R., Ramli, T. S., & Permata, R. R. (2022). Masa Depan Hak Cipta: Tinjauan Keabsahan Hasil Karya Kecerdasan Artifisial di Indonesia. *CITIZEN: Jurnal Ilmiah Multidisiplin Indonesia*, *2*(1), 118–128. DOI: 10.53866/jimi.v2i1.51

Fehér, K., & Katona, A. I. (2021). Fifteen shadows of socio-cultural AI: A systematic review and future perspectives. *Futures*, *132*, 102817. Advance online publication. DOI: 10.1016/j.futures.2021.102817

Fei, Q. (2022). Analysis of Traditional Cultural Acceptance Based on Deep Learning. *Computational Intelligence and Neuroscience*, *2022*, 1–8. Advance online publication. DOI: 10.1155/2022/2373842 PMID: 35707191

Ferrara, E. (2024). Fairness and Bias in Artificial Intelligence: A Brief Survey of Sources, Impacts, and Mitigation Strategies. In *Sci* (Vol. 6, Issue 1). DOI: 10.3390/sci6010003

Ferrara, E. (2024). The butterfly effect in artificial intelligence systems: Implications for AI bias and fairness. *Machine Learning with Applications*, *10*, 100430. Advance online publication. DOI: 10.1016/j.mlwa.2024.100525

Finn, E., & Wylie, R. (2021). Collaborative imagination: A methodological approach. *Futures*, *132*, 102788. Advance online publication. DOI: 10.1016/j.futures.2021.102788

Fleckenstein, J., Meyer, J., Jansen, T., Keller, S. D., Köller, O., & Möller, J. (2024). Do teachers spot AI? Evaluating the detectability of AI-generated texts among student essays. *Computers and Education Artificial Intelligence*, *6*, 100209. DOI: 10.1016/j.caeai.2024.100209

Foucault, M. (1961). *Madness and civilization: A history of insanity in the age of reason*. Pantheon Books. DOI: 10.4324/9780203278796

Fraser, N. (2014). *Justice interruptus: Critical reflections on the "postsocialist" condition*. Routledge. DOI: 10.4324/9781315822174

FREE *AI Poem Generator | ToolBaz.com*. (n.d.). [FREE] AI Poem Generator | ToolBaz.com. https://toolbaz.com/writer/poem-generator

Frye, N. (1957). *Anatomy of criticism: Four essays*. Princeton University Press. DOI: 10.1515/9781400866908

Fukuda-Parr, S., & Gibbons, E. (2021). Emerging consensus on 'ethical AI': Human rights critique of stakeholder guidelines. *Global Policy*, *12*(S6), 32–44. DOI: 10.1111/1758-5899.12965

Fusillo, M., & Lino, M. (2024). Inter-mediality in digital media environment. *New Techno-Humanities*, *4*(1), 58–64. DOI: 10.1016/j.techum.2024.11.002

Gadamer, H.-G. (2013). *Truth and method*. Bloomsbury Academic.

Gaffar, H., & Al-Barashdi, S. (2024). Copyright protection for AI-generated works: Exploring originality and ownership in a digital landscape. *Asian Journal of International Law*, *15*(1), 23–46. DOI: 10.1017/S2044251323000735

Gandhi, A., Adhvaryu, K., Poria, S., Cambria, E., & Hussain, A. (2023). Multimodal sentiment analysis: A systematic review of history, datasets, multimodal fusion methods, applications, challenges and future directions. *Information Fusion*, *91*, 424–444. DOI: 10.1016/j.inffus.2022.09.025

Gandhi, M. (1938). *Hind Swaraj*. Navajivan Publishing.

Gasparini, A. A., & Kautonen, H. (2022). Understanding artificial intelligence in research libraries: An extensive literature review. *LIBER Quarterly*, *32*(1), 1–36. DOI: 10.53377/lq.10934

Ge, B., De Massis, A., & Kotlar, J. (2022). Mining the past: History scripting strategies and competitive advantage in a family business. *Entrepreneurship Theory and Practice*, *46*(1), 223–251. DOI: 10.1177/10422587211046547

Geiger, C., Gervais, D. J., & Senftleben, M. (2015). *Understanding the "three-step test", In book: International Intellectual Property*, 167-189, http://dx.doi.org/DOI: 10.4337/9781782544807.00014

Gema, A. J. (2022). Masalah Penggunaan Ciptaan Sebagai Data Masukan dalam Pengembangan Artificial Intelligence di Indonesia. *Technology and Economics Law Journal, 1*(1), 1–17. DOI: 10.21143/TELJ.vol1.no1.1000

Gero, K. I. (2023). *AI and the Writer: How Language Models Support Creative Writers*. Columbia University.

Gero, K. I., & Chilton, L. B. (2019, May). Metaphoria: An algorithmic companion for metaphor creation. In *Proceedings of the 2019 CHI conference on human factors in computing systems* (pp. 1-12). DOI: 10.1145/3290605.3300526

Gervais, D. J. (2022). AI Derivatives: The Application to the Derivative Work Right to Literary and Artistic Productions of AI Machines. *SSRN, 52*(4), 1111–1136. DOI: 10.2139/ssrn.4022665

Gibson, B., & Green, C. N. (2025). Teaching literature in the age of AI: A collaborative approach to engaged learning. In *Navigating AI in Academic Libraries: Implications for Academic Research* (pp. 179–210). IGI Global.

Ginsburg, J. C. (2018). People Not Machines: Authorship and What It Means in the Berne Convention. [IIC]. *IIC; International Review of Industrial Property and Copyright Law, 49*(2), 131–135. DOI: 10.1007/s40319-018-0670-x

Ginsburg, J. C., & Budiardjo, L. A. (2019). Authors and machines. *Berkeley Technology Law Journal, 34*, 343.

Glass, G. (n.d.). Fidelity, remix, and the adaptive potential: Leveraging AI and ML techniques in literary adaptation theory. Source Name. Retrieved from https://www.proquest.com/openview/b157b50eb80b8a8d41cb21c37c443001/1?pq-origsite=gscholar&cbl=18750&diss=y

Gogula, S. D., Rahouti, M., Gogula, S. K., Jalamuri, A., & Jagatheesaperumal, S. K. (2023). An Emotion-Based Rating System for Books Using Sentiment Analysis and Machine Learning in the Cloud. *Applied Sciences (Basel, Switzerland), 13*(2), 773. DOI: 10.3390/app13020773

Gonsalves, C. (2024). Addressing student non-compliance in AI use declarations: Implications for academic integrity and assessment in higher education. *Assessment & Evaluation in Higher Education*, •••, 1–15. DOI: 10.1080/02602938.2024.2415654

Gopidi, A. (2020). Poetry in the Age of Mechanical Reproduction: A Computational Study (Doctoral dissertation, International Institute of Information Technology).

Griffin, S. M. (2023). Special Issue: Epigraphy and Paleography: Bringing Records from the Distant Past to the Present. In *International Journal on Digital Libraries* (Vol. 24, Issue 2). DOI: 10.1007/s00799-023-00371-4

Guerberof-Arenas, A., & Toral, A. (2022). Creativity in translation. *Translation Spaces*, *11*(2), 184–212. DOI: 10.1075/ts.21025.gue

Haase, J., & Hanel, P. H. P. (2023). Artificial muses: Generative artificial intelligence chatbots have risen to human-level creativity. *Journal of Creativity*, *33*(3), 100066. Advance online publication. DOI: 10.1016/j.yjoc.2023.100066

Habermas, J. (1984). *The theory of communicative action*. Beacon Press.

Hadinezhad, S., Garg, S., & Lindgren, R. (2024). Enhancing inclusivity: Exploring AI applications for diverse learners. In Kourkoulou, D., Tzirides, A.-O., Cope, B., & Kalantzis, M. (Eds.), *Trust and Inclusion in AI-Mediated Education: Where Human Learning Meets Learning Machines* (pp. 163–182). Springer Nature., DOI: 10.1007/978-3-031-64487-0_8

Hamat, A. (2024). The Language of AI and Human Poetry: A Comparative Lexicometric Study. *3L, Language, Linguistics. Literature*, *30*(2), 1–20.

Hanna, M. G., Pantanowitz, L., Jackson, B., Palmer, O., Visweswaran, S., Pantanowitz, J., Deebajah, M., & Rashidi, H. H. (2025). Ethical and bias considerations in Artificial Intelligence/Machine Learning. *Modern Pathology*, *38*(3), 100686. DOI: 10.1016/j.modpat.2024.100686 PMID: 39694331

Harris, F. (2010). *Akselerasi Transformasi Perlindungan Hak Kekayaan Intelektual Melalui Inovasi*. Badan Pembinaan Hukum Nasional.

Harwood, N. (2022). 'Teaching the writer to fish so they can fish for the rest of their lives': Lecturer, English language tutor, and student views on the educative role of proofreading. *English for Specific Purposes*, *68*, 116–130. DOI: 10.1016/j.esp.2022.07.002

Hashemi, A., Shi, W., & Corriveau, J. P. (2024). AI-generated or AI touch-up? Identifying AI contribution in text data. *International Journal of Data Science and Analytics*, *8*(4), 1–12. DOI: 10.1007/s41060-024-00693-9

Hassan, S. U., Ahamed, J., & Ahmad, K. (2022). Analytics of machine learning-based algorithms for text classification. *Sustainable Operations and Computers*, *3*, 238–248. DOI: 10.1016/j.susoc.2022.03.001

Hatzel, H. O., Stiemer, H., Biemann, C., & Gius, E. (2023). Machine learning in computational literary studies. *IT-Information Technology*, *65*(4–5), 200–217. DOI: 10.1515/itit-2023-0041

Hawin, M., & Riswandi, B. A. (2020). *Isu-Isu Penting Hak Kekayaan Intelektual di Indonesia*. UGM Press.

Hegel, G. W. F. (2017). *Elements of the philosophy of right*. Cambridge University Press.

Hegghammer, T. (2021). OCR with Tesseract, Amazon Textract, and Google Document AI: A benchmarking experiment. *Journal of Computational Social Science*, *5*(1), 861–882. DOI: 10.1007/s42001-021-00149-1

Herawati, Y. W., & Masitoh, S. (2024). Quantifying literary works: Is it possible?. *Jurnal Ilmiah Bahasa dan Sastra, 11*(1), 40-52.

Hermann, I. (2021). Artificial Intelligence in fiction: Between narratives and metaphors. *AI &amp. AI & Society*, *38*(1), 319–329. DOI: 10.1007/s00146-021-01299-6

Hobbs, R. (2020). Propaganda in an age of algorithmic personalization: Expanding literacy research and practice. *Reading Research Quarterly*, *55*(3), 521–533. DOI: 10.1002/rrq.301

Hollanek, T. (2023). AI transparency: A matter of reconciling design with critique. *AI & Society*, *38*(5), 2071–2079. DOI: 10.1007/s00146-020-01110-y

Holyoak, K. (2019). The Spider's Thread: Metaphor in Mind, Brain and Poetry. MIT Press

Holzinger, A., Zatloukal, K., & Müller, H. (2025). Is human oversight to AI systems still possible? *New Biotechnology*, *85*, 59–62. DOI: 10.1016/j.nbt.2024.12.003 PMID: 39675423

Hossain, K. I. (2024). Reviewing the role of culture in English language learning: Challenges and opportunities for educators. *Social Sciences &amp. Social Sciences & Humanities Open*, *9*, 100781. DOI: 10.1016/j.ssaho.2023.100781

Hosseini, M., Resnik, D. B., & Holmes, K. (2023). The ethics of disclosing the use of artificial intelligence tools in writing scholarly manuscripts. *Research Ethics*, *19*(4), 449–465. DOI: 10.1177/17470161231180449 PMID: 39749232

Hristov, K. (2017). *Artificial Intelligence and Copyright Dilemma*. IDEA: the Journal of the Franklin Pierce Center for Intellectual Property 57(3), 431-454, https://www.researchgate.net/publication/316761384_Artificial_Intelligence_and_the_Copyright_Dilemma

Hu, Y. (2023). Literature in the Age of Artificial Intelligence. In *2023 9th International Conference on Humanities and Social Science Research (ICHSSR 2023)* (pp. 1781-1787). Atlantis Press. DOI: 10.2991/978-2-38476-092-3_228

Huang, B., Chen, C., & Shu, K. (2025). Authorship attribution in the era of LLMs: Problems, methodologies, and challenges. *SIGKDD Explorations*, *27*(1), 45–63. DOI: 10.1145/3715073.3715076 PMID: 40276161

Huffaker, J. (2023). Social Reference Processing with Collaborative Human-AI Systems (Doctoral dissertation, University of Michigan). DOI: 10.7302/8321

Hugenholtz, P. B., & Quintais, J. P. (2021). Copyright and Artificial Creation: Does EU Copyright Law Protect AI-Assisted Output? *IIC; International Review of Industrial Property and Copyright Law*, *52*(9), 1190–1216. DOI: 10.1007/s40319-021-01115-0

Hu, N., Li, S., Li, L., & Xu, H. (2022). The Educational Function of English Children's Movies From the Perspective of Multiculturalism Under Deep Learning and Artificial Intelligence. *Frontiers in Psychology*, *12*, 759094. Advance online publication. DOI: 10.3389/fpsyg.2021.759094 PMID: 35140652

Hunkele, C., & Smith, V. (2024). An analysis of the accuracy and bias of a generative ai model. *International Journal of Advanced Research*, *12*(04), 989–1019. DOI: 10.21474/IJAR01/18640

Hussain, A., & Qazi, K. A. (2023). Textual alchemy: AI, authorship and the shifting paradigms of interpretation. *Rupkatha Journal on Interdisciplinary Studies in Humanities*, *15*(4), 1–12. DOI: 10.21659/rupkatha.v15n4.08

Hutson, J., & Schnellmann, A. (2023). The poetry of prompts: the collaborative role of generative artificial intelligence in the creation of poetry and the anxiety of machine influence. *Global Journal of Computer Science and Technology: D, 23*(1).

Hutson, J., Jeevanjee, T., Vander Graaf, V., Lively, J., Weber, J., Weir, G., & Edele, S. (2022). Artificial intelligence and the disruption of higher education: Strategies for integrations across disciplines. *Creative Education*, *13*(12), 3953–3980. Advance online publication. DOI: 10.4236/ce.2022.1312253

Ichien, N., Stamenković, D., & Holyoak, K. (2024). Interpretation of Novel Literary Metaphors by Humans and GPT-4. In *Proceedings of the Annual Meeting of the Cognitive Science Society* (Vol. 46).

Imamguluyev, R. (2023). The rise of gpt-3: Implications for natural language processing and beyond. *Int J Res Pub Rev*, *2582*(3), 7421. DOI: 10.55248/gengpi.2023.4.33987

Imami, T. R., & Mu'in, F., & Nasrullah. (2023). Proceedings of the 2nd International Conference on Education, Language and Art (ICELA 2022). In *Proceedings of the 2nd International Conference on Education, Language and Art (ICELA 2022)*. DOI: 10.2991/978-2-38476-004-6

Imran, M., & Almusharraf, N. (2023). Analyzing the role of ChatGPT as a writing assistant at higher education level: A systematic review of the literature. *Contemporary Educational Technology*, *15*(4), ep464. DOI: 10.30935/cedtech/13605

Indonesia, C. N. N. (2023, January 30). AI Milik Google Bisa Ciptakan Musik, Bakal Rilis dan Saingi ChatGPT? cnnindonesia.com. https://www.cnnindonesia.com/teknologi/20230130140149-185-906599/ai-milik-google-bisa-ciptakan-musik-bakal-rilis-dan-saingi-chatgpt

Intahchomphoo, C., & Gundersen, O. E. (2020). Artificial Intelligence and Race: A Systematic Review. *Legal Information Management*, *20*(2), 74–84. Advance online publication. DOI: 10.1017/S1472669620000183

Isayeva, S. (2024). Democratizing education AI and OpenAI models for global access to knowledge. In *Enhancing Higher Education and Research With OpenAI Models* (pp. 79–92). IGI Global. DOI: 10.4018/979-8-3693-1666-5.ch004

Jafery, N. N., Keikhosrokiani, P., & Asl, M. P. (2023). An Artificial Intelligence Application of Theme and Space in Life Writings of Middle Eastern Women: A Topic Modelling and Sentiment Analysis Approach. In Keikhosrokiani, P., & Pourya Asl, M. (Eds.), *Handbook of Research on Artificial Intelligence Applications in Literary Works and Social Media* (pp. 19–35). IGI Global Scientific Publishing., DOI: 10.4018/978-1-6684-6242-3.ch002

Jebaselvi, C. E., Mohanraj, K., & Anitha, T. (2024). The rise of AI in English language and literature. *Shanlax International Journal of English*, *12*(2), 53–58. DOI: 10.34293/english.v12i2.7216

Jerrin, N. B., & Bhuvaneswari, G. (2024). Comprehending AI's Role in Literature and Arts from a Transhumanist Perspective. [IRJMS]. *International Research Journal of Multidisciplinary Scope*, *5*(2), 846–859. DOI: 10.47857/irjms.2024.v05i02.0670

Jin, J., Yang, M., Hu, H., Guo, X., Luo, J., & Liu, Y. (2025). Empowering design innovation using AI-generated content. *Journal of Engineering Design*, *36*(1), 1–18. DOI: 10.1080/09544828.2024.2401751

Johnson, R. L., Pistilli, G., Menédez-González, N., Duran, L. D. D., Panai, E., Kalpokiene, J., & Bertulfo, D. J. (2022). The Ghost in the Machine has an American accent: value conflict in GPT-3. *The Ghost in the Machine Has an American Accent: Value Conflict in GPT-3.* http://arxiv.org/abs/2203.07785

Joubin, A. A. (2023). Screens as Anthropomorphic Interfaces: How AI Changes Shakespearean Theatrical Publics. *Shakespeare Bulletin, 41*(4), 529–553. DOI: 10.1353/shb.2023.a920571

JOURNEY, W. T. A. T. (2024). Preface: A Writing Transformation. Best Practices to Prepare Writers for Their Professional Paths.

Jung, K. (2023). Good readers, good writers, and AI: Tool, collaborator, author? *Fordham Intell. Prop. Media & Ent. LJ, 34*, 1029.

Kammerath, J. (2025). Decolonizing AI: Countermeasures against model biases. *Medium.* https://medium.com/@jankammerath/decolonizing-ai-countermeasures-against-model-biases-e25d95b826ea

Kangasharju, A., Ilomäki, L., Lakkala, M., & Toom, A. (2022). Lower secondary students' poetry writing with the AI-based poetry machine. *Computers and Education: Artificial Intelligence, 3*, 100048. DOI: 10.1016/j.caeai.2022.100048

Kant, I. (1785). *Groundwork of the metaphysics of morals.* Harper & Row.

Karaban, V., & Karaban, A. (2024). AI-translated poetry: Ivan Franko's poems in GPT-3.5-driven machine and human-produced translations. In *Forum for Linguistic Studies* (Vol. 6, No. 1). DOI: 10.59400/fls.v6i1.1994

Karjus, A. (2025). Machine-assisted quantitizing designs: Augmenting humanities and social sciences with artificial intelligence. *Humanities & Social Sciences Communications, 12*(1), 1–18. DOI: 10.1057/s41599-025-04503-w

Kar, S. K., Bansal, T., Modi, S., & Singh, A. (2024). How Sensitive Are the Free AI-detector Tools in Detecting AI-generated Texts? A Comparison of Popular AI-detector Tools. *Indian Journal of Psychological Medicine, XX*(X), 1–4. DOI: 10.1177/02537176241247934 PMID: 39564235

Kaur, G., Singh, M., & Singh, S. (2021). Mapping the literature on financial well-being: A systematic literature review and Bibliometric analysis. *International Social Science Journal, 71*(241–242), 217–241. DOI: 10.1111/issj.12278

Keikhosrokiani, P., & Asl, M. P. (2023). *Introduction to artificial intelligence for the analytics of literary works and social media: A review. Handbook of research on artificial intelligence applications in literary works and social media.* 1–17.

Kerr, I., Maurushat, A., & Tacit, C. S. (2003). Mesures de protection techniques: Partie I" Tendances en matiÃ¨re de mesures de protection technique et de technologies de contournement. *Les Cahiers De Propriete Intellectuelle, 15*(2), 575-617. https://cpi.openum.ca/files/sites/66/Mesures-de-protection-technique.pdf

Khalifa, M., & Albadawy, M. (2024). Using artificial intelligence in academic writing and research: An essential productivity tool. *Computer Methods and Programs in Biomedicine Update*, *5*, 100145. Advance online publication. DOI: 10.1016/j.cmpbup.2024.100145

Khallaf, R., & Khallaf, M. (2021). Classification and analysis of deep learning applications in construction: A systematic literature review. *Automation in Construction*, *129*(103760), 103760. DOI: 10.1016/j.autcon.2021.103760

Khan, W., Daud, A., Khan, K., & Muhammad, S. (2023). Exploring the frontiers of deep learning and natural language processing: A comprehensive overview of key challenges and emerging trends. *Journal of Natural Language Processing*.

Khan, A. M. (2025). Exploring the Role of Artificial Intelligence in the Creation of Literary Characters: A Comparative Analysis of Human and AI-Generated Characters in "Raja Gidh.". *Review Journal of Social Psychology & Social Works*, *3*(1), 24–32.

Kharispublishing (2023, December 19). Exploring the Impact of AI on Literature - Kharis Publishing. *Kharis Publishing - Inspirational Book Publisher*. https://kharispublishing.com/kp/exploring-the-impact-of-ai-on-literature/

Khomais, S. F. (2014). Enhancing preschool children's number knowledge: The suitability of an intervention programme for Saudi practice. *Early Child Development and Care*, *184*(1), 32–49. Advance online publication. DOI: 10.1080/03004430.2013.768238

Khurana, D., Koli, A., Khatter, K., & Singh, S. (2023). Natural language processing: State of the art, current trends and challenges. *Multimedia Tools and Applications*, *82*(3), 3713–3744. DOI: 10.1007/s11042-022-13428-4 PMID: 35855771

Kim, H. (2022). Computational approaches in the humanities: From sentiment analysis to deep learning colorization (Doctoral dissertation, Texas A&M).

Kim, S.-J. (2024). Research ethics and issues regarding the use of CHATGPT-like artificial intelligence platforms by authors and reviewers: A narrative review. *Science Editing*, *11*(2), 96–106. DOI: 10.6087/kcse.343

Kim, S., Whitford, M., & Arcodia, C. (2019). Development of intangible cultural heritage as a sustainable tourism resource: The intangible cultural heritage practitioners' perspectives. *Journal of Heritage Tourism*, *14*(5–6), 422–435. Advance online publication. DOI: 10.1080/1743873X.2018.1561703

KJ. Sathwik. A Journey through Generative Poetry: A Historical Overview of Generative Poetry's Odissey.(2024*). Research Trends in Language, Literature & Linguistics.* IIP Series, Vol 3. https://iipseries.org/assets/docupload/rsl20245FF8E74BFEFC545.pdf

Klingbeil, A., Grützner, C., & Schreck, P. (2024). Trust and reliance on AI: An experimental study on the extent and costs of overreliance on AI. *Computers in Human Behavior*, *160*, 108352. DOI: 10.1016/j.chb.2024.108352

Kobierski, M. (2023). AI the Creator? Analysing Prose and Poetry Created by Artificial Intelligence. Journal of Young English Philology Thought and Review, 9.

Korteling, J. H., van de Boer-Visschedijk, G. C., Blankendaal, R. A., Boonekamp, R. C., & Eikelboom, A. R. (2021). Human-versus artificial intelligence. *Frontiers in Artificial Intelligence*, *4*, 622364. Advance online publication. DOI: 10.3389/frai.2021.622364 PMID: 33981990

Koytak, H. Z. (2024). Ethnicity on the table: A content analysis of online reviews for Syracuse's cuisines. *Sociology Compass*, *18*(3), e13195. Advance online publication. DOI: 10.1111/soc4.13195

Krugmann, J. O., & Hartmann, J. (2024). Sentiment analysis in the age of Generative AI. *Customer Needs and Solutions*, *11*(1), 3. Advance online publication. DOI: 10.1007/s40547-024-00143-4

Kühl, N., Schemmer, M., Goutier, M., & Satzger, G. (2022). Artificial Intelligence and machine learning. *Electronic Markets*, *32*(4), 2235–2244. DOI: 10.1007/s12525-022-00598-0

Kuleto, V., Ilić, M., Dumangiu, M., Ranković, M., Martins, O. M., Păun, D., & Mihoreanu, L. (2021). Exploring opportunities and challenges of artificial intelligence and machine learning in higher education institutions. *Sustainability (Basel)*, *13*(18), 10424. DOI: 10.3390/su131810424

Kumar, A., Saudagar, A. K. J., Alkhathami, M., Alsamani, B., Khan, M. B., Hasanat, M. H. A., Ahmed, Z. H., Kumar, A., & Srinivasan, B. (2023). Gamified learning and assessment using ARCS with next-generation AIoMT integrated 3D animation and virtual reality simulation. *Electronics (Basel)*, *12*(4), 835. Advance online publication. DOI: 10.3390/electronics12040835

Kunst, J. R., & Bierwiaczonek, K. (2023). Utilizing AI questionnaire translations in cross-cultural and intercultural research: Insights and recommendations. *International Journal of Intercultural Relations*, *97*, 101888. DOI: 10.1016/j.ijintrel.2023.101888

Kyngäs, H., Mikkonen, K., & Kääriäinen, M. (Eds.). (2020). *The Application of Content Analysis in Nursing Science Research.*, DOI: 10.1007/978-3-030-30199-6

Lansford, J. E. (2021). Annual research review: Cross-cultural similarities and differences in parenting. *Journal of Child Psychology and Psychiatry, and Allied Disciplines*, *63*(4), 466–479. DOI: 10.1111/jcpp.13539 PMID: 34763373

Lanz, J. A. (2023, June 6). *AI Art Wars: Japan Says AI Model Training Doesn't Violate Copyright, Decrypt.* https://decrypt.co/143461/ai-art-wars-japan-says-ai-model-training-doesnt-violate-copyright

Lau, P. L., Nandy, M., Chakraborty, S., & Accelerating, U. N. (2023). Sustainable Development Goals with AI-Driven Technologies: A Systematic Literature Review of Women's Healthcare. *Health Care*, *11*(3), 401. DOI: 10.3390/healthcare11030401 PMID: 36766976

Lavrič, F., & Škraba, A. (2023). Brainstorming will never be the same again—A human group supported by artificial intelligence. *Machine Learning and Knowledge Extraction*, *5*(3), 105–122. DOI: 10.3390/make5040065

Law Number 28 of 2014 concerning Copyright.

Law, L. (2024). Application of generative artificial intelligence (GenAI) in language teaching and learning: A scoping literature review. *Computers and Education Open*, *6*, 100174. Advance online publication. DOI: 10.1016/j.caeo.2024.100174

Lee, D. C., Jhang, J., & Baek, T. H. (2025). AI-generated news content: The impact of AI writer identity and perceived AI human-likeness. *International Journal of Human-Computer Interaction*, •••, 1–13. Advance online publication. DOI: 10.1080/10447318.2025.2477739

Lehan, R. (2023). *The city in literature: an intellectual and cultural history.* Univ of California Press. DOI: 10.2307/jj.5973091

Lehman, J., Clune, J., Misevic, D., Adami, C., Altenberg, L., Beaulieu, J., Bentley, P. J., Bernard, S., Beslon, G., Bryson, D. M., Cheney, N., Chrabaszcz, P., Cully, A., Doncieux, S., Dyer, F. C., Ellefsen, K. O., Feldt, R., Fischer, S., Forrest, S., & Yosinski, J. (2020). The surprising creativity of digital evolution: A collection of anecdotes from the evolutionary computation and artificial life research communities. *Artificial Life*, *26*(2), 274–306. DOI: 10.1162/artl_a_00319 PMID: 32271631

Lehtimäki, M. L. (2024). Navigating Ethical and Practical Challenges in AI-Driven Visual Content Creation.

Li, D., Wu, K., & Lei, V. L. (2024). Applying topic modeling to literary analysis: A review. *Digital Studies in Language and Literature*, *1*(1–2), 113–141. DOI: 10.1515/dsll-2024-0010

Li, H., Jiao, H., & Yang, Z. (2023). Ship trajectory prediction based on machine learning and deep learning: A systematic review and methods analysis. *Engineering Applications of Artificial Intelligence*, *123*, 105488. Advance online publication. DOI: 10.1016/j.engappai.2023.107062

Lilja, E. (2023). Rhythm in Modern Poetry.

Linardaki, C. (2022). Poetry at the first steps of Artificial Intelligence. *Humanist Studies & the Digital Age*, *7*(1), 1. DOI: 10.5399/uo/hsda/7.1.6

Lincke, H. J., Vomstein, M., Lindner, A., Nolle, I., Häberle, N., Haug, A., & Nübling, M. (2021). COPSOQ III in Germany: Validation of a standard instrument to measure psychosocial factors at work. *Journal of Occupational Medicine and Toxicology*, *16*(Article 50), 1–15. DOI: 10.1186/s12995-021-00331-1

Lin, Z., & Ng, Y. L. (2024). Unraveling gratifications, concerns, and acceptance of generative artificial intelligence. *International Journal of Human-Computer Interaction*, •••, 1–18. Advance online publication. DOI: 10.1080/10447318.2024.2436749

Liu, C. C., Liao, M. G., Chang, C. H., & Lin, H. M. (2022). An analysis of children'interaction with an AI chatbot and its impact on their interest in reading. *Computers & Education*, •••, 189.

Liu, J., Niu, Y., Jia, Z., & Wang, R. (2023). *Assessing the ethical implications of artificial intelligence integration in media production and its impact on the creative industry*. MEDAAD. DOI: 10.70470/MEDAAD/2023/005

Livingstone, J. (2016). The Unsolvable Mysteries of the Voynich Manuscript. *New Yorker (New York, N.Y.)*.

Lotfi, F., Beheshti, A., Farhood, H., Pooshideh, M., Jamzad, M., & Beigy, H. (2023). Storytelling with image data: A systematic review and comparative analysis of methods and tools. *Algorithms*, *16*(3), 135. DOI: 10.3390/a16030135

Luchen, F., & Zhongwei, L. (2023). ChatGPT begins: A reflection on the involvement of AI in the creation of film and television scripts. *Frontiers in Art Research*.

Lu, D. (2023). Architecture in the age of playfulness: Mapping a framework for global historiography. In *The Routledge Companion to Contemporary Architectural History* (pp. 1–80). Routledge. DOI: 10.4324/9781315674469-1

Luger, G. F. (2021). Association and connectionist approaches to AI. In *Book Title* (pp. 105–141). Springer., DOI: 10.1007/978-3-030-71873-2_5

Luo, J. (2024). A critical review of GenAI policies in higher education assessment: A call to reconsider the "originality" of students' work. *Assessment & Evaluation in Higher Education.* Advance online publication. DOI: 10.1080/02602938.2024.2436748

Luther, T., Kimmerle, J., & Cress, U. (2024). Teaming up with an AI: Exploring human–AI collaboration in a writing scenario with ChatGPT. *AI, 5*(2), 210–225. DOI: 10.3390/ai5030065

Madiega, T. (2024). *EU Legislation in Progress Artificial Intelligence Act.* European Parliament: European Parliamentary Research Service, 1-13, https://www.europarl.europa.eu/RegData/etudes/BRIE/2021/698792/EPRS_BRI(2021)698792_EN.pdf

Mahadevkar, S. V., Patil, S., Kotecha, K., Soong, L. W., & Choudhury, T. (2024). Exploring AI-driven approaches for unstructured document analysis and future horizons. *Journal of Big Data, 11*(1), 92. DOI: 10.1186/s40537-024-00948-z

Mandour, W. S. (2025). AI-powered tools for linguistic and sentiment analysis in language learning: Applications using Google Sheets and large language models. In *Using AI tools in text analysis, simplification, classification, and synthesis* (pp. 67–112). IGI Global Scientific Publishing. DOI: 10.4018/979-8-3693-9511-0.ch003

Manghani, S. (2022). Notes on structuralism: Introduction. *Theory, Culture &amp. Theory, Culture & Society, 39*(7–8), 117–131. DOI: 10.1177/02632764221141823

Manurung, R., Ritchie, G., & Thompson, H. (2012). Using genetic algorithms to create meaningful poetic text. *Journal of Experimental & Theoretical Artificial Intelligence, 24*(1), 43–64. DOI: 10.1080/0952813X.2010.539029

Mao, Y., Liu, Q., & Zhang, Y. (2024). Sentiment analysis methods, applications, and challenges: A systematic literature review. *Journal of King Saud University. Computer and Information Sciences, 36*(4), 102048. DOI: 10.1016/j.jksuci.2024.102048

Marangoz, E. Ö. (2023, October 21). The Transformative Role of Artificial Intelligence and Machine Learning in Interpreting and Language Services. *RumeliDe Dil ve Edebiyat Arastirmalari Dergisi, 36*(36), 1591–1598. DOI: 10.29000/rumelide.1372500

Marcus, G. (2020). The next decade in AI: four steps towards robust artificial intelligence. arXiv preprint arXiv:2002.06177.

Margoni, T. (2018). *Artificial Intelligence, Machine learning and EU copyright law: Who owns AI? Machine Learning and EU Copyright Law: Who Owns AI.* CREATe Working Paper 2018/12 (December 2018), 1-21, https://doi.org/DOI: 10.5281/zenodo.2001763

Martínez-Olmo, F., & Catalán, F. G. (2024). Revisión sistemática de tendencias en la aplicación de la inteli-gencia artificial al ámbito de la escritura académica en las ciencias sociales. *Digital Education Review*, *45*(45), 37–42. DOI: 10.1344/der.2024.45.37-42

Martins, R. M., & Wangenheim, C. (2023). Findings on teaching machine learning in high school: A ten-year systematic literature review. *Informatics in Education*, *22*(3), 421–440.

Marx, K. (1859). *A contribution to the critique of political economy*. Progress Publishers.

Marx, K., & Engels, F. (1848). *The communist manifesto*. Progress Publishers.

Marzuki, W., Widiati, U., Rusdin, D., Darwin, , & Indrawati, I. (2023). The impact of AI writing tools on the content and organization of students' writing: EFL teachers' perspective. *Cogent Education*, *10*(2), 2236469. DOI: 10.1080/2331186X.2023.2236469

Mawhorter, P. A. (2016). Artificial intelligence as a tool for understanding narrative choices.

Mazzi, F. (2024). Authorship in artificial intelligence-generated works: Exploring originality in text prompts and AI outputs through philosophical foundations of copyright and collage protection. *The Journal of World Intellectual Property*, *27*(3), 410–427. DOI: 10.1111/jwip.12310

Mbiti, J. S. (1990). *African religions and philosophy*. Heinemann.

McArthur, J. (2023). Rethinking authentic assessment: Work, well-being, and society. *Higher Education*, *85*(1), 85–101. DOI: 10.1007/s10734-022-00822-y PMID: 35194229

McGuire, J., De Cremer, D., & Van de Cruys, T. (2024). Establishing the importance of co-creation and self-efficacy in creative collaboration with artificial intelligence. *Scientific Reports*, *14*(1), 18525. DOI: 10.1038/s41598-024-69423-2 PMID: 39122865

McMahon, P. (2024). Prague Structuralism and the Poetic Function. In *Structuralism and Form in Literature and Biology*. Palgrave Macmillan., DOI: 10.1007/978-3-031-47739-3_6

Meyl, V. (2023). Artificial Intelligence and the Metamorphosis of Beauty: A Philosophical Inquiry. *Open Journal of Philosophy*, *14*(1), 180–200. DOI: 10.4236/ojpp.2024.141015

Mezei, P. (2022). Jyh-An Lee/Reto M. Hilty/Kung-Chung Liu (eds.) Artificial Intelligence and Intellectual Property. *GRUR International, 71*(4), 390–392. https://doi.org/DOI: 10.1093/grurint/ikab145

Miller, B. (2020). " All of the rules of jazz": Stylistic Models and Algorithmic Creativity in Human-Computer Improvisation. Music Theory Online, 26(3).

Miller, A. I. (2019). *The artist in the machine: The world of AI-powered creativity*. Mit Press. DOI: 10.7551/mitpress/11585.001.0001

Mindner, L., Schlippe, T., & Schaaff, K. (2023, December). Classification of human- and AI-generated texts: Investigating features for ChatGPT. In Abbas, M., & Freihat, A. A. (Eds.), *Proceedings of the 6th International Conference on Natural Language and Speech Processing (ICNLSP 2023)* (pp. 1–10). Association for Computational Linguistics. https://doi.org/DOI: 10.1007/978-981-99-7947-9_12

Mohammad, S. M. (2021, January 14). *Sentiment analysis: Automatically detecting valence, emotions, and other affectual states from text*. arXiv.org. https://arxiv.org/abs/2005.11882v2

Mukminin, M. S., Putra, L. D., Muhhit, A. A., & Tenis, A. B. (2024). Personification Language Style in The Poem Created by ChatGPT. *Journal of Education and Contemporary Linguistics*, *1*(02), 21–31. DOI: 10.111322/hyy8v981

Mundre, A. (2025). Epistemic injustice in AI-generated histories. *eScholarship*. https://escholarship.org/content/qt92z102k6/qt92z102k6.pdf

Murfianti, F. (2020). *Hak Cipta Dan Karya Seni Di Era Digital*. Acintya. *Jurnal Penelitian Seni Budaya*, *12*(1), 44–58. DOI: 10.33153/acy.v12i1.3147

Murphy, K., Di Ruggiero, E., Upshur, R., Willison, D. J., Malhotra, N., Cai, J. C., Malhotra, N., Lui, V., & Gibson, J. (2021). Artificial Intelligence for Good Health: A scoping review of the ethics literature. *BMC Medical Ethics*, *22*(1), 14. Advance online publication. DOI: 10.1186/s12910-021-00577-8 PMID: 33588803

Naeem, A., Rehman, A. S., & Rasheed, A. (2025). Evaluating Cultural Adaptation in AI Translations: A Framework and Implications for Literary Works. In Ali, M., Anwar, M., Fazal, S., & Ayyaz, S. (Eds.), *AI Applications for English Language Learning* (pp. 223–252). IGI Global Scientific Publishing., DOI: 10.4018/979-8-3693-9077-1.ch010

Nanduri, D. K. (2024). *Exploring the Role of Generative Artificial Intelligence in Culturally Relevant Storytelling for Native Language Learning Among Children* (thesis).

Nanduri, D. K., & Bonsignore, E. M. (2023). *Revitalizing Endangered Languages: AI-powered language learning as a catalyst for language appreciation.*

Nandwani, P., & Verma, R. (2021). A review on sentiment analysis and emotion detection from text. *Social Network Analysis and Mining*, *11*(1), 81. DOI: 10.1007/s13278-021-00776-6 PMID: 34484462

Nanetti, A. (2021). Defining Heritage Science: A Consilience Pathway to Treasuring the Complexity of Inheritable Human Experiences through Historical Method, AI, and ML. *Complexity*, *2021*(1), 4703820. Advance online publication. DOI: 10.1155/2021/4703820

Nasser El Erafy, A. (2023). Applications of artificial intelligence in the field of media. *International Journal of Artificial Intelligence and Emerging Technology*, *6*(2), 19–41. DOI: 10.21608/ijaiet.2024.275179.1006

Nazer, L. H., Zatarah, R., Waldrip, S., Ke, J. X., Moukheiber, M., Khanna, A. K., Hicklen, R. S., Moukheiber, L., Moukheiber, D., Ma, H., & Mathur, P. (2023). Bias in artificial intelligence algorithms and recommendations for mitigation. *PLOS Digital Health*, *2*(6), e0000278. Advance online publication. DOI: 10.1371/journal.pdig.0000278 PMID: 37347721

Negus, K., & Astor, P. (2022). Authenticity, empathy, and the creative imagination. *Rock Music Studies*, *9*(2), 157–175. DOI: 10.1080/19401159.2021.1989272

Neumann, A., Sims, E., & Conrad, R. (n.d.). An Examination of the Impact of Stylometry. In *Artificial Intelligence/Machine Learning (AI/ML) on Privacy in Social Media.*

Ng, D. T. K., Luo, W., Chan, H. M. Y., & Chu, S. K. W. (2022). Using digital story writing as a pedagogy to develop AI literacy among primary students. *Computers and Education: Artificial Intelligence*, *3*, 100054. Advance online publication. DOI: 10.1016/j.caeai.2022.100054

Nguyen, A., Hong, Y., Dang, B., & Huang, X. (2024). Human–AI collaboration patterns in AI-assisted academic writing. *Studies in Higher Education*, *49*(5), 847–864. DOI: 10.1080/03075079.2024.2323593

Nguyen, H., Nguyen, V., Ludovise, S., & Santagata, R. (2024). Misrepresentation or inclusion: Promises of generative artificial intelligence in climate change education. *Learning, Media and Technology*, *49*(1), 1–17. DOI: 10.1080/17439884.2024.2435834

Nield, D. (2016, March 24). *A Novel Written by AI Passes the First Round in a Japanese Literary Competition, Science Alert*. https://www.sciencealert.com/a-novel-written-by-ai-passes-the-first-round-in-a-japanese-literary-competition

Ni, J., Young, T., Pandelea, V., Xue, F., & Cambria, E. (2023). Recent advances in deep learning based dialogue systems: A systematic survey. *Artificial Intelligence Review*, *56*(4), 3055–3155. DOI: 10.1007/s10462-022-10248-8

Nishant, R., Schneckenberg, D., & Ravishankar, M. N. (2024). The formal rationality of artificial intelligence-based algorithms and the problem of bias. *Journal of Information Technology*, *39*(1), 19–40. DOI: 10.1177/02683962231176842

NPR STAFF. (2016, April 05), New Rembrandt: From the Frontiers of AI and Not the Artist's Atelier. https:// www.npr.org/sections/alltechconsidered/2016/04/06/473265273/a-new-rembrandt-from-the-frontiers-of-ai-and-not-the-artists-atelier

Oberbichler, S., Boroş, E., Doucet, A., Marjanen, J., Pfanzelter, E., Rautiainen, J., Toivonen, H., & Tolonen, M. (2021). Integrated interdisciplinary workflows for research on historical newspapers: Perspectives from Humanities Scholars, computer scientists, and librarians. *Journal of the Association for Information Science and Technology*, *73*(2), 225–239. DOI: 10.1002/asi.24565 PMID: 35873357

Odden, T. O. B., Marin, A., & Rudolph, J. L. (2021). How has Science Education changed over the last 100 years? An analysis using natural language processing. *Science Education*, *105*(4), 653–680. DOI: 10.1002/sce.21623

ÓhÉigeartaigh, S. S., Whittlestone, J., Liu, Y., Zeng, Y., & Liu, Z.ÓhÉigeartaigh. (2020). Overcoming Barriers to Cross-cultural Cooperation in AI Ethics and Governance. *Philosophy & Technology*, *33*(4), 571–593. Advance online publication. DOI: 10.1007/s13347-020-00402-x

Okada, T., & Ishibashi, K. (2017). Imitation, Inspiration, and Creation: Cognitive Process of Creative Drawing by Copying Other' Artworks. *Cognitive Science*, *41*(7), 1804–1837. DOI: 10.1111/cogs.12442 PMID: 28914472

Oliveira, H. G. (2017). A survey on intelligent poetry generation: Languages, features, techniques, reutilisation and evaluation. In *Proceedings of the 10th international conference on natural language generation* (pp. 11-20). DOI: 10.18653/v1/W17-3502

Otero, J. (2022). Heritage Conservation Future: Where We Stand, Challenges Ahead, and a Paradigm Shift. *Global Challenges (Hoboken, NJ)*, *6*(1), 2100084. Advance online publication. DOI: 10.1002/gch2.202100084 PMID: 35024170

Ożegalska-Łukasik, N., & Łukasik, S. (2023). Culturally Responsive Artificial Intelligence – Problems, Challenges and Solutions. *Intercultural Relations*, *7*(2(14)), 106–119. Advance online publication. DOI: 10.12797/RM.02.2023.14.07

Özmutlu, M. (2025). Uncovering historical silences with AI. *Historica*. https://www.historica.org/blog/ai-unexpected-role-in-uncovering-historical-silences

Oztabak, C. (2025). AI-Generated Folklore for Culturally Resonant Storytelling in the Digital Age: Bridging Tradition and Technology in Storytelling. In Saka, E. (Ed.), *Understanding Generative AI in a Cultural Context: Artificial Myths and Human Realities* (pp. 161–184). IGI Global Scientific Publishing., DOI: 10.4018/979-8-3693-7235-7.ch007

Pack, A., & Maloney, J. (2023). Using generative artificial intelligence for language education research: Insights from using OpenAI's ChatGPT. *TESOL Quarterly*, *57*(4), 1571–1582. DOI: 10.1002/tesq.3253

Palace, V. M. (2019). What If Artificial Intelligence Wrote This: Artificial Intelligence and Copyright Law. *Florida Law Review*, *71*(1), 217–242. https://scholarship.law.ufl.edu/flr/vol71/iss1/5

Pansoni, S., Tiribelli, S., Paolanti, M., Di Stefano, F., Frontoni, E., Malinverni, E. S., & Giovanola, B. (2023). Artificial intelligence and cultural heritage: Design and assessment of an ethical framework. *International Archives of the Photogrammetry, Remote Sensing and Spatial Information Sciences - ISPRS Archives, 48*(M-2–2023). DOI: 10.5194/isprs-archives-XLVIII-M-2-2023-1149-2023

Papp-Zipernovszky, O., Mangen, A., Jacobs, A., & Lüdtke, J. (2021). Shakespeare Sonnet reading: An empirical study of emotional responses. *Language and Literature*, *31*(3), 296–324. DOI: 10.1177/09639470211054647

Pataranutaporn, P., Danry, V., Leong, J., Punpongsanon, P., Novy, D., Maes, P., & Sra, M. (2021). AI-generated characters for supporting personalized learning and well-being. *Nature Machine Intelligence*, *3*(12), 1013–1022. DOI: 10.1038/s42256-021-00417-9

Patwardhan, N., Marrone, S., & Sansone, C. (2023). Transformers in the real world: A survey on NLP applications. *Information (Basel), 14*(4), 242. DOI: 10.3390/info14040242

Pellegrino, A., Wang, R., & Stasi, A. (2023). Exploring the intersection of sustainable consumption and the Metaverse: A review of current literature and future research directions. *Heliyon, 9*(9), e19190. Advance online publication. DOI: 10.1016/j.heliyon.2023.e19190 PMID: 37681133

Poem Generator. (n.d.). Www.editpad.org. https://www.editpad.org/tool/poem-generator

Poetic Sound Devices. (2025). *Poem Generator - Capitalize My Title*. Capitalize My Title. https://capitalizemytitle.com/poem-generator/

Poetry Generator. (2023). Boredhumans.com. https://boredhumans.com/poetry_generator.php

Pondelíková, I., & Luprichová, J. (2024). AI-assisted enhancing of gender awareness through reading comprehension in history and literature courses of Anglophone cultures. In Sampson, D. G., Ifenthaler, D., & Isaias, P. (Eds.), *Proceedings of the 21st International Conference on Cognition and Exploratory Learning in Digital Age (CELDA 2024)* (pp. 198–208). IADIS Press.

Porter, B., & Machery, E. (2024). AI-generated poetry is indistinguishable from human-written poetry and is rated more favorably. *Scientific Reports, 14*(1), 26133. DOI: 10.1038/s41598-024-76900-1

Prada, L. (2024). People Can't Tell the Difference Between Human Poetry and AI. *Vice Magazine*. https://www.vice.com/en/article/people-cant-tell-difference-human-poetry-ai/

Premkumar, B. (2024). The Impact of artificial intelligence on literary creation and criticism: Emerging trends and implications. *International Journal of Language Literature and Culture, 1*(1), 37–41. Advance online publication. DOI: 10.22161/ijllc.4.4.5

Preuß, K. (2022). 'legal formalism' and western legal thought*. *Jurisprudence, 14*(1), 22–54. DOI: 10.1080/20403313.2022.2112457

Priya, A. (2020). Case study Methodology of Qualitative Research: Key attributes and navigating the conundrums in its application. *Sociological Bulletin, 70*(1), 94–110. DOI: 10.1177/0038022920970318

Pruneski, J. A., Pareek, A., Nwachukwu, B. U., Martin, R. K., Kelly, B. T., Karlsson, J., Pearle, A. D., Kiapour, A. M., & Williams, R. J.III. (2023). Natural language processing: Using artificial intelligence to understand human language in orthopedics. *Knee Surgery, Sports Traumatology, Arthroscopy : Official Journal of the ESSKA*, *31*(4), 1203–1211. DOI: 10.1007/s00167-022-07272-0 PMID: 36477347

Purwandoko, P. H., & Imanullah, M. N. (2017). Application of Natural Law Theory (Natural Right) To Protect the Intellectual Property Rights. *Yustisia*, *6*(1), 134–158. DOI: 10.20961/yustisia.v6i1.11516

Puspitasari, D. R., & Pratama, A. (2024). *Implementasi Perjanjian TRIPS dan Dampaknya terhadap Perlindungan Hak Cipta Industri Kreatif Lokal di Indonesia.* Book Chapter, 121-129, https://e-journal.janabadra.ac.id/index.php/bookchapter-2023/article/view/3952/2414

Qiao, Y., & Zhou, L. (2023). Implications of Artificial Intelligence Technology for the External Communication of Chinese Ethnic Cultures. *Mobile Information Systems*, *2022*, 1–13. Advance online publication. DOI: 10.1155/2022/3539332

Radanliev, P. (2024). Artificial intelligence: Reflecting on the past and looking towards the next paradigm shift. *Journal of Experimental & Theoretical Artificial Intelligence*, *36*(2), 1–18. DOI: 10.1080/0952813X.2024.2323042

Rahman, R. A., Al-Farouqi, A., & Tang, S. M. (2020). *Should Indonesian Copyright Law be Amended Due to Artificial Intelligence Development? Lesson Learned from Japan.* NTUT Journal of Intellectual Property Law and Management 9(1), 34-57, https://iip.ntut.edu.tw/var/file/92/1092/img/2036/v1-1.pdf

Rajendra, A., ... (2023, June 8). "Generative AI: is its output protectable by intellectual property rights?" *Osborne Clarke*. https://www.osborneclarke.com/insights/generative-ai-its-output-protectable-intellectual-property-rights

Rama, B. G. A., Prasada, D. K., & Mahadewi, K. J. (2023). Urgensi Pengaturan Artificial Intelligence (AI) dalam Bidanghukum Hak Cipta di Indonesia. *Jurnal Rechtens*, *12*(2), 209–224. DOI: 10.56013/rechtens.v12i2.2395

Ramesh, R., Venkatesh, M., & Girish, G. P. (2023, October). The symbiosis of AI and human agency in digital authorship: Redefining the landscape of contemporary literature. In *International Conference on Intelligent Computing & Optimization* (pp. 255–262). Springer Nature Switzerland. https://doi.org/DOI: 10.1007/978-3-031-50887-5_12

Ramli, T. S., Ramli, A. M., Mayana, R. F., Ramadayanti, E., & Fauzi, R. (2023). Artificial Intelligence as Object of Intellectual Property in Indonesian Law. *The Journal of World Intellectual Property*, *26*(2), 142–154. DOI: 10.1111/jwip.12264

Ramsay, S. (2011). *Reading Machines: Toward and Algorithmic Criticism*. University of Illinois Press. DOI: 10.5406/illinois/9780252036415.001.0001

Ranade, N., Saravia, M., & Johri, A. (2025). Using rhetorical strategies to design prompts: A human-in-the-loop approach to make AI useful. *AI & Society*, *40*(2), 711–732. DOI: 10.1007/s00146-024-01905-3

Ranke, L. (1981). *The secret of world history: Selected writings on the art and science of history*. Harvard University Press.

Rapp, C., Heilmann, T., & Kruse, O. (2023). Beyond MS Word: alternatives and developments. In Kruse, O., Rapp, C., Anson, C. M., Benetos, K., Cotos, E., Devitt, A., & Shibani, A. (Eds.), *Digital writing technologies in higher education: Theory, research, and practice* (pp. 33–47). Springer., DOI: 10.1007/978-3-031-36033-6_3

Rathore, M. M., Shah, S. A., Shukla, D., Bentafat, E., & Bakiras, S. (2021). The role of AI, machine learning, and big data in digital twinning: A systematic literature review, challenges, and opportunities. *IEEE Access : Practical Innovations, Open Solutions*, *9*, 32030–32052. DOI: 10.1109/ACCESS.2021.3060863

Ratna, P. (2021, October 14). Wamenkumham: AI Berimplikasi Terhadap UU Hak Cipta." Republika Online. https://www.republika.co.id/berita/r0ynzg428/wamenkumham-ai-berimplikasi-terhadap-uu-hak-cipta

Régis, C., Denis, J. L., Axente, M. L., & Kishimoto, A. (Eds.). (2024). *Human-centered AI: A multidisciplinary perspective for policy-makers, auditors, and users*. CRC Press. DOI: 10.1201/9781003320791

Reidenberg, J. R. (1998). Lex Informatica: The Formulation of Information Policy Rules through Technology. *Texas Law Review*, *76*(3), 553–593. https://ir.lawnet.fordham.edu/faculty_scholarship/42

Riedl, M. O. (2016). Computational Narrative Intelligence: A Human-Centered Goal for Artificial Intelligence. *ArXiv Preprint ArXiv*. http://arxiv.org/abs/1602.06484

Rife, M. C. (2007). The Fair Use Doctrine: History, Application, and Implications For (New Media) Writing Teachers. *Computers and Composition*, *24*(2), 154–178. DOI: 10.1016/j.compcom.2007.02.002

Riswandi, B. A. (2017). *Pembatasan dan Pengecualian Hak Cipta di Era Digital*. Citra Aditya Bakti.

Riyanto, G. P., & Yudha, P. (2023, January 19). *Getty Images Gugat Perusahaan AI, Diduga Pakai Gambar Tanpa Izin Untuk Latih Kecerdasan Buatan*, Kompas. Kompas.com. https://tekno.kompas.com/read/2023/01/19/12010047/getty-images -gugat-perusahaan-ai-diduga-pakai-gambar-tanpa-izin-untuk-latih

Rockwell, G., & Sinclair, S. (2022). *Hermeneutica: Computer-assisted interpretation in the humanities*. MIT Press.

Roos, M., & Reccius, M. (2024). Narratives in economics. *Journal of Economic Surveys*, *38*(2), 303–341. DOI: 10.1111/joes.12576

Rustandi, N. (2019). The Plurality and Minority in Religiousity (A Study on the Civil Right of Sunda Wiwitan Followers In Cigugur Kuningan). *Hanifiya: Jurnal Studi Agama-Agama*, *2*(1), 28–41. DOI: 10.15575/hanifiya.v2i1.4269

Saddhono, K., Nugrahani, F., & Syamsuri, A. S., Ermanto, Rahim, A. R., & Sarimanah, E. (2024). The ethics of AI in literature: Reflections on representation and responsibility. *2024 International Conference on IoT, Communication and Automation Technology (ICICAT)*, 755–760. DOI: 10.1109/ICICAT62666.2024.10923247

Saddhono, K., Rosa, S., Martiningsih, E., & Judijanto, L. Sultan, & Rahmat, W. (2024). From words to algorithms: The to get evolution of Indonesia in terms of literature via AI technology. *2024 4th International Conference on Advance Computing and Innovative Technologies in Engineering (ICACITE), 30*, 1568–1572.

Saddhono, K., Rosa, S., Martiningsih, E., Judijanto, L., & Rahmat, W. (2024). From Words to Algorithms: To Get Evolution of Indonesia in Terms of Literature via AI Technology. In *2024 4th International Conference on Advance Computing and Innovative Technologies in Engineering (ICACITE)* (pp. 1568-1572). IEEE. DOI: 10.1109/ICACITE60783.2024.10616427

Saddhono, K., Saputra, N., ... (2024). A New way to Create Virtual Authors/Writers using AI Based Technology with Optimized Voice and Style. In *2024 4th International Conference on Advance Computing and Innovative Technologies in Engineering (ICACITE)* (pp. 1509-1514). IEEE. DOI: 10.1109/ICACITE60783.2024.10616853

Sadek, M., Kallina, E., Bohné, T., Mougenot, C., Calvo, R. A., & Cave, S. (2024). Challenges of responsible AI in practice: Scoping review and recommended actions. *AI & Society*, *40*(1), 199–215. DOI: 10.1007/s00146-024-01880-9

Safa, B. M. (2024). *Look Like the Innocent Flower, but be the Serpent under't.": The Imbroglio of Betrayal in George R. R Martin's Storm of Swords and William Shakespeare's Macbeth. A Comparative Study* (Doctoral dissertation, University of Martyr Sheikh Larbi Tebessi Tebessa).

Salah, M., Al Halbusi, H., & Abdelfattah, F. (2023). May the force of Text Data Analysis be with you: Unleashing the power of Generative AI for Social Psychology Research. *Computers in Human Behavior: Artificial Humans*, *1*(2), 100006. DOI: 10.1016/j.chbah.2023.100006

Salzmann-Erikson, M. (2024). The intersection between logical empiricism and qualitative nursing research: A post-structuralist analysis. *International Journal of Qualitative Studies on Health and Well-being*, *19*(1), 2315636. Advance online publication. DOI: 10.1080/17482631.2024.2315636 PMID: 38346230

Sampaio, H. A., Correia, A. I., Melo, C., Brazão, L., & Shehada, S. (2021). Analyzing Tourism Agents' Perceptions of the Use of Artificial Intelligence. *Smart Innovation. Systems and Technologies*, *208*, 245–254. Advance online publication. DOI: 10.1007/978-981-33-4256-9_22

Sandu, A., Cotfas, L.-A., Stănescu, A., & Delcea, C. (2024). A Bibliometric Analysis of Text Mining: Exploring the Use of Natural Language Processing in Social Media Research. *Applied Sciences (Basel, Switzerland)*, *14*(8), 3144. DOI: 10.3390/app14083144

Sangapu, I. (2019). Artificial Intelligence in Education - From a Teacher and a Student Perspective. SSRN *Electronic Journal*. DOI: 10.2139/ssrn.3372914

Sarker, I. H. (2021). Deep Learning: A Comprehensive Overview on Techniques, Taxonomy, Applications and Research Directions. *SN Computer Science*, *2*(6), 420. DOI: 10.1007/s42979-021-00815-1 PMID: 34426802

Sarker, I. H. (2021). Machine learning: Algorithms, real-world applications and research directions. *SN Computer Science*, *2*(3), 160. Advance online publication. DOI: 10.1007/s42979-021-00592-x PMID: 33778771

Sarker, I. H. (2022). AI-based modeling: Techniques, applications and research issues towards automation, intelligent and smart systems. *SN Computer Science*, *3*(2), 158. DOI: 10.1007/s42979-022-01043-x PMID: 35194580

Sartre, J.-P. (2018). *Being and nothingness: An Essay in phenomenological ontology*. Routledge.

Schäffer, B., & Lieder, F. R. (2023). Distributed interpretation-teaching reconstructive methods in the social sciences supported by artificial intelligence. *Journal of Research on Technology in Education*, *55*(1), 111–124. DOI: 10.1080/15391523.2022.2148786

Schober, R. (2022). Passing the Turing test? AI generated poetry and posthuman creativity. *Artificial Intelligence and Human Enhancement: Affirmative and Critical Approaches in the Humanities*, *21*, 151–166. DOI: 10.1515/9783110770216-009

Scott, R. (2024). Imagined lives: Formal implications for creative writing in the age of ai. *New Writing*, *21*(4), 468–477. DOI: 10.1080/14790726.2024.2377549

Sejnowski, T. J. (2024). *ChatGPT and the Future of AI: The Deep Language Revolution*. MIT Press. DOI: 10.7551/mitpress/15580.001.0001

Senior thesis spotlight: AI and Italian. (2024, June 17). Princeton University. https://www.princeton.edu/news/2024/06/17/senior-thesis-spotlight-perfect-marriage-science-and-humanities

Shalevska, E. (2024). The Digital Laureate: Examining AI-Generated Poetry. RATE Issues, vol. 31, issue no. 1.

Sharma, C., Batra, I., Sharma, S., Malik, A., Hosen, A. S., & Ra, I. H. (2022). Predicting trends and research patterns of smart cities: A semi-automatic review using latent Dirichlet allocation (LDA). *IEEE Access : Practical Innovations, Open Solutions*, *10*, 121080–121095. DOI: 10.1109/ACCESS.2022.3214310

Sharma, C., Sharma, S., & Sakshi, . (2022). Latent DIRICHLET allocation (LDA) based information modelling on BLOCKCHAIN technology: A review of trends and research patterns used in integration. *Multimedia Tools and Applications*, *81*(25), 36805–36831. https://doi.org/. DOI: 10.1007/s11042-022-13500-z PMID: 36035323

Sharples, M., & Pérez, R. P. (2022). *Story machines: How computers have become creative writers*. Routledge. DOI: 10.4324/9781003161431

Shewell, C. (2020). Poetry, voice, brain, and body. *Voice & Speech Review*, *14*(2), 143–166. DOI: 10.1080/23268263.2020.1743502

Shin, H. (2023). The space between 1s and 0s: Intentional patiency in computational creativity. *Science Fiction Studies*, *50*(151), 454–473. DOI: 10.1353/sfs.2023.a910330

Shrivastava, R., Jain, M., Vishwakarma, S. K., Bhagyalakshmi, L., & Tiwari, R. (2023). Cross-Cultural Translation Studies in the Context of Artificial Intelligence: Challenges and Strategies. In Kumar, A., Mozar, S., & Haase, J. (Eds.), *Advances in Cognitive Science and Communications. ICCCE 2023. Cognitive Science and Technology*. Springer., DOI: 10.1007/978-981-19-8086-2_9

Singarimbun, F. I. (2024). Implikasi Hukum Penggunaan AI dalam Seni Grafis Terhadap Hak Kekayaan Intelektual. [Jurnal Penelitian Pendidikan Indonesia]. *JPPI*, *10*(3), 886–893. DOI: 10.29210/020243889

Singh, A., Sethu, S. G., & Chaudhary, R. (2024). Artificial intelligence in storytelling: A critical analysis of narrative authenticity, cultural impact, and the future of creative industries. *Library of Progress – Library Science, Information Technology & Computer, 44*(3).

Singh, V. (2022). Minding the machine: Technological change, typographic resistance and print journalism in pre-independence India. *Südasien-Chronik – South Asia Chronicle, 18*(1), 97–117.

Singh, S. (2025). Futuristic Perspective of AI in Literary Academia. *Journal of East-West Thought*, *15*(1), 141–147.

Sin-Wai. (2024). *Kin-Wah, C., & Ming, M.* Routledge Encyclopedia of Technology and the Humanities.

Sismanto, S., Bakri, M., & Huda, A. M. (2022). Implementation of Multicultural Islamic Education Values. *Proceedings of the International Conference on Madrasah Reform 2021 (ICMR 2021),* 633. DOI: 10.2991/assehr.k.220104.048

Skrynnikova, I. V. (2024). Interpreting metaphorical language: A challenge to artificial intelligence. Vestnik Volgogradskogo Gosudarstvennogo Universiteta, Seriya 2. *Yazykoznanie*, *23*(5), 99–107. DOI: 10.15688/jvolsu2.2024.5.8

Slocombe, W., & Liveley, G. (2024). Introduction: Why AI and literature? In The Routledge handbook of AI and literature (pp. 3–16). Routledge.

Smith, H. (2020). *The writing experiment: strategies for innovative creative writing*. Routledge. DOI: 10.4324/9781003118244

Soekanto, S. (2007). *Pengantar Peneltian Hukum*. Universitas Indonesia Press.

Sönmez, S. (2025). Artificial Intelligence in screenplay: ChatGPT application. In *Transforming Cinema with Artificial Intelligence* (pp. 37–52). IGI Global Scientific Publishing., DOI: 10.4018/979-8-3693-3916-9.ch003

Soori, M., Arezoo, B., & Dastres, R. (2023). Artificial Intelligence, Machine Learning and deep learning in advanced robotics, a review. *Cognitive Robotics*, *3*, 54–70. DOI: 10.1016/j.cogr.2023.04.001

Spencer, T. D., & Pierce, C. (2023). Classroom-based oral storytelling: Reading, writing, and social benefits. *The Reading Teacher*, *76*(5), 525–534. DOI: 10.1002/trtr.2144

Spivak, G. C. (1988). Can the subaltern speak? In C. Nelson & L. Grossberg (Eds.), *Marxism and the interpretation of culture* (pp. 271–313). University of Illinois Press.

Srivastava, P., & Hopwood, N. (2009). A practical iterative framework for qualitative data analysis. *International Journal of Qualitative Methods*, *8*(1), 76–84. DOI: 10.1177/160940690900800107

Stanford, H. A. I. (2022). The movement to decolonize AI: Centering dignity over dependency. *Stanford HAI*. https://hai.stanford.edu/news/movement-decolonize-ai-centering-dignity-over-dependency

Stein, A. (2022). *The Art of Presence: The Poet and Paradise Lost*. Univ of California Press.

Stelmach, M. (2025). Canonization/quantification: Film canon as an empirical matter. *Studies in Eastern European Cinema*, *16*(1), 136–148. DOI: 10.1080/2040350X.2024.2430798

Stöckli, L., Joho, L., Lehner, F., & Hanne, T. (2024).The Personification of ChatGPT

Stöckli, L., Joho, L., Lehner, F., & Hanne, T. (2024, May 24). (GPT-4)—Understanding Its Personality and Adaptability. *Information (Basel)*, *15*(6), 300. DOI: 10.3390/info15060300

Stokel-Walker, C. (2022). AI bot ChatGPT writes smart essays — Should professors worry? *Nature*. Advance online publication. DOI: 10.1038/d41586-022-04397-7 PMID: 36494443

Subagiyo, D. T., & Wibisono, H. (2025). The urgency of artificial intelligence regulation from a joint authorship perspective on copyright infringement. *Indonesia Private Law Review*, *5*(2), 135–156. DOI: 10.25041/iplr.v5i2.3962

Supranto, J. (2003). *Metode Penelitian Hukum dan Statistik*. Rineka Cipta.

Susanti, D., Sari, L. Y., & Fitriani, V. (2022). Increasing student learning motivation through the use of interactive digital books based on Project Based Learning (PjBL). *Jurnal Penelitian Pendidikan IPA*, *8*(4), 1730–1735. DOI: 10.29303/jppipa.v8i4.1669

Susanti, R. D. I. (2017). *Hak Cipta: Kajian Filosofis dan Historis*. Setara Press.

Świerczyńska-Kaczor, U. (2024). Empirical insights into traditional and AI-enhanced interactive narratives based on children's fables. *Journal of Economics and Management*, *46*(1), 25–54. DOI: 10.22367/jem.2024.46.02

Taherdoost, H., & Madanchian, M. (2023). AI advancements: Comparison of innovative techniques. *AI*, *5*(1), 38–54. DOI: 10.3390/ai5010003

Tan, D. N. L., & Mante-Estacio, M. J. (2021). Reader-text connection: Reporting the engagement of high school students with culturally relevant texts. *Teflin Journal, 32*(2), 342. Advance online publication. DOI: 10.15639/teflinjournal.v32i2/342-361

Tang, A., Li, K., Kwok, K. O., Cao, L., Luong, S., & Tam, W. (2023). The importance of transparency: Declaring the use of generative artificial intelligence (AI) in academic writing. *Journal of Nursing Scholarship, 56*(2), 314–318. DOI: 10.1111/jnu.12938 PMID: 37904646

Tatar, K., Ericson, P., Cotton, K., Del Prado, P. T. N., Batlle-Roca, R., Cabrero-Daniel, B., Ljungblad, S., Diapoulis, G., & Hussain, J. (2024). A Shift in Artistic Practices through Artificial Intelligence. *Leonardo, 57*(3), 293–297. Advance online publication. DOI: 10.1162/leon_a_02523

Tektona, R. I., Sari, N. K., & Alfaris, M. R. (2021). Quo Vadis Undang-Undang Hak Cipta di Indonesia: Perbandingan Konsep Ciptaan Artificial Intelligence di Beberapa Negara. *Negara Hukum, 12*(2), 285–305. DOI: 10.22212/jnh.v12i2.2144

The Agreement on Trade-Related Aspects of Intellectual Property Rights (TRIPs)

Thorp, H. H. (2023). ChatGPT is fun, but not an author. *Science, 379*(6630), 313–313. DOI: 10.1126/science.adg7879 PMID: 36701446

Tian, D., Wang, Q., Law, R., & Zhang, M. (2020). Influence of cultural identity on tourists' authenticity perception, tourist satisfaction, and traveler loyalty. *Sustainability (Basel), 12*(16), 6344. Advance online publication. DOI: 10.3390/su12166344

Tresnawati, D., Guno, Y., Satwika, I. P., Prihatmanto, A. S., & Mahayana, D. (2022). Artificial Intelligence serta Singularitas Suatu Kekeliruan atau Tantangan. *Jurnal Algoritma, 19*(1), 172–179. DOI: 10.33364/algoritma/v.19-1.1028

Triandis, H. C. (1993). Collectivism and Individualism as Cultural Syndromes. *Cross-Cultural Research, 27*(3–4), 155–180. Advance online publication. DOI: 10.1177/106939719302700301

Triatmojo, F., Hamzani, A. I., & Rahayu, K. (2021). *Perlindungan Hak Cipta Lagu Komersil*. Penerbit Nem.

Troiano, E. (2023). Where are emotions in text? A human-based and computational investigation of emotion recognition and generation. Source Name. https://doi.org/ DOI: 10.21248/jlcl.37.2024.253

Tsai, C. W., Ma, Y. W., Chang, Y. C., & Lai, Y. H. (2022). Integrating Multiculturalism Into Artificial Intelligence-Assisted Programming Lessons: Examining Inter-Ethnicity Differences in Learning Expectancy, Motivation, and Effectiveness. *Frontiers in Psychology*, *13*, 868698. Advance online publication. DOI: 10.3389/fpsyg.2022.868698 PMID: 35769741

Tsai, C.-H., & Wang, C.-P. (2019). An Analysis of the Development of Cultural Augmented Reality Education in Taiwanese Aboriginal Literature. *International Journal of E-Education, e-Business, e-. Management Learning*, *9*(4), 357–365. DOI: 10.17706/ijeeee.2019.9.4.357-365

Tsao, J., & Nogues, C. (2024). Beyond the author: Artificial intelligence, creative writing and intellectual emancipation. *Poetics*, *102*, 101865. DOI: 10.1016/j.poetic.2024.101865

Turner, M. L. (2023). *An in-depth exploration of the field of book ghostwriting*. Temple University.

Tu, X., He, Z., Huang, Y., Zhang, Z., Yang, M., & Zhao, J. (2024). An overview of large AI models and their applications. *Visual Intelligence*, *2*(1), 34. Advance online publication. DOI: 10.1007/s44267-024-00065-8

Ueno, T. (2017). *Copyright Issues on Artificial Intelligence and Machine Learning*. In: International Joint Conference on Artificial Intelligence 2017 Workshop: The First International Workshop on Sharing and Reuse of AI Work Products (2017), https://alai-paris2023.org/wp-content/uploads/2023/06/Reply-of-the-japan-ALAI-Group.pdf

Umphrey, R., Roberts, J., & Roberts, L. (2024). *Investigating Expert-in-the-Loop LLM Discourse Patterns for Ancient Intertextual Analysis*. ArXiv.org. https://arxiv.org/abs/2409.01882 DOI: 10.18653/v1/2024.nlp4dh-1.4

Unal, F. Z., Guzel, M. S., Bostanci, E., Acici, K., & Asuroglu, T. (2023). Multilabel genre prediction using deep-learning frameworks. *Applied Sciences (Basel, Switzerland)*, *13*(15), 8665. DOI: 10.3390/app13158665

University of the Philippines Principles for Responsible and Trustworthy Artificial Intelligence. (2023, November 10). University of the Philippines. https://up.edu.ph/up-principles-for-responsible-artificial-intelligence/

UPOU releases Guidelines on AI Use for Teaching and Learning - University of the Philippines Open University. (2024, January 19). University of the Philippines Open University. https://www.upou.edu.ph/news/upou-releases-guidelines-on-ai-use-for-teaching-and-learning/

Vallor, S. (2024). *The AI mirror: How to reclaim our humanity in an age of machine thinking*. Oxford University Press. DOI: 10.1093/oso/9780197759066.001.0001

Van Heerden, I., & Bas, A. (2021). Ai as author-bridging the gap between machine learning and literary theory. *Journal of Artificial Intelligence Research*, *71*, 175–189. DOI: 10.1613/jair.1.12593

Van Woudenberg, R., Ranalli, C., & Bracker, D. (2024). Authorship and ChatGPT: A Conservative View. *Philosophy & Technology*, *37*(1), 34. Advance online publication. DOI: 10.1007/s13347-024-00715-1 PMID: 38419827

Varsha, P. S. (2023). How can we manage biases in artificial intelligence systems–A systematic literature review. *International Journal of Information Management Data Insights*, *3*(1), 100165. Advance online publication. DOI: 10.1016/j.jjimei.2023.100165

Vassilakopoulou, P., & Hustad, E. (2023). Bridging Digital Divides: A Literature Review and Research Agenda for Information Systems Research. *Information Systems Frontiers*, *25*(3), 955–969. DOI: 10.1007/s10796-020-10096-3 PMID: 33424421

Verhaal, J. C., & Dobrev, S. D. (2022). The authenticity paradox: Why the returns to authenticity on audience appeal decrease in popularity and iconicity. *Journal of Management*, *48*(4), 873–899. DOI: 10.1177/0149206320950414

Victoria, M. (2025). Multimodal communication in intercultural interaction: edited by Ulrike Schroeder, Elisabetta Adami and Jennifer Dailey-O'Cain, New York, Routledge, 2023, 1–249 pp., £125.00 (hardback), ISBN: 9781032130170. *Language and Intercultural Communication, 25*(2), 306–308. https://doi.org/DOI: 10.1080/14708477.2025.2464477

Vincent, J. (2022, November 15). *The Scary Truth About AI Copyright is Nobody Knows What What Will Happen Next. The Verge*, https://www.theverge.com/23444685/generative-ai-copyright-infringement-legal-fair-use-training-data

Vinchon, F., Lubart, T., Bartolotta, S., Gironnay, V., Botella, M., Bourgeois-Bougrine, S., Burkhardt, J.-M., Bonnardel, N., Corazza, G. E., Glăveanu, V., Hanchett Hanson, M., Ivcevic, Z., Karwowski, M., Kaufman, J. C., Okada, T., Reiter-Palmon, R., & Gaggioli, A. (2023). Artificial intelligence & creativity: A manifesto for collaboration. *The Journal of Creative Behavior*, *57*(4), 472–484. DOI: 10.1002/jocb.597

Vinodini, S., & Adithya Pothan Raj, V. (2024). Enhancing literary analysis through artificial intelligence and machine learning: Insights from The Alchemist. In 2024 2nd International Conference on Recent Advances in Information Technology for Sustainable Development (ICRAIS) (pp. 136–141). Publisher Name. DOI: 10.1109/ICRAIS62903.2024.10811737

Vinodini, S. (2024a). The analysis of language, sentiment, and themes in Paulo Coelho's 'brida' using textblob. *2024 Ninth International Conference on Science Technology Engineering and Mathematics (ICONSTEM)*, 1–8. DOI: 10.1109/ICONSTEM60960.2024.10568869

Vondy (2025). Vondy.com. https://www.vondy.com/lyric-poem-generator-

Wagner, G., Lukyanenko, R., & Paré, G. (2022). Artificial intelligence and the conduct of literature reviews. *Journal of Information Technology*, *37*(2), 209–226. DOI: 10.1177/02683962211048201

Walter, Y. (2024). Embracing the future of Artificial Intelligence in the classroom: The relevance of AI literacy, prompt engineering, and critical thinking in modern education. *International Journal of Educational Technology in Higher Education*, *21*(1), 15. Advance online publication. DOI: 10.1186/s41239-024-00448-3

Wang, H., Li, Z., & Yang, C. (2023). Interpreting technologies in the artificial intelligence era. In *Conference Interpreting in China* (pp. 232–250). DOI: 10.4324/9781003357629-16

Wang, N. (2022). The rise of a new paradigm of Literary Studies: The Challenge of Digital Humanities. *New Techno Humanities*, *2*(1), 28–33. DOI: 10.1016/j.techum.2022.11.001

Wangsa, J. J., Fortunata, K. F., & Hanunisa, S. Z. (2023). *Impact of Artificial Intelligence on Intellectual Property Rights in Indonesia*. Anthology: Inside Intellectual Property Rights 1(1), 52-71, https://ojs.uph.edu/index.php/Anthology/article/view/6689/3021

Wang, Y., Singgih, M., Wang, J., & Rit, M. (2019). Making sense of blockchain technology: How will it transform supply chains? *International Journal of Production Economics*, *211*, 221–236. DOI: 10.1016/j.ijpe.2019.02.002

Watiktinnakorn, C., Seesai, J., & Kerdvibulvech, C. (2023). Blurring the lines: How AI is redefining artistic ownership and copyright. *Discover Artificial Intelligence*, *3*(1), 37. Advance online publication. DOI: 10.1007/s44163-023-00088-y

Werdiningsih, I., Wibisono, H., & Rusdin, D. (2024). Balancing AI and authenticity: EFL students' experiences with ChatGPT in academic writing. *Cogent Arts & Humanities, 11*(1), 2392388. Advance online publication. DOI: 10.1080/23311983.2024.2392388

White, H. (1973). *Metahistory: The historical imagination in nineteenth-century Europe*. Johns Hopkins University Press.

White, H. (1988). *The content of the form: Narrative discourse and historical representation*. Johns Hopkins University Press.

Wiboolyasarin, W., Wiboolyasarin, K., Suwanwihok, K., Jinowat, N., & Muenjanchoey, R. (2024). Synergizing collaborative writing and AI feedback: An investigation into enhancing L2 writing proficiency in wiki-based environments. *Computers and Education: Artificial Intelligence, 6*, 100228. Advance online publication. DOI: 10.1016/j.caeai.2024.100228

Williams, R. (2024). Impact. AI: Democratizing AI through K-12 Artificial Intelligence Education (Doctoral dissertation).

Woodgate, R. L., & Busolo, D. S. (2021). African refugee youths' experiences of navigating different cultures in canada: A "push and pull" experience. *International Journal of Environmental Research and Public Health, 18*(4), 1–13. DOI: 10.3390/ijerph18042063 PMID: 33672518

World Intellectual Property Organisation. (2019). The Story of AI in Patents. https://www.wipo.int/tech_trends/en/artificial_intelligence/story.html

World Intellectual Property Organization. (2008). *WIPO Intellectual Property Handbook*. Jenewa: WIPO Publication.

Xue, T. (2020). Using big data technology to assist in analyzing the influence of cultural context on the translation of english and American literature. *Journal of Physics: Conference Series, 1648*(3), 032058. Advance online publication. DOI: 10.1088/1742-6596/1648/3/032058

Yadav, D. (2024). *The Role of Artificial Intelligence in Literary Analysis: A Computational Approach to Understand Literary Styles*.

Yadav, D. (2024). The role of artificial intelligence in literary analysis: A computational approach to understand literary styles. Source Name. https://doi.org/xxxxx

Yang, D., Zhou, Y., Zhang, Z., Li, T. J. J., & Lc, R. (2022, March). AI as an Active Writer: Interaction strategies with generated text in human-AI collaborative fiction writing. In Joint Proceedings of the ACM IUI Workshops (Vol. 10, pp. 1-11). CEUR-WS Team.

Yang, G., & Kim, J. (2025). The ethics of reading revisited in the age of Artificial Intelligence. *ANQ: A Quarterly Journal of Short Articles, Notes and Reviews*, 1–9. DOI: 10.1080/0895769X.2025.2453815

Yang, D., Zhou, Y., Zhang, Z., Li, T. J. J., & Lc, R. (2022, March). AI as an Active Writer: Interaction strategies with generated text in human-AI collaborative fiction writing. In *Joint proceedings of the ACM IUI workshops* (Vol. 10, pp. 1–11). CEUR-WS Team.

Yang, L., Wang, G., & Wang, H. (2024). Reimagining literary analysis: Utilizing artificial intelligence to classify modernist French poetry. *Information (Basel)*, *15*(2), 70. DOI: 10.3390/info15020070

Yang, S., Chen, S., Zhu, H., Lin, J., & Wang, X. (2024). A comparative study of thematic choices and thematic progression patterns in human-written and AI-generated texts. *System*, *126*, 103494. Advance online publication. DOI: 10.1016/j.system.2024.103494

Ye, X., Huang, L., & Wang, Z. (2025). Exploration of the human-computer synergy paradigm for literary creation via the lens of digital humanities. *Humanities and Social Science Research*, *8*(2), 1–1. DOI: 10.30560/hssr.v8n2p1

Younas, A., Fàbregues, S., Durante, A., Escalante, E. L., Inayat, S., & Ali, P. (2023). Proposing the "MIRACLE" Narrative Framework for Providing Thick Description in Qualitative Research. *International Journal of Qualitative Methods*, *22*, 16094069221147162. Advance online publication. DOI: 10.1177/16094069221147162

Youvan, D. C. (2024). *AI for All: The Socioeconomic and Cultural Impacts of a 50-Year Leap into Democratized Artificial Intelligence*.

Yue, D., Meng, X., Kuoshu, H. H., & Hunter, I. (2023a). *Chinese thought in a multi-cultural world: Cross-cultural communication, comparative literature and beyond*. Routledge.

Zaki, M. Z., & Ahmed, U. (2024). Bridging linguistic divides: The impact of AI-powered translation systems on Communication Equity and inclusion. *Journal of Translation and Language Studies*, *5*(2). Advance online publication. DOI: 10.48185/jtls.v5i2.1065

Zhang, R., Zhao, W., & Eger, S. (2024). How good are LLMs for literary translation, really? Literary translation evaluation with humans and LLMs. arXiv. https://doi .org//arXiv.2410.18697DOI: 10.48550

Zhang, C., & Lu, Y. (2021). Study on Artificial Intelligence: The state of the art and future prospects. *Journal of Industrial Information Integration*, *23*, 100224. DOI: 10.1016/j.jii.2021.100224

Zhang, M., & Chen, W. (2022). Assessing collaborative writing in the digital age: An exploratory study. *Journal of Second Language Writing*, *57*, 100868. DOI: 10.1016/j.jslw.2022.100868

Zhao, D. (2024). The impact of AI-enhanced natural language processing tools on writing proficiency: An analysis of language precision, content summarization, and creative writing facilitation. *Education and Information Technologies*, *30*(6), 8055–8086. DOI: 10.1007/s10639-024-13145-5

Zhao, D. (2024). The impact of AI-enhanced natural language processing tools on writing proficiency: An analysis of language precision, content summarization, and creative writing. *Education and Information Technologies*.

Zhao, Y., Cheng, B., Huang, Y., & Wan, Z. (2023). Beyond Words: An intelligent human-machine dialogue system with multimodal generation and emotional comprehension. *International Journal of Intelligent Systems*, *38*(1), 1–15. DOI: 10.1002/int.20386

Zhao, Y., & Zhou, W. (2025). Unlocking ancient wisdom with modern tools: A new approach to the revitalization of ancient texts based on Generative Artificial Intelligence. *Journal of Academic Librarianship*, *51*(3), 111–120, 103055. DOI: 10.1016/j.acalib.2025.103055

Zheng, W. (2024). AI vs. Human: A Comparative Study of Cohesion and Coherence in Academic Texts between Human-Written and ChatGPT-Generated Texts.

Zheng, S., Liu, H., & Yang, H. (2021, August). A survey of story-generation apps and online systems between 2017 and 2020. In *Proceedings of the 2021 8th International Conference on Dependable Systems and Their Applications (DSA)* (pp. 390–398). IEEE. DOI: 10.1109/DSA52907.2021.00059

Zhu, T. (2021). From Textual Experiments to Experimental Texts: Expressive Repetition in "artificial Intelligence Literature. *Theoretical Studies in Literature and Art, 41*(5).

Zhuk, A. (2023). Navigating the legal landscape of AI copyright: A comparative analysis of EU, US, and Chinese approaches. *AI and Ethics*. Advance online publication. DOI: 10.1007/s43681-023-00299-0

Zhu, S., Wang, Z., Zhuang, Y., Jiang, Y., Guo, M., Zhang, X., & Gao, Z. (2024). Exploring the impact of ChatGPT on art creation and collaboration: Benefits, challenges and ethical implications. *Telematics and Informatics Reports*, *14*, 100138. Advance online publication. DOI: 10.1016/j.teler.2024.100138

Zimeta, M. (2023). Why AI must be decolonized to fulfill its true potential. *Chatham House*. https://www.chathamhouse.org/publications/the-world-today/2023-10/why-ai-must-be-decolonized-fulfill-its-true-potential

Zong, Z., & Guan, Y. (2024). AI-driven intelligent data analytics and predictive analysis in Industry 4.0: Transforming knowledge, innovation, and efficiency. *Journal of the Knowledge Economy*, *16*(1), 864–903. DOI: 10.1007/s13132-024-02001-z

Zou, D., & Lin, Z. (2024). Research on innovative applications of AI technology in the field of Cultural Heritage Conservation. *Academic Journal of Humanities &amp. Social Sciences*, *7*(10). Advance online publication. DOI: 10.25236/AJHSS.2024.071020

About The Contributors

Andi Asrifan, S.Pd, M.Pd, a distinguished figure in the realm of education, particularly in English Language Education, has made significant contributions through his extensive research, teaching, and leadership roles. As the Head of the Institute for Cooperation and International Affairs at Universitas Muhammadiyah Sidenreng Rappang and now a lecturer in Universitas Negeri Makassar (UNM), Dr. Asrifan's academic journey is marked by a rich tapestry of achievements, including a Doctor of Education in English Language Education. His work spans various facets of education, language, and technology, reflecting the diverse topics covered in his publications and research endeavors. These include, but are not limited to, the impact of the COVID-19 pandemic on educational practices, methodologies in English as a Foreign Language (EFL) classrooms, and the integration of technology in teaching and learning processes. Dr. Asrifan's commitment to advancing educational standards and practices is further evidenced by his active participation in international conferences, webinars, and workshops across countries like India, the Philippines, and Pakistan. These events, organized by various institutions and associations, underscore his role as a global educator and thought leader. His dedication to professional development is also highlighted through his involvement in numerous courses and certifications in personal branding, public speaking, and literacy teaching. Moreover, Dr. Asrifan's leadership extends beyond academia into organizational and educational development, where he has served in various capacities, including as an external examiner for Ph.D. dissertations and a reviewer for scientific journals. His accolades, memberships in professional organizations, and roles as an ambassador for international associations speak volumes of his influence and commitment to fostering educational excellence and sustainable development goals globally.

***

Philip Donald P. Herrera is an instructor, researcher, and linguist whose research interests include applied linguistics, literary studies, needs analysis, and teacher development.

Vishal Jain is presently working as Professor at the Department of Computer Science and Engineering, School of Engineering and Technology, Sharda University, Greater Noida, India. Before that, he worked for several years as an Associate Professor at Bharati Vidyapeeth's Institute of Computer Applications and Management (BVICAM), New Delhi. He has more than 18 years of experience in the academics. He has earned degrees: Ph.D (CSE), M.Tech (CSE), MBA (HR), MCA, MCP, and CCNA. He has more than 2200 research citations with Google Scholar (h-index score 24 and i-10 index 55) and has authored more than 150 research papers in professional journals and conferences. He has authored and edited more than 60 books (most of them are indexed at the Scopus) with various reputed publishers, including Elsevier, Springer, IET, Apple Academic Press, CRC, Taylor and Francis Group, Scrivener, Wiley, Emerald, NOVA Science, River Publishers, IGI-Global and Bentham Science. He has more than 200 Scopus publications. His research areas include machine learning, information retrieval, semantic web, ontology engineering, data mining, ad hoc networks, sensor networks and network security.

Junaidi, S.H., M.H., C.L.A., C.B.P.A., a Legal Practitioner, Writer and Lecturer at the Faculty of Law, Sjakhyakirti University Palembang. Born in 1978 in Palembang. Graduated from Muhammadiyah 9 Elementary School (1992), State Junior High School 8 (1995) and State Senior High School 7 (1998) all completed in Palembang. Bachelor of Laws completed at the Faculty of Law, Bhayangkara University, Greater Jakarta (2013) and Postgraduate Law completed at Krisnadwipayana University Jakarta (2016) with a Business Law Study Programme. Completed his Legal Auditor Education at Jimly School of Law and Government (JSLG), batch 13 (2014). The author is also a resource person in various national seminars. Active in writing scientific papers published in various national journals, national and international level proceedings and Book Chapters with various universities and research study institutions. The author is also a reviewer and editor for several national journals in the field of law. The author is also active as a book editor in various fields, especially in the field of law.

Sooraj Kumar Maurya currently holds the position of Assistant Professor of Philosophy and serves as the Teacher-in-Charge at the Department of Philosophy within Zakir Husain Delhi College (Evening), affiliated with the University of Delhi. He boasts an illustrious academic background, having earned his B.A., M.A., and D. Phil degrees from the esteemed Department of Philosophy at the University of

Allahabad. Dr. Maurya exhibits an unwavering commitment to scholarly pursuits and has significantly enriched the field of philosophy. His scholarly achievements include over 35 published research papers featured in esteemed international and national journals and conferences. Dr. Maurya's research interests span a broad spectrum of philosophical themes, with a particular focus on social philosophy, political philosophy, and moral philosophy.

Archan Mitra is an Assistant Professor at School of Media Studies (SOMS) at Presidency University, Bangalore. He is the author of two book "Cases for Classroom Media and Entertainment Business" and "Multiverse and Media", he also has other several edited books to his credit. He has done his doctorate from Visva-Bharati Santiniketan, West Bengal in the field of "environmental informatics and communication for sustainability". In addition to that he is a certified Science Communicator and Journalism from Indian Science Communication Society (ISCOS), certified Corporate Trainer with Amity Institute of Training and Development, Certified Social Media Network Analyst. He has a strong interest in environmental communication. He was awarded certificate of merit by PRSI, Kolkata Chapter and Medal of Honor by Journalistic Club of Kolkata. He was working as a research assistant with the World Bank's "Environmental Capacity Building in Southeast Asia" project at IIM Kashipur. He was instrumental in launching the World Bank's Green MBA MOOC, he has also assisted in the research project on Uttarakhand disaster mitigation by ICSSR, the leading research on Uttarakhand disaster.

St. Zulaiha Nurhajarurahmah, Academics and researchers who have expertise in the field Mathematics education. As a lecturer at the University Makassar State, she actively guides students In research and writing various scientific articles that Published in national and international journals. Interest The main research includes learning strategies Interactive, human resource development through Education, and technology integration in the learning process Teaching. Outside of his academic activities, she also often Become a speaker in seminars and workshops, share Insight into effective and innovative teaching. Book This comes as a form of commitment to continueContributing to the Indonesian education world, especially In curriculum development that is relevant to Global challenge." ChatGPT bilang: Sure! Here's a polished and professional version of the biography for Dr. St. Zulaiha Nurhajarurahmah, M.Pd.: Dr. St. Zulaiha Nurhajarurahmah, M.Pd. is an academic and researcher specializing in Mathematics Education. As a dedicated lecturer at Universitas Negeri Makassar, she actively mentors students in conducting research and authoring scientific articles, many of which have been published in both national and international journals. Her primary research interests include interactive learning strategies, human resource development through education, and the integration of technology in the teaching and learning process. Beyond her academic commitments, Dr. Zulaiha is also a sought-after speaker at seminars and workshops, where she shares insights on effective and innovative teaching practices. This book reflects her unwavering commitment to contributing to the advancement of education in Indonesia, particularly in the area of curriculum development that aligns with the demands of global challenges.

Sanchita Paul is a dedicated and accomplished content strategist with extensive experience in managing diverse content formats across different digital platforms. With a strong background in content strategy, editing, and UX writing, she has honed her skills in branding, social media management, and technical writing. Holding an MA in Communication and Journalism from Visva-Bharati University, Ms. Paul is proficient in tools like Google Analytics, Canva, and MS Office Suite, making her a versatile professional committed to producing high-quality, impactful content to improve brand visibility.

Muhammad Rapi, M.S. is a distinguished academic and Professor at the Faculty of Language and Literature at Universitas Negeri Makassar (UNM). Born on December 30, 1960, in Enrekeng, Kabupaten Soppeng, he has dedicated his career to the advancement of Indonesian language and literature. He completed his undergraduate studies at IKIP Ujung Pandang in 1986, followed by a Master's degree and a Doctorate in Literature from Universitas Padjadjaran, achieved in 1991 and 2001, respectively. Prof. Rapi specializes in philology, literary history, and hermeneutics, and has made significant contributions to the field through his research, focusing on themes such as nationalism in classical literature and the readability of educational texts. His scholarly work includes numerous publications in reputable journals, addressing critical issues in language education and cultural representation. In addition to his teaching responsibilities, Prof. Rapi is actively involved in community service initiatives aimed at improving educational practices and promoting cultural literacy. He has authored several influential books, including works on Bugis literature and the integration of cultural discourse in language education. His extensive experience and dedication to the field position him as a leading figure in the promotion of Indonesian literature and education.

Vikash Ranjan Singh is a faculty member in the Department of History at Zakir Husain Delhi College (Evening), University of Delhi. His academic interests include the study of historical narratives and their intersection with contemporary issues. Dr. Singh is dedicated to enriching the learning experience of his students, emphasizing critical thinking and historical analysis. He is actively involved in research and contributes to the academic community with his insights and publications. Dr. Singh can be reached at vikashatdelhi@gmail.com for further academic inquiries.

Supriadi, S.Pd., M.Pd., is a dedicated academic and expert in the field of Indonesian language and literature education. Born in Barru on February 11, 1982, he has built an impressive career as a lecturer and educator, currently serving as a permanent faculty member at Universitas Islam Makassar. Dr. Supriadi completed his undergraduate, master's, and doctoral studies at Universitas Negeri Makassar, specializing in Indonesian language education. His academic journey reflects a deep commitment to enhancing the quality of language education in Indonesia. Dr. Supriadi has a wealth of experience in teaching various subjects, including Scientific Writing, Language Skills, and the Development of Indonesian Language Learning in Primary Schools. He has been actively involved in research, focusing on innovative teaching strategies, such as the effectiveness of the Synectic Model in poetry appreciation and the use of Mind Mapping to improve listening skills in elementary students. His research has contributed significantly to the advancement of teaching methodologies and the promotion of critical discourse in language education. In addition to his teaching and research, Dr. Supriadi has played a crucial role in community service, particularly in enhancing literacy and language skills in rural areas. His efforts include providing language training to village officials and promoting the use of correct Indonesian spelling in elementary schools. Dr. Supriadi's dedication to education is also evident in his involvement in national and international seminars, where he has contributed as both a participant and a presenter. Through his work, Dr. Supriadi continues to impact the field of education, striving to improve the quality of language instruction and fostering a greater appreciation for Indonesian literature among students and educators alike.

Andi Sukri Syamsuri, A.Md., S.Pd., M.Hum. is a prominent academic and educator, born on June 26, 1971, in Kabupaten Wajo, Indonesia. He is currently a Professor at Universitas Muhammadiyah Makassar, where he has made significant contributions to the fields of Indonesian language and literature education. Prof. Syamsuri earned his Doctorate in Indonesian Language from Universitas Hasanuddin in 2006, following his Master's degree in the same discipline in 1997. His extensive career includes various leadership roles, such as Dean of the Faculty of Teacher Training and Education and Vice Rector at Universitas Muhammadiyah Makassar. He has been actively involved in research, focusing on pedagogical competencies and the integration of local culture into educational materials, with numerous publications in reputable journals. Prof. Syamsuri has also participated in numerous national and international seminars, contributing his expertise on language education and cultural preservation. His commitment to community service is evident through initiatives aimed at enhancing literacy and educational quality. He has received several accolades, including the Satya Lencana award from the President of Indonesia for his dedication to education. His scholarly work and leadership continue to influence the advancement of language education in Indonesia.

Sahrul Syawal, S.Pd., M.Pd., is a committed scholar in the field of educational sciences with a strong foundation in mathematics education and educational management. Born in Makale on October 8, 1985, he completed his undergraduate studies in Mathematics Education at Universitas Negeri Makassar, followed by a Master's degree in Educational Management. His academic pursuit culminated in a Ph.D. in Educational Sciences from the same university. Currently, Dr. Sahrul Syawal serves as a lecturer in the Doctoral Program of Educational Sciences at Universitas Negeri Makassar, where he actively engages in teaching, academic supervision, and research. His scholarly work explores topics in educational leadership, curriculum development, and innovations in teaching and learning. Through his dedication to advancing the field of education, Dr. Sahrul has made significant contributions to academic discourse and continues to inspire future educators and researchers across Indonesia.

Fathullah Wajdi, M.Pd, is an esteemed academic with a comprehensive background in Indonesian Language Education. Born on April 10, 1978, in Serang, Indonesia, he has dedicated over two decades to the field of education, beginning his career as a teacher in 2001. He holds a Doctorate in Indonesian Language Education from Universitas Pendidikan Indonesia, obtained in 2017, complementing his earlier degrees from Universitas Negeri Semarang and Universitas Negeri Sultan Ageng Tirtayasa. Currently, Dr. Wajdi serves as a lecturer at Universitas Negeri Makassar, where he is involved in various educational initiatives. His extensive teaching experience spans multiple institutions, including his roles as a permanent teacher and school principal at MA Al-Khairiyah Pipitan and other schools. His leadership in education is further highlighted by his administrative positions, demonstrating his commitment to enhancing academic standards. Dr. Wajdi is also an active researcher, contributing to national journals with publications focusing on innovative teaching methodologies, such as authentic assessment in drama learning and contextual approaches in literature. His scholarly work aims to improve pedagogical practices and enrich the educational landscape in Indonesia, reflecting his dedication to both teaching and research.

Index

A

C

www.ingramcontent.com/pod-product-compliance
Lightning Source LLC
LaVergne TN
LVHW062219200926
848484LV00006B/1432